108 Greenfield
MAS 02126
6172980167

SOCIAL STRUCTURE
and
SOCIAL PROBLEMS
in America

Consulting Editor:
Amitai Etzioni

SOCIAL STRUCTURE
and
SOCIAL PROBLEMS
in America

D. STANLEY EITZEN
The University of Kansas

Allyn and Bacon, Inc.   Boston

To KEITH, MIKE, AND KELLY

ACKNOWLEDGEMENTS

The author wishes to thank copyright owners and publishers of the following writers for permission to adapt or reprint their work:

ALFORD, R. H. Adapted from Robert R. Alford and Harry M. Scoble, "Sources of Local Political Involvement," *American Political Science Review* 62 (December, 1968), p. 1195, by permission of the publisher.

ALLPORT, G. W. Reprinted from Gordon W. Allport, *The Nature of Prejudice,* 1954, Addison-Wesley Publishing Company, Reading, Mass., by permission of the publisher.

BANFIELD, E. C. Reprinted from Edward C. Banfield, *The Unheavenly City* (Boston: Little, Brown and Company); copyright © 1968, 1970 by Edward C. Banfield, by permission of the publisher.

BECKER, H. S. Reprinted from H. S. Becker and I. L. Horowitz, "The Culture of Civility," *Transaction,* April, 1970, p. 12–14, by permission of the publisher.

BERGER, P. L. Adapted from Peter L. Berger and Brigitte Berger, "The Blueing of America," *The New Republic* (April 3, 1971), p. 20–23, by permission of the publisher.

BLAUNER, R. Reprinted from Robert Blauner, "Work Satisfaction and Industrial Trends in Modern Society," in *Labor and Trade Unionism,* Walter Galenson and Seymour Martin Lipset (eds.), (New York: John Wiley & Sons, Inc., 1960), p. 343, by permission of the publisher.

BLOOD, R. O. Reprinted with permission of The Macmillan Company from *Husbands and Wives* by Robert O. Blood, Jr., and Donald M. Wolfe. Copyright 1960 by The Free Press, A Corporation.

BOND, H. M. Adapted from Horace Mann Bond, "The Productivity of National Merit Scholars by Occupational Class," *School and Society* 85, (September 28, 1957), p. 268, by permission of the publisher.

CARMICHAEL, S. From *Black Power* by Stokely Carmichael and Charles V. Hamilton. Copyright © 1967 by Stokely Carmichael and Charles V. Hamilton. Reprinted by permission of Random House, Inc.

CBS NEWS Adapted from data supplied by CBS News from a poll conducted March 20, 1970, and published in *Public Opinion: Changing Attitudes on Contemporary Political and Social Issues,* 1972, R. R. Bowker Company. Reprinted by permission of CBS News.

CONVERSE, P. E. Adapted from Phillip E. Converse, "The Concept of a Normal Vote," *Elections and the Political Order,* by Angus Campbell, Philip E. Converse, Warren E. Miller, and Donald E. Stokes; copyright © 1966 by John Wiley & Sons, Inc.

CROSS AND FLAG Reprinted from "We Are In Trouble!!! The Crisis from A to Z," *The Cross and the Flag* (December, 1963), p. 3, by permission of the publisher.

DAVIS, O. Reprinted from Ossie Davis, "The English Language Is My Enemy," *IRCD Bulletin* 5 (Summer, 1969), p. 13, by permission of the publisher.

DENTLER, R. A. From Robert A. Dentler, "Equality of Educational Opportunity: A Special Review," *The Urban Review* 1 (December, 1966), p. 27; a publication of the Center for Urban Education; reprinted by their permission.

DOMHOFF, G. W. From *The Higher Circles* by G. William Domhoff. Copyright © 1970 by G. William Domhoff. Reprinted by permission of Random House, Inc.

DONNER, F. From Frank Donner, "The Theory and Practice of American Political Intelligence," *The New York Review of Books* 16 (April 22, 1971). Reprinted with permission from *The New Yorker Review of Books.* Copyright © 1971, The New York Review Inc.

DUTTON, F. G. Reprinted from *Changing Sources of Power: American Politics in the 1970s* by Frederick G. Dutton. Copyright © 1971 by McGraw-Hill Book Company. Used with permission of McGraw-Hill Book Company.

EPSTEIN, B. R. Reprinted from Benjamin R. Epstein and Arnold Foster, *"Some of My Best Friends . . ."* (New York: Farrar, Straus and Cudahy, 1962) p. 111–112, by permission of the Publications Department, the Anti-Defamation League.

FISCHER, J. Reprinted and adapted from John Fischer, "The Easy Chair," *Harper's Magazine* 240 (April, 1970), p. 18–28, by permission of the publisher.

FORBES MAGAZINE Adapted from a series of tables appearing in *Forbes* 109 (May 15, 1972), by permission of the publisher.

FORM, W. H. Adapted from William H. Form and Joan Huber (Rytina), "Ideological Beliefs on the Distribution of Power in the United States," *American Sociological Review* 35 (February, 1969), p. 27, by permission of the authors and the publisher.

FREE, L. A. Adapted from *The Political Beliefs of Americans: A Study of Public Opinion,* by Lloyd A. Free and Hadley Cantril, Rutgers University Press, New Brunswick, N.J., 1967, by permission of the publisher.

GALLUP, G. H. Adapted and reprinted from *Gallup Opinion Index,* Report No. 49 (July, 1969), p. 22, by permission of author and publisher.

GANS, H. J. Reprinted from Herbert J. Gans, "The Uses of Power: The Poor Pay All," *Social Policy* 2 (July–August, 1971), p. 20–24; copyright ©, Social Policy Corporation; reprinted by permission of the publisher.

GLOCK, C. Y. Based on data in Charles Y. Glock and Rodney Stark, *Religion and Society in Tension* (Chicago: Rand McNally and Company, 1965); adapted from Tables 5-1, 5-2, 5-3, 5-5, 5-6, 5-7, and 5-9, by permission of the publisher.

GREELEY, A. M. Reprinted from *What Do We Believe?: The Stance of Religion in America* by Andrew Greeley, Martin E. Marty, and Stuart E. Rosenberg; copyright by Hawthorne Books, Inc., and reprinted with their permission.

Acknowledgements

HACKER, H. M. Adapted from Helen Meyer Hacker, "Women as a Minority Group," *Social Forces* 30, (October, 1951), p. 65, by permission of the publisher.

HANSEN, W. L. Adapted from W. Lee Hansen and Burton A. Weisbrod, "The Distribution of Costs and Direct Benefits of Public Higher Education: The Case of California," *The Journal of Human Resources* 4 (Spring, 1969), p. 190, by permission of the publisher.

HAVIGHURST, R. J. Reprinted from Table 1, "Socioeconomic Area and Pupil Achievement in High Schools," *The Public High Schools of Chicago*, p. 208–209, by permission of the Board of Education, City of Chicago.

HEILBRONER, R. L. Reprinted from Robert L. Heilbroner, "Controlling the Corporation," *In the Name of Profit* by R. L. Heilbroner et al. (eds.), (New York: Doubleday and Company, Inc., 1972), by permission.

HENRY, J. Reprinted from *Culture against Man* by Jules Henry. Copyright © 1963 by Random House, Inc. Reprinted by permission of the publisher.

HOLLINGSHEAD, A. B. Adapted from August B. Hollingshead and Frederick C. Redlick, *Social Class and Mental Illness: A Community Study* (New York: John Wiley & Sons, Inc., 1958), by permission of the publisher.

LIPSET, M. Reprinted from Martin Lipset and Earl Raab, "The Wallace Whitelash," *Transaction*, December, 1969, p. 28, by permission of the publisher.

LORINKAS, R. Adapted from Robert Lorinkas, Brett Hawkins, and Stephen Edwards, "The Persistence of Ethnic Voting in Rural and Urban Areas," *Social Science Quarterly*, 49, (March, 1969), p. 895, by permission of the publisher.

MADOLE, J. H. Reprinted from James H. Madole, "The Unholy Romance of the Chinese Dragon and the American Eagle," *National Renaissance Bulletin* 22, (Nov.–Dec., 1971), p. 5, 7, 8, by permission of the author.

MALCOLM X Reprinted by permission of Grove Press, Inc. and of The Hutchinson Publishing Group, Ltd.; copyright © 1964 by Alex Haley and Malcolm X; copyright © 1965 by Alex Haley and Betty Shabazz.

MEAD, M. Reprinted from Margaret Mead, "Future Family," *Transaction* (September 1971) p. 52, by permission of the publisher.

MERTON, R. K. Reprinted with permission of The Macmillan Company from *Social Theory and Social Structure* by Robert K. Merton. © Copyright 1957 by The Free Press, A Corporation. Copyright 1949 by The Free Press.

MILLER, H. From *Rich Man, Poor Man* by Herman Miller; copyright © 1971 by Thomas Y. Crowell Company, Inc.; reprinted by permission of the publisher.

NADER, R. From Ralph Nader, "*A Citizen's Guide to the American Economy*," *The New York Review of Books* 17 (September 2, 1971), p. 15. Reprinted with permission from *The New York Review of Books*. Copyright © 1971, The New York Review, Inc.

NICKEL REVIEW Reprinted from *The Nickel Review*, Syracuse, New York (April 13, 1970), p. 3, by permission of the publisher, Harper & Row.

RAINWATER, L. Reprinted from Lee Rainwater, "Post-1984 America," *Society* 9 (February, 1972), p. 20, by permission of the author.

RYAN, W. From William Ryan, *Blaming the Victim* (New York: Pantheon Books, 1971); p. 60; copyright © 1971 by Pantheon Books, a Division of Random House, Inc., and reprinted with their permission.

REISS, I. L. From *The Family System in America* by Ira L. Reiss. Copyright © 1971 by Holt, Rinehart and Winston, Inc. Adapted and reprinted by permission of Holt, Rinehart and Winston, Inc.

SCHAFER, W. E. Abstracted from W. E. Schafer, C. Olexa, and K. Polk, *Society* (October, 1970) p. 40–42; copyright October 1970, *Society* magazine by Transaction, Inc., New Brunswick, New Jersey; by permission of the publisher.

SCHNEIDER, H. Adapted from Herbert Schneider, *Religion in Twentieth Century America* (Cambridge, Mass. Harvard University Press, 1952), p. 288, by permission of the President and Fellows of Harvard University.

SEXTON, P. C. Reprinted from Patricia Cayo Sexton, *The American School: A Sociological Analysis* (Englewood Cliffs, N.J.: Prentice-Hall, Inc., 1967), p. 54, by permission of the publisher.

SILBERMAN, C. E. From *Crisis in the Classroom: The Remaking of American Education*, by Charles E. Silberman. Copyright © 1970 by Charles E. Silberman. Reprinted by permission of Random House, Inc.

SLATER, P. E. Reprinted from Philip E. Slater, *The Pursuit of Loneliness*, (Boston: Beacon Press, 1970), p. 9, by permission of Beacon Press, 1970), p. 9, by permission of Beacon Press, Boston, and Penguin Books, Ltd., London.

STARK, R. From Rodney Stark, Bruce D. Foster, Charles Y. Glock, and Harold Quinley, "Sounds of Silence," reprinted from *Psychology Today* Magazine, April, 1970, © Communications/Research/Machines, Inc., by permission of the publisher.

TOFFLER, A. From "Education in the Future Tense," in *Future Shock*, by Alvin Toffler. Copyright © 1970 by Alvin Toffler. Reprinted by permission of Random House, Inc.

THUNDERBOLT Reprinted from *The Thunderbolt* (June 25, 1961), p. 1, by permission of the publisher.

ZINN, H. Reprinted from Howard Zinn, "How Democratic Is America?" in *How Democratic Is America?*, Robert A. Goldwin (ed.), (Chicago: Rand McNally and Co., 1969), by permission of the author.

Contents

Preface

This book is guided by the assumption that there is an inherent duality in all societies. The realistic analysis of any one society must include both the integrating and stabilizing forces on the one hand and the forces that are conducive to malintegration and change on the other. American society is characterized by harmony *and* conflict; integration *and* division; stability *and* change. This synthesis is crucial if the intricacies of social structure, the mechanisms of social change, and the sources of social problems are to be understood fully.

This objective of achieving a balance between the order and conflict perspectives is not fully realized in this book, however. Although both perspectives are incorporated into each chapter, the scales tend to be tipped in favor of the conflict perspective. This slight imbalance is the conscious product of the way I view the structure and mechanisms of society. In addition to presenting what I think is a realistic analysis of society, it counters the prevailing view presented in contemporary sociology textbooks—the order perspective with its implicit sanctification of the status quo. Such a stance is untenable to me, given the spate of social problems that persist in American society. The emphasis of the conflict approach, on the other hand, questions the existing social arrangements, viewing them as sources of social problems, a position with which I agree. Implicit in such a position is the goal of re-structuring society along more humane lines.

The fact that I stress the conflict approach over the order model does not suggest that this book is a polemic. To the contrary, the social structure is also examined from a sympathetic view. The existing arrangements do provide for the stability and maintenance of the system. But the point is that by including a relatively large dose of the conflict perspective the discussion *is* a realistic appraisal of the system rather than a look through rose-colored glasses.

Although I have striven for a balanced appraisal of American society, it could be argued that the selection of topics, the ordering of these topics, and the evidence presented has subtly "stacked the deck" in favor of my own view. Because of this possibility I would hope that the reader will "interact" with this book. The reader should constantly ask: is the writer correct? is the evidence sufficient? is the writer biased? do the conclusions stack up in the light of new facts? To encourage this, I have included in each chapter several "Panels" that illustrate problems, research findings, and controversial ideas in some depth. They supplement the narrative in a way that I hope will promote controversy and debate. This questioning attitude will lead the serious reader to become a more objective observer and keen analyst of social life—a primary goal of the social sciences.

Acknowledgements. Although the final responsibility for this book is mine, it reflects the influence, work, and support of many persons. I owe a special debt to my colleagues at the University of Kansas, especially Norm Yetman, George Ritzer, and Gary Maranell, who through their ideas, expertise, wit, and friendship aided in the shaping of this product. This book and my career in sociology have been helped immeasurably by my good fortune to have Ken Kammeyer in an adjoining office. His ideas, support, good judgment, and scholarship have served me in many manifest and subtle ways for which I am grateful.

Several secretaries at the University of Kansas have worked at turning out the various phases of this manuscript. My thanks to Peggy Bartee Brockington, Linda Stanwix, Debbie Supancic, Nann Weaver, and especially Barbara Johnson.

Finally, the criticism is often made that for a male author to thank his wife for her support is both patronizing and sexist. So it may be, but when one genuinely appreciates that support and feels that without it, the book would be not only less but probably unfinished, then he must acknowledge it publicly. So I must do for my wife, Florine, is unusually supportive of my scholarly efforts.

Lawrence, Kansas   D. S. E.
August, 1973

PART I

The United States:
A Nation of Uniformity
and Diversity,
Consensus and Dissensus

Every generation of Americans has had its critics and skeptics who expected the structure of the society to break down. The number now is growing and with apparent good reason. Racial injustice continues and integration is no longer the goal of many minority group members. Poverty is still with us and the gap widens. The large American city is so ripe with problems—crime, erosion of its tax base, traffic, pollution, and inadequate services—that unless major changes are made it will be populated only by the very poor and a few of those rich enough to insulate themselves from its problems. Economic crises of inflation, unemployment, and strikes continue to plague the stability of American social life. American political institutions often seem too removed from the people and therefore seem unresponsive to their wishes. In the name of defense the United States intrudes in the affairs of other nations, gives military aid to governments in highly volatile areas, and sends Americans to fight in unpopular wars.

Many Americans are particularly upset by the breakdown of

values they hold sacred—the sanctity of the home and family is challenged by the increase in communes and trial marriages; organized religion is threatened by the rise of underground churches and atheism; patriotism is undermined by draft dodgers and flag defilers; old fashioned sexual morality is challenged by coeducational dormitories, the Pill, and an ever increasing bombardment of pornography; the highly valued work ethic is under siege by many of the young who scoff at their parents for measuring achievement by the accumulation of material things; and finally, the legitimacy of traditional authority roles (e.g., parents, teachers, ministers, coaches, and elected officials) is increasingly being questioned.

The discontent among Americans is particularly acute now because of a unique combination of historical and structural factors. No American generation but the present has faced possible extinction from the effects of the population bomb, the pollution bomb, and the hydrogen bomb. No generation has undergone such a rapid rate of change. Americans have gone from the horse and buggy to space travel in seventy years. Television is a recent phenomenon which has had tremendous impact upon American life. The trend toward greater bureaucratization continues in business, labor, school, and government. All Americans are caught in its impersonal clutches.

While these and other changes have occurred with fantastic speed, American institutions have become afflicted with old age, unwilling to change. The intransigence of American institutions in the face of rapid social and technological change has caused a gap which, if not breached, will lead to increasing despair, discontent, alienation, and hostility by the dislocated.

The problems of American society are of great magnitude, and solutions must be found. But understanding must precede action—and that is the goal of this book.

The analysis of American society is a challenging task. It is frustrating because of the heterogeneity of the population and the complexity of the forces impinging upon American social life. It is frustrating because the diversity within the United States leads to many inconsistencies and paradoxes. Furthermore, it is difficult if not impossible for a native American to be objective and consistently rational about his society.

The study of American society becomes absorbing as one gains insights about his own actions and the behavior of others. Understanding the intricate complex of forces leading to a particular type of social structure or social problem can be very rewarding. This book will attempt to give the reader just such a sociological perspective.

Part I sets the stage for an analysis of the structure (organization) and process (change) of American society. The focus will be on the characteristics of societies in general and the United States in particular. Part II analyzes the various manifestations of inequality present in American society. The final part examines the basic American institutions, focusing on the contradictory forces of stability and change found within each.

CHAPTER 1

The Duality of Social Life

SOCIAL SYSTEMS: ORDER AND CONFLICT

The analyst of society begins with a mental picture of its structure. For the scientist, this image (or model) influences what he looks for, what he sees, and how he explains the phenomena that occur within the society.

Among the characteristics of societies is one—the existence of segmentation—that is the basis for the two prevailing models of society. Every society is composed of parts. This differentiation may result from differences in age, race, sex, physical prowess, wisdom, family background, wealth, organizational membership, economic specialty, or any other characteristic considered to be salient by the members. The fundamental question concerning differentiation is this: what is the basic relationship among the parts of society? The two contradictory answers to this question provide the rationale for the two models of society—order and conflict.

One answer is that the parts of society are in harmony. They cooperate because of similar or complementary interests and because they need each other to accomplish those things beneficial to all (e.g., production and distribution of goods and services, protection). Another answer is that the subunits of society are basically in competition with each other. This view is based on the assumption that the things men desire most (wealth, power, autonomy, resources, high status) are always in short supply; hence competition and conflict are ubiquitous social phenomena.

5

The Order Model

The order model* attributes to societies the characteristics of cohesion, consensus, cooperation, reciprocity, stability, and persistence. Societies are viewed as social systems, composed of parts that are linked together into a boundary-maintaining whole. The parts of the system are basically in harmony with each other. The high degree of cooperation (and societal integration) is accomplished because there is a high degree of consensus on societal goals and on cultural values. Moreover, the different parts of the system are assumed to need each other because of complementary interests. Because the primary social process is cooperation and the system is highly integrated, all social change is gradual, adjustive, and reforming. Societies are therefore basically stable units.

For order theorists, the central issue is: What is the nature of the social bond? What holds the group together in a boundary-maintaining whole? This was the focus of one of the most important figures in sociology, Emile Durkheim, the French social theorist of the early 1900s. The various forms of integration were used by Durkheim to explain differences in suicide rates, social change, and the universality of religion.[2]

One way to focus on integration is to determine the manifest and latent consequences of social structures, norms, and social activities. Do these consequences contribute to the integration (cohesion) of the social system? Durkheim, for example, noted that the punishment of crime has the manifest (intended) consequences of punishing and deterring the criminal. The latent consequence of punishment, however, is the societal reaffirmation of what is to be considered moral. The society is thereby integrated through belief in the same rules.[3]

Taking Durkheim's lead, sociologists of the order persuasion have made many penetrating and insightful analyses of various aspects of society. By focusing on *all* the consequences of social structures and activities—intended and unintended, as well as negative (mal-integrative)—we can see behind the facades and thereby understand more fully such disparate social arrangements and activities as ceremonials (from rain dances to sporting events), social stratification, fashion, propaganda, and even political machines.**

---

* This model is most often referred to in sociology as the functional or structural-functional model. It is the basis for the analysis of American society by Robin M. Williams, Jr.[1]
** See Robert K. Merton's *Social Theory and Social Structure* for an excellent discussion of sociological research from the order (functionalist) perspective.[4]

The Conflict Model

The assumptions of the conflict model are opposite from those of the order model. The basic form of interaction is not cooperation but rather competition which often leads to conflict. Because the individuals and groups of society compete for advantage, the degree of social integration is minimal and tenuous. Social change results from the conflict among competing groups and therefore tends to be drastic and revolutionary. The ubiquitousness of conflict results from the dissimilar goals and interests of social groups. It is, moreover, a result of social organization itself.

The most famous conflict theorist was Karl Marx, who, after examining history, theorized that there exists in every society (except, Marx believed, in the last historical stage of communism) a dynamic tension between two groups—those who own the means of production and those who work for the owners. The powerful will use and abuse the powerless, thereby "sowing the seeds" of their own destruction. The destruction of the elite is accomplished when the dominated unite and overthrow the dominants.

Ralf Dahrendorf, a contemporary conflict theorist, has also viewed conflict as a ubiquitous phenomenon, not because of economic factors as Marx believed, but because of other aspects of social organization. Organization means, among other things, that power will be distributed unequally. The population will therefore be divided into the "haves" and the "have-nots" with respect to power. Since organization also means constraint, there will be a situation in all societies where the constraints are determined by the powerful, thereby further ensuring that the "have-nots" will be in conflict with the "haves." Thus, the important insight that conflict is endemic to social organization.*

One other emphasis of conflict theorists is that the unity present in society is superficial because it results not from consensus but coercion. The powerful, it is asserted, use force and fraud to keep society running smoothly, with benefits mostly accruing to those in power (see Panel 1–1).

The basic duality of social life can be seen by summarizing the opposite ways in which order and conflict theorists view the nature of society. If asked, "What is the fundamental relationship among the parts of society?" the answers of order and conflict theorists would disagree. This disagreement leads to and is based upon a

---

* The above is a very superficial account of a complex process that has been fully described by Ralf Dahrendorf.[5]

number of related assumptions about society. These are summarized in Table 1–1 on page 10.

One interesting but puzzling aspect of Table 1–1 is that these two models are held by different scientific observers *of the same phenomenon*. How can such different assumptions be derived by experts of society? The answer is that both models are correct. Each focuses on reality—but only part of that reality. Scientists have tended to accept one or the other of these models, thereby focusing on only part of social reality for at least two reasons: (1) one model

PANEL 1–1

"THE POLITICAL NATURE OF VIOLENCE"

Source: Jerome Skolnick, *The Politics of Protest* (New York: Ballantine Books, Inc., 1969), pp. 3–8.

Jerome Skolnick, an analyst of American society who is highly sensitive to the role of the powerful, has observed (in his report to the National Commission on the Causes and Prevention of Violence) that what is considered violence and what is not will actually be determined by those in power.

First, "violence" is the term used for any act that threatens the power structure. In this way the lynching of a black is less shocking (and therefore less violent) than the behavior of the black that provoked it. In other words, violence is perceived as a quality of those individuals and groups who challenge existing arrangements rather than those who uphold them. Thus, what the victimized group may see as "police brutality" is viewed by those in power as legitimate and not as violence.

Violence always refers to a disruption of some condition of order. But Skolnick has pointed out that order, like violence, is also politically defined. "Order" itself can be very destructive to some categories of persons. Carmichael and Hamilton illustrated this in their book *Black Power.* They noted that when white terrorists bombed a black church as they did in Birmingham, Alabama, and killed five children, the act was deplored by most elements of American society. But when hundreds of black babies die each year in Birmingham because of the effects of racism, no one in the power structure gets upset and calls this violence.[6] Although high infant mortality and rates of preventable disease, which are perpetuated through discrimination, take many times more lives than civil disorder, the term violence is not applied. Skolnick has suggested that we should indeed identify such outcomes

or the other was in vogue at the time of the scientist's intellectual development;* or (2) one model or the other made the most sense for the analysis of the particular problems of interest—e.g., the interest of Emile Durkheim, who devoted his intellectual energies to determining what holds society together, or the fundamental con-

* Order theorists have dominated American sociology since the 1930s. This has led to the charge by so-called radical sociologists that the contemporary sociology establishment has served as the official legitimator of the system— not the catalyst for changing the system.[7]

as "institutional violence," implying that the system itself injures and destroys.

Violence is also defined politically through the selection process. Some acts of force (to injure persons, or to destroy property) are not always forbidden or condemned in American society. Property damaged during football games, Halloween, or the Mardi Gras is often overlooked. Even 10,000 beer drinking, noisy, and sometimes destructive college students on the beaches of Florida are allowed to go on such a binge because "boys will be boys." But if the same 10,000 college students were to destroy the same amount of property in a demonstration where the goal was to change the system, then the acts would be defined as "violent" and the police called to restore order by force if necessary (which, of course, would not be defined as violence by the authorities). Thus, violence is condemned or condoned through political pressures and decisions. The basic criterion is whether the act is in approved channels or is supportive of existing social and political arrangements. If not supportive, then the acts are by definition to be condemned and punished.

The decision of whether or not to use violence to control protest is also a political one. Although the use of force by those in power ("official violence") is violent, it is not usually perceived as such. When the mayor of a large city tells his police to shoot looters, or when police officers injure persons for alleged violations of the law, then we have instances of official violence.

Skolnick's analysis of the relationship between the power structure and violence is important and useful to the analyst of any society. It highlights the benefits accruing to those persons and groups highly situated because of existing social arrangements. It also aids in understanding the behavior of those not well situated who work to change the existing system.

cern of Karl Marx, who explored the causes of revolutionary social change. The analysis of social problems is one important area where sociologists have been influenced by the order and conflict models. Let us turn to these contrary ways to view social problems before examining a synthesis of the two models.

Social Problems from the Order and Conflict Perspectives

There is general agreement among sociologists that a social problem reflects a violation of normative expectations.[8] It is a situation that is incompatible with the values of a significant number of people who agree that the situation should be altered. Put another way, a social problem is anything that is assumed to disturb the routine functioning of society. Under this rubric fall such different phe-

TABLE 1–1.   The Duality of Social Life: The Assumptions of the Order and Conflict Models of Society

	Order Model	Conflict Model
Question:	What is the fundamental relationship among the parts of society?	
Answer:	Harmony and Cooperation.	Competition and conflict.
Why:	The parts have complementary interests. Basic consensus on societal norms and values.	The things people want are always in short supply. Basic dissensus on societal norms and values.
Degree of Integration:	Highly integrated.	Loosely integrated. Whatever integration is achieved is the result of force and fraud.
Type of Social Change:	Gradual, adjustive, and reforming.	Abrupt and revolutionary.
Degree of Stability:	Stable.	Unstable.

nomena as unemployment, poverty, crime, prejudice, drug addiction, political extremism, and mental illness.

The order and conflict perspectives constrain their adherents to view the causes, consequences, and remedies to social problems in opposing ways. The order perspective focuses on deviants themselves. This approach (which has been the conventional way of studying social problems) asks: Who are the deviants? What are their social and psychological backgrounds? With whom do they associate? Deviants somehow do not conform to the standards of the dominant group; they are assumed to be out of phase with conventional behavior. This is believed to occur most often as a result of inadequate socialization. In other words, deviants have not internalized the norms and values of society because they are either brought up in an environment of conflicting value systems (as are children of immigrants or the poor in a middle class school) or are under the influence of a deviant subculture such as a gang. Since the order theorist uses the prevailing standards to define and label deviants, the existing practices and structures of society are accepted implicitly. The remedy is to rehabilitate the deviants so that they conform to the societal norms.

The conflict theorist takes a quite different approach to social problems. The adherents of this perspective criticize order theorists for "blaming the victim."[9] To focus on the individual deviant is to locate the symptom, not the disease. Individual deviants are a manifestation of a failure of society to meet the needs of individuals. The sources of crime, poverty, drug addiction, and racism are found in the laws, the customs, the quality of life, the distribution of wealth and power, and in the accepted practices of schools, governmental units and corporations. In this view, then, the schools are the problem, not dropouts; the quality of life, not mental illness; the maldistribution of wealth, not poverty; the roadblocks to success for minority group members, not apathy on their part. The established system, in this view, is not "sacred." Since it is the primary source of social problems, it, not the individual deviant, must be restructured.

Although most of this book attempts to strike a balance between the order and conflict perspectives, the conflict model is clearly favored when social problems are brought into focus. This is done explicitly for three reasons: (1) the focus on the deviant has dominated sociology and there is a need for balance; (2) the subject matter of sociology is not individuals, who are the special province of psychology, but society. If sociologists do not make a critical analysis of the social structure, then who will? Also (3) I am convinced that the source of social problems is found within the institutional framework of society. Thus, a recurrent theme of this book is that social problems are societal in origin and not the exclusive function of individual pathologies.

A Synthesis of the Order and Conflict Models

The assumptions of both models are contradictory for each comparison shown in Figure 1–1, and their contradictions highlight the duality of social life. Social interaction can be harmonious or acrimonious. Societies are integrated or divided, stable or unstable. Social change can be fast or slow, revolutionary or evolutionary.

Taken alone, each of these perspectives fosters a faulty perception and interpretation of society, but taken together, they complement each other and present a complete and realistic model. A synthesis that combines the best of each model would appear, therefore, to be the best perspective for understanding the structure and process of society.[10]

The initial assumption of a synthesis approach is that *the processes of stability and change are properties of all societies.* There is an essential paradox to human societies: they are always ordered; they are always changing. These two elemental properties of social life must be recognized by the observer of society. Within any society there are forces providing impetus for change *and* there are forces insisting on rooted permanence. Allen Wheelis has labelled these two contrary tendencies as the instrumental process and the institutional process, respectively.[11]

The instrumental process is based upon man's desire for technological change—to find new and more efficient techniques to achieve man's goals. The institutional process, on the other hand, designates all those activities that are dominated by the quest for certainty. Man is bound in his activities often by customs, traditions, myths, and religious beliefs. So there are rites, taboos, and mores that persons obey without thinking. So, too, are there modern institutions such as monotheism, monogamy, private property, and the sovereign state, all of which are coercive in that they limit freedom of choice but they are assumed proper by almost all individuals in American society.

These two processes constitute the dialectic of society. As contrary tendencies, they generate tension because the instrumental forces are constantly prodding the institutions to change when it is not their nature to do so.

The second assumption is that *societies are organized but that the very process of organization generates conflict*. Organization implies, among other things, differential allocation of power. Inequalities in power are manifested in at least two conflict-generating ways: differentials in decision-making, and inequalities in the system of social stratification (social classes and minority groups). Scarce resources can never be distributed equally to all persons and groups in society. The powerful are always differentially rewarded and make the key decisions as to the allocation of scarce resources.

A third basic assumption for a synthesis model is that *society is a social system*. The term "social system" has several important implications: (1) that there is not chaos but some semblance of order—that action within the unit is, in a general way, predictable; (2) that boundaries exist which may be in terms of geographical space or membership; and (3) that there are parts which are interdependent—thus, conveying the reality of differentiation and unity. A society is a system made up of many subsystems (e.g., groups, organizations, communities). Although these are all related in some way, some are strongly linked to others while others have only a remote linkage. The interdependence of the parts implies further that events and decisions in one sector may have a profound influence on the entire system. A strike in the transportation industry, for example, eventually impinges upon all individuals and groups. But some events have little or no effect upon all of American society. Most important for the synthesis approach is the recognition that the parts of the system may have complementary interests with other parts but may also have exclusive, incompatible interests and goals. There is generally some degree of cooperation and harmony found in society because of consensus over common goals and because of similar interests (e.g., defense against external threats). Some degree of competition and dissensus is also present because of incompatible interests, scarcity of resources and unequal rewards. Societies, then, are imperfect social systems.

A fourth assumption is that *societies are held together by complementary interests, by consensus on cultural values, but also by coercion*. Societies do cohere. There are forces that bind diverse groups together into a single entity. The emphasis of both order and conflict models provides twin bases for such integration—consensus and coercion.

Finally, *social change is a ubiquitous phenomenon in all societies*.

13

It may be gradual or abrupt, reforming or revolutionary. All social systems change. Order theorists have tended to view change as a gradual phenomenon occurring either because of innovation or because of differentiation (e.g., dividing units into subunits to separate activities and make the total operation more efficient within the society). This view of change is partially correct. Change can also be abrupt, it can come about because of internal violence, or it may result from forces outside the society (i.e., reaction to events outside the system, or accepting the innovations of others).

To summarize, a synthesizing of the order and conflict models views society as having ". . . two faces of equal reality—one of stability, harmony, and consensus and one of change, conflict, and constraint."[12]

The remainder of this chapter illustrates the duality of social life by examining American society from the perspectives of the conflict and order theorists. We will consider the sources of disunity in the United States and the major instances of violence that have occurred throughout American history. Despite the existence of division and violence the United States is unified at least minimally. We will, therefore, also consider the factors that work to unify.

DIVISION AND VIOLENCE IN AMERICAN SOCIETY

Societies are integrated but disunity and disharmony also exist to some degree in all societies. It is especially important to examine the segmenting influences in American society for they aid in explaining contemporary conflict and social change.

The Divisive Forces in American Society

Social scientists have found that in small groups the more heterogeneous the group, the more likely cliques will form. A group composed of members of one religion, for example, cannot form cliques on the basis of religion, but one with three religions represented has the potential of subdividing into three parts.[13] This principle applies to larger organizations as well, including societies. The United States, then, has the potential of many, many subgroups since it is so diverse. The United States is in effect a mosaic of different groups—different on a number of dimensions such as occupation, racial background, education, and economic circumstances. Let us briefly examine these and other dimensions and the manner in which they bring about segmentation in American society.

1. *Size*. The United States is large in size in the number of people and the expanse of land. Both of these facts have a segmenting influence in American society. With respect to population size, there is an accepted sociological proposition that states: "As the population of a social organization increases, the number of its parts and the degree of their specialization also increase."[14] If, as in the United States, there is not only a large population (well over 210 million) but a high level of technology as well, then the division of labor becomes very refined. This division is so refined that there are over 30,000 different occupations recognized and catalogued by the United States Census Bureau.

If people have specialized occupations they will probably interact most often with persons like themselves. Because of similar interests they will tend to cooperate with each other and perhaps compete with other groups for advantage. The important social theorist of the early 1900s, Robert Michels, wrote about this tendency for exclusion and conflict as a universal tendency in all social organizations.

> By a universally applicable social law, every organ of the collectivity, brought into existence through the need for the division of labor, creates for itself, as soon as it becomes consolidated, interests peculiar to itself. The existence of these special interests involves a necessary conflict with the interests of the collectivity.[15]

A second segmenting factor related to size has to do with land rather than population. The United States, excluding Alaska and Hawaii, has an area of 3,615,123 square miles. Found within this large territory is a wide range in topography and climate. Some areas are sparsely settled, others not. Some regions are attracting new residents at a much faster rate than others.

Traditionally there have been pronounced regional differences (and sometimes rivalries) because each region had its own economic specialization (i.e., its own industry and agriculture) and each was relatively isolated from the influences of the others. The revolutions in manufacturing, transportation, and communication have helped to break down this regionalism.

Although regionalism has been declining, it remains a force that sometimes divides Americans. As evidence of this, many votes in Congress show that regional considerations often outweigh national ones. Many non-southern Americans have stereotyped ideas of southerners. Southerners often hold stereotypes of the "Yankee" that may cause the rejection of ideas and innovations from such a source. Consequently, communication within American society is often blocked and interaction stifled because persons from one region feel not only physically separate from and but also superior to persons from other regions.

2. *Social class.* Economic differences provide important sources of division in American society. There is the natural resentment of persons without the necessities of life toward those with a bountiful supply of not only the necessities but luxuries as well. There is also hostility toward a system that provides excessive benefits (or excessive hurdles) to persons not on the basis of demonstrated skills but on family background.

Status (prestige) differentials also divide Americans. Organizations, residential areas, and social clubs sometimes exclude certain persons and groups because of their social "inferiority."

3. *Race.* Throughout human history race has been used as a criterion for differentiation. If any factor makes a difference in American society it is race. Blacks, American Indians, Mexican Americans, and other minority racial groups have often been systematically excluded from residential areas, occupations, organizations and even sometimes denied equal rights under the law.* Although the overt system of racial discrimination has changed, racist acts continue in American society with the result that these disadvantaged groups continue to be second class citizens.

Racial strife has occurred throughout American history. Slave revolts, Indian battles, race riots, and lynchings have occurred with regularity. Racial conflict continues today not only in the ghettos of large cities but in most neighborhoods where the minority group is large enough to be perceived by the majority as a threat, in univer-

---

* The 1970 Census revealed the following racial distribution for the United States:

Race	Number	Percentage
white	177,748,975	87.5
black	22,580,289	11.1
Am. Indian	792,730	.4
Japanese	591,290	.3
Chinese	435,062	.2
Filipino	343,060	.2
all other	720,520	.3

sities and secondary schools, in factories and other places of work, and in the armed forces. The rhetoric of violence has been escalated recently by minority group leaders. The appeal of militant groups is ever greater, particularly among the young. Minority group members are no longer willing to wait for slow racial reform. They are bent upon seeing justice done now. It is equally clear that many majority group members will do virtually anything to keep the status quo (i.e., to retain an advantageous position for themselves). Many minority persons seeking to shake the status quo may participate in various acts of violence. This violence brings repression by the powerful which further angers and frustrates the minority— thus a treadmill of violence and division.

4. *Ethnic groups.* The United States is inhabited by a multitude of ethnic groups that migrated to this country in different waves. It has been assumed that the mixture of these diverse peoples would in time blend into a homogeneous type. Glazer and Moynihan, however, have pointed out forcefully that the "melting pot" did *not* happen.[16] To the contrary, many ethnic groups have retained the customs and ideas brought to this country from another society. Many Americans continue to vote for or against candidates based on their ethnicity. Some groups have preferred isolation while others have experienced forced segregation.

5. *Religion.* Religion, like race and ethnicity, evokes an emotional response in individuals. It is difficult to be neutral about religion. It is almost impossible to accept the idea that religious beliefs other than one's own are equi-legitimate. Religion also has a polarizing effect because it is often the basis for selecting (or rejecting) mates, friends, neighbors, schools, and employees. Therefore religious differences in the United States not only differentiate persons but also may provide the basis for conflict.[17]

Religious intolerance is not unknown in American history. Although the nation was founded on the principle of religious freedom, at various times and places Jews, Catholics, Quakers, Mennonites, and atheists have been targets of religious bigotry.

There have been political parties (Know-Nothing Party), organizations (Ku Klux Klan and the American Nazi Party), and demagogues (Gerald L. K. Smith, George Lincoln Rockwell) that have been anti-Catholic and anti-Semitic. Their moderate success in attracting followers demonstrates that some Americans are susceptible to such appeals. The effect has been to lessen the probability of inter-faith cooperation and enhance the likelihood of conflict.

6. *Age structure.* Young people, particularly college students, tend to feel alienated from an economic and political system they perceive as hypocritical and inequitable.*

Young people are especially alienated today by political impotence. They feel they have no impact on a political system that is undemocratic and that has ever increasing power over their lives. Persons typically respond to feelings of alienation in one of three ways: (1) apathy—to repress the problem and say it does not matter; (2) escape—to physically withdraw (e.g., join a commune) or repress the problem through drugs, alcohol, religion, television, or novels; or (3) attempt to change the alienating conditions. Americans of all ages have reacted to their own alienation by apathy or escape. Some, particularly young intellectuals, have chosen the third alternative.

How can these persons change the system if they are self-defined as powerless? A first step is legitimate, polite protest which usually takes the form of voting, petitions, or writing Congressmen. A second option is to use impolite yet legitimate forms of protest (e.g., peaceful demonstrations, picket lines, boycotts, and marches). The third alternative, used when others fail, is to employ illegitimate forms of protest (e.g., civil disobedience, riots, bombings, and guerilla warfare).[19]

Illegitimate protest is selected by dissident groups because of the intransigence of those in power to change. The dissident groups consider their actions legitimate because it is for a just cause ("the ends justify the means") but these protests are perceived as illegitimate by those in power. Those in authority resort to force, oftentimes intensifying the zeal and purpose of the protestor, and frequently rallying previously uncommitted persons to the cause of the dissidents.

Implicit in this section is the notion that highly differentiated social systems, like that in the United States, must cope with the realities of disharmony, conflict of interest, and even violence. There is no alternative to conflict because of the diverse conditions of American social structure. This is not to say that conflict is altogether bad. There can be positive consequences of conflict for both parties to the conflict and the society as well.[20]

All societies have the potential for cleavage and conflict because of the differential allocation of power. Concomitant with having power is the holding of other advantages (prestige, privilege, and

---

* Although the student movement is a worldwide phenomenon, the present discussion focuses on the American scene. For analyses of student revolt in international perspective see especially the entire issue of *Daedalus* 97.[18]

economic benefits). Persons with advantage almost invariably wish to keep it, and those without often want to change the reward system.

Coupled with the stratification system in the United States are other aspects of social structure that increase the probability of conflict. The United States, perhaps more than any other society, is populated by a multitude of ethnic groups, racial groups, and religious groups. The diversity is further increased by the existence of regional differences and a generation gap. Although assimilation has occurred to some degree, the different groups and categories have not blended into a homogeneous mass, but continue to remain separate—often with a pride that makes assimilation unlikely and conflict possible.

Violence in the United States and the Myth of Peaceful Progress

There are two beliefs held typically by Americans that combine to make the "myth of peaceful progress."[21] First, there is a widely held notion that the United States is made up of diverse groups that have learned to compromise differences in a peaceful manner. Second, there is the belief that any group in the United States can gain its share of power, prosperity, and respectability merely by playing the game according to the rules. Hence, there is no need for political violence in America since the system works for the advantage of all.

It is precisely because these beliefs are widely shared that most Americans do not understand such confrontations as those between the National Guard and students, the police and black snipers in city ghettos, or the five year grape boycott by Cesar Chavez and his followers. These are believed to be aberrations, and are explained away by saying that they are communist-inspired, or that some groups (e.g., blacks) are exceptions to the rule because they are basically immoral and irrational. Perhaps the most prevalent explanation locates the source of all violence in the individual psyches of the persons involved.

These explanations are incomplete because they locate the blame outside the system itself. American history shows that, with but few exceptions, powerless and downtrodden groups seeking power have not achieved it without a struggle. American institutions, Rubenstein has noted, are better designed to facilitate the upward mobility of talented individuals than oppressed groups. "Most groups which have engaged in mass violence have done so only after a long period of fruitless, relatively nonviolent struggle in which established procedures have been tried and found wanting."[22] The problem is that the United States, like all other societies, has not and does not allow for the nonviolent transfer of power.

Throughout American history groups that were oppressed resorted to various legitimate and illegitimate means to secure rights and privileges which they believed to be rightfully theirs. The power structure typically reacted either by doing nothing or by repression—the choice depending upon the degree to which the minority groups' actions were perceived as a real threat. The following is a partial list of groups which at various times in American history have resorted to violence to achieve social, economic or political objectives.[23]

Revolutionary colonists. The most notable case of violence by a minority in early American history was the Revolutionary War. The United States was literally born through violence. The American colonists first petitioned the King of England to redress grievances and when this failed they turned to acts of civil disobedience and finally eight years of war. "The Declaration of Independence," clearly a revolutionary document, provided the rationale for mass violence:

> We hold these truths to be self-evident, that all men are created equal, that they are endowed by their Creator with certain unalienable Rights, that among these are Life, Liberty, and the pursuit of Happiness. That to secure these rights, Governments are instituted among Men, deriving their just powers from the consent of the governed. That whenever any Form of Government becomes destructive of these ends, it is the Right of the People to alter or to abolish it, and to institute new Government, laying its foundation on such principals and organizing its powers in such form as to them shall seem most likely to effect their Safety and Happiness. Prudence, indeed, will dictate that Governments long established should not be changed for light and transient causes; and accordingly all experiences hath shewn that mankind are more disposed to suffer, while evils are sufferable, than to right themselves by abolishing the forms to which they are accustomed. But when a long train of abuses and usurpations, pursuing invariably the same Object evinces a design to reduce them under absolute Despotism, it is their right, it is their duty, to throw off such Government, and to provide new Guards for their future security . . .

This document, a cornerstone of American heritage, legitimates the use of violence by oppressed peoples. It could have been written by a modern day militant. While still revered, its content is no longer taken literally by those in power or by the bulk of the American citizenry.

American Indians. Long before the Revolutionary War, and continuing to the present day, Indians have attempted to change the order established by whites. When white settlers took their land, ruined their hunting, and imprisoned them on reservations, the Indians fought these occurrences and were systematically suppressed by the United States government.* Currently, Indians will occasionally boycott, or make demands, or even try to reclaim territory.

Exploited farmers. Farmers have used violence on occasion to fight economic exploitation. Between the Revolutionary War and 1800, for example, three such revolts took place—Shay's Rebellion, the Whiskey Rebellion, and Fries Rebellion. The protesting farmer has used various forms of violence (destruction of property, looting, and killing) throughout American history. Some modern farmers have resorted to acts of violence to publicize their demands and to terrorize other farmers in order to present a united front against their opponents.

Slaveholders. Feeling the threat of the abolitionist movement, white southerners beginning in about 1820 used violent means to preserve slavery. In the early stages this amounted to civil disobedience, and later it burst out into fighting in places like "bleeding Kansas." Eventually the South seceded and the Civil War was waged—a classic example of a minority group using violence to force a change and being suppressed by the power of the majority.

WASP supremacists. Following the Civil War and continuing to the present day, some whites have engaged in guerilla warfare, terrorism, and lynching in order to maintain the subjugation of blacks.** From 1882 to 1903, for example, 1,985 blacks were killed by southern lynch mobs.[25]

Riots, lynchings and mob actions are not solely southern phenomena. Many Americans from other sections of the country have used these techniques against various "alien" groups (usually Catholics and immigrants from non-Teutonic Europe) in order to maintain their superiority. American history is rife with examples of this

---

* For the Indian's end of the "winning" of the American West, see the powerful indictment of the whites by Dee Brown.[24]
** Some examples of alleged white violence toward blacks in the recent past are: the assassinations of Medgar Evers and Martin Luther King, Jr., the bombing of a black church in Birmingham, Alabama, during the Sunday school hour killing five children.

phenomenon: "Native Americans" tore apart the Irish section of Philadelphia in 1844; a Catholic Church and homes of Irish Catholics were destroyed in Boston in 1854; Chinese and Japanese immigrants were victims of both riots and discrimination particularly on the West Coast; Japanese, even those who were American citizens, were put in "concentration camps" during World War II because their patriotism was suspect; and Jews have been the objects of physical attack, boycotts, intimidation, and discrimination throughout American history. Perhaps the best contemporary example of mob violence against intruders can be seen in some communities where an all-white neighborhood is faced with one or more black families moving in. Threats, burning crosses, ostracization, and occasional physical violence have occurred with alarming regularity where black "invasion" of previously all-white areas has taken place. This is not a southern phenomenon but an American one.*

Ethnic minorities. Immigrant groups (i.e., those groups most recently immigrant) as well as racial groups, because they have been the target of discrimination, threats, and physical violence, have themselves participated in violence. Sometimes gangs have attacked the groups responsible for their deprived condition. Most often, however, hostility by immigrants has been aimed at groups with less power, either toward blacks or more newly arrived immigrants.

Violence by blacks has occurred throughout American history. Always the victims, they have sometimes responded to violence in kind. During the years of slavery more than 250 insurrections took place. Mass black violence has occurred in many major cities (e.g., Chicago and Washington, D.C., in 1919, Detroit in 1943, and again in 1967, Los Angeles in 1965, and Newark in 1967).

The rage that blacks must feel against whites has surfaced sporadically in small and diffuse ways as well. Most commonly it has been manifested in individual crimes (murder, theft, and rape) or gang assaults on whites or in destruction of property owned by whites.

Labor disputants. Another relatively powerless group resorting to violence to achieve their aims was American labor. The working men of the 1870's attempted to organize for collective action against unfair policies of the industrialists. Unions such as the Knights of

---

* Ironically, this type of violence usually occurs in blue-collar areas (black "invasion" is not a threat in the more expensive neighborhoods) where individuals are more prone toward "law and order" political candidates. Apparently when individuals feel personally threatened "law and order" becomes vigilantism.

Labor, American Federation of Labor, and the Industrial Workers of the World formed. Their primary tactic was the strike, which in itself is non-violent. But strikers often used force to keep persons from crossing the picket lines. Nor were the owners blameless. Their refusal to change existing wages, hours, and working conditions was the source of grievance. They sometimes turned to violence themselves to suppress the unions (e.g., threats and hiring persons to physically break up picket lines).

The intransigent refusal of the owners to change the truly awful conditions of nineteenth century workers resulted in considerable violence in many industries, particularly in the coal mining, steel, timber, and railroad industries.

Labor violence, as in other cases mentioned previously, was ultimately effective. Working conditions, wages, and security of the workingman improved. Legislation was passed providing for arbitration of differences, recognition of unions, and so on. Clearly, the use of force was necessary to gain advances for the laboring man.

Given the evidence just cited, it is remarkable that people still hold to the "Myth of Peaceful Progress." Violence was necessary to give birth to the United States. Violence was used both to keep the blacks in servitude and to free them. Violence was used to defeat rebellious Indians and to keep them on reservations. Additionally, violence has been a necessary means for many groups in American society to achieve equality or something approaching parity in power and in the rights that all Americans are supposed to enjoy.

The powerful have not been munificent in giving a break to the powerless. To the contrary, much effort has been expended by the powerful to keep the powerless in that condition. Many times in American history, violence has been the only catalyst for change. Minority groups in the United States (e.g., blacks, women, farmers) have repeatedly gone outside of existing law. To these groups, the use of force was justified because of the need to right insufferable wrongs—the very reason the colonists gave for breaking from England. We should note, however, that violence does not always work. The Indian revolts were not beneficial in any way to the Indians. Moreover, some groups such as the Jews have advanced with comparatively little violence.[26] Historically, however, "violence" is, as H. Rap Brown, the black militant, has said, "as American as cherry pie." The Presidential Commissions on Civil Disorders and Violence have laid bare the inaccuracies of the "peaceful progress" idea held by so many Americans. The uniform remedy suggested by these commissions for minimizing violence is to solve the cause of social unrest and perceived injustice. Minority groups

23

cannot be blamed for revolt if they are reacting against a system that systematically disadvantages them.

THE INTEGRATIVE FORCES IN AMERICAN SOCIETY

Most order theorists recognize that conflict, disharmony and division occur within societies, particularly in complex, heterogeneous societies. They stress, however, the opposite societal characteristics of cooperation, harmony, and unity. They see American society as "We the people of the United States . . ." rather than a conglomerate of sometimes hostile groups.

In particular, order theorists focus on what holds society together. What are the forces that somehow keep anarchy from becoming a reality—or as the philosopher Hobbes asked long ago, "Why is there not a war of all against all?" The answer to this fundamental question is found in the combined effects of a number of factors.

Functional integration. Probably the most important unifying factor is the phenomenon of "functional integration." In a highly differentiated society such as the United States with its very specialized division of labor, interaction among different segments occurs with some regularity. Interdependence often results because no group is entirely self-sufficient. The farmer needs the miller, the processor, and retail agents, as well as the fertilizer manufacturer and the agricultural experimenters. Manufacturers need raw materials on the one hand and customers on the other. Management needs workers and the workers need management.

These groups, because they need each other, because each gains from the interaction, work to perpetuate a social framework that maximizes benefits to both parties and minimizes conflict or the breaking of the relationship. Written and unwritten rules emerge to govern these relationships, usually leading to cooperation rather than either isolation or conflict, and to linkages between different (and potentially conflicting) groups.

Consensus on societal values. A second basis for the unification of diverse groups in American society is that almost all Americans hold certain fundamental values in common.* Order theorists as-

* The common value orientations of Americans will be explored in detail in Chapter 2.

sume that commonly held values are like social glue binding other-wise diverse people in a cohesive societal unit. Unlike functional integration, unity is achieved here through similarity rather than through difference.

Most Americans believe that democracy is the best possible gov-ernment. Americans accept the wishes of the majority on election day. Defeated candidates, for example, do not go off into the hills with their followers to blow up bridges and otherwise harass the government. Most Americans are patriotic. They revere American heritage and believe strongly in individualism, free enterprise, and the Judeo-Christian ethic.

There are many symbols that epitomize the consensus of Ameri-cans with respect to basic values. One such unifying symbol is the American flag. Although a mere piece of cloth, the flag clearly symbolizes something approaching the sacred. Reverence for the flag is evidenced by the shock shown when it is defiled and by the punishment given to defilers. The choice of the flag as an object to spit on, or burn, is a calculated one by dissident groups. They choose to defile it precisely because of what it represents and because most Americans revere it so strongly.

Similarly, such documents as the Declaration of Independence and the Constitution are held in high esteem and serve to unify Americans.

The American heritage is also revered through holidays such as Thanksgiving or Independence Day. Consensus is also achieved through the collective "worship" of American heroes such as George Washington, Abraham Lincoln, and Dwight Eisenhower.

The social order. A third factor that unifies all Americans, at least minimally, is that they are all subject to similar influences and "rules of the game." Americans are answerable to the same body of law (at the national level) and they are under the same govern-ment. Additionally, Americans use the same language, the same system of monetary exchange, the same standards for measure-ment, and so on. The order in society is evidenced by the fact that Americans take for granted such assorted practices as obeying traffic lights, the use of credit, and the acceptance of checks in lieu of money.

Group membership. A source for unity (as well as cleavage) is group memberships. Some groups are exclusive, since they limit membership to a particular race, ethnic group, income category, religion, or other characteristic. The existence of exclusive organizations creates tension if persons are excluded who want to be included, because exclusiveness generally implies feelings of superiority. Country clubs, fraternities, some churches, and some neighborhoods are based on the twin foundations of exclusiveness and superiority. In American society, however, there are groups whose membership consists of persons from varying backgrounds (i.e. the membership includes rich and poor or black and white). Consequently, heterogeneous organizations such as political parties, religious denominations or churches, and veterans organizations allow members the chance not only to interact with persons unlike themselves but also to join together in a common cause.

Many, if not most, Americans who belong to several organizations belong to organizations with different compositions by race, religion or other salient characteristics. To the extent that these cross-cutting memberships and allegiances exist, they tend to "cancel out" potential cleavages along social class, race, or other lines. Individuals belonging to several different organizations will probably feel some "cross-pressures" (i.e. pulls in opposite directions), thereby preventing polarization.

Additionally most Americans belong to at least one organization such as a school, church, or civic group with norms that support those of the total society. These organizations support the government and what it stands for and they expect their members to do the same.

International competition and conflict. External threats to the society's existence unify. The advice Machiavelli gave his "prince" is a regrettable truth: "if the Prince is in trouble he should promote a war." This was the advice that Secretary of State Seward gave to President Lincoln prior to the Civil War. Although expedient advice from the standpoint of preserving unity, it was, Lincoln noted, only a short-term solution.

A real threat to security unifies those groups, no matter how diverse, who feel threatened. Thus a reasonable explanation for lack of unity in America's involvement in an Indo-China war would be that the Viet Cong are not perceived by most Americans as a real threat to their security.

The mass media. The world is in the midst of a communications revolution. Only in very recent times has television, for example, expanded to encompass virtually every home in the United States. This phenomenon—universal exposure to television—has been blamed, among other things, for the rise in juvenile delinquency, lowering cultural tastes, contributing to general moral deterioration, and suppressing creativity.[27] These damning criticisms are countered by order theorists who see television and the other forms of mass media as performing several integrative functions. Government officials, for example, can use the media to shape public opinion (e.g. to unite against an "enemy" or to sacrifice by paying higher taxes). The media also reinforce the values and norms of society. Newspaper editorials extol certain persons and events while decrying others. Soap operas are stories involving moral dilemmas with virtue winning out. Newspaper and magazine stories under the caption, "It Could Only Have Happened in America," abound. The media do not, except for a few exceptions, "rock the boat." American heroes are praised and her enemies vilified. The American way is the right way; the ways of others are considered incorrect, or downright immoral.

Planned integration. Charismatic figures or other persons of influence may work to unite segmented parts of the system (conversely, they can also promote division). Thus, a union leader or the archbishop of a Catholic diocese can, through personal exhortation or by example, convince his members to cooperate rather than compete, or to open membership requirements rather than maintain exclusiveness.

Public officials on the local, state, and national levels can use their power to integrate the parts of the society in three major ways: (1) by passing laws to eliminate barriers among groups; (2) by working to solve the problems that segment the society; (3) by providing mediators to help negotiate settlements between feuding groups such as management and labor.[28] High officials such as the President utilize various means of integration. First, there is the technique of cooptation (i.e., appointing a member of a dissident group to a policy-making body to appease the dissenting group). Second, he can use his executive powers to enforce and interpret the laws in such a way as to unite groups within the society. Finally, the President may use the media to persuade the people. The President can request television time on all networks during prime time, thereby reaching most of the adult population in order to use whatever powers of persuasion he has to unite diverse groups.

Expanding economy. A final integrating factor in contemporary American society is that the majority have a relatively high standard of living. Most Americans do not feel oppressed. Even many persons who do not have many material blessings tend to believe in the American creed that anyone can be upwardly mobile—if not themselves, then at least their children.

Thus, contrary to Karl Marx's prediction over a century ago that capitalism would be overthrown by an oppressed majority, most Americans today consider themselves as "haves" rather than as "have-nots." There has been no polarization along purely economic lines because blue collar workers are often relatively well-off financially (many make more money than persons with more prestigious jobs).

SUMMARY

The order and conflict models of society are both significant, and they will be utilized in the remainder of this book. While each, by itself, is important, a realistic analysis must include both. The order model must be included because there is integration, order, and stability, because the parts are more or less interdependent, and because most social change is gradual and adjustive. The conflict model is equally important because society is not always a harmonious unit. To the contrary, much of social life is based on competition. Societal integration is fragile; it is often based on subtle or blatant coercion.

A crucial difference between the two models is the implicit assumption of each as to the nature of the social structure (rules, customs, institutions, social stratification, and the distribution of power). The order perspective assumes that the social structure is basically right and proper because it serves the fundamental function of maintaining society. There is, therefore, an implicit acceptance of the status quo, assuming that the system works. As we examine the major institutions of society in this book, one of the tasks will be to determine how each of these institutions aids in societal integration.

Although order theorists also look for the dysfunctions of institutions, rules, organizations, and customs (dysfunctions refer to those consequences that are malintegrative), the critical examination of society is the primary thrust of conflict theorists. While this book will describe the way American society is structured and how this arrangement works for societal integration, a major consideration will center around the questions, "who benefits under these arrangements and who does not?" Thus, the legitimacy of the system will always be doubted. This is, in the words of Skolnick and Currie, appropriate to the values of a democratic society:

> Democratic conceptions of society have always held that institutions exist to serve man, and that, therefore, they must be accountable to men. Where they fail to meet the tests imposed on them, democratic theory holds that they ought to be changed.[29]

SUGGESTED FURTHER READING

Johnson, Chalmers, *Revolutionary Change* (Boston: Little, Brown and Company, 1966). A political scientist examines revolutionary change incorporating the insights of the order and conflict perspectives.

Lenski, Gerhard E., *Power and Privilege: A Theory of Social Stratification* (New York: McGraw-Hill Book Company, 1966). Chapters 1 and 2 provide an excellent discussion of the order and conflict perspectives with the author's synthesis of the two.

Rubenstein, Richard E., *Rebels in Eden: Mass Political Violence in the United States* (Boston: Little, Brown and Company, 1970). This is an account of the history of violence in the United States that destroys the "myth of peaceful progress."

Skolnick, Jerome, *The Politics of Protest* (New York: Ballantine Books, 1969). This is a task force report to the National Commission on the Causes and Prevention of Violence. It provides an excellent survey of the sources of contemporary protest in American society from a conflict perspective.

Williams, Robin M., Jr., *American Society: A Sociological Interpretation*, Third Edition (New York: Alfred A. Knopf, 1970). This text examines American society from the order (functionalist) perspective.

NOTES AND REFERENCES

1. Robin M. Williams, Jr., *American Society: A Sociological Interpretation*, Third Edition (New York: Alfred A. Knopf, 1970).

2. Emile Durkheim, *Suicide*, John A. Spaulding and George Simpson (trans.), (New York: The Free Press, 1951), originally published in 1897; Emile Durkheim, *The Division of Labor in Society*, George Simpson (trans.), (New York: The Free Press, 1933), first published in 1893; and Emile Durkheim, *The Elementary Forms of Religious Life*, Joseph Ward Swain (trans.), (New York: Collier Books, 1961), first published in 1912.

3. Emile Durkheim, *The Rules of the Sociological Method*, (Eighth Edition), (Glencoe: The Free Press, 1938), pp. 64–75.

4. Robert K. Merton, *Social Theory and Social Structure*, (Second Edition), (Glencoe: The Free Press, 1957), pp. 19–84.

5. Ralf Dahrendorf, *Class and Class Conflict in Industrial Society* (Stanford, Calif.: Stanford University Press, 1959).

6. Stokely Carmichael and Charles V. Hamilton, *Black Power: The Politics of Liberation in America* (New York: Vintage Books, 1967), p. 4.

7. *Sociological Inquiry* 40 (Winter, 1970).

8. This section depends largely on the insights from three sources: John Horton, "Order and Conflict Theories of Social Problems as Competing Ideologies," *American Journal of Sociology* 71 (May, 1966), pp. 701–713; Jerome H. Skolnick and Elliott Currie, "Approaches to Social Problems," *Crisis in American Institutions*, Jerome H. Skolnick and Elliott Currie (eds.), (Boston: Little, Brown and Company, 1970), pp. 1–16; and Earl Rubington and Martin S. Weinberg (eds.), *The Study of Social Problems: 5 Perspectives* (New York: Oxford University Press, 1971).

9. William Ryan, *Blaming the Victim* (New York: Pantheon Books, 1971).

10. A number of analysts in recent years have attempted such a synthesis: Pierre van den Berghe, "Dialectics and Functionalism: Toward a Theoretical Synthesis," *American Sociological Review* 28 (October, 1963), pp. 697–705; Gerhard E. Lenski, *Power and Privilege: A Theory of Social Stratification* (New York: McGraw-Hill, 1966); and Chalmers Johnson, *Revolutionary Change* (Boston: Little, Brown and Company, 1966).

11. Allen Wheelis, *The Quest for Identity* (New York: W. W. Norton and Co., Inc., 1958).

12. Ralf Dahrendorf, "Out of Utopia: Toward a Reorientation of Sociological Analysis," *American Journal of Sociology*, 64 (September, 1968), p. 127.

13. James A. Davies, "Structural Balance, Mechanical Solidarity, and Interpersonal Relations," *Sociological Theories in Progress I*, Joseph Berger, Morris Zelditch, Jr., and Bo Anderson (eds.), (Boston: Houghton Mifflin Company, 1966), pp. 74–101.

14. Paul E. Mott, *The Organization of Society* (Englewood Cliffs, N.J.: Prentice-Hall, Inc., 1965), p. 50.

15. Robert Michels, *Political Parties*, Eden and Cedar Paul (trans.), (New York: The Free Press, 1966), p. 389.

16. Nathan Glazer and Daniel Patrick Moynihan, *Beyond the Melting Pot: The Negroes, Puerto Ricans, Jews, Italians, and Irish of New York City*, (Cambridge, Massachusetts: The M.I.T. Press, 1963). See also, Andrew M. Greeley, "White Against White: The Enduring Ethnic Conflict," *The White Majority*, Louise Kapp Howe, (ed.) (New York: Vintage Books, 1970), pp. 111–118.

17. Earl Raab (ed.), *Religious Conflict in America* (Garden City, New York: Doubleday & Company, Inc., Anchor Books, 1964); and

Robert Lee and Martin E. Marty (eds.), *Religion and Social Conflict* (New York: Oxford Univ. Press, 1964).

18. *Daedalus* 97 (Winter, 1968) entitled, "Students and Politics."

19. ·David O. Arnold, "The American Way of Death: The Roots of Violence in American Society," *The Age of Protest,* Walt Anderson (ed.), (Pacific Palisades, Calif.: Goodyear Publishing Company, Inc., 1969), pp. 262–268.

20. Lewis Coser, *The Functions of Social Conflict* (New York: The Free Press, 1956); and Joseph S. Himes, "The Functions of Racial Conflict," *Social Forces* 45 (September, 1966), pp. 1–10.

21. The following discussion is drawn largely from three staff reports to the National Commission on the Causes and Prevention of Violence: Jerome H. Skolnick, *The Politics of Protest* (New York: Ballantine Books, Inc., 1969); Hugh Davis Graham and Ted Robert Gurr, *The History of Violence in America* (New York: Bantam Books, 1969); and James F. Kirkham, Sheldon G. Levy, and William J. Crotty, *Assassination and Political Violence* (New York: Bantam Books, 1970). Also helpful were: Richard E. Rubenstein, *Rebels in Eden: Mass Political Violence in the United States* (Boston: Little, Brown and Company, 1970), and a series of analyses by a number of eminent social scientists appearing in the *New York Times Magazine* (April 28, 1968) under the title, "Is America by Nature a Violent Society?"

22. Rubenstein, *Rebels in Eden,* p. 8.

23. Graham and Gurr, *The History of Violence in America;* Skolnick, *The Politics of Protest,* pp. 10–15; Kirkham, Levy, and Crotty, *Assassination and Political Violence,* pp. 212–237; John Higham, *Strangers in the Land* (New Brunswick, N.J.: Rutgers University Press, 1955); David W. Chalmers, *Hooded Americanism* (Chicago: Quadrangle, 1968); Graham Adams, Jr., *Age of Industrial Violence* (New York: Columbia University Press, 1966); and Arthur I. Waskow, *From Race Riot to Sit-In* (Garden City, New York: Doubleday and Company, 1966).

24. Dee Brown, *Bury My Heart At Wounded Knee* (New York: Holt, Rinehart & Winston, Inc., 1971).

25. James E. Cutler, *Lynch-Law: An Investigation into the History of Lynching in the United States.* (New York: Longmans, Green, 1905), p. 177.

26. Rubenstein, *Rebels in Eden,* p. 18.

27. Melvin L. De Fleur, *Theories of Mass Communication,* Second Edition (New York: David McKay Company, Inc., 1970), p. 5.

28. Paul E. Mott, *The Organization of Society* (England Cliffs, N.J.: Prentice-Hall, Inc., 1965), pp. 283–284.

29. Skolnick and Currie, "Approaches to Social Problems," (see note 8 above), p. 15.

CHAPTER 2

Culture

CULTURE: THE KNOWLEDGE THAT PEOPLE SHARE

To know the culture of a society is to understand fully that society. Culture explains most individual and group behavior as well as the persistence of most aspects of social life.

The Characteristics of Culture

Social scientists studying a society foreign to them must spend months, perhaps years, learning the culture of that group. They must learn the meanings for the symbols (written and spoken language, gestures, and rituals) the individuals in that society employ. They must know the feelings people share as to what is appropriate or inappropriate behavior. Additionally, they need to know the rules of the society: which activities are considered important, the skills members have in making and using tools, as well as the knowledge members need to exist in that society. In short, the analyst must discover all the knowledge that people share—that is, he must know the culture. Let us examine each of the characteristics of this important social concept.

1. *Culture is an emergent process.* As individuals interact on any kind of sustained basis, they exchange ideas about all sorts of things. In time they develop common ideas, common ways of doing

things, and common interpretations for certain actions. In so doing, the participants have created a culture. The emergent quality of culture is an on-going process; it is built up slowly rather than being present at the beginnings of social organization. The culture of any group is constantly undergoing change because the members are in continuous interaction. Culture, then, is never completely static.

2. *Culture is learned behavior.* Culture is not instinctive or innate in the human species; it is not part of the biological equipment of man. The biological equipment of man, however, makes culture possible. That is, man is a symbol-making creature capable of attaching meaning to particular objects and actions and communicating these meanings to others. When any person joins a new social organization he must learn the culture of that group. This is true for the infant born into a society as well as a college girl joining a sorority or a young man inducted into the armed forces, or for immigrants to a new society. This process of learning the culture is called socialization.

3. *Culture channels human behavior.* Culture, since it emerges from social interaction, is an inevitable development of human society. More important, it is essential in the maintenance of any social system because it provides two crucial functions—predictability of action and stability. To accomplish these functions, however, culture must restrict man's freedom (although as we will see, cultural constraints are not normally perceived as such); through cultural patterns the individual is expected to conform to the expectations of his group.

How does culture work to constrain individuals? Or put another way, how does culture become internalized in the individual so that his actions are controlled? Somehow culture operates not only outside the individual but also inside him. Sigmund Freud recognized this process when he conceptualized the "superego" as that part of the personality structure that inhibits the individual from committing acts considered wrong by his parents, his group, or his society.

The process of internalization (and therefore control) is accomplished mainly in three ways. First, culture becomes part of the human makeup through the belief system into which a child is born. This belief system, provided by parents and those persons immediately in contact with youngsters, shapes their ideas about the surrounding world as well as giving them certain ideas about themselves. The typical American child, for example, is taught to accept Christian beliefs without reservation. These beliefs are literally "force fed," since alternative belief systems are considered by the "feeders" as unacceptable. It is interesting to note that after Christian beliefs are internalized by the child, they are often used by the "feeders" as levers to keep the child in line.

Second, culture is internalized through psychological identification with the groups to which individuals belong (membership groups), or to which they want to belong (reference groups). Individuals want to belong; they want to be accepted by others. Therefore, they tend to conform to the behavior of their immediate group as well as the wishes of society at large.

Finally, culture is internalized by providing the individual with an identity. People's age, sex, race, religion, and social class have an effect upon the way others perceive them and the way they perceive themselves. To be a male, for example, requires in American society that one be aggressive, ambitious, and competitive. Berger has said, ". . . in a sociological perspective, identity is socially bestowed, socially sustained, and socially transformed."[1]

Culture, then, is not freedom but rather constraint. Of the entire range of possible behaviors (which probably are considered appropriate by some society somewhere) the person of a particular society can only choose from a narrow range of alternatives. The paradox, as Peter Berger has pointed out, is that while society is like a prison to the persons trapped in its cultural demands and expectations, it is not perceived as limiting to individual freedom. Berger has stated it well in the following passage:

> For most of us the yoke of society seems easy to bear. Why? . . . because most of the time we ourselves desire just what society expects of us. We *want* to obey the rules. We *want* the parts that society has assigned to us.[2]

Individuals do not see the prison-like qualities of culture because they have·internalized the culture of their society. From birth children are shaped by the culture of the society into which they are born. They retain some individuality because of the configuration of forces unique to their experience (gene structure, peers, parents' social class, religion, and race), but the behavioral alternatives deemed appropriate for them are narrow.

Culture even shapes thought and perception. What we see and how we interpret what we see is determined by culture. CBS News staged an experiment several years ago that illustrates this point. A black man with something in his hand ran down a crowded city street. White by-standers were asked what they saw. The typical response was that they had perceived the black as carrying a gun, knife, or stolen property, and running from the authorities. In fact, the man was running to catch a bus with a rolled-up newspaper in his hand. Would the respondents have interpreted the actions differently if the person was white? Many white Americans believe that blacks tend toward criminal activity. This stereotype can, therefore, affect negatively the interpretation of a socially accept-able act.

For a dramatic illustrative case of the kind of mental closure that may be determined by culture, consider the following riddle about a father and son driving down a highway:

> There is a terrible accident in which the father is killed, and the son, critically injured, is rushed to a hospital. There the surgeon approaches the patient and suddenly cries, 'My God, that's my son!'

How is it possible that the critically injured boy is the son of the man in the accident as well as the son of the surgeon? Answers might involve the surgeon being a priest, or a stepfather, or even artificial insemination. The correct answer to this riddle is that the surgeon is the boy's mother. Americans, male and female alike, have been socialized to think of women as occupying roles less important than physician/surgeon. If Russians were given this riddle they would almost uniformly give the correct answer since approximately three-fourths of Russian physicians are women. So culture may be confining—not liberating. It not only constrains actions but also thinking.

4. *Culture is boundary maintaining.* Culture not only limits the range of acceptable behavior and attitudes but it instills in its adherents a sense of "naturalness" about the alternatives peculiar to a given society (or other social organization). Thus there is a universal tendency to deprecate the ways of persons from other societies as wrong, old-fashioned, inefficient or immoral, and to think of the ways of one's own group as superior (as the only right way). The concept for this phenomenon is *ethnocentrism.* The word combines the Greek word *ethnikos*, which means nation or people, and the English word for center. So one's own race, religion or society is the center of all and therefore superior to all.

Ethnocentrism is demonstrated in statements such as "My fraternity is the best," "Reincarnation is a weird belief," "We are God's chosen people," or "Polygamy is immoral." To name the playoff between the American and National Leagues the "World Series" implies that baseball outside the United States (and Montreal) is inferior. Religious missionaries provide a classic example of one among several typical groups convinced that their own faith is the only correct one.

A resolution passed at a town meeting in Milford, Connecticut, in 1640 is a blatant example of ethnocentrism. It stated:

> Voted, the earth is the Lord's and the fulness thereof
> Voted, the earth belongs to the saints
> Voted, we are the saints.

Further examples of ethnocentrism taken from American history are: "manifest destiny," "white man's burden," exclusionary immigration laws such as the Oriental Exclusion Act, and "Jim Crow" laws. A current illustration of ethnocentrism can be seen in the activities of the United States as it engages in exporting the "American way of life," because it is believed that democracy and capitalism are necessities for the good life and therefore best for all peoples.

Ethnocentrism, because it implies feelings of superiority, leads to division and conflict between subgroups within a society and between societies, each of which feels "superior."

Ethnocentric ideas are real because they are believed and they influence perception and behavior. Analysts of American society (whether they are Americans or not) must recognize their own ethnocentric attitudes and the way these affect their own objectivity.

To summarize, culture emerges from social interaction. The paradox is that though culture is man-made, it exerts a tremendous complex of forces that constrain the actions and thoughts of mankind. The analyst of any society must be cognizant of these two qualities of culture, for they combine to give a society its unique character; culture explains social change as well as stability; culture explains existing social arrangements (including many social problems); culture explains a good deal of individual behavior because it is internalized by the individual members of society and therefore has an impact (substantial but not total) on their actions and personalities.

The Components of Culture

The concept "culture" refers to knowledge that is shared by the members of a social organization. In analyzing any social organization and, in this case, any society, it is helpful to conceive of culture as combining six types of shared knowledge—symbols, technology, roles, ideologies, norms, and values.

1. *Symbols.* By definition, language refers to symbols that evoke similar meanings in different people. Communication is possible only if persons attribute the same meaning to stimuli such as sounds, gestures, or objects. Language, then, may be written, spoken, or unspoken. A shrug of the shoulders, a pat on the back, the gesturing with a finger (which one may be significant), a wink, or a nod are examples of unspoken language and vary in meaning from society to society.

2. *Technology.* Technology refers to the information, techniques, and tools used by men to satisfy their varied needs and desires. For analytic purposes two types of technology can be distinguished— material and social. *Material technology* refers to knowledge of how to make and use things. It is important to note that the things produced are not part of the culture but represent rather the knowledge that people share and that make it possible to build and use the object. The knowledge is culture, not the object.

Social technology is the knowledge about how to establish, maintain, and operate the technical aspects of social organization. Examples of this are procedures for operating a university, a municipality, or a corporation through such operations as Roberts Rules of Order, bookkeeping, or the kind of specialized knowledge citizens must acquire to function in society (knowing the laws, how to complete income tax forms, how to vote in elections, how to use credit cards and banks).[3]

3. *Roles.* The concept "role" is very important in the analysis and understanding of human behavior. It refers to the behavioral expectations and requirements attached to a position in a social organization (e.g., the father in a family, a janitor in a school, a bookkeeper in a corporation, or a citizen in a society). The shared expectations for the behavior of the members in the various positions in that social organization are part of that organization's culture.

Regardless of whom the incumbent in the position is, certain behaviors are expected of that person by others in the organization. These expectations constrain the behavior of the "actors" so that behavior tends to be predictable. Specific roles, however, vary with the degree of latitude allowed. A monk may have virtually all of his duties prescribed precisely, whereas a college professor has a good deal of freedom in his role.

Although the roles in society are less specific in their demands than are those found in other types of social organizations, they have an important impact on social life within the society. Generally, behavioral expectations differ markedly in American society for age, sex, and racial roles. To be a male in American society, for example, is quite different from being a female in the behaviors expected.

The larger society also expects certain behaviors from one occupational category that it does not from others. Compare what is expected of professional people to what is expected of blue collar workers in speech, manners, and philanthropy (in time and money). Consider further the societal demands made on parents. Parents do not have total control over their offspring. The society has certain minimal expectations for parents that if not met will lead to punishment, the ultimate being removal from the parental role.

4. *Ideologies*. These are shared beliefs about the physical, social, and metaphysical worlds. They may, for example, be statements about the existence of supernatural beings, the best form of government, or racial pride.

Ideologies help individuals interpret events. They also provide the rationale for particular forms of action. They can justify the status quo or demand revolution. A number of competing ideologies exist within American society—e.g., fundamentalism and atheism, capitalism and socialism, and white supremacy and black supremacy. Clearly, ideology unites as well as divides and is therefore a powerful man-made (cultural) force within societies.

5. *Norms*. This aspect of culture refers to rules that specify appropriate and inappropriate behavior. In essence, norms are the behavioral expectations that members of a particular group collectively share. The norms are rules that persons have internalized to insure that certain behaviors will occur and other behaviors will probably not occur in specific situations. In other words, norms insure predictability of action.

Some rules (norms) are not considered to be important and consequently are not severely punished if violated. These norms are called *folkways*. Examples of folkways in our society are: it is expected that men should rise when a lady enters the room (unless she is the maid); women should not wear curlers to work; one should not drink whiskey in church (wine is all right at the appropriate time—communion—but one does not bring his own bottle).

It is easy to see that folkways involve etiquette, customs, and regulations, which if violated do not threaten the fabric of society.

Violation of the *mores,* on the other hand, is considered important enough by society that it must be punished severely. This type of norm involves morality—in fact they can be thought of as moral imperatives. Some examples of mores are: one must have only one spouse at a time; "thou shalt not kill" (unless defending one's country or one's own property); one must be loyal to the United States.

There is a problem, however, for many Americans in deciding the degree of importance for some norms. Figure 2–1 shows the criteria for deciding whether a norm should be classified as a folkway or a *mos* (the singular of the Latin term *mores*).

Figure 2–1 shows that on the basis of the two defining criteria there are four possibilities, not just two. It is difficult to imagine cases that would be located in cell (b). The only possibilities are activities that have only recently been designated as very harmful but laws have not yet been passed for strict punishment (either because of the natural lag in the courts and legislatures or because powerful influence groups have been influential in blocking the necessary legislation). The best current example of cases that would fall in cell (b) would be the pollution of lakes, streams, and air by large commercial enterprises. These acts are recognized as having serious consequences for present and future generations but either go unpunished or receive only minor fines.

Cell (c), on the other hand, is interesting because there are acts not important to the survival of society or the maintenance of its institutions that receive severe punishments (at least relative to the crime). Some examples would be a student being suspended from school until he gets his hair cut; persons caught smoking marijuana being sentenced to a jail term; young men burning their draft cards being jailed or drafted; and a woman being fired from her job for not wearing a bra.

FIGURE 2–1   *Classification of Norms*

Severity of Punishment

		High	Low
Degree of Importance	High	Mores (a)	(b)
	Low	(c)	Folkways (d)

Both criteria used to delineate types of norms—degree of importance and severity of the punishments—are determined by those in power. Consequently, activities that are perceived by the powerful as disruptive of the power structure or institutional arrangements that benefit some and not others are viewed as illegitimate and punished severely. Dick Gregory, the black political satirist, has provided an example of this. He has noted that the 15,000 young people at the 1968 Democratic convention in Chicago were perceived as a threat to change the system and therefore were jailed, beaten and generally harassed by the police. Compare the treatment of these young people who were there because of their moral convictions with that of the 15,000 attending a Shriner's Convention in Chicago. Many of the Shriners got drunk, were sexually promiscuous, and just generally "raised hell." Is it not strange that the moral are punished while the immoral go virtually unscathed?[4]

6. *Values.* Another aspect of culture is values, which are the bases for the norms. These are the criteria used in evaluating objects, ideas, acts, feelings or events as to their relative desirability, merit, or correctness.

Man is a valuing being. He continually evaluates himself and others. What objects are worth owning? What makes a man successful? What activities are rewarding? What is beauty? Of course, different societies have distinctive criteria (values) for evaluating. A man is considered successful in the United States, for example, if he accumulates many material things as a result of hard work. In other societies a man might be considered successful if he attains total mastery of his emotions or if he totally rejects materialism.

One objective common to any social science course is the hope that students will become aware of the various aspects of social life in an analytical way. For Americans studying their own society this means that while immersed in the subject matter, they also become participant observers. This implies an objective detachment (as much as possible) so that one may understand better the forces which in large measure affect human behavior, individually and in groups.

The primary task for the participant observer interested in societal values is to determine what the values are. There are a number of clues that are helpful for such a task.* The first clue is to determine what most preoccupies people in their conversations and

* A good but partial list of methods to determine empirically the values of American society has been developed in a text by Robin M. Williams.[5]

actions. So one might ask: toward what do people most often direct their action? Is it, for example, contemplation and meditation or physical fitness or the acquiring of material objects? In other words, what gives the individual high status in the eyes of his fellows?

A second technique that might help delineate the values is to determine the choices that people make consistently. The participant observer should ascertain what choices tend to be made in similar situations. For example, how do individuals dispose of surplus wealth? Do they spend it for self aggrandizement or for altruistic reasons? Is there a tendency to spend it for the pleasure of the present, save it for security in the future, or spend it on others?

A third procedure is used typically by social scientists—that is, to find out through interviews or written questionnaires what people say is good, bad, moral, immoral, desirable, or undesirable. There is often a difference between what people say and what people do. This is always a problem in the study of values because there will sometimes be a discrepancy between values and actual behavior. Even if there is a difference between what people write on a questionnaire or say in an interview and their actual behavior, they will probably say or write those responses they feel are appropriate, and this by itself is a valid indicator of what the values of the society are.

One may also observe the reward-punishment system of the society. What behavior is rewarded with a medal, or a bonus, or public praise? Alternatively, what behavior brings condemnation, ridicule, public censure, or imprisonment? The greater the reward or the punishment, the greater the likelihood that important societal values are involved. Consider, for example, the extraordinary punishment given to Americans who willfully destroy the private property of others (e.g., a cattle rustler, a thief, a looter, or a pyromaniac).

Closely related to the reward-punishment system are the actions that cause individuals to feel guilt or shame (e.g., losing your job, living on welfare, declaring bankruptcy) or those actions which bring about ego enhancement (a better paying job, getting an educational degree, or owning a business). Individuals feel guilt or shame precisely because they have internalized the norms and values of society. When values and behavior are not congruent, feelings of guilt will be a typical response.

Another technique is to examine the principles that are held as part of "the American way of life." These principles are enunciated in historical documents such as the Constitution, the Declaration of Independence, and the Bible. We are continually reminded of these principles in speeches by elected officials, by editorials in the mass media, and from pulpits. The United States has gone to war in order to defend such principles as democracy, equality, freedom and the free enterprise system. One question the analyst of values should ask, therefore, is, "For what principles will the people fight?"

The remainder of this chapter is devoted to the description of the American system of values. The understanding of American values is essential to the analysis of American society for it provides the basis for America's uniqueness as well as the source for many of its social problems.

AMERICAN VALUES AS SOURCES OF SOCIETAL INTEGRATION AND SOCIAL PROBLEMS

American society, while similar in some respects to other advanced industrial societies, is also fundamentally different. Given the combination of geographical, historical, and religious factors found in the United States, it is not surprising that its cultural values are unique.

Geographically, the United States has remained relatively isolated from other societies for most of its history. Americans have also been blessed with an abundance of rich and varied resources (land, minerals, and water). Until only recently, Americans were unconcerned with conservation and the careful use of resources (as many societies must be to survive) because there was no need. The country provided a vast storehouse of resources so rich they were often used wastefully.

Historically, the United States was founded by a revolution that grew out of opposition to tyranny and aristocracy. Hence, Americans have verbally supported such principles as freedom, democracy, equality, and impersonal justice.

Another historical factor that has led to American culture having its particular nature is that it has been peopled largely by immigrants. This fact has led, on the one hand, to a blending of many cultural traits such as language, dress, and customs, and alternatively, to the existence of ethnic enclaves that resist assimilation.

A final set of forces that has affected American culture stems from its religious heritage. First is the Judeo-Christian ethic that has prevailed throughout American history. The strong emphases on humanitarianism, the inherent worth of all individuals, a morality based on the Ten Commandments, and even the Biblical injunction to "have dominion over all living things," have had a profound effect upon how Americans evaluate each other.

Another aspect of America's religious heritage, the Protestant (Puritan) work ethic, has been an important determinant of the values that are believed to typify most Americans.[6] The majority of early European settlers in America tended to believe in a particular set of religious beliefs that can be traced back to two individuals, Martin Luther and John Calvin. Luther's contribution was essentially twofold: each person was considered to be his own priest (stressing man's individuality and worth), and each person was to accept his work as a "calling." To be "called" by God to do a job, no matter how humble, was to give the job and the individual dignity. It also encouraged everyone to work very hard to be successful in that job.

The contribution of John Calvin was based upon his belief in "Predestination." God, because He is all-knowing, knows who will be "saved." Unfortunately, individuals do not know whether they are "saved" or not, and this is very anxiety-producing. Calvinists came to believe that God would look with more favor upon those preordained to be "saved" than those who were not. Consequently, success in one's business became a sign that one was "saved," and this was therefore anxiety-reducing. Calvinists worked very hard to be successful. As they prospered, the capital they accumulated could only be spent on necessities, for to spend on luxuries was another sign that one was not "saved." The surplus capital was therefore invested in the enterprise (purchasing more property or better machinery, hiring a larger work force or whatever).

Luther and Calvin produced an ethic that flourished in America. This ethic stressed the traits of self-sacrifice, diligence, and hard work. It stressed achievement, and most importantly, it stressed a self-orientation rather than a collectivity orientation. Indirectly, this ethic emphasized private property, capitalism, rationality, and growth.

These forces, in a combination peculiar to the United States, have influenced the way in which Americans solve what Florence Kluckhohn has suggested are the basic dilemmas faced by all societies. Every society through its culture must provide answers about certain basic questions: (1) man's basic human nature; (2) man's relationship to nature; (3) to what degree the significant time dimension should be the past, present, or future; (4) what activities are important; and (5) to what extent the relationship of man to other men should be cooperative or competitive.

Every society, because of its unique combination of geography (amount and type of available resources), history, and the impact of outsiders, develops a culture that includes societal values and the choices to the various societal dilemmas mentioned by Kluckhohn.[7] It is difficult to say whether the choices to these dilemmas are the bases for societal values or vice-versa. Most likely the influences are reciprocal, and one is not always antecedent to the other.

The remainder of this chapter will examine each of the societal dilemmas and the typical modes of American response to them. We will see how particular values are clearly related to the modal responses as well as the social problems that often result. This approach will aid in understanding not only social problems, but also social change, since persons particularly affected by social problems will question the values that lead to such problems.

As a note of caution, in the analysis presented below, generalizations are made about the values of the majority of Americans—those found in the broad middle class (but these generalizations will probably not hold for all of them either). The values mentioned should *not* be construed to be those held by all Americans.

Man's basic nature. Of the several possible ways to conceptualize man's basic nature, three are especially important for the understanding of American society and the origin of social problems. The first two views coincide with the order and conflict perspectives.[8] Order theorists have generally assumed that man is basically evil (selfish) and that the function of society is to constrain the individual. Through the socialization process and the threat of negative sanctions, persons learn (except for deviants) to serve the common good. This view, that individuals, not institutions, are to be blamed for crime, poverty, racism, and ignorance, is held by the majority of Americans. Individuals are capable of good and evil and are therefore responsible for their own actions. A quote from the 1964 Presidential candidate, Barry Goldwater, illustrates this belief:

> Every man . . . is responsible for his *own* development. The choices that govern his life are choices that *he* must make; they cannot be made by any other human being, or by a collectivity of human beings.[9]

The persons holding such a view believe that social problems will be eliminated if the "hearts and minds" of individuals are changed. The focus, for example, of those interested in changing the pattern in race relations has been, typically, to change the racist attitudes of individuals rather than to make meaningful structural changes that would lessen the probability of racist acts.

Conflict theorists, on the other hand, maintain a more optimistic view that man is basically good, but that society through the influence of corrupting institutions and an unjust system of stratification is the source of evil. Hence, they urge the belief that social problems can be solved if society is restructured to meet the needs of man. In other words, institutions should exist to serve man, not the obverse. Along this line, many of today's youth believe that if man is left in freedom he is good. Communes and some experiments in education are based on the assumption that man is good, that he can live peaceably with others, and that he does not need the constraints of society to make him good. Many believe in the statement by A. S. Neill that gives the philosophy behind his famous educational experiment.

> We have a complete belief in the child as a good not an evil, being. . . . My view is that the child is innately wise and realistic. If left to himself without adult suggestion of any kind, he will develop as far as he is capable of developing.[10]

Another view of man, sometimes held simultaneously with other views, is especially important because it helps to explain a good deal of typical American behavior. This is the conception of man as a machine, a view which (according to Richard Means) is widely accepted by many Americans.[11] This metaphor suggests, first of all, that man is only what he produces. Americans tend, generally, to evaluate others in terms of superficial criteria (e.g. amount of education, the amount and type of possessions). Man is known and evaluated by his external qualities only. This implies a superficial quality to interaction and the relationships that result. As will be pointed out in a later chapter, this superficiality is a result of the increased urbanization and bureaucratization in American life. A bureaucracy, for example, is by definition an organization designed to accomplish a goal as efficiently as possible (in turning out a product, saving souls, or whatever). This means individuals occupying positions in the hierarchy will be constantly evaluated—not as individuals but as producers.

Several indicators in American society are shown by Means to suggest that man is generally conceived of as a machine. Advertising demonstrates this, as it tends to stress the importance of external symbols of status. Advertisers and businessmen tend to see man as an object to be manipulated. Like Pavlov's dog consumers will "salivate" at the appropriate time if properly conditioned by advertising.

Playboy and other "skin" magazines emphasize that sex is a transitory pleasure—that women are objects for men to use without any lasting relationship. Commercial television with its plastic, superficial view of people (soap operas, quiz shows, situation comedies) demonstrates the image of man as a machine. Means sees this image of man especially in the emphasis on violence in movies, television, and even cartoons. He has stated:

> It is the very essence of violence to think of man as a machine. The act of violence is made possible by assuming that man *is* a machine. Machines do not show pain, or dream, or smile, or laugh. In consequence we do not have to dream or laugh with them. Man as machine is easy to do violence to; he does not really respond. The example par excellence is the animated cartoon of the "Tom and Jerry" and "Road Runner" and even the Walt Disney variety. The plot is an unending series of pushing one another off cliffs, hitting, beating, smashing, flattening—but it never hurts. There is no human response. The creature returns again and again to its own demise. A strange form of cultural humor![12]

What does it mean to view man as a machine? An important implication is the emphasis in the natural and social sciences to stress the scientific method—i.e., to stress knowledge for its own sake, to remain ethically neutral. This notion allows the scientist to avoid the negative outcomes of his findings (the hydrogen bomb, chemical-biological warfare, or the social disorganization caused by urban renewal). The social scientist is thereby absolved from any guilt for not trying to solve social ills. He is enjoined, rather, to remain neutral and detached in his ivory tower.

A view of man as a machine implies that people can rationalize the use of hydrogen bombs, chemical-biological warfare, napalm bombs in a war, or indiscriminate gassing to break up a riot, or the beating of demonstrators. This view of man is summed up in a statement made by an ex-army sergeant turned professional golfer —Orville Moody—about the college riots of 1970.

> Tell you one thing . . . Kent State and the rest. I'm gettin' sick of it. Next time they try somethin', might save more lives in the long run if we get out the machine guns and shoot 'bout 50 of them fools. That'll stop 'em hollerin'. I wish the President would make an amendment to the Constitution to say, all right, you can demonstrate, but we're gonna shoot you if you do. That'd stop them pussyfooters.[13]

This points to a basic problem of any society—the handling of dissent. The prevailing view in the United States appears to be to "get tough," to not "pussyfoot around." The consequence of this attitude (which stems from viewing man as a machine or man as evil and in need of control) is that demonstrators are sometimes beaten and jailed when the demonstration was peaceful.

Man's relationship to nature. There are three basic ways in which man relates to nature. Man can consider himself controlled by nature, thereby accepting the environment and the forces that impinge upon him in a fatalistic manner. He can be in harmony with nature—man needs nature and nature needs man. Finally, man can try to attain mastery over nature.

The view of man having mastery over nature is clearly a characteristic of most Americans. Rather than accepting the environment as given, Americans have sought to change and conquer it. Damming rivers, cutting down timber, digging tunnels, conquering space, and seeding clouds with silver nitrate are but a few examples of this life-orientation to overcoming nature's obstacles rather than acquiescing to them. Nature is viewed by most Americans, then, as something to be subdued and used.

What Richard Means has called the "cornucopian view of nature" is also held by most Americans.[14] Nature is conceived as a vast storehouse of "things" waiting only to be used by man. The natural world is regarded as a bountiful preserve totally dedicated to serving mans' needs.

The typical American view of nature as something to be controlled for man's benefit and as something in bountiful supply accounts for several American value orientations: capitalism, progress, and applied science.

Capitalism, with its twin emphases on the private ownership of property and self aggrandizement, seems especially appropriate where persons believe nature to be abundant and something to be conquered. In the search for higher profits, consequently, nature is abused (e.g., strip mining, and the disposal of harmful wastes into rivers). Further evidence is seen for this in the unwillingness of many individuals and corporations to change practices that are harmful to nature unless forced by the government to do so.

Progress is highly valued by Americans. They dislike the status quo. They tend to be never entirely satisfied. There is always something better. This desire (which is encouraged by the advertising industry) causes Americans to discard items that are still usable and to purchase new things. Thus, industry is "forced" to turn out more products, thereby using up natural resources.

Applied science is highly esteemed by Americans. It is only through the application of scientific knowledge that man can purposely change his environment. Americans esteem the acquisition of new scientific knowledge (experimentation) and its application (engineering). Coupled with this emphasis on science is the American emphasis on rationality—i.e. efficiency. Americans continuously search out more "reasonable," "time saving," and "effort-saving" ways of doing things. This dual emphasis on science and rationality is evidenced by the tendency of many Americans to be suspicious of anything that does not have direct utility (or that will not make money). Americans tend, therefore, to emphasize the practical rather than the contemplative or artistic as do some other societies.

The common American approach to nature, and the values emanating from this approach, have led to several interrelated contemporary problems—pollution, the ecology crisis, overpopulation, and the depletion of natural resources.

It is fairly easy to trace how Americans have come to this condition of environmental abuse, since until fairly recently the country was a land of open wide spaces, clear air and water, virgin forests, and with rich and varied minerals. If the water became polluted or the land no longer fertile, or the timber used up, people just moved to virgin territory. But now there is no more new land, virgin forests, or clear water.

The related values of capitalism, private property, and self-aggrandizement (individualism) have also led to an ecology crisis. Industries fouling the air and water with refuse, farmers spraying pesticides that kill weeds and harm animal and human life, are but two examples of how individual persons and corporations look out for themselves with an almost total disregard for the short and long range effects of their actions on life. As long as Americans hold a narrow self-orientation rather than a collectivity orientation this crisis will not only continue but steadily worsen. The use a man makes of his land (and the water on it or running through it, and the air above it) has traditionally been his to decide because of the American belief in private property. This belief in private property has meant in effect that individuals have had the right to pave a pasture for a parking lot, tear up a lemon grove for a housing development, put down artificial turf for a football field, dump waste products into the air and water, and so on. Consequently, individual decisions have had the collective effect of taking millions of acres of arable land out of production permanently, polluting the air and water, covering land where vegetation once grew with asphalt, concrete buildings, and astroturf even though green plants are the only source of oxygen.[15]

The commonly held value of progress has also had a negative effect on contemporary American life. Progress is typically defined to mean either growth or new technology. Every city wants to grow. Chambers of Commerce want more industry and more people (and incidentally more consumers). No industry can afford to keep sales at last year's figures. Everyone agrees that the Gross National Product must increase each year. If all these things are to grow as Americans wish, then concomitant with such growth must be increased population, more products turned out (using natural resources), more electricity, more highways, and more waste. Continued growth will inevitably throw the tight ecological system out of balance since there are but limited supplies of air, water, and places to dump waste materials. Not only are these limited but they diminish as the population increases.

Progress also means a faith in technology. It is commonly believed by Americans that scientific knowledge will solve problems. Scientific breakthroughs and new technology have solved some problems and do aid in saving labor. But often new technology creates problems that were unanticipated.* Although the automobile is of fantastic help to man, it has polluted the air, and it kills about 50,000 Americans each year in accidents. It is difficult to imagine life without electricity, but the creation of electricity pollutes the air or causes the thermal pollution of rivers. Insecticides and chemical fertilizers have performed miracles in agriculture but have polluted food and streams (and even "killed" some lakes). Obviously, the slogan of the Du Pont Corporation—"better living through chemistry"—is not entirely correct. Jet planes, while helping man in many ways, pollute the air (viz. one jet taking off emits the same amount of hydrocarbon as the exhausts from 10,000 automobiles), and also make life miserable for those living along the flight paths near busy airports.

There have always been individuals in American society who have rejected the notion that nature is something to be subdued. Currently, organizations such as Zero Population Growth and the Sierra Club finance lobbying activities in Washington and the state capitals. They also exert moral pressure on the citizenry to limit family size, to not use throw-away containers, and to be responsible to future generations by not abusing the natural resources.

---

* Sociologists have a term for this phenomenon—"latent functions"—which means, in effect, unintended consequences. The intended consequences of an activity or social arrangement are called "manifest functions."

Recently there appears to be an ever-increasing number of Americans who prefer to be in tune with nature rather than to subdue it. Consider, for example, the increasing numbers of "flower children" who practice Oriental-style religions which stress man's oneness with nature, not his dominion over it. Some also eat only organic foods and live as closely to nature as possible.

Only time will tell how large this movement will become. The problems of pollution and population can be conquered if Americans change their basic attitudes toward nature. Currently, most persons do not consider it immoral to use non-returnable bottles, DDT, or to have large families. Ultimately nature will force Americans to change, but it then will be too late.

Predominant time dimension. All societies give attention to the past, the present, and the future. Societies differ, however, in emphasis. Some societies (and some segments within American society such as the Amish) are "tradition-directed." They tend to be primarily interested in customs, traditions and re-doing ceremonies as they have been passed down to them by their forefathers. Obviously the people in such a society would not be interested in change.

Other societies are primarily interested in the present time dimension. Persons and societies with such an emphasis pay little attention to the past and regard the future as vague and unpredict-

PANEL 2–1

ZERO GROWTH?

Source: John Fischer, "The Easy Chair," *Harper's Magazine* 240 (April, 1970), pp. 18–28.

John Fischer has become distressed enough about the ecology crisis in the United States to propose the following drastic steps:

—a zero growth rate in people, Gross National Product, and the consumption of products;

—the creation of an Anti-Patent Office that forbids any technological discovery to be put to use until *all* the side effects are known and controlled; and

—the use of land, water, and air cannot be left to private decision but must be controlled by the Federal Government.

Most Americans have also become quite concerned about what is happening to their environment. But would they be willing to take the steps toward a solution as outlined by Fischer? This really becomes a

able. These people tend to be fatalistic about the future and spend little time planning for it. They also tend toward hedonism. Kluckhohn's studies have shown that Mexican-Americans tend toward a present time-orientation.

Americans, for the most part, are future oriented. They neither make the past sacred nor are they content with the present. This emphasis by Americans on the future is seen in several value configurations. The first is that *progress* (change) is highly valued. As individuals, Americans work toward a brighter tomorrow, a better job, a bigger home, college education for their children, and a move to the suburbs. Individuals ever strive to improve—not being satisfied with the status quo.

A second value orientation related to a future orientation is *security*. As a nation, the United States is very much preoccupied with security. Much more than half of the United States Government's budget is spent on defense.* There are elaborate and expensive schemes for protection against attack. This includes radar installations, planes, submarines, and rockets ready at all times to destroy the enemy. By the early 1970s the U.S. had stockpiles of arms enormous enough to kill every Russian twenty times. Apparently

* The defense appropriation for fiscal 1972 was $70.5 billion compared to $39.2 billion in 1960 and $12.9 billion in 1950.

test of how tenacious are the American values of growth and progress, materialism, and individualism. Or put another way, just how committed are we to these values? For example, would you be willing to let the government:

—set a limit of two children per family?

—freeze the number of job and income levels for all business enterprises because growth must be curtailed and profits stabilized?

—set a quota for consumption of consumer goods per individual?

—limit the amount of travel per year?

—prohibit the use of an effective long term cure for the common cold until it is tested for many years to determine and control all of the side effects?

—severely limit what an owner can do with his property (e.g., pour concrete, spray insecticides, burn trash, remove trees)?

These are difficult questions. Assent to them would mean that the quality of American life would change dramatically. Severe constraints on individual freedom, the absence of luxuries and many labor-saving devices, and the tremendous slowing down of technological progress may, however, be the price of survival.

this desire for protection cannot ever be satiated, since the Pentagon continues to make the stockpile bigger and devise more efficient means to kill and to deliver the killing mechanisms.**

A third value configuration related to the focus on the future is *success*. Americans place great stress on personal achievement. It is believed that hard work and initiative will bring success. There is a tendency to sacrifice in the present for the rewards that await in the future ("deferred gratification"). Many Americans will sacrifice by working days and going to school at night so that they might get a better job. Parents may make great sacrifices so that their children will have the opportunity for a college education or other advantages the parents never received. In this manner success is accomplished vicariously through the achievements of one's children.

Many people today are reacting against some of the values that stem from this future-time orientation. Many reject the emphasis on security. Some young people ridicule the efforts of their parents directed at security. Perhaps young people who have lived their lives under the shadow of the H-bomb, the "pollution bomb" and the "population bomb" see no need to look for the future. "Live," rather, "for the present," they say. For some, then, there is a preoccupation with broadening sensory experiences found in music, drugs, and sex. For others, there is a preoccupation with an "other world" of science fiction, mysticism, or religion, all of which eschew individual ambition.

The rejection of security by some is also seen in the goals they profess. They seek self-fulfillment. They either reject the materialistically-oriented work world for jobs that only provide maintenance, or they seek low paying altruistic jobs. Several contemporary social commentators[16] have predicted that more and more young people will be rejecting the technocratic society with its emphases on materialism, rationality, and progress for lives of meaningfulness and genuineness with regard to others and oneself.

Valued personality type. What type of individual action is most highly rewarded (in money, respect, and honor) in American society? Kluckhohn has enumerated three types of action orientations. First, there is the hedonistic type who is oriented toward the

** This build-up of arms, although done in the name of security, actually leads, in my opinion, to insecurity. If the United States adds to its defense system, its enemies must do so also, for it would appear to them that the United States is preparing for an act of aggression. The enemies' build-up justifies America's build-up and the arms race spirals, making everyone quite insecure (and giving us a "self-fulfilling prophecy" in our need for arms).

52

satisfaction of desires. This type tends toward an acceptance of life as it is.

Another type of orientation—being-in-becoming—has the fundamental goal of self-realization or self-development in the sense of understanding oneself. This is the goal of many Far Eastern religions.

The third personality type is oriented toward action itself. In this orientation there is the demand for accomplishment by the acting individual. This action-orientation is the dominant one in American society. Americans scoff, for example, at activities such as contemplation and meditation because they do not seem to bring tangible results.

There are several typically American value configurations that emanate from this emphasis on action. *Work and activity* have been highly valued throughout American history. The early settlers, many of them Puritans, had religious beliefs that promoted attitudes of diligence and hard work. Not only was work considered a virtue but non-work was considered a sin ("idle hands are the Devil's workshop"). Also, both for early American settlers and later residents, there was a tendency to work hard because of the vast opportunities to make profit open to those willing to work.

Although there is some evidence that contemporary Americans have lost some of their compulsiveness with regard to work, this quality remains for many. Those people who make it to the top of their professions do so precisely because, typically, they have been compulsive in their quest. This is true in business, in academia, in sports, in virtually all areas of life.

Ceaseless activity rules not only the work situation but also leisure time. Many Americans are not content unless busy at something, whether it be their job, a do-it-yourself project, playing 18 (or 36) holes of golf, or driving 500 miles a day while on vacation.

The demand for action that is characteristic in American society is related also to the value configuration of *accomplishment and success*. Hard work, ambition, and industry are traits that not only result in ceaseless activity, but also usually contribute to success in terms of money, security, and upward mobility. Success, as defined in these terms is highly esteemed.* Americans feel justified, then, in condemning and disparaging those individuals who are not suc-

---

* There is a monthly magazine entitled *Success Unlimited* that offers its 125,-000 subscribers (1971) a potpourri of personal success stories and self-improvement sermons.

cessful and who do not coincidentally exhibit the qualities of ambition, hard work, thriftiness—those who drop out of school, who take jobs that do not challenge, who do not "save for a rainy day" but spend on unimportant things. Free and Cantril have reported the results of a Gallup Poll that illustrates this tendency on the part of most Americans. The question asked of the national sample was: "In your opinion, which is generally more often to blame if a person is poor—lack of effort on his part, or circumstances beyond his control?" The respondents replied:[17]

Circumstances	25%
Lack of effort	34%
Both	38%
Don't know	3%
	100%

Seventy-two percent of this sample felt that the poor were at least partially to blame for their own situation—certainly an indication that Americans tend to feel anyone can rise above his situation if he will only try. It is easy to see, then, why there generally is resistance by the populace to increasing the dole to welfare recipients.

Some Americans, particularly young people but also many members of the lower classes, reject the high value placed on the "action" type of personality. For many young people there is a focus, rather, on the "hedonistic" type where persons are valued for their authenticity and spontaneity. So for these persons a hedonistic life style is most desirable. For others there is a search for understanding self. This may be accomplished through the studying and practicing of Zen Buddhism or yoga. Or it may be done with the use of mind-expanding drugs through which one perceives himself and life in a new way.

Many persons who are either lower class or minority group members (or both as is most common) see no need for hard work because they are not rewarded as are middle and upper-class whites. They tend, therefore, toward a "hedonistic" orientation—living for the present, not achieving, and not exerting much effort.

Man's relationship to other men. Perhaps the most basic decision men must make is how to relate to other men. There are two polar extremes—man can consider himself as an autonomous unit in competition with others; or alternatively the goals and welfare of the individual can be considered secondary to those of his group (the relationship is thereby one in which the basic social process is cooperation). Societies can be characterized as promoting one or the other of these views.

Every society must have a minimum of cooperation among its members if anarchy and a "war of all against all" is to be avoided. American society, while achieving a degree of harmony and cooperation among its members, has been and remains primarily a society that favors individualism and competition. Competition, it is often said, is the basis for the United States being the strongest nation (economically and militarily) the world has ever known. Consequently, although there are socialistic features present (e.g., schools, post office, public utilities, and social security), socialism with its emphasis on collective rather than individual goals has been minimized and is even believed by many to be "evil."

This self-orientation (as opposed to collectivity orientation) is the basis for a number of value configurations that prevail in American society. It is related to the value configurations of work, activity, and success that have been mentioned above. The individual is successful through his own initiative and hard work. The stress on individualism is, of course, related to *capitalism*. The individual through his own efforts, business acumen, and luck can (if successful) own property and pyramid profits. This goal of great monetary success ("the American Dream") is believed by most Americans. It is believed that anyone can make it. Curiously, individuals who do not make it commonly do not reject capitalism. Instead, they wait in the hope that "their ship will come in" or that their children will prosper under the system.

The belief that private property and capitalism are not to be restricted has led to several social problems: (1) unfair competition (monopolies, interlocking directorates, price-fixing); (2) a philosophy by many entrepreneurs of *caveat emptor* ("let the buyer beware") whereby the aim is profit with total disregard for the welfare of the consumer; and (3) the current ecology crisis, which is due in great measure to the standard policy of many Americans and most corporations to do whatever is profitable—thus a total neglect for conservation of natural resources.

All of these practices have forced the federal and state governments to enact and enforce regulatory controls. Clearly, Americans have always tended to abuse nature and their fellow men in the name of profit. Freedom if so abused must be curtailed, and the government (albeit somewhat reluctantly, given the pressures from various interest groups) has done this.

The primacy given to individuals in American society is related to another value configuration—*democracy.* Democracy rests upon the assumption that individuals are capable of making rational decisions. Americans believe strongly that democracy is the best form of government. They believe, in fact, that the "Founding Fathers" provided a government based on a perfect theory—one based on representative democracy, majority rule, and limited centralized rule.

Individualism in the form of democracy and capitalism is felt to be so much of what is American and what is good that Americans want to export it to the rest of the world. This ethnocentric notion involves a sense of mission to the entire world. It is confidently believed by many Americans that democracy and capitalism, if established universally, would solve many of the world's problems (e.g., poverty, backwardness, and despotism). Americans, therefore, have an "illusion of rightness." There is no question but that the American way is not only the best way but the *only* path to peace and prosperity for *all* societies. This kind of thinking (strongly supported by business interests,) provides the ideological fuel for America's world-wide commitments, its role as international policeman, and its giving of foreign aid.

The emphasis on individualism has also led to an extraordinary amount of competition in American society. Competition is built into virtually all spheres of activity (e.g. in education, business, courtship, sports, occupations and professions, and government). The structural and social emphasis on competition assures that many persons will fail in some areas while some will be successful in virtually all areas. Failure is, of course, psychologically damaging because the person is defined by others and himself as a loser. While failure is an individual phenomenon, its basis has social roots in the pervasiveness of competition in American society.

The focus on individualism places responsibility on the individual for his acts—not on society or its institutions. The individual is blamed for being poor, not the maldistribution of wealth and other socially perpetuated disadvantages which blight many families generation after generation. The black is blamed for his aggressive behavior and not the limits placed on social mobility for blacks by the social system. The individual is blamed for dropping out of high school before graduation, not the educational system which fails to meet his needs. This attitude helps to explain the reluctance by persons in authority to provide adequate welfare, health care, and compensatory programs to help the disadvantaged. This common tendency of individuals to focus on the deviant rather than the system that produces deviants has also been true of American social scientists analyzing social problems.*

The traditional assumption has been that deviants, not society, need to be changed. It can be argued, however, that important changes can be accomplished only if society itself is changed. By this argument, society and its institutions are man-made. They exist to serve man. Thus, when they fail man, they must be changed.

Finally, Philip Slater has noted that there is a curious relationship between individualism and conformity. Individualism and competition lead to uniformity and conformity. "Our society gives far more leeway to the individual to pursue his own ends, but, since *it* defines what is worthy and desirable, everyone tends, independently but monotonously, to pursue the same things in the same way."[19] Everyone wants peace and privacy, so when they can afford it they move to the suburbs—but so does everyone else. Individuals in making autonomous decisions are seeking status (and proof of status, which means owning particular material items) in the manner defined by the values of society. Thus there is a "cultural press" to buy certain things and do certain things. So while free to choose, Americans are in fact constrained. What looks like conformity in the United States is really a number of individuals making the same kinds of decisions somewhat autonomously.

There are many pressures to move away from the value orientations associated with individualism. Some people, for example, want more and more governmental control over actions that take advantage of consumers or rape the environment. Some favor doing away with much (or all) private property, as they see this as inherently evil and the cause of social inequality and deprivation.** Some persons are working to eliminate competition. Some educational experiments are attempting to find methods of motivating students without using competition.

Many Americans are reacting against the competitive, status striving, materialistic life of their elders. They prefer "authentic" to what they believe to be "superficial" interaction, cooperation to competition, and meeting group goals to achieving individual goals.

* For an excellent discussion of how social problems textbooks have focused on the deviants rather than the institutions, see an appeal for the opposite perspective by Jerome H. Skolnick and Elliott Currie.[18]
** This argument, briefly, is that the ownership of property leads to privilege and power as well—the more property the more privilege and power. Since property is passed to the next generation—power and privilege become attached to family position and are therefore ascribed rather than achieved. Thus the offspring of the wealthy will have many advantages over the offspring of the poor, regardless of their other qualifications.

Values and Behavior

There are a number of American values that relate to active mastery over nature, a doing orientation to life, an emphasis on the future, and individualism. The specific value configurations are often intertwined with each other, but sometimes they are inconsistent. Moreover, there is often a very large gap between the values and actual behavior. American culture has therefore been labelled "dualistic" or even "schizoid."[20]

The discrepancy between values and behavior has probably always existed in American society. Inconsistencies have always existed, for example, between the Christian ethic of love, brotherhood, and humanitarianism on the one hand and the realities of religious bigotry, the maximization of self-interest, and property rights over human rights on the other. The gap may be widening because of the tremendous rate of social change taking place (the rush toward urbanization, the increased bureaucratization in all spheres of social life). Values do not change as rapidly as do other elements of the culture. Although values often differ from behavior, they remain the criteria for evaluating objects, persons, and events. It is important, however, to mention behaviors that often contradict the values because they demonstrate the hypocrisy prevalent in American society that so often upsets young people (and others) who in turn, then, develop countercultures (a topic we will cover shortly).

Perhaps most illustrative of the inconsistency between values and behavior is the belief in the American Creed held by most Americans—generally assumed to encompass equality of all men, freedom of speech and religion, and the guarantees of life, liberty and prosperity—as against the injustices perpetuated by the system and individuals in the system on members of minority groups.[21]

Americans glorify individualism and self-reliance. These related traits, however, are not found in bureaucracies, where the watchword is "don't rock the boat." Whyte in his classic *The Organization Man* has noted that bureaucracies are not tolerant of individualists (except at the highest levels). They desire persons who adjust to the wishes of the group. They generally prefer that committees reach decisions, not individuals.[22]

The value placed on "hard work" is still found in many Americans. But for many it has been replaced by a philosophy of "getting by." Unions sometimes enforce a policy of restricted output so as not to embarrass slower (or lazier) workers. Some observers have noted that the current generation, unlike its predecessor, is overrepresented by either: (1) "corner cutters" and "angle players"—

persons interested in "easy money"; or (2) persons who value a subsistence existence.

Successful persons in America have always been self-made. They have been the ones who achieved wealth, fame, and power through their own achievements. The value placed on achievement rather than ascription began in American history as an anti-aristocracy bias. This has changed over time, and now the wealthy are considered successful whether they made the money or not. Americans now tend to give great weight to the opinions expressed by wealthy men, as evidenced by the electorate's tendency to elect the wealthy to public office.

Americans have always placed high value on the equality of all men (in the courts or in getting a job). This value is impossible to reconcile with the racist and superiority themes held by some individuals and groups. It is also impossible to reconcile with many of the formal and informal practices on jobs, in the schools, and in the courts.

Related to the stated belief in equality are the other fundamental beliefs enunciated by the "Founding Fathers": the freedoms guaranteed in the Bill of Rights and the Declaration of Independence. Ironically, although the United States was founded by revolutions, the same behavior (called for by the Declaration of Independence) by dissident groups is now squelched (in much the same way as King George III did).

Americans value "law and order." This reverence for the law has been overlooked throughout American history whenever "law-abiding" groups, such as vigilante groups, occasionally took the law in their own hands (by threatening that anyone who disobeys vigilante law will be lynched). Currently, the very groups to make the loudest demands for "law and order" are ones who disobey certain laws—e.g., southern politicians blocking federal court orders to integrate schools, American Legion posts that notoriously ignore local, state and federal laws about gambling and liquor, and school administrators allowing prayer in public schools despite the ruling of the Supreme Court.

A final example of disparity between American values and behavior involves the pride Americans have in solving difficult problems. Americans are inclined to be realists. They are pragmatic, down-to-earth problem-solvers ready to apply scientific knowledge and expertise to handle such technical problems as getting man to and from the moon safely. This realism tends to be replaced by mere gestures, however, when it comes to social problems. Americans have a compulsive tendency to avoid confrontation with chronic social problems. They tend to think that social problems will be solved if one has "nice" thoughts, such as "ban the bomb," "the population problem is everybody's baby," or "black is beautiful." Somehow the verbal level is mistaken for action. If one hears his favorite television personality end his weekly program with a statement against pollution, then the problem will be somehow solved.

This is evidenced at another level by proclaiming a "war on poverty," or setting up a commission to study violence, pornography, or civil disorders. Philip Slater has said that the typical American approach to social problems is to decrease their visibility—out of sight, out of mind.

> When these discarded problems rise to the surface again—a riot, a protest, an expose in the mass media—we react as if a sewer had backed up. We are shocked, disgusted, and angered. We immediately call for the emergency plumber (the special commission, the crash program) to ensure that the problem is once again removed from consciousness.[23]

Slater has also suggested the interesting hypothesis that the avoiding tendency lies at the very root of American character.

> This nation was settled and continuously repopulated by people who were not personally successful in confronting the social conditions obtained in their mother country, but fled these conditions in the hope of a better life. This series of choices (reproduced in the westward movement) provided a complex selection process—populating America disproportionately with a certain kind of person.[24]

The examples just presented make clear that while Americans express some values, they often behave differently. The values do, however, still provide the standards by which individuals are evaluated. These inconsistencies are sometimes important in explaining individual behavior (guilt, shame, aggression), and the emergence of insulating personal and social mechanisms such as compartmentalization and racial segregation.

Not only is there an inconsistency between values and behavior, but there is also a lack of unity among some of the values themselves. Some examples of this phenomenon, which Record and Record have called "ethical schizophrenia," are individualism *vs.* humanitarianism, materialism *vs.* idealism, and pragmatism *vs.* utopianism.[25]

CULTURAL DIVERSITY

Despite the inconsistencies and ambiguities just noted, Americans do tend to believe in certain things—e.g., that democracy is the best form of government; that capitalism is the best economic system; that success can be defined in terms of hard work, initiative, and the amassing of wealth and property; that Christianity should be the country's dominant religion; and that there should be equality of opportunity and equal justice before the law. It is important to note that while these values are held generally by the American populace, there is never total agreement on any of them. The primary reason for this is the tremendous diversity found within the United States.

It is composed of too many people that differ on important social dimensions: age, sex, race, region, social class, ethnicity, religion, rural/urban, and so on. These variables suggest that groups and categories will differ in values and behavior because certain salient social characteristics imply differential experiences and expectations. These will be noted often in the remainder of this book.

Let us examine a few differences held by various groups and categories to illustrate the lack of consistency among Americans. Values are the criteria used to determine, among other things, morality. A Gallup survey asked a national sample in the summer of 1969, "Would you find pictures of nudes in magazines objectionable?" The reply was: Yes—73% ; No—27%. Almost three-fourths of Americans, then, judge such pictures to be inappropriate or immoral, a high percentage but still indicative of a rather substantial minority. Table 2–1 breaks down the data by sex, age, and education. Clearly on this issue, Americans differ significantly,by sex, age, income, occupation, amount of education, region, and community size. There remains, however, a majority in each of these categories who find nudity objectionable (at least when answering a Gallup pollster).

There are rural-urban differences that are well known. An interesting example is the probability that rural people are, on the one hand, more humanitarian yet, on the other, more intolerant of deviance among their fellows than are urban dwellers. But there are variations among rural communities as there are among urban places on these and other differences. Compare, for example, the degree of tolerance for eccentricity and deviant behavior by persons in San Francisco with that by persons from New York or Chicago (see Panel 2–2).

Region of the country accounts for some variation in values held.[26] But the generalizations made about southerners, easterners, and midwesterners, while having some validity, gloss over many real differences. Within any one region there are differences between rural and urban people, between different religious groups, between different ethnic groups, and so on. Perhaps the best study of cultural variation within the United States (and even within one geographical region) was done by Kluckhohn and Strodtbeck.[27] These researchers studied five small communities in the same general area in the American southwest—a Mormon settlement, a Texan settlement, a village of Spanish-Americans, a Zuni reservation and a Navaho reservation. They found that these groups were quite different with respect to individual versus collective orientation, time dimension, the relationship of man to nature, and so on. Because each of these communities differed in their answer to various human dilemmas, their values also differed significantly.

Kluckhohn and Strodtbeck, of course, did not choose American communities at random. They were very selective, hoping to demonstrate the existence of real cultural differences within the United States. What they found were four subcultures (all but the

TABLE 2–1.   Nudes in Magazines

Question: "Would you find pictures of nudes in magazines objectionable?"   (Late May, 1969).

	% Yes	% No
NATIONAL	73	27
Sex		
Men	66	34
Women	80	20
Education		
College	59	41
High School	74	26
Grade School	86	14
Occupation		
Prof. & Bus.	64	36
White Collar	64	36
Farmers	89	11
Manual	76	24

Texas community) within one geographical region within the border of the United States.

The concept, subculture, has been defined typically as a relatively cohesive cultural system that varies in form and substance from the dominant culture. Under the rubric "subculture," then, there are ethnic groups, delinquent gangs, and religious sects. Milton Yinger has proposed that the concept "subculture" be defined more precisely. He has suggested that it be used for one type of group and "contraculture" for another type that had been previously called a subculture.[28] For Yinger the concept "subculture" should be limited to relatively cohesive cultural systems that differ from the dominant culture in such things as language, values, religion, and style of life. Typically, a group that is a subculture differs from the larger group because it has immigrated from another society and because of physical or social isolation it has not been fully assimilated. The cultural differences, then, are usually based on ethnicity. Tradition keeps the culture of this group somewhat unique from the dominant culture. There are a number of examples of such subcultures in the United States—the Amish, the Hutterites, some Orthodox Jewish sects, many Indian tribes, Appalachian snake handlers, and

Age	% Yes	% No
21–29 years	56	44
30–49 years	73	27
50 & over	83	17
Region		
East	68	32
Midwest	81	19
South	79	21
West	62	38
Income		
$10,000 & over	66	34
$ 7,000 & over	69	31
$ 5,000–$6,999	76	24
$ 3,000–$4,999	79	21
Under $3,000	80	20
Community size		
1,000,000 & over	67	33
500,000 & over	67	33
50,000–499,999	65	35
2,500–49,999	82	18
Under 2,500, Rural	84	16

Source: Gallup Opinion Index, Report No. 49 (July, 1969), p. 22.

Poles, Croatians, Hungarians, Italians, Greeks, and Irish groups at one time or another in American history. The existence of numerous subcultures within the United States explains much of the lack of consistency with respect to American values.

A contraculture, as defined by Yinger, is a culturally homogeneous group that has developed values and norms that differ from the larger society because the group opposes the larger society. This type of group is in conflict with the dominant culture. The particular values and norms can only be understood by reference to the dominant group.

The values held by delinquent gangs are commonly believed to be a reaction against the values held by the larger society (and hence would represent a contraculture). Albert K. Cohen has noted, for example, that lower-class juvenile gangs not only reject the dominant value system but they exalt the exact opposite values.[29] These boys, Cohen argued, are ill-equipped because of their lower class

PANEL 2–2

TOLERANCE FOR DEVIANT BEHAVIOR IN SAN FRANCISCO

Source: Howard S. Becker and Irving Louis Horowitz, "The Culture of Civility," *Transaction* 7 (April, 1970), pp. 12–14.

Deviants of many kinds live well in San Francisco—natives and tourists alike make that observation. The city's apparently casual and easygoing response to "sex, dope and cheap thrills" (to crib the suppressed full title of Janis Joplin's famous album—itself a San Francisco product) astounds visitors from other parts of the country who can scarcely credit either what they see happening or the way natives stroll by those same events unconcerned.

—Walking in the Tenderloin on a summer evening, a block from the Hilton, you hear a black whore cursing at a policeman: "I wasn't either blocking the sidewalk! Why don't you motherfucking fuzz mind your own goddamn business!" The visiting New Yorker expects to see her arrested, if not shot, but the cop smiles good-naturedly and moves on, having got her back into the doorway where she is supposed to be.

—You enter one of the famous rock ballrooms and, as you stand getting used to the noise and lights, someone puts a lit joint of marijuana in your hand. The tourist looks for someplace to hide, not wishing to be caught in the mass arrest he expects to follow. No need to worry. The police will not come in, knowing that if they do they will have to arrest people and create disorder.

origins and other related drawbacks to be successful in the game as it is defined by the dominant society. They, therefore, repudiate the commonly held values for a new set that have meaning for them and under which they can perform satisfactorily. These values differ from the values of the larger culture because the delinquents actually want the larger values but cannot attain them. If Cohen's thesis is correct, then delinquent gangs indeed form a contraculture (although Cohen specifically names them subcultures).

Many young Americans have rejected the dominant values not because they are ill-equipped to succeed under them but rather because they have come to view them as inhibiting, causing in-authentic interaction, and channeling individual goals so as to maximize competition and conflict and minimize cooperation and harmony. The values accepted by these persons reverse many of the fundamental values of Americans—hence they provide an example of a contraculture (or counterculture as the term is now more

—Candidates for the city's Board of Supervisors make their pitch for the homosexual vote, estimated by some at 90,000. They will not be run out of town; the candidates' remarks are dutifully reported in the daily paper as are the evaluations of them by representatives of SIR, the Society for Individual Rights.

—The media report (tongue in cheek) the annual Halloween Drag Ball, for which hundreds of homosexuals turn out at one of the city's major hotels in full regalia, unharassed by police.

—One sees long-haired, bearded hippies all over the city, not just in a few preserves set aside for them. Straight citizens do not remark their presence, either by gawking, hostility or flight.

—Nudie movies, frank enough to satisfy anyone's curiosity, are ex-hibited in what must be the largest number of specialty movie houses per capita in the country. Periodic police attempts to close them down (one of the few occasions when repression has been attempted) fail.

The items can be multiplied indefinitely, and their multiplicity demands explanation. Most cities in the United States refuse to let deviants in-dulge themselves publicly, let alone tolerate candidates who seek their bloc votes. Quite the contrary. Other cities, New York and Chicago being good examples, would see events like these as signs of serious trouble, omens of a real breakdown in law enforcement and deviance control, the forerunner of saturnalia and barbarian take-over.

popularly known). There really are two strains of this counterculture: those who have retreated from the "world" to live life as they
feel it should be lived, and those who remain in the "world" and
actively try to change it. Both of these categories reject patriotism,
they lack respect for authority figures (political leaders, police,
teachers, parents), they cast off puritan sexual codes, they spurn
the hard work–success ethic, and they discredit the system because
of its inequities they feel are a result of capitalism, force and fraud.
Most importantly they reject the notion that the American social
order is good and just.[30]

SUMMARY FOR PART I

Part I has focused on the properties of societies. The special emphasis has been on the inherent duality of these properties. Thus, the
inclusion of both the order and conflict perspectives was shown to
be necessary if the examination of a complex, heterogeneous society
such as the United States was to be realistic.

The importance of culture as an integrating force was the highlight of Chapter 2. But since the cultural values that most represent
Americans (e.g., capitalism, materialism, progress, and rationality)
are not shared by all in the society and, moreover, are the sources of
some social problems, the culture is also a source of division.

Part II continues these themes by examining the actual structure
of American society as expressed in the distribution of rewards
(property, prestige, and power). These inequalities, which are
found in all societies to varying degrees, have integrating and
divisive functions. They are especially important because they contribute to the explanation of social conflict and social change.
Additionally, they provide the foundation for understanding American institutions, the subjects of Part III of this book.

SUGGESTED FURTHER READING

Berger, Peter L., *Invitation to Sociology: A Humanistic Perspective*
(Garden City, N.Y.: Doubleday and Company Anchor Books, 1963).
Chapters 4 and 5 of this book are entitled "Man in Society" and
"Society in Man," respectively. They provide an insightful sociological
treatment of culture.

Henry, Jules, *Culture Against Man* (New York: Random House, 1963). An anthropologist looks at American culture and its impact on the family, education, and other institutions.

Kluchhohn, Florence, and Fred L. Strodtbeck, *Variation in Value Orientation* (New York: Harper and Row, 1961). An interesting account of the subcultural variations found within one geographical region, using Kluckhohn's societal dilemmas as the bases for comparison.

Means, Richard L., *The Ethical Imperative: The Crisis in American Values* (Garden City, N.Y.: Doubleday and Company Anchor Books, 1970). This book examines American values and social problems in an atypical and insightful manner.

Olsen, Marvin E., *The Process of Social Organization* (New York: Holt, Rinehart and Winston, 1968). Chapters 4 and 5 of this book are especially helpful for understanding the emergence of culture and, concomitantly, social organization.

Roszak, Theodore, *The Making of a Counter Culture: Reflections on the Technocratic Society and its Youthful Opposition* (Garden City, New York: Doubleday and Company Anchor Books, 1969). This book examines the sources of alienation among youth in American society and their reactions to it.

Slater, Philip, *The Pursuit of Loneliness: American Culture at the Breaking Point* (Boston: Beacon Press, 1970). This book provides a valuable analysis and critique of American culture.

NOTES AND REFERENCES

1. Peter L. Berger, *Invitation to Sociology* (Garden City, New York: Doubleday and Company, Inc., Anchor Books, 1963), p. 98; see also, R. P. Cuzzort, *Humanity and Modern Sociological Thought* (New York: Holt, Rinehart and Winston, Inc., 1969), pp. 203–204.

2. Berger, *Invitation to Sociology*, p. 93.

3. Marvin E. Olsen, *The Processes of Social Organization* (New York: Holt, Rinehart and Winston, Inc., 1968), p. 60; and Gerhard Lenski, *Human Societies: A Macrolevel Introduction to Sociology* (New York: McGraw-Hill Book Company, 1970), pp. 37–38.

4. Dick Gregory, "Dick Gregory: The Light Side: The Dark Side," (New York: Poppy Industries, Inc., 1969).

5. Robin M. Williams, *American Society: A Sociological Interpretation,* Third Edition (New York: Alfred A. Knopf, 1970), pp. 444–446.

6. See especially the insights of Max Weber, *The Protestant Ethic and the Spirit of Capitalism,* Talcott Parsons (trans.), (New York: Charles Scribner's Sons, 1958). This work was first published in 1904.

7. Much of the discussion about societal dilemmas is based on the insightful scheme first elaborated by Florence Rockwood Kluck-

hohn, "Dominant and Variant Value Orientations," in *Personality in Nature, Society, and Culture*, Second Edition, Clyde Kluckhohn and Henry A. Murray (eds.), (New York: Alfred A. Knopf, 1955), pp. 342–357. See also Florence Kluckhohn and Fred L. Strodtbeck, *Variation in Value Orientation* (New York: Harper and Row, 1961).

8. Gerhard Lenski, *Power and Privilege: A Theory of Social Stratification* (New York: McGraw-Hill Book Company, 1966), pp. 25–32, for a brief discussion of the way order and conflict theorists view the nature of man and a realistic synthesis of the two.

9. Barry Goldwater, *The Conscience of a Conservative* (New York: Hillman Books, 1960), p. 12.

10. A. S. Neill, *Summerhill: A Radical Approach to Child Rearing* (New York: Hart Publishing Company, 1960), p. 4.

11. Richard L. Means, *The Ethical Imperative: The Crisis in American Values* (Garden City, New York: Doubleday and Company, Inc., Anchor Books, 1970), Chapter 6.

12. Means, *The Ethical Imperative*, pp. 155–156.

13. Curry Kirkpatrick, "The Nontransmogrification of Orville Moody," *Sports Illustrated*, (June 22, 1970), p. 37.

14. Means, *The Ethical Imperative*, Chapter 5, but especially p. 119.

15. For discussions of the ecology crisis see especially: Robert Disch *et al.* (ed.), *The Ecological Conscience: Values for Survival* (Englewood Cliffs, New Jersey: Prentice-Hall, Inc., Spectrum Books, 1970); Paul R. Ehrlich and Anne H. Ehrlich, *Population Resources, Environment: Issues in Human Ecology* (San Francisco: W. H. Freeman and Company, 1970); The Editors of *Ramparts*, *Eco-Catastrophe* (San Francisco: Canfield Press, 1970); and *Man and the Ecosphere: Readings from Scientific American* (San Francisco: W. H. Freeman and Company, 1971).

16. Most notably, Theodore Roszak, *The Making of a Counter Culture* (Garden City, New York: Doubleday and Company, Inc., Anchor Books, 1969); and Charles Reich, *The Greening of America* (New York: Bantam Books, 1971).

17. Lloyd A. Free and Hadley Cantril, *The Political Beliefs of Americans: A Study of Public Opinion* (New York: Simon and Schuster, Clarion Book, 1968), p. 28.

18. Jerome H. Skolnick and Elliott Currie, "Approaches to Social Problems," in *Crisis in American Institutions*, Jerome H. Skolnick and Elliott Currie (eds.), (Boston: Little, Brown and Company, 1970), pp. 1–16.

19. Philip Slater, *The Pursuit of Loneliness: American Culture at the Breaking Point* (Boston: Beacon Press, 1970), p. 9.

20. Harold J. Laski, *The American Democracy* (New York: The Viking Press, 1948); Read Bain, "Our Schizoid Culture," *Sociology and Social Research* 19 (1935), pp. 266–276; and Jane C. Record and Wilson Record, "Ideological Forces and the Negro Protest," *The Annals* 357 (January, 1965), pp. 89–96.

21. Gunnar Myrdal, *An American Dilemma* (New York: Harper and Row, 1944); *Report of the National Advisory Commission on Civil Disorders* (New York: Bantam Books, 1968); and Raymond W. Mack, *Transforming America: Patterns of Social Change* (New York: Random House, 1967), especially Chapter 7, "The American Dream and the American Dilemma."

22. William H. Whyte, Jr., *The Organization Man* (Garden City, New York: Doubleday and Company, Inc., Anchor Books, 1956), p. 150.

23. Slater, *The Pursuit of Loneliness*, p. 15.

24. Slater, *The Pursuit of Loneliness*, pp. 13–14.

25. Record and Record, "Ideological Forces and the Negro Protest," pp. 89–96.

26. John Gillin, "National and Regional Cultural Values in the United States," *Social Forces* 34 (December, 1955), pp. 107–113.

27. Florence Kluckhohn and Fred L. Strodtbeck, *Variations in Value Orientations* (New York: Harper and Row, 1961).

28. J. Milton Yinger, "Contraculture and Subculture," *American Sociological Review* 25 (October, 1962), pp. 625–635. The following discussion relies principally upon this article.

29. Albert K. Cohen, *Delinquent Boys: The Culture of the Gang* (Glencoe, Illinois: The Free Press, 1955).

30. Robert E. Lane and Michael Lerner, "Why Hard-Hats Hate Hairs," *Psychology Today* 4 (November, 1970), pp. 45–49 and 104–105; and Roszak, *The Making of a Counter Culture*.

PART II

Inequality in the United States

There is a vertical dimension to all societies. Individuals and groups are considered to be equal to, superior to, or inferior to others with respect to power, possessions, privileges, and prestige. Curiously, this fact is sometimes overlooked or minimized by analysts of American society. Instead of focusing on the power elite, the existence and persistence of poverty for a sizeable proportion of Americans, or the racism that prevails, many choose to elaborate on "positive" aspects of society. They stress the Democratic creed of liberty and justice for all, the pluralistic (democratic) system with one man equalling one vote, the relative prosperity of the large American middle class, or the vast progress made in recent years in the area of civil rights. This emphasis on the positive is exemplified by S. M. Lipset in his book, *The First New Nation*[1] where the harsh facts of inequality are finally noted in the Epilogue. As Dusky Lee Smith has so aptly said of Lipset, "He ends where sociologists should begin."[2]

We begin the analysis of American society with inequality for several reasons. First, the United States is not (and has never been) a classless society. The notion that all Americans are born equal is a myth that should be dispelled. Second, an understanding of the inequalities of American society is essential to understanding its institutions. The decision-making process at all levels of government and the distribution of goods and services are but two examples of the relationship between inequality and American institutions. Finally, the phenomenon of inequality is one of the fundamental keys to understanding human behavior. Why do life styles differ? Why do some persons accept the system while others reject it? Why do some persons and groups adopt values antithetical to the dominant American values? Why are the members of certain social categories more likely to be labelled "criminals" than members of other categories? While the answers to these questions are indeed complex, we can be assured that a significant portion of the answers can be attributed to the phenomenon of social inequality.

CHAPTER 3

The American System
of Social Stratification

Inequality is a fact of social life. All known societies have some system of ranking individuals and groups along a superiority-inferiority scale. The thrust of this chapter is that the particular placement of individuals in the ranking system makes a significant difference—a difference in life style, behavior, attitude, and self-images.

Major Concepts and Assumptions

People differ in age, physical attributes, and in what they do for a living. The process of categorizing persons by age, height, occupation or whatever is called *social differentiation*. When people are ranked in a vertical arrangement (hierarchy) that differentiates them as superior or inferior, then we have *social stratification*. The key difference between differentiation and stratification is that the process of ranking or evaluation occurs only in the latter. What is ranked and how it is ranked is dependent upon the values of the society.

Social stratification refers, in essence, to structured social inequality. The term "structured" refers to stratification being socially patterned.[3] This implies that inequalities are not caused by biological differences (e.g., sex, or race). Biological traits do not become

73

relevant in patterns of social superiority or inferiority until they are socially recognized and given importance by being incorporated into the beliefs, attitudes, and values of the people in the society. Americans, for example, tend to believe that sexual and racial characteristics make a difference—therefore they do.

The social patterning of stratification is also found in the distribution of rewards in any community or society, since that distribution is governed by social norms. In American society few individuals seriously question the income differential between medical doctors and primary school teachers because the norms and values of society dictate that such inequities are just.

Patterned behavior is also achieved through the socialization process. Each generation is taught the norms and values of the society and of its social class. The children of slaves and the children of the ruling family in a society are each taught the behavior "proper" for persons of their station in life.

Finally, the system of stratification is always connected with other aspects of the society. The existing stratification arrangements are affected by and have effects upon such matters as politics, marriage and the family, economics, education, and religion.

An individual's position (*social status*) in the social stratification system is determined by the degree to which he possesses those qualities highly valued by the society. The important criteria by which people are evaluated and ranked in the United States are (1) family background, which includes the status of the preceding generations of one's family, their ethnic and racial background, and religious affiliation, (2) the amount and type of an individual's wealth, (3) personal qualities such as sex, age, beauty, and intelligence, (4) personal achievements such as amount of education, type of job, and job performance, and (5) the amount of power and authority of the individual.

These criteria for evaluation can be viewed as either ascribed or achieved characteristics. Ascribed characteristics befall individuals regardless of their efforts. Individuals cannot control their age, their sex, their race, or their family background—therefore these characteristics are ascribed. Achieved characteristics, on the other hand, are those attained by individuals because of their own efforts, such as amount of education and type of job.*

---

* This distinction between ascribed and achieved characteristics is a somewhat artificial one made for analytical purposes, since abscribed characteristics can and do have an effect upon educational attainment, type of job, and the other achieved characteristics.

When a number of persons occupy the same relative economic rank in the stratification system they form a *social class*. Persons of similar status form a *status group*. The members of a status group view one another as social equals. Interaction tends to occur most frequently among status equals. Although social classes and status groups often overlap, they may not—leading to the phenomenon of *status inconsistency*.

The rigidity of the stratification system varies from society to society. The key indicator of rigidity is the extent to which ascribed characteristics "lock" the individual into a social class or status group. The more that achieved characteristics determine class or status position, the more open the system—the more movement is possible from one rank to another (*social mobility*).

Probably the most rigid stratification system ever devised by man was the caste system of India. In brief, this system (1) determined status by heredity, (2) allowed marriage to occur only within one's status group (endogamy), (3) determined occupation by heredity, and (4) restricted interaction among the status groups. Even the Indian caste system, however, was not totally rigid for some mobility has been allowed under certain circumstances.*

In contrast to the closed stratification system of India, the United States is a relatively open system. Social mobility is not only permitted but it is part of the American values that upward mobility is good and should be the goal of all Americans.

The United States, however, is not a totally open system. All American children have the social rank of the parents while they are youths. As we shall see in the four chapters of this section, the status of parents has a tremendous influence on a child's attitudes and behaviors (particularly performance in school) and these determine in large measure whether the child can be mobile (upward or downward).

Suzanne Keller has argued forcefully that the hereditary transmission of elite status, while still important, is on the decline in the United States.[5] She has suggested that relatively recent social and technological changes have deprived the family of the capacity to transfer elite status to offspring. There is a tremendous need for expertise in specialized areas in a technological society. Since experts are made—not born—persons of talent regardless of the social class of their parents will be upwardly mobile. Keller argues,

* Some observers have charged that the stratification system of the United States is caste-like with reference to race. Race, in many ways, presents a barrier that determines status, the range of marriage partners, and discriminatory treatment of all kinds.[4]

then, that achieved characteristics are becoming more and more important, while the importance of ascribed characteristics is receding at the same rate. It is important to note, however, that ascribed and achieved characteristics remain important in social placement. In the words of Keller, "The recruitment of elites in American society today reflects the pull of social class, the push of individual merit, and the invisible hand of tradition."[6]

The stratification system in the United States presents a paradox. On the one hand there is rigidity—there is a high probability that the children of the wealthy will be wealthy when they become adults while children of poverty-stricken families spend a lifetime in the same condition—but yet there is fluidity. Any person with talent, and there is a growing need for trained specialists, can move up the stratification hierarchy quite rapidly.[7] See Panel 3–1 for a discussion about the prospects of mobility increasing dramatically in the near future.

Social Stratification from the Order and Conflict Perspectives

As we examine inequality in American society, let us keep in mind the alternative ways order and conflict theorists view this phenomenon. The position of the order theorists is basically supportive of inequality, since the unequal distribution of rewards is assumed to be not only inevitable but necessary. Conflict theorists, on the other hand, tend to denounce the distributive system as basically unjust, unnecessary, and the source of many social problems.

Adherents of the order model begin with the fact that social inequality is a ubiquitous and apparently unavoidable phenomenon. They reason that inequality must, therefore, serve a useful function for society. The argument, as presented in the classic statement by Davis and Moore, is as follows:[8] The smooth functioning of society requires that various tasks be accomplished through a division of labor. There is a universal problem, then, of allocation—of getting the most important tasks done by the most talented people. Some jobs are more important for social survival than others (typically persons involved in decision-making, medicine, religion, teaching, and the military). The societal problem is how to get the most talented people motivated to go through the required long periods of training and to do these important tasks well. The universally found answer, according to Davis and Moore, is differential rewards. Society must provide suitable rewards (money, prestige, and power) to induce individuals to fill these positions. The rewards

PANEL 3-1

"THE BLUEING OF AMERICA"

Source: Adapted from Peter L. Berger and Brigitte Berger, "The Blueing of America,"
The New Republic (April 3, 1971), pp. 20–23; and Peter and Brigitte Berger, "The Eve
of the Blueing of America," *The New York Times* (February 15, 1971), p. 23.

Two sociologists, Peter and Brigitte Berger, have speculated that the increased interest of American young people in the counterculture will have some unusual consequences, the most important of which is dramatic upward mobility for the children of blue-collar workers.

Participation in the counterculture means rejection of basic American values such as capitalism, onward and upward technology (progress), and materialism. Additionally, the Protestant work ethic is replaced by a hedonistic ethic that stresses liberation from traditional customs (sex taboos, cleanliness, hard work).

Attraction to the counterculture is not randomly distributed. Almost exclusively, these adherents are college-educated children of the upper-middle class. Most commonly, they have attended the more prestigious schools. Their parents are quite successful by traditional standards. Ordinarily, these persons would at least match their parents in education, prestige of job, and income. But the members of the counterculture deliberately set out on a course guaranteed to make them poorer than their parents; in other words they will be downwardly mobile. They are doing this in a variety of ways: (1) by totally "dropping out" of "straight" society; (2) by seeking low paying jobs that provide enough money to survive but make only minimum demands on one's time and emotions; or (3) shifting college majors from business, advertising, law, and scientific technology to the social sciences and humanities.

What will be the consequences of this trend (assuming that it becomes more and more widespread)? First, since many of the children of the well-to-do who have attended the best schools will be downwardly mobile, there will be room at the top. The scientific, technological, and bureaucratic roles will be filled by the newly college-educated children of the lower-middle and working classes. Second, social change will not be dramatic since the power structure will be filled by "straights" who are happy with the system. Third, the stratification system will remain very open and fluid. There will be the immediate filling of the vacuum created by the "drop-outs." Those from blue-collar backgrounds who are upwardly mobile will, however, because of their affluence raise their children differently than they themselves were raised. This, in turn, will make their children highly susceptible to the appeals of the counterculture—thereby leaving a vacuum that may be filled by the children of the present generation's "drop-outs."

must, it is argued, be distributed unevenly to various positions because the positions are not equally pleasant nor equally important. Thus, a differential reward system guarantees that the important societal functions are fulfilled, thereby insuring the maintenance of society. In this way, differential ranks actually serve to unify society (functional integration through a division of labor and through the socialization of persons to accept their positions in the system). Although there probably is some truth to this argument, the analyst of American society must also ask: is inequality primarily integrative or divisive? Is it necessary? Must the poor always be with us?[9]

Conflict theorists view stratification in a wholly different manner. Rather than accepting stratification as a source of societal integration, the conflict perspective assumes it to be a major source of discord and coercion. It is a source of discord because the "have-nots" will not be satisfied but rather resentful of their lowly position and lack of rewards. Coercion results from stratification as the powerful (who are coincidentally the wealthy) prey on the weak. The powerful make and enforce the laws, determine the distribution of rewards, and through control of the media and education make their value system paramount. Thus, stratification is unjust and is a primary source of revolutionary change as the "have-nots" rebel against the system.

While it is true that social stratification is an important source of societal friction, the conflict theorists have not answered the important question as to its necessity (neither have the order theorists for that matter, although they address themselves directly to that question). Both models have important insights that we must consider. the order theorists see stratification serving the useful function of societal maintenance by providing a mechanism (differential rewards) to insure that all the slots in the division of labor are filled. Conflict theorists are equally valid in their contention that stratification is unjust, divisive, and a source of social instability or change.

THE SOCIAL CLASSES IN THE UNITED STATES

There are several questions to be raised in this section: is the United States a classless society? and if not, how many classes are there and what are their characteristics? are there real gaps between each of these classes? and finally, are the classes national in scope or are they community-specific?

Economic and Status Differences in the United States

There is a great deal of evidence that Americans differ greatly on a number of socioeconomic dimensions. Americans are also very status-conscious. Let us examine some of the documentation for the existence of economic and status differences in the United States.

In the first place, wealth is unquestionably maldistributed in the United States. There exists in the United States unbelievable wealth in the hands of a few and wretched poverty for some others. This is not to say that the bulk of Americans lack enough wealth to live comfortably for most are reasonably comfortable. The median income in 1968 was $8,632, when 67 percent of American families had incomes between $4,000 and $14,999. It is important to note, however, the proportions of Americans at either extreme. In 1968, 16 percent earned less than $4,000 and 15 percent had incomes of more than $15,000.[10] At the low end of the wealth continuum some Americans die each day of malnutrition and inadequate health care while a few others have a superabundance of material blessings.*

Americans also vary considerably in educational attainment. The amount of formal education an individual receives is a major determinant in his occupation and in his income. Despite the standard belief by Americans in free mass education and the almost uniform requirement that persons complete at least eight years of formal schooling, very real differences in educational attainment exist. In 1972 the median number of school years completed was 12.2 for whites and 10.3 for blacks.** Although the proportion who have completed four years of high school has more than doubled since 1940, still one-fourth of the adult population has not gone to high school at all.[11]

There is an obvious correspondence between being inadequately educated and receiving little or no income. There is not only a generational correlation between these two variables but an inter-generational one as well. The children of the poor and uneducated tend to not do well in school and eventually drop out (regardless of ability) while the children of the educated well-to-do tend to continue in school (regardless of ability). Thus, the cycle of inequality is maintained.

---

* Chapter 11 provides much greater detail about the unequal distribution of income in American society. See the Appendix, Figures 74 and 75, for the 1969 data on family income broken down by race and region (page 431).
** See the Appendix, Figures 55, 56, and 57, for the 1970 data on education broken down by age, region, and race (page 429).

Another demonstration that persons diverge in status is that occupations vary systematically in prestige. The degree of prestige and difference accorded to occupations is variable. A justice of the Supreme Court obviously enjoys more prestige than a bartender. But society makes much more subtle prestige distinctions. There is a rather uniform tendency to rate physicians slightly higher than college professors who in turn are somewhat higher in rank than dentists. Further down the prestige scale, mail carriers outrank carpenters who in turn have higher prestige than automobile repairmen.*

The culture provides "the man in the street" with a ready-made and well understood ranking system. It provides a relatively uniform system based on several related factors. These are (1) the importance of the task performed—(i.e., how vital the consequences of the task are for the society), (2) the degree of authority and responsibility inherent in the job, (3) the native intelligence required, (4) the knowledge and skills required, (5) the dignity of the job, and (6) the financial rewards of the occupation.

Occupation, then, is a very important variable that sorts people into hierarchically arranged categories. It is highly correlated with income and educational level. There is a strong probability that highly educated persons will also have a high prestige job and have a good deal of wealth. Of these three variables, occupational level is considered the best single indicator of status position in the United States.

Additional evidence for Americans being status-conscious is the importance attached to family background. An individual's social status is not immutably fixed by birth in American society, but family background remains an important determinant of status. Race and ethnicity are inherited from one's parents, and they have had and continue to have a profound effect upon socioeconomic status. Offspring almost invariably adopt the religion of their parents, and this, too, may have consequences for placement in the status hierarchy. Most importantly, the extent of family wealth determines in very large measure the life style, amount and type of education, with whom one associates as equals, whom one marries,

---

* C. C. North and Paul K. Hatt, the two sociologists who gathered these prestige rankings in 1947, found some degree of variation but a substantial agreement among a cross-section of American adults (N = 3,000).[12] This study was replicated in 1963 to ascertain if Americans had changed their ranking of occupations. The correlation between the two studies of 0.99 suggests that the rating of occupations by Americans has remained remarkably stable.[13] Incidentally, sociologists have found a high correlation in the ratings for occupations for a number of industrialized nations.[14]

and the occupational niche one occupies. Family status is especially important at either extreme of the status hierarchy. In the middle range there is much greater fluidity, with family background being less important either as an obstacle, (as with the lowest social category) or as a passport to prestige and wealth, (as with the very highest category).

There is no doubt that most Americans are status seekers. They spend a great amount of effort seeking to rise in status. Many Americans "moonlight" (i.e., work at two jobs), or both husband and wife work to get ahead financially. Others sacrifice to further their education so that they might be better able to secure a more prestigious (and better paying) job.

There is also the propensity of Americans to purchase material goods that they feel will impress others. Presumably this is done in order that persons might be accepted as social equals by others higher in the stratificational "pecking order." The purchase of jewelry, furs, large homes, art objects, luxury cars, the latest in clothing styles, and other ostentatious displays are examples of this phenomenon of "conspicuous consumption."

A final piece of evidence leading to the conclusion that social inequality is a real phenomenon in American society is the existence of patterns of deference. Persons of wealth are treated differently than poor persons in schools, churches, and community organizations. With few exceptions, their opinions are given greater weight, they are more likely to be elected or appointed to official posts, and they are automatically treated with greater respect.

American Social Classes: Statistical Categories or Social Groups?

The preceding section established that Americans are conscious of their position in the status hierarchy and that the range in status is quite large with respect to income, education, and occupation. This means in effect that there is social inequality in the United States and that it can be perceived as a continuum of status. This raises a question upon which social scientists are not in agreement: are there breaks in this continuum that allow us to distinguish social classes and/or status groups? Put another way, are American social classes real, or are they artificial constructs?

The techniques employed by many sociologists insure that the social strata they delineate are not real. Persons are assigned a social class position on the basis of their education, occupation, income level, place of residence, or other status characteristics.

With such a technique placement is arbitrary, to say the least. The procedure is invalid if the goal is to delineate the exact boundaries of classes and their memberships. It is a valid technique, however, if the goal is to compare the behaviors and/or attitudes of persons at different status levels. The sociologists who use this technique tend either to accept the continuum approach to stratification, or to use it as a quick method to delineate approximately the members of real classes.

The "classes are real" adherents claim that there are distinct social strata whose members are conscious of their unity. They share common goals, interests, and values. Furthermore, they contend that there are boundaries separating each of the strata. The problem is that class consciousness, class unity, and the understanding of class boundaries are variables. They may be quite pronounced in some communities and not so in others. The valid point made by proponents of the "realist" perspective, however, is that persons in communities tend to think in terms of classes. They see themselves in a class and they can place others in the stratification system.

There is conflicting evidence for the "classes are real" thesis. A. B. Hollingshead found evidence in his study of Morris, Illinois, for the existence of five discrete classes. He found that respondents in that community believed in the existence of social classes, identified persons as members of specific classes, thought of themselves as members of classes, and associated behavior with class level. At one point in the research Hollingshead asked twelve knowledgeable persons to rank 20 representative families into classes. No instructions were given regarding the number of strata into which the families should be divided. Ten of the twelve raters divided the families into five strata. This Hollingshead interpreted as conclusive evidence for the existence of five discrete social class groups in that community.[15]

In contrast, Gerhard Lenski's study of Danielson, Connecticut, suggests the very opposite of that found by Hollingshead. Lenski selected 24 residents who were old enough (between 20 and 70) and who had lived in the community long enough (at least 7 years) to be considered "well-informed" members of that community of 6,000. Each rater was given a pack of cards with the names and addresses of 173 families. They were asked to select from the pack only the names they knew and rank these families according to their relative "standing." They were not given any instructions regarding the number of classes or levels into which the families were to be divided. The raters, it was found, lacked a consensus on the number of strata and the placement of families within strata. For example, one rater identified three strata in the community, four raters discerned four strata, seven raters noted five strata, eight raters perceived six strata, and four raters believed the community to have seven strata. Lenski noted that the raters, in the course of the rating interview, constantly changed the number of strata they were using to classify the sample families. He concluded that, for this community at least, there was no system of discrete social classes. But Lenski delved further into his data. Perhaps some of the raters perceived the actual number of classes while others just were not keen observers of the community. If this were so then perhaps all the raters who agreed on the number of strata would agree as to the families belonging in each. There was virtually no agreement, however, among the raters who perceived the same number of strata. For example, the most common number of strata perceived was six, but some raters defined the top stratum in very narrow terms including only two or three families in it. Others, by contrast, defined the top stratum so as to include twelve families in it. Lenski's findings, therefore, present the consistent conclusion that although status differences occur in the community, there are no real social classes.[16]

The studies by Hollingshead and Lenski suggest that the extent of class boundaries varies from community to community. The analyst of any particular community or the total society should look for two basic indicators of the existence of separate classes: the existence of *class consciousness* and *class segregation*.

1. *The extent of class consciousness.* Karl Marx believed that capitalist societies were composed of two broad classes—those persons who owned the instruments of production (bourgeoisie) and those who worked for the owners (proletariat). In other words, there would be a dichotomy based on the relationship to the means of production. Marx predicted (based upon his analysis of history and of how capitalism was working in mid-nineteenth-century England) that persons in these two classes would develop class consciousness —a necessary precondition for class conflict. The essential characteristics of class consciousness for Marx were, first of all, that persons in a similar economic position should realize they have common interests. In Marx's analysis, the proletariat will be profoundly dissatisfied with the distribution of economic rewards while the bourgeoisie will work to keep the status quo. The bourgeoisie will cooperate among themselves because they are outnumbered and fear the potential power of the lower class. These

feelings of common interests lead naturally to the second characteristic of class consciousness—each class becomes hostile to the
other. Marx designated these two classes as the oppressors and the
oppressed. If these words describe the situation accurately, then
hostility between them would be a natural outcome. Finally, class
consciousness entails a collective commitment to a political ideology
for the attainment of economic interests.

Implied in these three characteristics of class consciousness is the
uniformity of belief by persons in a similar economic situation.
Marx believed this would occur because of the unequal distribution
of economic rewards. Because of similar economic interests, the
bourgeoisie would unite to exert control over the proletariat, while
the proletariat would band together for power. Finally, the relative
ease of communication among the individuals in the same class
position should lead to relatively uniform beliefs within each class.

Marx predicted that the natural development of class consciousness would lead ultimately to class conflict in capitalist societies.
Does his prediction appear to hold for the United States? To answer
this, we need to ask: Do Americans identify themselves with a
class? Are blue collar workers (or businessmen) unified? Are they
allied in a common cause? Do they vote for the same candidates
and perceive issues in the same way? Are they organized? Is it clear
who are members and who are not?

The empirical evidence for the existence of class consciousness
suggests that this phenomenon is relatively low in the United States
but not absent.

TABLE 3–1.   Interest Groups Which Ought to Be Most Powerful, by
Years of Education (in percentages)

Years of Education	All Should Be Equal	Big Business	Labor Unions	All Other	Don't Know	Total %
0–7	52	2	4	23	19	100
8–11	48	4	13	22	13	100
12–15	38	19	10	25	8	100
16+	38	14	0	41	7	100

Source: William H. Form and Joan Huber (Rytina), "Ideological Beliefs on
the Distribution of Power in the United States," American Sociological Review,
34 (February, 1969), p. 27.

Many studies have documented that people in various occupational, educational, and income levels differ significantly in the opinions on a number of social and political issues. Let us examine several examples of this evidence. Table 3–1 shows how persons with different educational levels feel power should be divided among various interest groups. These data were from a sample of Muskegon, Michigan, residents.

These data suggest that nothing approaching unanimity of opinion is found at any one educational level. This lack of consistency is also found in the vote for President in 1968. Table 3–2 gives these data including the important variables of occupation and income as well as education.

Table 3–2 shows the lack of unanimity among persons at the various socioeconomic levels. The vote for Wallace is especially important to consider in the context of class consciousness. Wallace sought support from the "common man." His appeal was populist. The common man was typically pictured in Wallace's speeches as a victim—a victim of the federal bureaucrats, intellectuals, mass media, student demonstrators, and the welfare chiselers. Wallace's

TABLE 3–2.   1968 Presidential Voting in the Non-South (in percentages)

| Occupation | Voted for | | | Total Percent |
	Humphrey	Nixon	Wallace	
Non-manual	42	53	5	100
Manual	49	42	9	100
union	57	34	9	100
nonunion	39	52	9	100
Education				
Grade school or less	53	40	7	100
High school or less	43	49	7	99
At least some college	43	52	5	100
Income				
less than $3,000	41	53	5	99
$3,000–$6,999	46	44	10	100
$7,000–$9,999	42	52	6	100
$10,000–$14,999	46	47	6	99
$15,000+	39	58	3	100

Source: adapted from Seymour Martin Lipset and Earl Raab, "The Wallace Whitelash," Trans-action 7 (December, 1969), p. 28.

appeal was simple—"us common folks against *them*." The results of that election (Table 3–2) show that this appeal was only very slight. Class consciousness as a political tactic did not work.

A final example of this lack of consensus within status ranks is taken from a CBS News poll in March 1970. The interviewees were asked: "Do you think everyone should have the right to criticize the government, even if the criticism is damaging to our national interests?" The replies by income and education are given in Table 3–3.

Table 3–3 affirms the contention that there are differences of opinion within each of the status levels. However, the data show a relationship between educational attainment or income level and belief in freedom of speech. For both status variables, the percentage of persons favoring free speech increases as the level of status increases. A relationship between status and some dependent variable, then, is not indicative by itself of class consciousness. Class consciousness can only be inferred when the persons within a status category approach unanimity with respect to an issue, or candidate, or political philosophy. The evidence is that substantial minorities at each status level do not share in the attitudes of those who are similarly situated.

Are Americans aware of class boundaries? Do they know what class they are in? Do they owe great allegiance to that class? These

TABLE 3–3.   Freedom of Speech (in percentages)

| | Oppose or favor | | | |
	For	Limited	No Opinion	Total
Education				
Grade school	28	68	4	100
Some high school	31	64	5	100
H.S. graduate	44	54	2	100
Some college	56	42	2	100
College graduate	61	34	5	100
Income				
Under $5,000	33	63	4	100
$5,000–$9,999	40	57	3	100
$10,000–$14,999	48	49	3	100
$15,000+	57	39	4	100

Source: adapted from Hazel Erskine, "The Polls: Freedom of Speech," *Public Opinion Quarterly* 34 (Fall, 1970), p. 491.

related questions lie at the core of class consciousness. Most of the evidence from studies of the United States suggests negative answers to these questions.

The study cited most often as a basis for the existence of class consciousness in the United States was conducted by Richard Centers.[17] Centers gathered data from a representative cross section of American adult white males in 1945. Among other things, he asked if they belonged to: the middle class, the lower class, working class, or upper class. Here are the results:

upper class	3%
middle class	43%
working class	51%
lower class	1%
don't know	2%

Centers felt that since only 2 percent of Americans did not know what class they belonged to he had overwhelming evidence of a strong class consciousness in the United States.

Centers' study, however, raises more questions than it answers. Let us look at several of the criticisms, because they weaken what on the surface appears to be a very strong argument for class consciousness.[18] First, self-identification as to class in a questionnaire may not be reliable. Some individuals may claim a class position which represents only wish fulfillment or fantasy. For instance, 18 percent of the unskilled workers in Centers' study said they were middle class. Conversely, some individuals may be inclined to downgrade their actual class position because they are influenced by equalitarian ideology. In Center's study 10 percent of the professionals identified themselves as working class instead of middle or upper.

A second criticism is the use of a forced-choice type of question. The situation was structured for the respondents, as they had four response categories. What if Centers had used five or six categories? Or better yet, what if the respondents were not given any prearranged choices? Neal Gross tested this in a study of 935 heads of households in Minneapolis. The respondents were asked to identify their social class with no hint as to what was meant by social class or how many the interviewer thought there might be. Over one-third of the responses were in the "don't know" category (Centers only found 2 percent in this category).[19] Obviously, the open-ended method provides an opportunity for the respondent to express his lack of class identification as well as identification. We must conclude, therefore, that Centers did not measure class consciousness.

Oscar Glantz conducted a study better designed than Centers' to determine the extent of class consciousness. He gathered data from 400 white, adult males in Philadelphia. But rather than a cross-section of citizens he selected occupational groups that would most likely be class-conscious in the Marxian sense—big and small businessmen on the one hand and union and non-union on the other. To get at class consciousness he asked: "To which of these groups do you feel you owe allegiance—business or labor?" He further asked them to respond to six questions, three of which were statements adopted by the National Association of Manufacturers and three from the Congress of Industrial Organizations. On the basis of group identification and the answers to the six questions, Glantz ascertained the degree of class consciousness. The methods, it would appear, were "stacked" in favor of finding class consciousness (as was the case for Centers) but the results revealed the opposite. He found that 40 percent of all big businessmen and 25 percent of small businessmen were class-conscious. Only 28 percent of all union members and 13 percent of non-union workers were so designated. These findings, striking because the percentages are so much less than expected in the most class-conscious-prone groups, indicate that class consciousness certainly must be at a relatively low level in the United States.[20] Although this is the obvious conclusion, we should not ignore its existence for some individuals and groups. The very upper-most stratum in American society, the group that has had a great deal of money over several generations, whose children go to exclusive schools, and where intermarriage is the highest, constitute a social class with a high degree of class identification by the members. Toward the other end of the continuum there are persons who feel oppressed and who lack economic security. It has been demonstrated that these persons are especially likely to be conscious of their class and feel antipathy toward other classes.[21]

Marx's prediction of the class consciousness and the polarization of the classes has occurred but only minimally in the United States. Class conflict occurs only rarely, and more in the context of specific issues rather than a proletarian revolution. There are labor disputes and strikes, but they do not threaten the fabric of American society. There is some indication that the poor are becoming more organized. They can, if organized, exert greater pressure for better living conditions. The Poor People's March on Washington, D.C., late in the 1960's is just such an example. Welfare mothers in various cities are also organizing to bring about change. This trend appears to be building momentum.

Perhaps the two best examples of group consciousness leading to conflict in American society are not based on economics (as Marx envisioned) but rather on race and age. Among blacks, for instance, more. and more leaders have recently emphasized racial pride, separateness, and violence. In-group solidarity (race consciousness) has been accomplished. Among different age groups there has also been building an "us" versus "them" feeling. There have been sporadic violent clashes between the young and the establishment, with the outcome generally being greater repression of the dissidents. The problem with "youth consciousness," of course, is that the young become the old, that is, the oppressed may become the oppressors, whether there is a revolution or not.

On the opposite end of the age scale, another relatively neglected group, the "senior citizens," have begun organizing and protesting on their own behalf.

Although racial and age groups approach the group consciousness that Marx envisioned, this consciousness has not really developed among social classes in the United States.* There are a number of possible explanations for the relatively low level of class consciousness in the United States. First, Americans, rich and poor alike, tend to share the belief that upward mobility is possible. Even workers who know they will never move to a better job often hold the hope that their children will be upwardly mobile. Because of this widespread belief in the opportunities for upward mobility, efforts to improve status are typically individual efforts rather than concerted collective effort.

A second reason for the low level of class consciousness is that the living standards of blue-collar workers have steadily improved. Skilled laborers (electricians, plumbers, masons) are paid more than many white collar workers (clerks, teachers). Even assembly line workers can make a more than adequate income.

Third, and related to the second reason, is that there has been a leveling of the differences in the life-styles of manual and nonmanual workers. Many manual workers can afford cars, homes, boats, and clothes similar to those owned by higher-status persons and therefore do not feel separate from them.

The development of class consciousness is also inhibited by the existence of organizations whose memberships cut across class lines. Religious denominations, local churches, and organizations

* Marx's theory, however, has provided a fairly accurate model for considering the development process in the emerging nations of Latin America, Africa, and Asia.

such as the American Legion have as members persons from a number of social strata.

Fifth, the blue-collar category, the most likely stratum to develop class consciousness according to Marx, is composed not only of white but all manner of racial and ethnic group members as well. The animosities among these groups within the ranks of the blue collars is often so great that the possibility of unity, coordinated effort, and group pride necessary for class consciousness is precluded.

2. *Class segregation.* A second empirical technique that may be employed to ascertain whether there are distinct boundaries among the social classes is to determine the extent to which there is class segregation. There are two types of segregation to look for: social and spatial. Social segregation refers to barriers that restrict social interaction to the members of a certain category. This is often accomplished by economic factors. High rent, high cost of property, entrance fees, and dues have the function of restricting residents in some parts of town and membership in some clubs. "Undesirables" may also be kept out of certain areas or clubs by the vote of the members. This practice of "blackballing," as well as the economic factors, explains the separation of the wealthiest from the rest of the population.

There is also a voluntary segregation by status that occurs at all levels in the hierarchy. The status character of many organizations is well known and is accomplished often without restrictive entrance requirements. People just feel more comfortable interacting with others like themselves (in wealth, amount of education, type of occupation). Society matrons just have no desire to belong to the women's auxiliary of plumbers local #371 and the wives of plumbers would probably not be comfortable sipping tea with the ladies of the Junior League. Lower class persons probably would feel uneasy in prestigious Episcopal, Presbyterian or Unitarian churches while the well-to-do probably might feel just as uncomfortable in a Pentecostal church.

In order to determine the extent of voluntary status separation the analyst can: (1) compare the status characteristics of marriage partners; (2) determine the status characteristics of persons who spend their leisure time together; (3) ascertain the status characteristics of the members of voluntary associations (from the African Violet Society to the Veterans of Foreign Wars); and compare the status characteristics of close friends.

Segregation also occurs in space. Residential segregation may be forced (as is often the case with minority racial groups) or voluntary. Some residential areas go to great lengths to remain exclusive. Devices such as "gentleman's agreements," restrictive covenants, and point systems have been used for such a purpose.

In summary, the evidence shows that class consciousness has not developed in the United States as Karl Marx predicted (i.e., to the point of political unity). The degree of class consciousness varies with locality and status group. The best evidence for the existence of class consciousness seems to be the social and spatial boundaries separating the highest classes from the rest of the populace.

The Hierarchy of "Classes"

Although class consciousness is relatively low in the United States, Americans do have a conception of a stratification structure, and evaluate persons as social superiors, equals, or inferiors.

Since actual class boundaries are virtually nonexistent (or fuzzy beyond recognition), we will put some artificial closure around a number of strata and call them social classes. The reason for this exercise is to enumerate the characteristics that tend to cluster in the persons located at particular points along the status hierarchy. These characteristics aid in the understanding of behavioral and attitudinal differences found when comparing persons in different strata. They also aid in understanding and analyzing power differentials on the community and national levels. Thus, we should keep in mind, however, that the dividing line between strata is arbitrary and that we should conceive of the stratification system as a continuum with artificial lines designating social classes for analytical purposes only.

The assumption of this analysis is that at different points on this "class" continuum persons will have more or less distinctive characteristics. The units designated as social classes are aggregates of individuals and families who are in similar economic positions and therefore have similar opportunities. Moreover, there is a strong likelihood that they probably consider other persons in the aggregate as social equals.

1. *The upper class* (*the old rich*). Of the various social classes in the United States, the upper class of the old rich is the only class with real boundaries. There is strong in-group solidarity and it is clear to the members who is and who is not included. G. William Domhoff, after an extensive analysis, concluded that this category

makes up .5 percent of the American population. His criteria for inclusion in the upper class are found in Panel 3–2.

Domhoff's criteria for inclusion suggest that the very uppermost stratum in American society is not only wealthy but exclusive. They belong to exclusive clubs and attended equally exclusive boarding schools. These clubs and schools are exclusive because they have very elaborate screening mechanisms to ensure that only certain people are allowed in—usually the persons whose parents were also wealthy. Great wealth by itself is not enough, for persons who acquired it only during their lifetime will never be fully accepted by the persons in the highest stratum.

One characteristic of the upper class is physical and social separation from the other strata. As mentioned above, members of the elite go to very private schools and they belong to private clubs where interaction is restricted to people like themselves. Living in restricted residential areas is another dimension of the exclusiveness prevalent in the upper strata. The life style of the very wealthy also distinguishes it from the other strata. Expensive clothes, jewelry, furs and cars, as well as distinctive speech and manners serve to further separate this group from others.

The possession of great wealth and the benefits concomitant to having great wealth serve to make the elite very powerful, both in the local communities where each of the members resides, and nationally.* Persons of wealth accumulate not only power, but also honor and deference. It is natural that such persons exude self-confidence, for their opinions are sought, their life style is emulated, and they, by their presence, can legitimize an otherwise questionable activity.

Upper class persons tend to be family-oriented. There is a sense of extended family solidarity. This is a consequence of the emphasis on family heritage among the elite. Family solidarity is also maintained often by the joint holding of property. The main source of wealth for the elite are interest and dividends from investment of inherited wealth. Their typical jobs are those of high-ranking executives in established corporations or banks.

Persons in this category tend toward attitudes of political and economic conservatism. Because they benefit so much from existing political and economic arrangements, they work to maintain the status quo. The holding of similar interests (e.g., maintaining the status quo) promotes class consciousness—a condition not found to any extent elsewhere in the stratification hierarchy.

* We will explore the power of the wealthy in detail in Chapter 4.

PANEL 3–2

THE CRITERIA FOR UPPER CLASS MEMBERSHIP

Source: G. William Domhoff, *The Higher Circles: The Governing Class in America* (New York: Random House, 1970), pp. 21–27.

G. William Domhoff provides a number of criteria that distinguish the uppermost social stratum from all others:

1. A person will be considered a member of the upper class if he, his parents, his wife's parents, or any of his siblings are listed in any of the following registers and blue books: *The Social Register* (which has editions in twelve major cities), *Social Secretary* (Detroit), *Social Register* (Houston), *Blue Book* (Los Angeles), *Social Register* (New Orleans), and the *Blue Book* (Seattle).

2. A person will be considered a member of the upper class if he, his father, brother, or father-in-law attended any of the following schools: thirty seven very private schools including Choate, (Wellingford, Connecticut), Deerfield (Deerfield, Massachusetts), Groton (Groton, Massachusetts), Milton (Milton, Massachusetts), and St. Mark's (Southborough, Massachusetts).

3. A person will be considered a member of the upper class if he, his father, brothers, or father-in-law belongs to any one of the following social clubs: forty exclusive clubs including the Century and Knickerbocker Clubs (New York), Pacific Union (San Francisco), Idlewild (Dallas), Somerset (Boston), and the Racquet Club (St. Louis).

4. A person will be considered a member of the upper class if his sister, wife, mother, or mother-in-law attended one of the following schools: sixty-seven private schools including: Abbot Academy (Andover, Massachusetts), Baldwin (Bryn Mawr, Pennsylvania), Chatham Hall (Chatham, Virginia), Lenox (New York), and Westover (Middlebury, Connecticut).

5. A person will be considered a member of the upper class if his sister, wife, mother, or mother-in-law belongs to one of the following clubs: ten including Acorn (Philadelphia), Chilton (Boston), Colony (New York), Fortnightly (Chicago), and Sulgrave (Washington, D.C.).

6. A person will be considered a member of the upper class if his or her father was a millionaire entrepreneur or a $100,000-a-year corporation executive or corporation lawyer, *and* (a) if he or she attended one of the 130 private schools listed in the back of Kavaler's *The Private World of High Society, or* (b) if he or she belongs to any of the exclusive clubs mentioned in Baltzell's *Philadelphia Gentleman: The Making of a National Upper Class* or in Kavaler. The list of private schools and exclusive clubs can be larger here than for the second, third, fourth, and fifth criteria because it is known that the person is a member of the second generation of a wealthy family.

Since the American system of social stratification is a continuum of social "classes," there are no rigid boundaries that mark this continuum into clearly defined classes except at the highest level. As Domhoff has asserted, ". . . the social structure is made up of strata that shade off one into the other until we arrive at the highest level, where the continuum hardens into a social class with more or less definite boundaries and class consciousness."[22]

Domhoff argued that through in-group interaction and differential life styles, class consciousness is intensified among the elite. Evidence of in-group interaction is found in the large proportion of intermarriage that occurs among the very rich. The marriage between two elite young people provides further linkage between the two families. The linked families are often widely separated in space, but the marriage occurred because the children attended the same or neighboring private boarding schools or colleges.

The prestigious private schools that provide the milieu for mate selection have stringent requirements that usually admit only the uppermost stratum. The evidence is also that these schools provide havens for the interaction of rich children from all over the country. As an example of this, ". . . Hotchkiss graduates are listed in the *Social Register* for the following cities: New York, 552; Chicago, 125; Philadelphia, 94; Cleveland, sixty-four; Pittsburg, sixty-four; Boston, fifty-nine; San Francisco, forty; Washington, thirty-five; and St. Louis, thirty-four."[23]

The nation-wide interaction of the rich is also found in club memberships. The exclusive clubs of the upper class have nation-wide memberships.

Summer resorts are further evidence for the cohesiveness of the national upper class. Around the island of Mt. Desert in Maine, for example, are found the summer homes of Social Register listees from the following cities: Philadelphia, ninety-two; New York, eighty; Boston, forty; Washington, twelve; Chicago, seven; Baltimore, seven; Cincinnati-Dayton, six; and St. Louis, five.[24] The same is true of such winter resorts as Palm Beach in Florida and Palm Springs in California.

In summary, the "old rich" are a distinct social class. They are separated from others in the stratification system by where they live, where they attend school, by life style, and by the deference they receive from others. There is, therefore, a clear-cut boundary between the "old rich" and others.

The persons within the "old rich" category form a real social class because the members consider themselves as such—they know who belongs and who does not. Additionally, there are linkages between the members—through marriage, business, school, neighborhood, club, and mutual acquaintance. The members interact and hence form a social group.

The "old rich" social class, unlike any of the other strata, is national in scope. There is a considerable amount of intermarriage and social interaction linking wealthy families living in different cities. While it is clear that not everyone in the "old rich" category knows each other, it is highly probable (as Domhoff has asserted after a great deal of research on the subject) that everyone has friends and relatives who know someone from the uppermost stratum in every major American city. The upper class person, therefore, has an entree into the highest social circles all over the country.[25]

2. *The "new rich."* We will inaccurately refer to the "new rich" and the remaining status categories as "classes." They are not classes in the sense that the "old rich" are. Class consciousness is weak, within-stratum interaction is not as restrictive as in the elite, and the boundaries, which are fuzzy in the minds of many citizens, are therefore set arbitrarily according to objective criteria by social researchers. This arbitrariness of the boundaries, however, does not negate the existence of status differentials.

The "new rich" differ from the uppermost stratum in prestige, not wealth. Great wealth alone does not insure acceptance by the elite as a social equal. A family tradition of wealth (of more than two generations) is a necessary condition for inclusion in the elite. The *nouveaux riches* of Houston, for example, could buy a membership in River Oaks Country Club with an initiation fee of $10,000 (in 1961) but membership in the Houston Country Club was closed except to members of old-guard families.[26] To have acquired wealth in one's lifetime means that one will not have had the time required to learn the ways of the wealthy (e.g., language, manners, grace). This is accomplished only if one has been totally immersed from birth in the ways of the wealthy (private schools, extensive travel, interaction limited to others of equivalent status and background).

The *nouveaux riches* often try to buy their way into elite circles by giving lavish parties, building very expensive homes and other forms of conspicuous consumption. Such overly ostentatious behavior is perceived typically by the elite as "too gauche" and therefore further evidence for exclusion from the most elite circles. One tenet of the "old rich" faith is that one should not have to prove himself with ostentatious displays. This behavior, although it is often motivated by a desire to be accepted by the "old rich," actually causes the opposite reaction.

The following is an account of Jim and Sally Hershberger of Wichita, Kansas. Jim, a self-made millionaire by the age of 29, and his new wife decided to have a house-warming for their new estate, to which they invited 1,400 guests. This, by itself, was somewhat gauche, but they went further in their efforts to impress others. Mrs. Hershberger sent letters inviting the press to her big party. This invitation included the following information about the new house:

> It's 192 feet long and 50 feet wide . . . not counting the basement and the four-car garage, we have 14,000 square feet of living space. As a matter of fact, this is the largest single resident structure to be built in the United States in the last 18 years. [The patio is] approximately 120 by 60 feet. [The tennis court is] considered the best court in Kansas. [We have] a trained masseur who is part of our household and a 500-piece chandelier from Europe, which, upon arrival, took over eight hours just to assemble.[27]

The obvious display of wealth and the invitation to the press giving the details of their palatial home are symptomatic of the attempt of the "new rich" to be envied by all and accepted by the "old rich."

The "new rich" stratum is thus composed of the self-made wealthy. These families have amassed fortunes typically through business ventures, or because of special talent in sports, music, or motion pictures. Additionally, some professionals (doctors, lawyers) may become wealthy because of their practice and/or investments. Finally, a few persons because of their own talent may become very wealthy by working their way in corporations to top executive positions where high salaries and stock options are common.

The "new rich" tend to be political conservatives. They are inclined toward the radical right groups that oppose the welfare state, the graduated income tax, and unions. They vigorously oppose communism and socialism because under these economic systems hard work and initiative are penalized while the ne'er-do-wells benefit. As the political sociologist S. M. Lipset has noted:

> New wealth most often tends to have extremist ideologies, to believe in extreme conservative doctrines in economic matters. The man who makes money himself feels more insecure about keeping it than do people who possess inherited wealth. He feels more aggrieved about social reform measures which involve redistribution

of the wealth, as compared with individuals, still wealthy, who have grown up in an old traditionalist background, which inculcates the values of tolerance traditionally associated with upper-class aristocratic conservatism. It is not without reason that the new millionaires, such as those in Texas, have given extensive financial support to radical right movements, politicians, and to such propaganda organizations as Facts Forum.[28]

3. *The upper-middle class.* The key distinguishing feature of this category are high-prestige jobs (but not the most remunerative in the society) that require a good deal of formal education and have a high degree of autonomy, responsibility, and security. This stratum is largely composed of professional people, business executives, and businessmen. They do not make nearly as much money as the new rich but, as a category, they are usually better educated. Education is of particular importance to persons in this class because the members have found it important to their own careers. The children of this class are expected by the parents to receive a college education.

Much like the two upper classes, the upper-middle class is a bastion of conservatism in American society. They believe in the work-success ethic and capitalism. They are self-made persons, having accomplished prestige and a comfortable economic situation through hard work and sacrifice. They tend, therefore, to oppose many socialistic programs, especially welfare. Many of the more highly educated, however, tend toward liberalism on civil rights, civil liberties, and internationalism issues (but some notable exceptions may be doctors, dentists, and engineers).

4. *The middle class.* This category is composed of white-collar workers who may work primarily in minor jobs in bureaucracies. Also included are clerks, technicians, the owners of small businesses, and salesmen.

These workers are paid an adequate wage, but substantially lower than upper-middle class persons. Their jobs require less skill, less responsibility, and do not involve as much decision making as the class above them in the stratification hierarchy.

These persons usually have some education beyond high school. Some college or training in specialized schools is typical. Most, however, have not graduated from college. This presents a severe limitation to career mobility unless they possess exceptional skills.

The heterogeneity of this stratum is clearly evident. There is a vast difference, for example, between white-collar workers in huge bureaucracies and the owners of small businesses. They differ in amount and type of education, income, degree of autonomy on the job, and job security. These differences affect attitudes, perceptions, motivation, and behaviors. Even child-rearing patterns are noticeably different between these two social categories. An interesting study by Miller and Swanson showed the diversity found within this stratum by comparing entrepreneurial parents (self employed) with bureaucratic parents (employed in large-scale organizations). The researchers assumed that the different settings and demands of each category would be revealed in the way children were reared.* They found that entrepreneurial families stressed self-control, self-reliance, and individual initiative because these traits were needed in the competitive business world. Bureaucratic parents, on the other hand, reared their children to adjust and accommodate to the wishes of others because these traits were especially appropriate for success in large organizations.[29]

The wide diversity found within the "middle class" demonstrates that this category is *not* a real social class. The persons designated as members by social scientists lack class consciousness and the boundaries are not well-defined.

5. *The lower-middle class.* This category is composed of skilled craftsmen such as mechanics, electricians, plumbers, cabinet makers, and masons, many of whom are self-employed. It also includes foremen in large industrial plants who have authority over other workers.

This category receives relatively high wages, often higher than white-collar workers, allowing them to own homes and other possessions typical of middle-class Americans.

They differ from white collar workers in that they are manual workers with less formal education. Although they rank relatively low in the hierarchy, they are "aristocrats" of the blue-collar workers.

Many persons in this stratum are likely to be *status inconsistents* (as are the "new rich"). This means that an individual's status attributes are unbalanced—i.e., their income is higher than their educational background would appear to warrant. This condition often leads to strain and hostility in individuals, since they may not be accepted as equals by persons they feel are their equals (neigh-

* A fuller discussion of child-rearing patterns by social class is found in Chapter 8.

bors, colleagues, customers) who have similar incomes but more education and different life styles.

6. *The upper-lower class.* Semi-skilled operatives who work in the mass production industries are the main component of this class. They are manual workers whose jobs allow little if any autonomy, are simple and repetitive, and require no creativity. Along with the boredom of these jobs is their relative insecurity because of strikes or because of unemployment brought about by economic recession.

These persons have not gone beyond high school and many have not even achieved that. Because of their lack of education and limited skills they are severely blocked if they have aspirations to be upwardly mobile. There is really quite a large gap between semi-skilled workers and white-collar workers. The gulf, for many, is too large to breach.

7. *The lower-lower class.* This class is composed of unskilled laborers whose formal education is often less than eight grades. The chronically unemployed are in this class. The bulk of those on welfare are in this class. Minority group members—blacks, Puerto Ricans, Mexican Americans, Indians—are disproportionately found in this category.

These persons are those that are looked down upon by all others in the community. They live "on the other side of the tracks." They are considered by others to be undesirable as playmates, friends, organization members, or marriage partners. Lower-lowers are viewed as lazy, shiftless, dependent, and immoral—traits exactly opposite of "good middle-class virtues."

THE CONSEQUENCES OF SOCIOECONOMIC STATUS

We have conceived of social strata as aggregates of individuals and families with more or less similar economic positions, similar educational attainment, and holding occupations similar in prestige. These aggregates are ranked, and this creates a stratification hierarchy. Even though these "classes" do not possess real boundaries and class consciousness (except, as we have noted, at the very top), there are very real differences between an aggregate of people at one level of the status hierarchy and persons at another level. This section will illustrate these differences from research that has focused on the life chances of the various strata.

Life Chances

Perhaps Marx was right that the key to the class structure is economics. The extent of one's wealth is the determining factor in a number of crucial areas, including the chance to live and the chance to obtain those things (e.g., possessions, education) that are highly valued in society. The term "life chances" refers to the chances throughout one's life cycle to live and to experience the good things in life. This is dependent almost exclusively on the economic circumstances of the family to which one is born. Gerth and Mills have contended that life chances refer to,

> Everything from the chance to stay alive during the first year after birth to the chance to view fine art, the chance to remain healthy and grow tall, and if sick to get well again quickly, the chance to avoid becoming a juvenile delinquent—and very crucially, the chance to complete an intermediary or higher educational grade . . .[30]

1. *Life expectancy.* Economic position has a great effect upon how long one will live or in a crisis who will be the last to die. For instance, the official casualty lists of the trans-Atlantic luxury liner, the "Titanic," which rammed an iceberg in 1912, listed three percent of the first class female passengers as lost; sixteen percent of the second class female passengers drowned, and among the third class females forty-five percent were drowned.[31] Apparently, even in a disaster, socioeconomic position makes a very real difference— the higher the economic status of the individual, the greater the probability of survival.

The greater advantage toward longer life by the well-to-do is not limited to disasters such as the "Titanic." A consistent research finding is that health and death are influenced greatly by social status.*

Probably the most complete and valid (methodologically) study in this area was conducted by Kitagawa and Hauser, who matched 340,000 death certificates (for deaths occurring during the months

---

* There is an excellent summary article (by Aaron Antonovsky) surveying over thirty studies done prior to 1950 in the United States and elsewhere which lead to the conclusion that socioeconomic status influences one's chance of staying alive.[32]

May–August, 1960) to the 1960 Census records.[33] Using educational attainment level as an indicator of socioeconomic status, the researchers found the expected strong inverse correlation between mortality and educational attainment. Among white women between the ages of 25 and 64 years, for example, the mortality rate for those with less than eight years of school was sixty-one percent higher than among college-educated women. Among white males in this age bracket, the mortality rate for those with less than eight years of school was forty-eight percent higher than for the college-educated men.

2. *Principal cause of death.* The data from Kitagawa and Hauser show very clearly the relationship between socioeconomic status (as measured by educational attainment) and the principal cause of death. The most striking finding was for white males between 25 and 64; those with less than eight years of education had a mortality rate from tuberculosis of more than 800 percent higher than the college-educated. This relationship, although not as strong as found for tuberculosis, was also noted for death from influenza, pneumonia, accidents (motor vehicle and all others), and cancer of the stomach, lung, bronchus, and trachea).

Among the women of this sample, the same general pattern of the less educated having higher mortality rates from specific diseases was found with one exception. Cancer of the breast was found to be the cause of death more frequently in the more educated category.

Among men over 65 there were two interesting differences. The lower educated persons were more likely to die of cardiovascular disease and cancer than the higher educated. But one form of cancer—cancer of the prostate—was much more likely to be the cause of death among the more highly educated men.

3. *Physical health.* The physical health of poor persons is more likely to be impaired than the health of the more well-to-do because of differences in diet, sanitation facilities, and adequate clothing and shelter. Poor persons also cannot afford the best medical care. Data from a 1964 survey compared the medical care of families making less than $2,000 annually and those making more than $7,000. Only 34 percent of the poor families had medical insurance while 90 percent of the others did. Children under 15 years of age in the poor families visited the doctor an average of 1.6 times a year while children of the affluent category averaged 5.7 visits.[34]

This difference has also been found for visits to the dentist.

Persons in families with annual incomes of less than $2,000 averaged .8 dental visits per year while individuals from families making in excess of $7,000 a year averaged 2.3 visits to the dentist.[35] This does not mean that the teeth of the well-to-do are worse than those of the poor but rather that they can afford to do more to insure that they will have good teeth. The inference is clear that the higher the socioeconomic status the greater the probability of having healthy teeth and gums.

The above statistics suggest that lower-income persons will get sick more often and stay sick longer than persons with greater income. Table 3–4 gives data to substantiate this claim.

These data show an inverse relationship between annual income and number of days away from work. It is difficult to know, however, whether the higher rate of absenteeism among the poorer people was a result of illness. This can be inferred from the consistent research findings that the lowest income categories have substantially higher rates of chronic disabilities (e.g., heart conditions, hypertension, arthritis and rheumatism, and visual and hearing impairments).[36]

4. *Mental health.* The most consistent relationship reported in social psychiatric studies is the inverse relationship between socioeconomic status and psychological disorder. Probably the most often cited study is that conducted by Hollingshead and Redlich in New Haven, Connecticut. Table 3–5 presents a portion of their results.

TABLE 3–4. Number of Days Away from Work per Year: Currently Employed Men and Women in the United States, According to Family Income

Annual Income	Men	Women
Under $2,000	9.8	6.5
2,000–4,000	6.4	6.6
4,000–7,000	4.5	5.4
7,000 or more	4.9	4.9

Source: U.S. National Health Service, "Currently Employed Persons, Illness and Work Loss Days, July, 1959–June, 1960," *Public Health Service Publication* 584, Series C, No. 7, 1962.

Hollingshead and Redlich used objective variables to determine social class—level of occupation and education and quality of neighborhood. Despite the artificiality of the class boundaries, the findings are dramatic in that they show that the prevalence of all types of psychoses increases as the index of occupation, education, and neighborhood decreases. This classic study by Hollingshead and Redlich is representative of the findings of countless other studies.[37]

5. *Family instability.* Research relating socioeconomic status to family discord and marital disruption has found an inverse relationship—the lower the status the greater the proportion of divorce or desertion.* An explanation for this relationship is that lower class families experience greater economic and job insecurity. Given the tremendous emphasis in the United States on success and achievement, the lower class person (particularly the male) will tend to define himself and be perceived by others in the society as a failure. Such a belief will, doubtless, hinder rather than help a marriage relationship.

6. *The draft.* The draft system works to the disadvantage of the uneducated. In 1969 only ten percent of the men drafted were college men—yet over forty percent of college-age men go to college. The Supreme Court has further helped the educated by ruling

TABLE 3–5.   Class, Status, and Rate of Different Types of Psychoses, Per 100,000 Population

Type of Disorder	Class			
	Upper & Upper Middle	Lower Middle	Upper Working	Lower Working
Affective psychoses	40	41	68	105
Psychoses due to alcoholism & drug addiction	15	29	32	116
Organic psychoses	0	24	46	254
Schizophrenic psychoses	111	168	300	895
Senile psychoses	21	32	60	175

Source: A. B. Hollingshead and F. C. Redlich, *Social Class and Mental Illness: A Community Study* (New York: John Wiley & Sons, 1958), p. 232.

* This relationship has been found after analyzing the 1950 and 1960 Census data.[38]

103

that a person çan be a conscientious objector either on basis of religion or philosophy. Young intellectuals can use their knowledge of history, philosophy, and even sociology to argue that they should not serve. The uneducated will not have the necessary knowledge or sharpened intellect to make such a case.

For those educated young men who end up in the armed services, there is a greater likelihood of their serving in noncombat supply and administrative jobs than for the non-college educated. Persons who can type, do bookkeeping, or know computer programming will generally be selected to do jobs where their skills can be used. Conversely, the non-skilled will generally end up in the most hazardous jobs. The chances for getting killed while in the service are greater, therefore, for the less educated than for the college educated.

7. *Justice.* There is very strong evidence that the administration of justice is unequal in the United States. Low-status persons are more likely to be arrested, to be found guilty, and to serve longer sentences for a given violation than persons of middle and upper status. Let us review a small but representative portion of the evidence.

Oaks and Lehman examined 5,579 indictments for felonies in Cook County, Illinois, for the year 1964. They compared the results of the cases according to whether the individual was defended by a court-appointed lawyer or a private counsel. They found that the chances of the indictment being dismissed or the defendant being declared not guilty were more than twice as great when the individual was defended by his privately-retained lawyer. Clearly, this gives affluent individuals a much greater probability of escaping a criminal record because they can afford the best defense.[39]

A study of California court decisions involving first-degree murder found blue-collar workers to stand a better chance of being sentenced to death than white collar workers. This study, conducted by five Stanford University Law School students, examined 200 separate factors that might be related to getting the death penalty. Occupation was found to be the most important determinant.[40]

White-collar crime (e.g., price fixing, using fraudulent advertising claims, embezzlement, and issuing fraudulent stock) often involves much more money than burglary or robbery, but the offenders of white collar crimes seldom receive proportionate jail sentences or fines. In 1969, for example, a partner in a New York stock brokerage firm pleaded guilty to trading illegally $20 million in Swiss banks. He hired a prestigious lawyer who got the judge to issue a fine of $30,000 and a suspended sentence. That same judge, when confronted a few days later with the case of an unemployed black shipping clerk who pleaded guilty to stealing a television set worth $100 from an interstate shipment, sentenced him to one year in jail.[41]

Why does justice let her blindfold slip? The rich can afford the services of the very best lawyers for their defense, detectives to gather supporting evidence, and expert witnesses such as psychiatrists. The rich can afford to appeal the decision to a series of appellate courts. The poor, on the other hand, must take court-appointed lawyers who are usually among the least experienced lawyers in the community. All of the evidence points to the regrettable truth that the wealth of a defendant makes a significant difference in the administration of justice.

There is a class bias held by most citizens, including arresting officers and judges, that affects the administration of justice. There is a set of assumptions about persons according to their socioeconomic status. In a study of a small South Dakota community, police officials were found to deal severely with lower-class delinquents on the theory that they came from bad stock and therefore required strict punishment. Upper-class teenagers who violated the same laws were deemed by officials to be "accidental" cases to which their families were not accountable, and the cases were consequently dismissed after a warning.[42]

A Philadelphia attorney who specializes in representing juveniles has said:

> A middle-class white juvenile delinquent—even if caught red-handed—almost never goes to jail, but for a poor kid, it's another story. I have represented many white middle-class girls caught shoplifting, and almost none of them went to prison. This isn't due to my talents, but to the system. I'd say to the court, "your honor, this girl wants to go to college, and her family is sending her to a psychiatrist." Then I'd put Momma on the stand, have her mention the psychiatrist's name—and that's all it would take.[43]

8. *Education.* In general, life chances are dependent upon wealth —they are purchased. The level of educational attainment (except for the children of the elite where the best in life is a birthright) is the crucial determinant of one's chances of income. The median income in 1968 for white families whose head had less than 8 years of school was $5,589; if the house head was a high school graduate, the earning was $9,680, and if a college graduate, $13,589.[44]

Even though upward social mobility is very possible in the United

States, socioeconomic status remains as the single most important determinant of educational success. Study after study has verified this denunciation of the "equal education for all" myth.* Educational opportunities are not equally available to all.[45]

Inequality of educational opportunity exists in all educational levels in many subtle and not so subtle ways. It occurs in the quality of education when schools are compared by district. The districts with a better tax base have superior facilities, better-motivated teachers (because the districts can pay more), and better techniques than the poorer districts. Within each school, regardless of the type of district, children are given standardized tests that have a middle-class bias. Armed with these data, children are placed in "tracks" according to "ability." These tracks thus become discriminatory because the lowest track is composed disproportionately of the lower socioeconomic category. These tracks are especially harmful in that they structure the expectations of the teacher.

The classic study that demonstrates empirically the reinforcement of the stratification system by the educational system was done by A. B. Hollingshead.[46] He found that the lower the socioeconomic status of the high school student's family—

1. the higher the drop-out rate
2. the lower the vocational aspirations
3. the lower the proportion planning on college
4. the lower the course grades and the higher the percentage of failures
5. the lower the I.Q. scores
6. the greater the number of recorded discipline problems

The net effect of these facts is that children tend to repeat the educational experience of their parents. Consequently even bright youngsters from the lower classes have difficulty in school and probably will not attend college. These data are interpreted by social scientists as demonstrating that American schools systematically disadvantage the lower class children in favor of upper and middle-class children.

Chapter Summary

There is a consistent relationship between socioeconomic status and achievement of the desirable things in life. The general pattern is that lower status persons are disadvantaged—in school, in mar-

* A complete discussion of this type of inequality appears in Chapter 10.

riage, in the courts, in health, and so on. The research findings are consistent, regardless of whether socioeconomic status is measured by income, educational attainment, or occupational prestige, or a combination of these status characteristics.

SELECTED GENERAL READINGS

Dobriner, William M., *Class in Suburbia* (Englewood Cliffs, New Jersey: Prentice-Hall, 1963). A comparative study of social class in two suburban communities, one on Long Island and the other in New England.

Domhoff, G. William, *The Higher Circles: The Governing Class in America* (New York: Random House, 1970). The first five chapters describe the American upper class. The remainder of the book demonstrates the power of this social class in foreign and domestic affairs.

Kohn, Melvin L., *Class and Conformity: A Study in Values* (Homewood, Illinois: The Dorsey Press, 1969). This book provides data from Turin, Italy, Washington, D.C., and a national sample of U.S. males on the differences in values and behavior among the social classes.

Roach, Jack L., Llewellyn Gross, and Orville Gursslin (eds.), *Social Stratification in the United States* (Englewood Cliffs, New Jersey: Prentice-Hall, 1969). This is an excellent compilation of articles on the American system of stratification.

Rushing, William A., *Class, Culture, and Alienation: A Study of Farmers and Farm Workers* (Lexington, Massachusetts: D. C. Heath and Company, 1972). An interesting and insightful study that compares middle-class farmers with lower-class farm workers on the effects of perceived deprivation and denied opportunity.

Tumin, Melvin M., *Social Stratification* (Englewood Cliffs, New Jersey: Prentice-Hall, 1967). This book is a concise survey of the theories, methods, and consequences of social stratification. Most of the examples provided are of the American case.

Vidich, Arthur J., and Joseph Bensman, *Small Town in Mass Society: Class, Power, and Religion in a Rural Community* (Garden City, New York: Doubleday & Company Anchor Books, 1960), This is a classic study of the class structure in one upper New York state community.

NOTES AND REFERENCES

1. Seymour M. Lipset, *The First New Nation: The United States in Historical and Comparative Perspective* (Garden City, New York: Doubleday and Company, Inc., Anchor Books, 1967).

2. Dusky Lee Smith, "The Sunshine Boys: Toward a Sociology of Happiness," *The Sociology of Sociology*, Larry T. Reynolds and Janice Reynolds (eds.), (New York: David McKay Company, Inc., 1970), p. 383.

3. The following discussion is indebted in part to the insights provided by Melvin M. Tumin, *Social Stratification: The Forms and Functions of Inequality* (Englewood Cliffs, New Jersey: Prentice-Hall, Inc., 1967), pp. 12–18.

4. For an excellent discussion of the extent to which American society parallels Indian society see: Gerald D. Berreman, "Caste in India and the United States," *American Journal of Sociology* 66 (September, 1960), pp. 120–127.

5. Suzanne Keller, *Beyond the Ruling Class: Strategic Elites in Modern Society* (New York: Random House, 1963).

6. Keller, *Beyond the Ruling Class*, p. 218.

7. Gideon Sjoberg, "Contradictory Functional Requirements and Social Systems," *Journal of Conflict Resolution* 4 (1960), pp. 198–208.

8. Kingsley Davis and Wilbert E. Moore, "Some Principles of Stratification," *American Sociological Review* 10 (April, 1945), pp. 242–249.

9. There are some powerful criticisms of the Davis-Moore argument. See especially Melvin M. Tumin, "Some Principles of Stratification," *American Sociological Review* 18 (August, 1953), pp. 387–393; and George A. Huaco, "The Functionalist Theory of Stratification: Two Decades of Controversy," *Inquiry* 9 (Autumn, 1966), pp. 215–240.

10. U.S. Bureau of the Census, *Statistical Abstract of the United States: 1970*, 91st edition (Washington, D.C., 1970), p. 322.

11. New York *Times* News Service Release (December 8, 1972).

12. C. C. North and Paul K. Hatt, "Jobs and Occupations: A Popular Evaluation," *Public Opinion News* 9 (September, 1947), pp. 3–13.

13. Robert W. Hodge, Paul M. Siegel, and Peter H. Rossi, "Occupational Prestige in the United States, 1925–63," *American Journal of Sociology* 70 (November, 1964), pp. 286–302.

14. Robert W. Hodge, Donald J. Treiman, and Peter H. Rossi, "A Comparative Study of Occupational Prestige," in *Class, Status, and Power*, Second Edition, Reinhard Bendix and S. M. Lipset (eds.), (New York: The Free Press, 1966), pp. 309–321.

15. A. B. Hollingshead, *Elmtown's Youth: The Impact of Social Classes on Adolescents.* (New York: John Wiley and Sons, Inc., 1949).

16. Gerhard Lenski, "American Social Classes: Statistical Strata on Social Groups," *American Journal of Sociology* 58 (September, 1952), pp. 139–144.

17. Richard Centers, *The Psychology of Social Classes: A Study of Class Consciousness* (Princeton, New Jersey: Princeton University Press, 1949).

18. For a summary of the criticisms of Centers' study see especially, Milton M. Gordon, *Social Class in American Sociology* (New York: McGraw-Hill Book Company, Inc., paperback edition, 1963), pp. 193–202.

19. Neal Gross, "Social Class Identification in the Urban Community," *American Sociological Review* 18 (August, 1953), pp. 398–404.

20. Oscar Glantz, "Class Consciousness and Political Solidarity," *American Sociological Review* 23 (August, 1958), pp. 375–382.

21. John C. Leggett, "Economic Insecurity and Working-Class Consciousness," *American Sociological Review* 29 (April, 1964), pp. 226–234.

22. G. William Domhoff, *The Higher Circles: The Governing Class in America* (New York: Random House, 1970), p. 74.

23. Domhoff, *The Higher Circles,* p. 78.

24. Domhoff, *The Higher Circles,* p. 80.

25. Domhoff, *The Higher Circles,* p. 871; cf., E. Digby Baltzall, *Philadelphia Gentlemen: The Making of a National Upper Class* (New York: The Free Press, 1958); and C. Wright Mills, *The Power Elite* (Fair Lawn, New Jersey: Oxford University Press, Inc., 1959).

26. Lucy Kavaler, *The Private World of High Society* (New York: Pyramid Books, 1961), p. 184.

27. Adapted from Lewis H. Lapham, "That So Necessary Ingredient," *Saturday Evening Post* 237 (September 5, 1964), pp. 56.

28. Seymour Martin Lipset, "The Sources of the 'Radical Right,'" in *The Radical Right,* Daniel Bell (ed.), (Garden City, New York: Doubleday Anchor Books, 1963), p. 341.

29. Daniel R. Miller and Guy E. Swanson, *The Changing American Parent* (New York: John Wiley and Sons, 1958).

30. Hans Gerth and C. Wright Mills, *Character and Social Structure: The Psychology of Social Institutions* (New York: Harcourt, Brace & World, Inc., 1953), p. 313.

31. Walter Lord, *A Night to Remember* (New York: Henry Holt, 1955), p. 107.

32. Aaron Antonovsky, "Social Class, Life Expectancy and Overall Mortality," *Millbank Memorial Fund Quarterly* 45 (April, 1967), pp. 31–73.

33. Evelyn M. Kitagawa and Philip M. Hauser, "Education Differentials in Mortality by Cause of Death: United States, 1960," *Demography* 5 (1968), p. 318–353.

34. Anselm Strauss, "Medical Ghettos," *Trans-action* 4 (May, 1967), pp. 32.

35. *Statistical Abstract of the United States,* 1966, Table 82.

36. U.S. National Center for Health Statistics, Series 10, No. 17, May, 1965, p. 28.

37. Robert Faris and H. Warren Dunham, *Mental Disorders in Urban Areas* (Chicago: University of Chicago Press, 1939); and Leo Srole, Thomas S. Langner, Stanley T. Michael, Marvin K. Oplea,

and Thomas A. C. Rennie, *Mental Health in the Metropolis* (New York: McGraw Hill Book Company, 1962).

38. For 1950 Census data: Paul C. Glick, *American Families* (New York: John Wiley and Sons, 1957); for the 1960 Census data: J. Richard Udry, "Marital Instability by Race, Sex, Education, and Occupation Using 1960 Census Data," *American Journal of Sociology* 72 (September, 1966), pp. 203–209.

39. Dallin H. Oaks and Warren Lehman, "Lawyers for the Poor," *Trans-action* 4 (July–August, 1967), p. 25–29.

40. "California Juries," *Parade Magazine* (November 2, 1969).

41. Glynn Mapes, "Unequal Justice: A Growing Disparity in Criminal Sentences Troubles Legal Experts," *The Wall Street Journal* (September 9, 1970), p. 21.

42. John Useem, Pierre Langent, and Ruth Useem, "Stratification in a Prairie Town," *American Sociological Review* 7 (June, 1942), p. 341.

43. Mapes, "Unequal Justice," p. 21.

44. *Statistical Abstract, 1970*, Table 494, p. 325.

45. For the most comprehensive documentation of educational inequality in the United States see, James S. Coleman, *et al., Equality of Educational Opportunity* (Washington, D.C.: U.S. Government Printing Office, 1966).

46. A. B. Hollingshead, *Elmtown's Youth: The Impact of Social Classes on Adolescents* (New York: John Wiley & Sons, Inc., 1949).

CHAPTER 4

The Distribution of Power in American Society

The compelling question of this chapter is—who are the real power wielders in American society? Is it an elite, or are the people sovereign? The location and exercise of power is difficult to determine especially in a large and complex society such as the United States. Decisions are necessarily made by a few people, but in a democracy these few are to be representatives of the masses and therefore subject to their influence. But what of non-representatives who aid in shaping policy? What about the pressure on the decision-makers by powerful groups? What about those pressures on the decision-maker which are so diffuse that the leaders may not even know who is applying the pressure?

MODELS OF THE NATIONAL POWER STRUCTURE

There are two basic views of the power structure—elitist and pluralist. The elitist view of power is that there is a pyramid of power. Those persons at the apex control the rest of the pyramid. The pluralists, on the other hand, see power as dispersed rather than concentrated. Power is broadly distributed among a number of organizations, special interests, and the voters. This chapter is devoted to the examination of different elitist and pluralist concep-

111

tions of power in the United States. As we survey each, the fundamental question we should ask ourselves is—how does this model mesh with the facts of contemporary America? Does the model portray things as they are or as they should be?

Pluralism I: Representative Democracy

Many Americans accept the notion promoted in high school civic books that the United States is a "government of the people, by the people, for the people." Democracy is the form of government in which the people have the ultimate power. In a complex society of over 200 million persons the people cannot make all decisions; they must elect representatives to make most decisions. So, decision-making is concentrated at the top—but it is to be controlled by the people who elect the decision-makers. This model is shown in Figure 4–1.

The most important component of a democratic model is that the representatives, because they are elected by the people, are responsive to the wishes of the people (see Panel 4–1 for other criteria of a democracy).

This model, however, does *not* conform to reality. The United States is undemocratic in many important ways. The people, although they do vote for their representatives every few years, are really quite powerless. For example, who makes the really important decisions about war and peace, economic policies, and foreign policy? The people certainly do not. And in the light of the Pentagon Papers released in 1971, which concerned the conduct of American leaders in the Indo-China War, it is clear that the American people have been deliberately misinformed by the leadership.

FIGURE 4–1   *Representative Democracy*

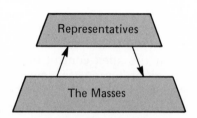

Not only have the American people been misinformed, but the basic democratic tenet that the public be informed has been defied. On the one hand, Congress has shown its contempt for the electorate by the use of secret meetings. The executive branch, too, has acted in secret. Recent Presidents have gone months without a press conference, have used "executive privilege" to keep presidential advisors from testifying before Congressional committees, and have refused to debate opponents in election campaigns.

Many persons who are appointed rather than elected wield tremendous power. Technical experts, for example, evaluate extremely complicated issues; they can virtually dictate to the President and Congress what is needed for defense, shoring up the economy, or winning friends abroad, because they are the experts. The coterie of advisors to the President may convince him to act in particular ways. The members appointed to the regulatory agencies have tremendous power to shape various aspects of the economy. A final example is that Supreme Court justices are appointed for life to that powerful post. The people have only a negligible voice in these appointments since only the Senate must approve.

Perhaps one of the most undemocratic features (at least in its consequences) of the American political system is a result of the manner in which campaigns are financed. Political campaigns are expensive, with state wide campaigns sometimes costing hundreds of thousands of dollars while a national campaign runs into the millions; (excluding primaries, President Nixon spent more than $36 million and McGovern spent in excess of $18 million in the 1972 election campaign). The trend is for these expenses to increase; (while $44.2 million was reported spent on the 1968 presidential election, over $54 million was spent in 1972). Because campaigns are expensive, candidates must either be independently wealthy or they must rely on the contributions of wealthy donors (either individuals or interest groups). In the 1972 presidential campaign individuals gave as much as $1 million to President Nixon's campaign budget. Such contributions are given for a number of reasons, including the hope of future favors or payoffs for past benefits. Thus, the passage of favorable laws, beneficial governmental rulings, maintenance of tax loopholes, or appointment to prestigious government posts such as ambassador may be the reward for financing candidates. Some individuals and interest groups even donate to the candidates of both parties to insure that their interests are served regardless of the election outcome. The result is that the wealthy have power while the less well-to-do and certainly the poor have no hold on office-holders.*

There are a number of other undemocratic features that belie the validity of this model. The "seniority system" in Congress gives extraordinary power to those individuals with longevity of service. The electoral college system is undemocratic. So is the party nomination system; the people choose from among the nominees for President, but they have little voice in their selection as nominees. The establishment of voting district boundaries is often "gerrymandered" by the party in power to keep themselves in power. Minority groups of all kinds may have little if any representation because of the many "winner-take-all" electoral systems.

Another objection, and a most telling one, is that the majority of citizens are relatively uninformed and apathetic about politics—thereby giving power to those already in office by default. Surveys ". . . show that 65 percent of the eligible voters do not regularly

* The obvious solution to this problem is to limit the cost of campaigns and provide each candidate with the same amount of funds from the government. This would insure that the winning candidate would at least take office without owing favors. Plans such as this have been defeated, however, presumably by powerful persons or groups who benefit under the existing arrangement.

PANEL 4–1

THE CRITERIA FOR A DEMOCRATIC SOCIETY

Source: Howard Zinn, "How Democratic is America?" How Democratic is America, Robert A. Goldwin (ed.), (Chicago: Rand McNally & Company, 1969), pp. 39–40.

I propose a set of criteria for the description "democratic" which goes beyond formal political institutions, to the quality of life in the society (economic, social, psychological), beyond majority rule to a concern for minorities, and beyond national boundaries to a global view of what is meant by "the people," in that rough, but essentially correct view of democracy as "government of, by, and for the people. . . ."

1. To what extent can various people in the society participate in those decisions which affect their lives: decisions in the political process and decisions in the economic structure?
2. As a corollary of the above: do people have equal access to the information which they need to make important decisions?
3. Are the members of the society equally protected on matters of life and death—in the most literal sense of the phrase?

vote, half cannot name their congressman, 68 percent cannot identify anything their congressman has ever done, 96 percent cannot identify any policy he stands for—all rather minimal tests of political activity, and the figures are worse for state and municipal levels."[1]

A final objection to this model is that it neglects the vast power of the various interest groups on specific issues. Organized labor, the American Medical Association, environmentalists, farmers, and other interest groups often mobilize and get beneficial legislation involving tariffs, taxes, contracts, subsidies or whatever.

Pluralism II: Veto Groups

Although some groups have more power than others and some individuals have more power than others, the power structure in the United States is viewed according to the "Veto Group" model as a plurality of interest groups.[2] Each interest group (e.g., the military, labor, business, farmers, education, medicine, law, veterans, the aged, blacks, and consumers) is primarily concerned with protecting its own interests. The group that primarily exercises power

4. Is there equality before the law: police, courts, the judicial process —as well as equality *with* the law-enforcing institutions, so as to safeguard equally everyone's person, and his freedom from interference by others, and by the government?

5. Is there equality in the distribution of available resources: those economic goods necessary for health, life, recreation, leisure, growth?

6. Is there equal access to education, to knowledge and training, so as to enable persons in the society to live their lives as fully as possible, to enlarge their range of possibilities?

7. Is there freedom of expression on all matters, and equally for all, to communicate with other members of the society?

8. Is there freedom for individuality in private life, in sexual relations, family relations, the right of privacy?

9. To minimize regulation: do education and the culture in general foster a spirit of cooperation and amity to sustain the above conditions?

10. As a final safety feature: is there opportunity to protest, to disobey the laws, when the foregoing objectives are being lost—as a way of restoring them?

varies with the issue at stake. There is a balance of power, since each "veto group" mobilizes to prevent the others from actions threatening its interests. Thus, these groups tend to neutralize each other.

The masses are sought as an ally (rather than dominated, as is the case in the various elitist models) by the interest groups in their attempts to exert power over issues in their jurisdiction. Figure 4–2 shows the relationship between the various levels in this model.

This pluralist model assumes that there are a number of sectors of power. The most powerful persons in each are usually wealthy— probably upper class. But, the pluralist view is that the upper class is not a unified group—there is considerable disagreement within the upper-class category because of differing interests. Power is not concentrated, but is viewed as a shifting coalition depending upon the issue. The basic difference between pluralists and elitists is on the question of whether there is a basic unity or disagreement among the powerful from different sectors (basically, those who are wealthy enough to be upper class).

There are several criticisms of this pluralistic model. They stem from the knowledge that it, like the other pluralistic model (for representative democracy), is an idealized conception of the distribution of power—as such, it does not conform with reality and is subject to question on several grounds. First, is the power structure so amorphous that power shifts constantly from one power source to another? Second, are the interest groups so equal in power that they neutralize each other? The special bias of this view is that it does not give attention to the power differentials among the various interest groups. It is absurd to claim that the power of big business is neutralized by the countervailing power of farmers. A more prob-

FIGURE 4–2   *The Veto Groups Model*

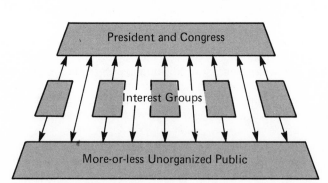

able occurrence is that there is a hierarchy of power among these so-called "veto-groups."

A final criticism is that the leaders in each sector come dispropor-tionately from the upper economic strata. If this assertion is correct, then the possibility of a power elite that transcends narrow interest groups is present, since they may know each other, tend to inter-marry, and have similar economic interests (as we will see later).

The pluralist models are not altogether faulty. There are a number of possible power centers that often compete for advantage. Shifting coalitions are possible. There are instances when selected officials are responsive to public opinion. However, it seems to this observer that most of the evidence supports an elitist view, although each of the three types described below also has its faults.

The elitist views of societal power are usually structured quite similarly to those of Karl Marx. For Marx economics was the basis for the stratification system (i.e., unequal distribution of rewards including power). The economic elite, because of similar interests (i.e., keeping the status quo) and limited social interaction patterns, is a unified group. The economic elite controls the state and its inhabitants.

Implicit in the Marxian conception of the powerful is the notion of conspiracy. The elite manipulate the masses through religion, nationalism, control of the media, and control of the visible govern-mental leaders.[3]

Power Elite I: Communist Conspiracy

The "Communist conspiracy" view is not taken seriously by social scientists, and most citizens would see little reality in its assump-tions. However G. William Domhoff has estimated that it is shared by five to fifteen million adult Americans.[4] In this ultra-conservative view of the power structure, the United States is led by a small, cohesive group of ideologues. This group is thought to be a "con-spiracy" which shares an ideology that is collectivist (anti-capi-talism and pro-welfare) and internationalist (one-world govern-ment), ridiculing the traditional virtues of rugged individualism and blind patriotism. Moreover, the elite conspiracy is believed to pro-mote the erosion of other traditional American values—morality, fundamentalist religion, hard work, and limited government.

An important component of this view is that the leaders act together, and secretly, to manipulate the masses so that certain agreed upon goals are accomplished. They are motivated by an ideology that is antithetical to all that America has stood for in the past.

Within the ultra right wing literature, some variations are found as to who comprises the conspiracy. For some it is composed of Jews (see Panel 4–2). For others it is the "Eastern Establishment" of bankers and industrialists who control the Republican Party. Another variation is that the leaders are either card-carrying Communists or the dupes of the Communists. The founder of the John

PANEL 4–2

THE INTERNATIONAL JEWISH CONSPIRACY

Sources: *The Thunderbolt* (June 25, 1961), p. 1.

Gerald L. K. Smith, "We Are in Trouble!!! The Crisis from A to Z," *The Cross and the Flag* 22 (December, 1963), p. 3.

James H. Madole, "Will a World Jewish Empire be Established Through Atomic Blackmail?" *National Renaissance Bulletin* (October-December, 1964), p. 3; *also* "The Unholy Romance of the Chinese Dragon and the American Eagle," (no. 22, November-December, 1971), pp. 5, 7, 8.

The following are several excerpts from publications of the most "extreme right" groups in America. These passages have been selected around a common theme—the international Jewish conspiracy to which American leaders are said to be a part.

Writing in 1961 about the John F. Kennedy appointees to the federal government, *The Thunderbolt* said:

> This is no longer a Gentile Government, but a completely Jew dominated conspiracy running the U.S.A. . . . Our Government has been taken over through a secret Jewish revolution. NOT ONE OF THE POWERFUL JEWS LISTED ABOVE [there were 22] WERE ELECTED TO POWER, THEY WERE APPOINTED BY A MAN WHO HAS BETRAYED HIS PEOPLE. THE JEWS HAVE TAKEN OVER, AND WE HAVE A COMPLETE STOOGE FOR PRESIDENT WHO HAS NO SAY SO ABOUT IT. WHITE MEN AWAKE, THE JEWS ARE DESTROYING AMERICA. JOIN THE NATIONAL STATES RIGHTS PARTY, AND FIGHT TO SAVE AMERICA WHILE THERE IS STILL TIME. THE HOUR IS LATE, BUT THE TRUTH CAN STILL DRIVE THESE TYRANTS FROM POWER AND SAVE OUR RACE, NATION AND FAITH!"

This theme was also enunciated by Gerald L. K. Smith but with the added assertion that the Jewish advisors of President Kennedy have convinced him to give in to the demands of Russia:

> The President of the United States is surrounded by a cabal of international Jews and appeasers in general who are determined

Birch Society, Robert Welch, has written, for example, that President Dwight D. Eisenhower was a Communist. He said, "My firm belief that Dwight Eisenhower is a dedicated, conscious agent of the Communist conspiracy is based on an accumulation of detailed evidence so extensive and so palpable that it seems to me to put this conviction beyond any reasonable doubt."[5]

Although there is a tendency by academics not to take this model seriously, there are at least two aspects of this view that make

that the American sovereign policy of independent and private initiative shall be destroyed. He is being advised by the Rostows, the Yarmolinskys, the Schlesingers, the Weinbergs and their ilk.

Serving as a puppet for these manipulators, the Secretary of State Dean Rusk, in cooperation with international bankers, such as the Jewish Secretary of the Treasury Dillon and a long list of domestic demagogues and left wing agitators—this nauseating cabal has sold America down the river. It is up to you and me and others like us to see to it that what they have sold is *not* delivered.

I am convinced that secret agreements have been reached between Khrushchev and Kennedy, and many things have been promised which have not been publicized.

An excerpt from the *National Renaissance Bulletin* suggested that the Jews in Russia and the United States will blackmail the rest of the world into submission:

Now that Nikita Khrushchev has been officially deposed and replaced by Leonid Brezhnev, who is married to a Russian Jewess, the American Jewish Power Structure is seeking to bring about a reconciliation between Washington and Moscow—A RECONCILIATION BASED ON A MONOPOLY OF ATOMIC WEAPONRY AND THERMONUCLEAR KNOWLEDGE HELD IN THE JOINT HANDS OF THESE FORMER ENEMIES! These two behemoths among nations will, under Jewish guidance, attempt to intimidate the non-aligned countries of the world, particularly West Germany and Red China, which are mutually feared by the Soviet government and the Jewish policy-makers in Washington, WITH THE HIDEOUS THREAT OF ATOMIC DEVASTATION SHOULD THEY SEEK TO DEVELOP THEIR OWN NUCLEAR RESOURCES FOR SELF DEFENSE.

Finally, the *National Renaissance Bulletin* has explained the recent United States-Communist China detente in terms of the international Jewish conspiracy:

Why, therefore, have we completely switched our policy to oppose the growing strength of Chinese power in Asia? Who is the sinister mastermind that has made the Aryan Slavs of Russia our main

sense. First, the ultra-rightwingers are convinced that the big money interests (heads of major banks, industrial giants, and insurance companies) actually run the country. This can make a good deal of sense, as we will see later, although the degree to which they are unified in trying to run the country is debatable. Second, both political parties are dominated largely by the same kinds of people—the wealthy. From that viewpoint it really does not make very much difference which party is in power or who is appointed to the highest government posts—the interests of the wealthy tend to be served.

PANEL 4–2 Continued

enemy while embracing a cunning Oriental foe? The sinister Zionist mastermind behind Nixon's absurd blueprint for an unholy alliance between the Red hordes of Asia, the hopelessly beguiled, drug and whisky-besotted Aryan masses of the USA, and the devilish conspirators and international wirepullers in Jerusalem, is the highly sensual little Jew, Henry Kissinger, whose family fled from Hitler's regime to our unfortunate shores in 1938.

. . . .

The Zionist wirepullers in Jerusalem, through their agent Henry Kissinger, have plotted a love match between the American Eagle and the Chinese Dragon whereby Mao-Tse-tung will have a seat in that great debating society, the United Nations, Taiwan will be turned over to Red China by the successor to the ancient and highly corrupt ex-warlord, Chiang-Kai-shek, Red China will be relieved of the American presence in Southeast Asia by the end of 1972 at which point the pitifully corrupt and inefficient bureaucrats, whose hedonistic excesses are bankrolled by stupid American taxpayers, will flee with their concubines and cadillacs to the French Riviera while Cambodia, Laos, and South Vietnam fall like ripe fruit into Hanoi's basket and most important of all, in the eyes of Peking, China will have hundreds of American warplanes, helicopters, and other war material formerly destined for American use in Southeast Asia!

. . . .

[This] will serve Eretz Israel by placing millions of American equipped Chinese on the 5000 mile border between Soviet Russia and Red China thus forcing Russian naval forces out of the Mediterranean and into the Pacific. This will leave Israel, and her American backers, with a free hand in the Middle East."

There are some notable points of this model that do not fit the facts. The government is not dominated by Jews or Communists who work for the overthrow of the government. As Domhoff has asked: is David Rockefeller a Communist? Is he against capitalism?—not likely. There is no "conspiracy." The leaders tend to have similar economic interests, and they work for what they consider best for the country and its economy; this means a strong defense, protected industry, prosperity, and economic growth. They are not a tightly knit organization that works secretly for the goal of America's downfall. This is a paranoid view of the world that is just plain false.

Power Elite II: The Thesis of C. Wright Mills

C. Wright Mills' view of the American structure of power posits that the key persons in three sectors—the corporate rich, the executive branch of the government, and the military—all combine to form a power elite that make all important decisions.[6]

The elite is a small group of persons who routinely interact together. They also, as Mills assumed, have similar interests and goals. The elite is the power elite because the members have key institutional positions—i.e., they command great authority and resources in a specific and important sector, and each sector is dependent upon the other sectors.

There are three levels in Mills' pyramid of power. The uppermost is the power elite—composed of the leaders of three sectors. Mills implied that of the three, the corporate rich are perhaps the most powerful (first among "equals"). The middle level of power is comprised of local opinion leaders, the legislative branch of government, and the plurality of interest groups. These bodies, according to Mills, do the bidding of the power elite. The third level is the powerless mass of unorganized people who are controlled from above. They are exploited economically and politically. The three levels of power are depicted in Figure 4–3.

Mills believed that the power elite was a relatively new phenomenon resulting from a number of historical and social forces that have enlarged and centralized the facilities of power, making the decisions of small groups much more consequential than in any other age.[7]

The two important and related factors giving rise to the recent emergence of the power elite are: (1) the means of power and violence are now infinitely greater than they were in the past; and

(2) they are also increasingly centralized. The decisions of a few become ultimately crucial when they have the power to activate a system that has the capabilities of destroying hundreds of cities within minutes. Transportation, communication, the economy, the instruments of warfare are examples of several areas that have become centralized—making a power elite possible. The federal government taxes, regulates, and passes laws so that the lives of almost all Americans are affected. This same bureaucratic process is evident in the military, where decisions are more and more centralized. The Pentagon, which oversees the largest and most expensive feature of the government, is a relatively new phenomenon. The economy in the United States was once composed of many, many small productive units that were more or less autonomous. But over time the number of semi-autonomous economic units has dwindled through mergers, interlocking directorates, and chainstores, putting the financial squeeze on the small businessman. The result is that the economy has become dominated by less than 200 giant corporations.

The tremendous advances in transportation and communication

FIGURE 4–3   *Mills' Pyramid of Power*

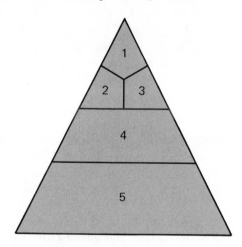

Legend:
1 = *corporate rich*
2 = *executive branch*
3 = *military leaders*
4 = *leaders of interest groups; legislative branch; local opinion leaders*
5 = *unorganized masses*

have made it much more likely that the persons holding key positions in the political, economic, and military hierarchies can be in contact with each other if they wish to do so. If, as Mills assumed, they have similar interests, then they must be in contact so that their activities can be coordinated to the best mutual advantage.

The key decision-makers also have instruments to influence the masses, such as television, public relations firms, and techniques of propaganda that are unsurpassed in the history of mankind. Hence, if there is a power elite and they want to manipulate the masses to accept their decisions, then they have the instruments of mass persuasion at their disposal.

Mills also contended that the importance of institutions has shifted. Whereas the family and religion were once the most important American institutions, they (along with education) have become subordinate to the three power institutions of the economy, polity, and military—thus making the leaders of these three domains the power elite. Mills said, "Families and churches and schools adapt to modern life; governments and armies and corporations shape it; and, as they do so, they turn these lesser institutions into means for their ends."[8] For example, religious institutions supply chaplains to the armed forces, where they increase the effectiveness of the combat units by raising morale. Schools train persons for their places in the giant corporations. Fathers and sons are sometimes taken from their homes to fight and die for their country. And, Mills said, the symbols of these lesser institutions are used to legitimate the decisions of the power elite who dominate the powerful institutions.

A most important impetus for the formation of the power elite was World War II. American participation in a war worldwide in scope and where the possibility of defeat was very real, meant, among other things, that a reorganization of various sectors had to be accomplished. The national government, particularly the executive department, had to be granted dictatorial powers so that the war could be conducted. Decisions had to be made quickly and in secret, two qualities not compatible with a democracy. The nation's corporations had to be mobilized for war. They made huge profits. Finally, the military became very prominent in decision-making. Their expertise was essential to the making of wartime strategy.

Following World War II, the United States was faced with another threat, the spread of Communism. This meant, in effect, that the Executive department, the corporations, and the military did not shift back to their peacetime ways. The military remained in the decision-making process, the corporations remained dependent upon lucrative defense contracts, and the Executive branch continued to exercise its autonomous or at least semi-autonomous powers.

All of the above factors, according to Mills, ensured that the domains of the polity, economy, and military were enlarged and centralized. Decisions made in each of these domains became increasingly crucial to all citizens, but particularly to the leaders of the other key domains. The result had to be a linkage between the key persons in each domain. It was in their interests to cooperate. Since each sector affected the others, the persons at the top of each hierarchy had to interact with the leaders from the other sectors, so that the actions and decisions would benefit all. Thus they have come to form a triangle of power, an interlocking directorate of persons in the three key domains making coordinated decisions—a power elite.

An important ingredient in Mills' view is that the elite is a self-conscious cohesive unit. This unity is based on three factors: psychological similarity, social interaction, and coinciding interests.

1. *Psychological similarity.* The institutional positions men occupy throughout their lifetimes determine the values they will hold. For example, career military men hold certain values by virtue of being socialized into the military subculture. The famous quote that "What's good for General Motors is good for the U.S." by Secretary of Defense (under President Eisenhower) Charles Wilson is also indicative of this probability (Wilson was former chairman of the Board of General Motors). Thus, for Mills, the psychology of these leaders is largely shaped by the values they develop in their institutional roles. Additionally, the psychological similarity among the members of the elite is derived from their similar social origins and style of life.

2. *Social interaction.* Mills stated that the ruling elite are involved in a set of overlapping groups and intricately connected cliques.

> The people of the higher circles may also be conceived as members of a top social stratum, as a set of groups whose members know one another, see one another socially and at business, and so, in making decisions, take one another into account. The elite, according to this conception, feel themselves to be, and are felt by others to be, the inner circle of "the upper social classes." They form a more or less compact social and psychological entity; they have become self-conscious members of a social class. People are either accepted into this class or they are not, and there is a qualitative split, rather

than merely a numerical scale, separating them from those who are not elite. They are more or less aware of themselves as a social class and they behave toward one another differently from the way they do toward members of other classes. They accept one another, understand one another, marry one another, tend to work and to think if not together at least alike.[9]

3. *Coinciding interests.* A third unifying condition hypothesized by Mills is the existence of similar interests among the elite. The interest of the elite is, among other things, maintenance of the capitalist system with themselves at the top. Additionally, the government needs adequate defense systems, to which the military agree and to which the corporations gladly sell for a profit. The huge corporations have large holdings in foreign countries. They therefore expect the government to make policy decisions that will be beneficial (profitable) for American interests. These similar interests result in a unity and a need for planning and coordination of their efforts. Since each sector affects the other, the persons at the top of each hierarchy must interact with leaders of the other sectors so that their actions will benefit all. Top decisions, Mills argued, thus become coordinated decisions.

Empirical Evidence for the Existence of a Military-Industrial Power Elite

Mills postulated that there was an interlocking directorate uniting key persons in the business, military, and economic sectors. The relationships among the three are therefore:

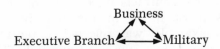

Business

Executive Branch ◄————► Military

There is much evidence supporting the linkages for each of the three relationships pictured above.

1. *Business-Government.* On the surface the Federal Government appears to have great power over business—through taxation, the power of the regulatory agencies (e.g., Federal Trade Commission, Interstate Commerce Commission, and Securities and Exchange Commission), the power to determine interest rates and the flow of money, and so on. But who are the people who wield power in the executive branch of the government? The evidence is that they tend

125

to be wealthy businessmen.[10] The leaders are either rich or they are dependent upon contributions from the wealthy. The important appointees of the President (cabinet members, members of regulatory agencies, Supreme Court justices, ambassadors) most often are executives in the large corporations, corporation lawyers, or bankers. The implication is clear, if Mills was correct, that the linkage between the executive branch and business is very strong and that the leaders in both areas are alike in attitudes and actions because of similar interests.

2. *The military-industrial alliance.* There are direct and obvious ties between the Pentagon and industry.* The military needs weapons, ammunition, vehicles, clothing and other materials. Industries gladly supply them for a profit.** The needs of both are apparently never satiated. The military continually seeks more sophisticated weaponry and delivery systems, while industry seeks more contracts and profit. But why is industry so interested in obtaining government contracts? Richard Kaufman has pointed out that producing goods for the military is more profitable, less competitive, and more susceptible to control through lobbying in Washington than commercial work.[11]

Kaufman stressed first that there is much less competition for defense contracts. The general rule for Government procurement is that purchases shall be made through written competitive bids obtained by advertising for the items needed. In World War II this rule was suspended. After the War the rule was put back into force, but with seventeen exceptions. According to Kaufman about 90 percent of the Pentagon's contracts in 1968 were negotiated under these seventeen exceptions. The meaning is clear that in all but 10 percent of the cases, contracts were made on a basis other than competitive bids. It was in this manner that the General Dynamics Corporation, for example, was selected to receive a multibillion dollar contract to produce the controversial TFX planes, even though Boeing submitted a lower bid.

What does it take to get a contract, if it is not being the lowest bidder? The answer is not easy, for there are many possibilities, including superior design, more efficient programs, performance on

---

* The thrust of the next two sections (the military-industrial alliance and the government-military alliance) is on the role of the military in American society. A full discussion of this is imperative because this role is so extensive and it is central to Mills' thesis.
** In 1969 the Pentagon signed agreements with 22 prime contractors (e.g., Lockheed—$2 billion, General Electric—$1.6 billion, and McDonnell Douglas —$1.07 billion), and some 100,000 subcontractors.

schedule, and better quality control. Perhaps more important is convincing a few key men in the Pentagon. A good deal of time and money is spent in trying to influence these men. Not the least of these methods is the practice in industry of hiring former military officers. Kaufman quoted a speech made by Senator Proxmire, who said that as of February, 1969, 2,072 retired military officers holding ranks of Army colonel or Navy captain were employed by the 95 top contractors for an average of 22 in each company.* The top ten companies in terms of military contracts employed an average of 106. It is difficult to say whether these men are instrumental in procuring government contracts after their retirement. But, at a minimum, there is a serious conflict-of-interest problem.

In addition to reduced competition, defense contractors receive other benefits from the government. Kaufman has said that the Pentagon generously provides capital to its contractors. More than $13 billion worth of government-owned property (land, buildings, and equipment) was in contractors' hands in 1969. In addition, the government reimburses a supplier during the life of his contract for as much as 90 percent of the costs. Congress may even "bail out" a contractor whose business faces bankruptcy, but only, it would seem, if the corporation is very large and a prime supplier of defense material. The Lockheed Corporation in 1971, for example, received a government loan of $250 million. Moreover, if a defense contractor has been inefficient or careless in its cost estimates, resulting in cost overruns, the government may absorb some of the additional cost. This is done under a 1958 law authorizing modification of defense contracts whenever such action is necessary to "facilitate the national defense" in times of declared national emergency. Thus, when Lockheed had cost overruns of approximately $1.1 billion on its C-5A jet transport and other procurement disasters, the government ruled that Lockheed's liability would be for only $200 million.

The gist of these assertions is that there are tremendous profits to be made in defense contracting, and many if not most of the risks are borne by the Government. The irony is that this is in opposition to the free enterprise system. Apparently, American capitalism is in fact a form of corporate socialism where very large corporations receive government aid while smaller business ventures must operate on the principle of "survival of the fittest."

The military-industrial complex has had a tremendous growth

---

* Senator Proxmire noted in 1972 that an additional 993 officers above the rank of major had been hired by defense contractors since 1969. Associated Press release (January 8, 1972).

since World War. II. The fear of Communism has caused the United States to spend $1,000 billion on defense from 1946 to 1969. The result has been the development of an economic behemoth to which a tremendous proportion of Americans are beholden either directly or indirectly. The impact of defense to the economy in a local area is seen when either: (1) a large industry does or does not receive a major government contract; or (2) the Pentagon decides to build or to deactivate a major defense installation. Virtually all segments of the community favor increased defense work or at least continuance of what they already have at the local level. We find that all segments of the community are affected—businessmen, teachers, home owners, blue collar workers, and professionals. It is for this reason that a critic of the military-industrial complex, Senator William Proxmire from Wisconsin, has suggested that the system should rather be called the "military-industrial-bureaucratic-labor-intellectual-technical-academic complex."[12] Proxmire's label indicates the interconnectedness and pervasiveness of the system in American life. Some examples from the year 1969 include:

1. The military payroll in Charleston, South Carolina, was $2 billion a year in 1969. Charleston is particularly favored because it was the district of the then chairman of the House Armed Services Committee, Mendel Rivers. Either because of Rivers or by chance, this district included an Air Force base, an Army depot, a Naval shipyard, a Marine air station, the Parris Island boot camp, two naval hospitals, a Naval station, a Naval supply center, a Naval weapon station, a fleet ballistic-missile-submarine training center, a Polaris missile facility, an Avco Corporation plant, a Lockheed plant, a General Electric plant, and Sikorsky Aircraft Division of United Aircraft, which recently purchased 800 acres for a plant.[13]

2. The budget for the Defense Department in fiscal 1969 was $78.4 billion. If the budgets for military assistance to other nations, atomic energy, the Selective Service System, and the National Aeronautics and Space Administration are added to that of the Defense Department, then there was a total of $85 billion, or more than one-tenth of the nation's Gross National Product that was spent on defense. The growth in expenditures on defense, space, and military assistance programs has grown enormously in recent years. In 1972 dollars, the cost has risen from $4.19 per capita in 1935, to $89.18 in 1950, to $245.97 in 1960, and to $387.75 in 1970.[14]

3. About one in every ten working Americans was directly or indirectly employed by the military machine. In addition to the millions in the Armed Services or in the reserves, the work force in

defense industries was 4 million in 1969. The Pentagon also hired 1.3 million civilians for its bureaucracy.

4. About 50 percent of all research financed by the government was for defense. Universities and professors have become particularly dependent upon government-sponsored research. Grant-winning professors are thrice blessed: they have money for research which, in turn, means more prestige, as well as higher salaries. Universities benefit because they often receive special equipment and about one-half of all grant monies for overhead. For the more prestigious universities, the overhead amounts in the millions of dollars annually. Graduate students benefit by getting research assistantships.

The above examples indicate the extent to which the United States is geared toward preparation for war. Even the land, 29 million acres of it (roughly the size of New York State), is controlled by the Pentagon. One-tenth of our manpower and one-tenth of the GNP are devoted to non-productive causes (although we should recognize that some benefits do accrue from military production, such as new inventions, more efficient computers, and faster air travel). This emphasis on military matters has resulted in a domestic "brain drain." Scientists work on projects of military significance rather than solving problems that will be of benefit to mankind. The result is a tremendous waste of human, monetary, and natural resources.

Aside from the monetary and manpower costs of the military, there is a more insidious danger. This danger is what General Shoup, the former commandant of the Marine Corps, has called the "new American militarism." By this he meant to suggest several trends involving the rise of the influence of the military. The first trend is the rise of a fantastically large and complex bureaucracy. In 1968, for example, the expenditures of the military were $10 billion greater than the gross revenue of America's five largest corporations combined—General Motors, Standard Oil of New Jersey, AT&T, Ford and General Electric. As with all bureaucracies, its goals are deflected so that maintenance of the bureaucracy itself becomes of prime concern. As the economist Galbraith has said of this trend in the military:

> The problem of the military power is not unique; it is merely a rather formidable example of the tendency of our time. That is for organization, in an age of organization, to develop a life and purpose and truth of its own. This tendency holds for all great bureaucracies, both public and private. And their action is not what serves a larger public interest, their beliefs do not reflect the reality of life.

What is done and what is believed are, first and naturally, what serve the goals of the bureaucracy itself. Action in the organization interest, or in response to the bureaucratic truth, can thus be a formula for public disservice or even public disaster.[15]

Or in the words of former Marine Commandant Shoup,

More so than many large bureaucratic organizations, the defense establishment now devotes a large share of its efforts to self-perpetuation, to justifying its organizations, to preaching its doctrines, and to self-maintenance and management.[16]

This principle of bureaucracies—that once created, their prime goal is always self-perpetuation—helps to explain many efforts and much of the excessive costs within the military establishment. For example, it explains the tremendous propaganda machine whose efforts are directed toward: (1) making the service look good by covering up mistakes; (2) increasing morale; (3) adding enlistees; (4) getting the public to accept the notion that Americans must have a better defense system; and (5) greater appropriations from Congress. According to a study conducted by the Twentieth Century Fund, the Pentagon spends $190 million annually for propaganda.[17]

But there is a second feature of the rise of militarism that, according to General Shoup, has even more frightening implications. This is the military stance that is found in various elements of American society: the belief that we must be tough, aggressive, and firm in the resistance to Communist aggression; hence the belief in the military solutions to world problems.[18] Because so many American political leaders have held this stance, America cannot give in at the conference table, or "lose face" in any way. A direct result of this stance is the arms race. America cannot rest on its present system of offense and defense, but must ever improve its capabilities along these lines. Such efforts, of course, strike fear in the enemy that the United States might attack, so they, too, build up their military strength, which, in turn, increases American paranoia. Additionally, there is the lack of trust in developing bona fide negotiatons or other diplomatic techniques. The enemy cannot be trusted except when "coerced"; hence negotiations are seen as unreliable except from a position of overwhelming strength.

Finally, this military posture means that American patriots must be ever vigilant domestically. Thus, the Defense Department admitted in 1971, after being questioned by Congress, that through a vast domestic network it kept records on 25 million persons (or one out of eight Americans).[19] Apparently the Defense Department, without any directive from the Executive Department or Congress, felt it necessary in the interests of defense to keep dossiers on Americans whose patriotism was to be doubted for some reason.

3. *Government-military alliance.* The Defense Department is dependent upon Congress for money, including the appropriations for new programs. The Defense Department, according to the Constitution, must be headed by a civilian appointed by the President and approved by the Senate. The President is also Commander-in-Chief of the Armed Forces. He is the final authority who makes important policy decisions.

The alliance between the government and the military is not a one-way relationship, however, since Congress and the Executive Department are influenced in many ways by the military. Frequently they must rely upon the testimony of military experts, and the assessment of America's spy network determines to a significant degree what course of action the government will take. Furthermore, the Pentagon (in 1967) had 6,140 public relations men around the world whose job was to convince the public and the government, among other things, of the importance of its programs and of the need for new weaponry. Additionally, the Pentagon employed 339 "legislative liaison" lobbyists with a budget of $4.1 million to promote its interests in Washington. The next largest lobby was the postal clerks union, which spent $277,524 in that year.[20]

The Pentagon estimated that it spent about $44 million in fiscal 1970 for public relations activities. But Congressman Jonathan Bingham of New York has asserted that if all the Pentagon's public relations activities were actually classified that way and not under other budget headings, the cost might exceed $70 million a year.[21] This money is spent by each service, both to persuade the public and officials that its brand of weaponry is needed against imminent Communist aggression, and to promote the position of the military through films, television programs and speakers' programs. This kind of promotion even goes so far as circling a plane over a football field on autumn Saturdays to suggest that young men join the Air Force ROTC—all at the expense of the taxpayer (even allowing, perhaps, some officer to get extra flight pay that month).

There is often a direct relationship between Pentagon suppliers in industry and Pentagon appointees. The Secretary of Defense under Eisenhower was Charles Wilson, former President of General

Motors. The Secretary of Defense under Kennedy and Johnson was Robert McNamara, former President of Ford Motor Company. Nixon's Deputy Defense Secretary, David Packard, was the former head of Hewlett-Packard Company, a defense-contract-oriented company. (Packard, by the way, was allowed by Congress to keep his large stock holdings in his company while he worked for the Defense Department.) The Deputy Defense Secretary under Kennedy was Roswell Gilpatric, a former lawyer for General Dynamics. It was Gilpatric along with Secretary of Defense McNamara and the Secretaries of the Navy and Air Force who overruled repeated recommendations for Boeing from the top military selection board, instead choosing General Dynamics in the ill-fated TFX fiasco.[22]

There are also two more subtle connections between government officials and the military. In 1969, 139 Congressmen and Senators were members of one or another of the military reserves. Additionally, Congressmen from 363 of the 435 districts had some defense work in their districts. This provides a more or less ready-made vote for defense budgets.

An even more indirect pressure on Congressmen and the President comes from the 20 percent of the adult population who are veterans of United States military service. These men have been affected to some degree by the indoctrination they received while in the service. General David M. Shoup, a critic of the militaristic trend, has said of these veterans:

> As they get older, many veterans seem to romanticize and exaggerate their own military experiences and loyalties. The policies, attitudes, and position of the powerful veterans' organizations such as the American Legion, Veterans of Foreign Wars, and AMVETS, totaling over 4 million men, frequently reflect this pugnacious and chauvinistic tendency Their memberships generally favor military solutions to world problems in the pattern of their own earlier experience, and often assert that their military service and sacrifice should be repeated by the younger generations.[23]

These veterans appear to be a powerful pressure group. To the power-elite proponents, these veterans are not reckoned as having much power by themselves, but are seen in a role allied to the militaristic programs of the government. Strong support from the veterans gives the appearance of "grass roots" democracy.

Critique of Mills' thesis. Much of Mills' argument seems to fit with the realities of American politics. Certainly the men at the top of the key sectors wield enormous power. The last several decades have seen shifts in this power with the decline of the role of Congress and the rise in military clout.

There are some elements to Mills' thesis, however, that are not consistent with the facts. First, Mills believed that the three sub-elites that comprise the power elite are more or less equal, with the corporate rich probably having the most power. The equality of these groups is not proved. Certainly the military seems second-rate compared to the Executive Branch, Congress, and the large corporations. Military leaders are influential only in their advisory capacities and their ability to convince the Executive Branch and Congress. What looks like military power is often actually the power of the corporations and/or the Executive Branch carried out in military terms. In the view of many observers (especially Domhoff, as we will see in the next section), the business leaders comprise the real power elite. While this is debatable, the fact is that they far surpass the military in power, and since the Executive Branch is composed of ex-businessmen, the logical conclusion is that business interests prevail in that sector as well.

Conflict occurs among the three sectors. There is often bitter disagreement between corporations and government, between military and Executive Branch, and between military and some elements in the business community. How is this conflict to be explained if, as Mills contended, the power elite is a group that acts in concert, with joint efforts planned and coordinated to accomplish the agreed-upon goals? There is a good deal of empirical evidence that the heads of the three major sectors do *not* comprise a group.

Mills relegates a number of powerful (or potentially powerful) forces to the middle ranges of power. What about the power of pressure groups that represent interests other than business or the military? Certainly organized labor, farmers, professional organizations such as the American Medical Association, and consumers exert power over particular issues. Sometimes business interests even lose. How is this to be explained?

Finally, is Congress only in the "middle level" of the power structure? In Mills' view, Congress is a rubber stamp for the interests of business, the Executive Branch, and the military. Congress is apparently not composed of "puppets" for these interests, although the laws most often seem to favor these interests. But Congress does have its mavericks, and some of these persons, by virtue of seniority, exert tremendous power (either for the blockage or passage of legislation). Should not the key Congressional leaders be included in the power elite? The problem is that they often have interests that do not coincide with those of the presumed "elite."

Power Elite III: Domhoff's "Governing Class" Theory

While in the Mills view, power is concentrated in a relatively small, cohesive elite, G. William Domhoff's model of power is more broadly based in a "governing class."[24] Domhoff defined this "governing class" as the uppermost social group (approximately .5 percent of the population) which owns a disproportionate amount of the country's wealth and contributes a disproportionate number of its members to the controlling institutions and key decision-making groups of the country. This status group is composed mainly of rich businessmen and their families, many of whom are, according to Domhoff's convincing evidence, closely knit through stock ownership, trust funds, intermarriages, private schools, exclusive social clubs, exclusive summer resorts, and corporation boards (see Chapter 3).

The "governing class" in Domhoff's analysis controls the Executive Branch of the federal government, the major corporations, the mass media, foundations, universities, and the important councils for domestic and foreign affairs (e.g., the Council on Foreign Relations, Committee for Economic Development, National Security Council, National Industrial Conference Board, The Twentieth Century Fund). If they can control the Executive Branch, this governing class can probably also control the very important regulatory agencies, the federal judiciary, the military, the Central Intelligence Agency, and the Federal Bureau of Investigation.

The "governing class" has greater influence (but not control) than any other group upon Congress and state and local governments. These parts of the formal power structure are not directly controlled by the "governing class" in Domhoff's analysis, but since he claims they control the executive and judicial branches, the Congress is effectively blocked by two of the three divisions of government. Thus, by Domhoff's thesis, American foreign and domestic policies are initiated, planned, and carried out by members and organizations of a power elite that serves the interests of an upper class of rich businessmen.[25] Decisions are made that are considered appropriate for the interests of the United States—a strong economy, an adequate defense, and social stability. While perhaps beneficial to all Americans, policies designed to accomplish these goals especially favor the rich. Consequently, American corporations overseas are protected, foreign trade agreements are made that benefit American corporations, and the tax structure benefits corporations or the very wealthy (by means of allowances

134

for oil depletion, for capital gains and capital losses, for depreciation of equipment, and for other business expenses).

Domhoff has demonstrated in detail the manner in which the governing class interacts (which we have already examined in Chapter 3). Once he established the interlocking ties brought about by common interests and through interaction, he cited circumstances that show the impact of individuals and subgroups within the elite upon the decision-making structure of the United States. To mention a few:

1. Control of presidential nominations through the financing of political campaigns: The evidence is clear that unless a person has large financial reserves or the backing of wealthy men, he cannot hope to develop a national following or compete in party primaries.
2. Control of both major political parties: Even though the Democratic Party is usually considered the party of the common man, Domhoff shows that it, like the Republican Party, is controlled by aristocrats.
3. Almost total staffing of important appointive governmental positions (cabinet members, members of regulatory agencies, judges, diplomats, and presidential advisors): These appointees are either members of the upper class or persons who have held positions in the major corporations, and are thereby persons who accord with the wishes of the upper class.

As a result of the above circumstances (and others), all the important foreign and domestic decisions are seen as made by the governing class. Domhoff's view of the power structure is reconstructed graphically in Figure 4–4.

In many ways Domhoff's model of the American power structure was a refinement of the one posited earlier by Mills. Domhoff's assessment of the power structure was similar to Mills' in that they both: (1) view the power structure as a single pyramid; (2) see the corporate rich as the most powerful interest group; (3) relegate Congress to a relatively minor role and place the Executive Branch in an important role in the decision-making process; and (4) view the masses as being dominated by powerful forces rather than having much grass-roots power.

The major difference between the views of Mills and Domhoff is that Domhoff has asserted the complete ascendancy of the upper class to the apex of power. The Executive Branch is controlled by upper-class businessmen, industrialists, and financiers rather than the two groups being more or less equal partners in the power elite,

135

as Mills saw it. Moreover, the placement of the military in the pyramid of power is quite different. Mills saw the military as part of the alliance of the "troika," while Domhoff saw the military as having much less power and being dominated by the corporate rich through the Executive Branch.

FIGURE 4–4   *Domhoff's View of the Structure of Power**

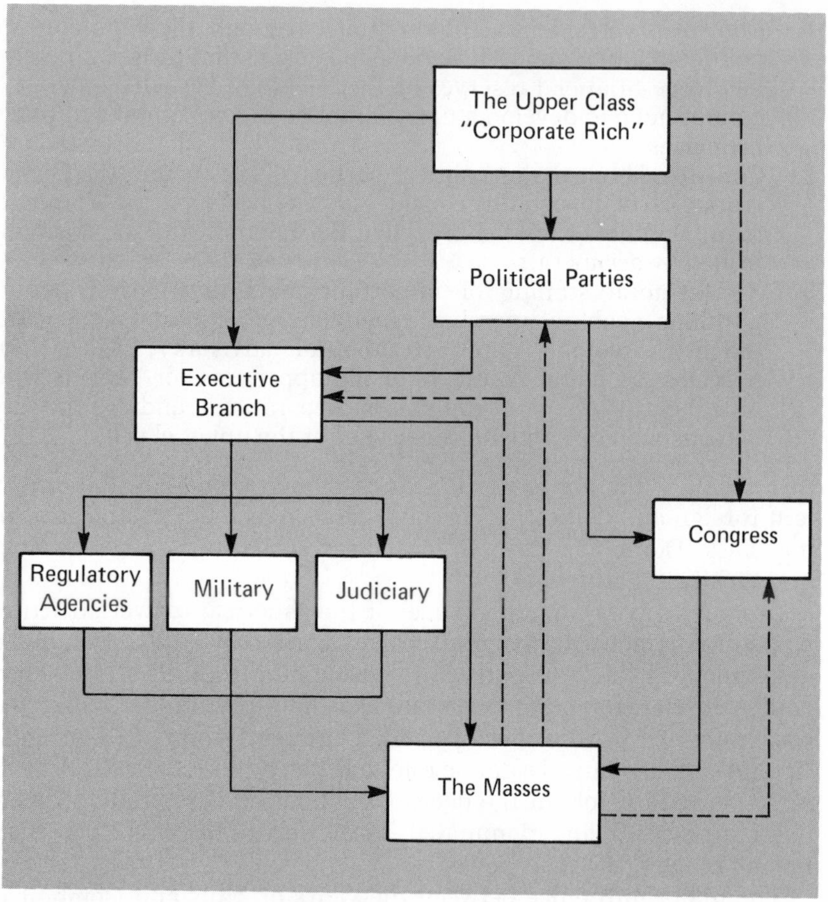

Legend: ———— Control
        - - - - - - - Influence

* This model is based on my interpretation of Domhoff and is therefore subject to minor errors in emphasis.

Critique of Domhoff's thesis. Domhoff's book is quite persuasive, but there are several criticisms that should be mentioned. First, much of Domhoff's proof is in the form of listing the upper class pedigrees of presidential advisors, cabinet members, ambassadors, regulatory agency members, and so on. While persons in these positions are disproportionately from upper-class backgrounds (as evidenced by their attendance at prestige schools, their membership in exclusive social clubs, and their placement in the various social registries), we are given no proof that these persons actually promote the interests of the corporate rich. This is an assumption by Domhoff that appears reasonable, but it is an oversimplification. There is always the possibility of wealthy persons making decisions on bases other than economics, such as religious or moral altruism or civil rights or human rights. Thus, Domhoff's assumption is one of Marxian economic determinism, and as such is subject to the criticism of oversimplification of a complex process. While an economic motive of some kind may explain a great deal of social behavior, its operation with other prestige factors may be very complex, and it will not explain all of human behavior.

Although Domhoff has denied his belief in an upper class conspiracy, his books strongly suggest that he does hold this view, at least implicitly. The upper class is shown to get its way either by force or fraud. His chapter on social legislation showed, for example, that workmen's compensation, social security, and collective bargaining were accomplished not by pressure from workingmen, but because the upper class felt it was in their long-range economic interest to pass such seemingly socialistic legislation. Domhoff, therefore, viewed the efforts of the upper class (assuming that they indeed form an elite) as only self-seeking, never altruistic. Moreover, the power of labor and other pressure groups in the forming of social legislation was virtually ignored.[26]

One glaring weakness of many pluralists and elitists is that they are not objective. Their writings tend often to be polemics because so much effort is spent attempting to prove what they believe is the nature of the power structure. The evidence is presented so as to insure the absolute negation of the opposite stance. This points to a fundamental research problem. Are the data reliable? Are our observations distorted by bias? The sociologist or political scientist is forced in the study of power to rely on either the perceptions of others (who are presumed to be knowledgeable) or his own observations, which are distorted by not being present during all aspects of the decision-making process. Unfortunately, one's perceptions are also affected by his model (conflict or order; Marxian or democratic). Ideological concerns often cause either faulty perceptions or a rigidity of thought that automatically rejects conflicting evidence.

A SYNTHESIS MODEL OF POWER

Given these problems with objectivity, we must ask ourselves: (1) what is the power structure really like? (2) what facts are consonant with the pluralist model and what facts fit the elitist model? With these questions in mind, let us attempt to develop a model for the distribution of power that fits the American case. The first step in this process is to enumerate some conditions of societies that affect the distribution of power.

All societies are composed of different segments. The bases for segmentation may be sex, age, race, religion, physical prowess, social class, occupational specialty, or special interest. The extent of segmentation and the degree of competition among such groups are variables. It is safe to assume that most segmented parts of a society would hope for and work toward greater power (and therefore advantage) in that society (although some may not if they have been socialized to accept their role and to accept that attempts to change it would bring serious religious or other sanctions).

The second basic condition of societies is that they all require some coordination among the various segments. The more complex the society, the greater the problem of coordination. Complex societies also require rapid decision-making. Both of these requirements—rapid decision-making and coordination—mean that decision-making *must* be concentrated in a few persons. It is an empirical question as to whether power is concentrated in one or several elites or whether the "people" retain power while not actually making most decisions.

Finally, the degree of power centralization is a variable. The logical range is from absolute equality of all individuals and groups on the one hand to total power in one person or group on the other. All societies are found somewhere between these two extremes. Various factors affect change in the degree of power centralization. As Mills noted, World War II and the Cold War were important factors giving increased power to the Executive Branch and the military sector of American society. Force and fraud may also be used by certain individuals and groups to increase their power.

These conditions are accepted by elitists and pluralists. Where both of these theorists go wrong is in their distorted interpretations of the real world. Let us examine the *real* situation which, hopefully, will aid in the formulation of a more realistic view of the power structure. First of all, what is there about the elitist position that fits reality?

1. A contemporary trend has been for federal government to assume more and more power, thereby lessening the power of the state and local governments.

2. The Executive Branch has a tremendous amount of power, particularly in foreign affairs. Congress has tried to reassert its historic role, but the Executive Branch continues to have great power in this area. Some examples are sending the military forces to various places, fighting undeclared wars, diplomatic decisions, and CIA activities.

3. There is no question but that the wealthy in America have great influence in Congress and in the Executive Branch. This influence is accomplished through campaign contributions, control of the political parties, occasional bribes, and either through being elected or appointed to high offices. It is also fair to say that American foreign and domestic policy is, for the most part, based on the assumption that if business interests benefit, all Americans benefit.

4. Even if there are a number of different sectors of power present (the pluralist position) the leaders of each are almost universally wealthy, members of the establishment who more or less favor the status quo. This is true, for example, in industry, in banking, for labor, and for the farm bloc. Because of great wealth they probably have some interests in common (the economic status quo, an adequate defense system, protecting American interests abroad, and an expanding economy).

What is there about the pluralist position that fits reality?

1. There are many separate power structures. Each operates generally within its own sphere of influence—the AFL-CIO in labor, the AMA in medicine, the NEA in public education, the NAM for large business concerns, and so forth. Each tries to influence Congress and the Executive Branch on issues affecting it. Within each of these domains there is a hierarchy of power. A powerful elite then makes decisions and in other ways influences its public (and this influence is often reciprocal).

2. The various power structures are unequal in power. The economic elite is the most powerful. But there are shifting coalitions that may at times effectively counter-balance the unequal power of the corporate rich. Or one group may band with the corporate rich against some other coalition. An example of this

latter case was when a committee called "American Industry and Labor for the SST" (Supersonic Transport) was formed in 1971 to lobby for a bill that would appropriate money for such a project. Here was a concerted effort by Boeing Aircraft and its subcontractors, united with various unions, to get legislation advantageous to both groups. They were opposed by a loose coalition of environmentalists worried about pollution, and many taxpayers worried about providing a government subsidy to certain industries and their workers.

3. Pressure groups exert a tremendous influence on decision-making. They may be organized or diffuse, but they can and do bring change. Blacks, migrant workers, young people, the aged, consumers, have by individual and collective efforts caused a shift in policy on occasion. The efforts of many young people have helped reverse American Indo-China policies. The grape boycott helped Cesar Chavez and his migrant workers gain a victory.

A realistic view of the power structure must incorporate the valid points mentioned above from both pluralistic and elitist views. The twin bases for a realistic view are (1) that power must be centralized in a complex society—for coordination, regulation, and rapid decision making; and (2) that there are several elites—one for each of the important sectors of society. The persons at the top of each sector influence Congress and the Executive Branch, either through contributions or by being elected or appointed to important government positions. The amount of power residing within any one of these sectors varies with the amount of support that can be mobilized from the masses and/or the coalitions that can be made with other sectors. Figure 4–5 gives a model that synthesizes the strengths of the elitist and pluralist models.

Figure 4–5 is conical in shape. The cone represents the centralization of power—diffuse with the masses at the base, but concentrated at the top in the Executive Branch of the Federal Government. The face of the cone is divided into sectors of varying degrees of power (the exact amount in each is an empirical question). Each sector is itself a pyramid of power, with power concentrated at the top. The elite at the apex of each pyramid is composed of wealthy, powerful persons who are members of the "old rich" or "new rich" socioeconomic strata. Because of their wealth and position, most are reluctant to change the status quo. They also tend to favor economic expansion and a strong military stance to protect their interests domestically and internationally. Each pyramid of power also is shown to have access (which is variable) to Congress and the

Executive Branch. The degree of access and influence is a function of power that each sector has (resources, mobilization of the masses, threat or use of sanctions such as strikes, boycotts, or the withholding of support). Each of the sectors, consequently, varies in the amount of power over time. Some of the sectors are closely aligned to others. The two-headed arrows symbolize that power and influence not only go up or down, but also laterally. Although the business sector is the most powerful segment in the political process, it is not all-powerful.

Finally, this view of the distribution of power depicts the masses as partners of the various sectors. The masses offer or withdraw their support in the various sectors depending upon the issue and

FIGURE 4–5   *A Synthesis Model of the Power Structure*

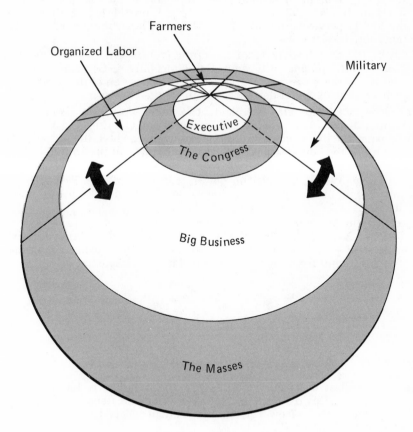

the efforts of the sectors to mobilize the public. Thus, there are shifting alliances that can occasionally affect the decision-making process.

SELECTED GENERAL READINGS

Domhoff, G. William, *The Higher Circles: The Governing Class in America* (New York: Random House, 1970). The presentation of an elitist view of power with empirical support.

Donovan, James A., *Militarism, U.S.A.* (New York: Charles Scribner's Sons, 1970). A highly critical examination of the American military by a retired Marine Corps colonel.

Fulbright, J. William, *The Pentagon Propaganda Machine* (New York: Random House, 1971). Senator Fulbright provides data that show the highly pervasive nature of the Defense Department's public relations activities.

Goldwin, Robert A. (ed.), *How Democratic Is America? Responses to the New Left Challenge* (Chicago: Rand McNally & Company, 1969). This is a series of essays by authoritative spokesmen of different viewpoints on the extent of democracy in the United States.

Newfield, Jack, and Jeff Greenfield, *A Populist Manifesto* (New York: Warner Books, 1972). This is a proposal for creating a coalition of the poor, the disaffected, and the white working class, the purposes of which are the equalization of wealth and power in the United States.

Olsen, Marvin E. (ed.), *Power in Societies* (New York: The Macmillan Company, 1970). A reader on power at the macrolevel. Parts III, IV, and V contain the classic statements on elitist and pluralistic power theories.

Rose, Arnold M., *The Power Structure: Political Process in American Society* (New York: Oxford University Press, 1967). An extensive critique of Mills' *Power Elite* and an attempt to provide a pluralist model different from the ones presented in this chapter.

NOTES AND REFERENCES

1. John Walton, "Economic Order," *Society Today Resource Letters* (Del Mar, California: CRM Books, 1971), p. 2.

2. The fullest description of this pluralistic model is found in the classic by David Riesman, Nathan Glazer and Reuel Denney, *The Lonely Crowd* (New Haven, Connecticut: Yale University Press, 1950), pp. 213–217.

3. Karl Marx and Friedrich Engels, *The German Ideology* (New York: International Publishers, 1947), p. 39. For a review of other

classical elitist theorists see Marvin E. Olsen, "Elitist Theory as a Response to Marx," *Power in Societies,* Marvin E. Olsen (ed.), (New York: The Macmillan Company, 1970), pp. 106–113.

4.   This model of the American power structure is described in G. William Domhoff, *The Higher Circles: The Governing Class in America* (New York: Random House Vintage Books, 1971), Chapter 8. Three ultra-conservative books provide the bases for Domhoff's description: Dan Smoot, *The Invisible Government* (Dallas: The Dan Smoot Report, Inc., 1962); Phyllis Schlafy, *A Choice Not an Echo* (Alton, Illinois: Pere Marquette Press, 1964); and William S. McBirnie, *Who Really Rules America: A Study of the Power Elite* (Glendale, California: Center for American Research and Education, 1968).

5.   Associated Press story in the *Christian Science Monitor* (April 1, 1961).

6.   The model described here was first put forth in the classic book by C. Wright Mills, *The Power Elite* (New York: Oxford University Press, 1956). It contains the first assertion of the existence and threat of a military-industrial complex in the United States.

7.   The following is taken from C. Wright Mills, "The Power Elite," *Reader in Political Sociology,* Frank Lindenfeld (ed.), (New York: Funk & Wagnalls, 1968), pp. 263–276.

8.   C. Wright Mills, "The Power Elite," p. 267.

9.   Mills, *The Power Elite,* p. 11.

10.   Mills, *The Power Elite,* Chapter 10 gives the evidence up to 1954. More recent evidence is found in G. William Domhoff, *Who Rules America?* (Englewood Cliffs, New Jersey: Prentice-Hall, Inc., 1967), Chapter 4.

11.   The following account is taken largely from Richard F. Kaufman, "The Military-Industrial Complex," *Crisis in American Institutions,* Jerome H. Skolnick and Elliott Currie (eds.), (Boston: Little, Brown and Company, 1970), pp. 178–192.

12.   William Proxmire, *America's Military-Industrial Complex* (New York: Praeger Publishers, 1970). This book is particularly valuable for an analysis of the role of Congress in the military-industrial alliance.

13.   "The Military-Industrial Complex," *Newsweek* (June 9, 1969), p. 76.

14.   Walter Dean Burnham, "Crisis in American Political Legitimacy," *Society* 10 (November/December, 1972), p. 28.

15.   John Kenneth Galbraith, "How to Control the Military," *Harper's Magazine* 238 (June, 1969), p. 32.

16.   David M. Shoup, "The New American Militarism," *The Atlantic* 223 (April, 1969), p. 56.

17.   Reported on C.B.S. television documentary, entitled, "The Selling of the Pentagon," shown to the public February 23, 1971. Cf. Dennis Farney, "War of Words: Pentagon's Promotion of its Own Activities Upsets Many Cities," *The Wall Street Journal* (Novem-

ber 13, 1970), p. 1; and William J. Fulbright, *The Pentagon Propaganda Machine* (New York: Random House Vintage Books, 1971).

18. Shoup, "The New American Militarism," p. 56.
19. United Press International release (March 3, 1971).
20. "The Military-Industrial Complex," p. 84.
21. Dennis Farney, "War of Words."
22. I. F. Stone, "In the Bowels of Behemoth," *The New York Review of Books* (March 11, 1971), p. 30.
23. Shoup, "The New American Militarism," p. 52.
24. The discussion below is taken from Domhoff's books *Who Rules America?* and *The Higher Circles: The Governing Class in America.*
25. See Chapter 5 of Domhoff's *The Higher Circles* for "how the power elite make foreign policy," and Chapter 6 for "how the power elite shape social legislation." Both of these chapters are persuasive in showing empirically the power of the upper class in the making of key decisions.
26. Domhoff, *The Higher Circles*, Chapter 6.

CHAPTER 5

Poverty in the United States

The United States is envied by most peoples of the world. It is blessed with great natural resources, the most advanced technology known, and a very high standard of living. Despite these facts, a significant portion of American citizens live in a condition of poverty. Millions of Americans are ill-fed, ill-clothed, and ill-housed. These same millions are discriminated against in the schools, in the courts, in the job market, and in the market place, all of which have the effect of trapping many of the poor in that condition. The "American Dream" is just that for millions of Americans—a dream that will not be realized.

The purpose of this chapter is both descriptive and practical. On the other hand, we will examine the facts of poverty—who are the poor, how many are poor, where the poor are located, is the proportion increasing or decreasing, and what it means to be poor. On the practical level, we will explore what needs to be done if extreme poverty is to be eliminated.

There are two underlying themes in this chapter. The first is important to consider as we examine the descriptive facts about the poor: The victims of poverty are not to be blamed for their condition, but rather the inequities present in American society are responsible. This is because the essence of poverty is inequality—in money and in opportunity. The second theme is most important when we take up the possible solutions to this social problem: The United States has the resources to eliminate poverty if it would give that problem a high enough priority.

The extent of poverty in America. What separates the poor from the non-poor? In a continuum there is no absolute standard for wealth. The line separating the poor from the non-poor is necessarily arbitrary. The Social Security Administration has set the yearly income of $3,553 for a non-farm family of four as the dividing line (in 1968), assessing that this figure was the minimal amount required for a subsistence level. Using this standard, 25.4 million Americans were in a poverty condition in 1968. In 1971, this figure was placed at $4,137 a year and 25.6 million persons were thereby defined as living in poverty.* In this chapter we will consider the poor as those persons below this arbitrary line established by the Social Security Administration. In effect, though, the poor are all those persons denied adequate health, diet, clothing, and shelter because of their lack of resources.

Exact figures on the poor are difficult to determine. For one thing, the amount of money needed for subsistence varies so drastically by locality. Compare, for example, the money needed for rent in New York City with that needed in rural Arkansas. Another difficulty is that those persons most likely to be missed by the U.S. Census are the poor. An estimated 5.7 million people were not counted in the 1960 Census. Those persons most likely to be missed in the Census live in the ghettos (where several families may be crowded into one apartment) or in rural areas where some homes are inaccessible and where some workers follow the harvest from place to place and therefore have no permanent home. Transients of any kind will probably be missed by the Census. The conclusion is inescapable that the proportion of the poor in the United States is underestimated because the poor tend to be invisible—even to the government.[1] This underestimate of the poor has important consequences, since the U.S. Census data are the basis for political representation in Congress. These data are also used as the facts for instituting new governmental programs or abandoning old ones. Needless to say, an accurate count of the total population is necessary if the Census is so used.

Despite these difficulties in exact measurement, there are statistics that demonstrate the unequal distribution of income in the United States. Table 5–1 presents these data for 1968.

The data in Table 5–1 show clearly the unequal distribution of income in the United States even though, as noted earlier, the number of very poor persons is under-estimated. They show further

* See the Appendix, Figures 77 and 78 for the characteristics of persons below the poverty line in 1969.

that blacks are found disproportionately in the lower income categories. Poverty, while found disproportionately in all minority groups, is pervasive among whites as well. About 70 percent of the poor are white.

WHO IS TO BLAME FOR POVERTY?

Basically there are two very different answers to this question. In the first instance, the poor themselves are believed to be at fault for their condition. Poverty is thus perceived as the result of persons being lazy, stupid, wasteful, and immoral. The second possibility places the blame on society. Some persons are poor because society has failed to provide equality in education, because of institutional discrimination against minorities, because of the failure of private industry to provide enough jobs, because automation has made some jobs obsolete, and so forth. In this view, society has worked in such a way as to trap certain persons and their offspring in a condition of poverty.

The weight of sociological evidence suggests strongly that the inequities of society are to blame for poverty, not the traits of indi-

TABLE 5–1.   Family Income—Percent Distribution: 1968

Income	All Races	White	Negro
Under $1,000	1.8	1.5	3.9
1,000–1,999	3.4	2.9	9.1
2,000–2,999	5.1	4.5	11.0
3,000–3,999	6.1	5.4	12.3
4,000–4,999	6.0	5.6	10.6
5,000–5,999	6.9	6.7	8.8
6,000–6,999	7.6	7.6	7.6
7,000–9,999	23.4	24.0	17.6
10,000–14,999	25.0	26.2	14.7
15,000 and over	14.7	15.7	6.3
Totals	100.0	100.0	100.0
Median income	$8,632	$8,937	$5,360
Percent with incomes less than $3,000	10.3	8.9	24.0

Source: Statistical Abstract of the United States, 1970, adapted from Tables 486 and 491, pp. 322 and 324.

viduals. The focus of this book is on the effects of social structure on social problems, and this chapter will provide an illustration of how the structure itself can work to the detriment of certain categories of persons. But the citizenry tend to view social problems and poverty in particular from the opposite perspective—blaming individuals for their plight. A recent study of a national cross section of adults (N = 1,017) examined beliefs about the cause of poverty. More than half (53 percent) gave the most weight to blaming the poor (because of their assumed loose morals, drunkenness, wastefulness, and lack of effort). Only 22 percent saw the workings of society as the fundamental reason for poverty.[2] Americans, then, tend to blame the victim for his condition. "We still blame the poor for being poor, which makes as much sense as blaming the sick for being diseased. Now that we have accepted no-fault auto insurance and even no-fault divorce, surely it is time to accept no-fault poverty as well."[3]

The prevalent view (blaming the victim) has extremely important ramifications for the way the war on poverty will be waged. Instead of looking for structural changes, this view focuses on changing the attitudes and behaviors of the individual poor. Thus it is imperative that we examine closely the rationale for blaming the poor because of its important implications.

Blaming the Poor

Although a number of causes are commonly given for why the poor themselves are at fault, they really boil down to two major reasons. One is that the poor have developed a deviant subculture that is antithetical to the American values of hard work, thriftiness, and morality. The other basis for blaming the poor is the belief that the poor are poor because they are inferior. Let us examine these in turn.

One explanation of poverty is called the "culture of poverty" hypothesis. This view contends that the poor are qualitatively different in values and life styles from the rest of society *and that these cultural differences explain continued poverty.* In other words, the poor, in adapting to their deprived condition, are found to be more or less permissive in the raising of their children, less verbal, more fatalistic, less apt to defer gratification, and less likely to be interested in formal education than the more well-to-do. Most important to this position is the contention that this deviant cultural pattern is transmitted from generation to generation. Thus, there is a strong implication that poverty is perpetuated by defects in the lifeways of the poor. If poverty itself were to be eliminated, the former poor would probably continue to defer gratification, be immoral by middle-class standards, and so on. Panel 5–1 provides an illustration by an eminent political scientist who views the poor in this manner.

Banfield in Panel 5–1 presents a classic example of "blaming the victim." To him the poor have a subculture with values that differ radically from the other social classes. He does not see the present-time orientation of the poor as a function of the hopelessness of their situation. Yet it seems highly unlikely that the poor see little reason to complain about the slums: What about the filth, the rats, the overcrowded living conditions, the high infant mortality? What about the lack of jobs and opportunity for upward mobility? This feeling of being trapped seems the primary cause of a hedonistic present-time orientation. If the structure were changed so that the poor could see that hard work and deferred gratification really paid off, they could adopt a future-time orientation. Needless to say, there have been many severe critiques of Banfield's position.[4]

Alternatives to "Blaming the Poor"

The alternative view to the "culture of poverty" hypothesis is the thesis that the poor are an integral part of American society. They do not abandon the dominant values of the society, but rather retain them while simultaneously holding an alternative set of values. This alternative set is a result of adaptation to the conditions of poverty. Elliot Liebow in his classic study of lower-class black men has taken this view. For him, street-corner men strive to live by American values but are continually frustrated by externally imposed failure.

> From this perspective, the streetcorner man does not appear as a carrier of an independent cultural tradition. His behavior appears not so much as a way of realizing the distinctive goals and values of his own subculture, or of conforming to its models, but rather as his way of trying to achieve many of the goals and values of the larger society, of failing to do this, and of concealing his failure from others and from himself as best he can.[5]

149

PANEL 5–1

"BLAMING THE POOR"

Source: Edward C. Banfield, *The Unheavenly City: The Nature and Future of Our Urban Crisis* (Boston: Little, Brown and Company, 1970).

A controversy that continues to rage is what to do about the urban poor. Edward Banfield, a distinguished professor of urban government at Harvard and chairman of President Nixon's task force on model cities has written a highly controversial book that presents the conservative assessment of the urban condition.

In Banfield's view, the urban poor have a culture of poverty that dooms them and their descendants to the lowest social class. The essence of the poor subcultures is a present-time orientation.

> . . . the lower-class individual lives from moment to moment. If he has any awareness of a future, it is of something fixed, fated, beyond his control: things happen *to* him, he does not *make* them happen. Impulse governs his behavior, either because he cannot discipline himself to sacrifice a present for a future satisfaction or because he has no sense of the future. He is therefore radically improvident: whatever he cannot consume immediately he considers valueless. His bodily needs (especially for sex) and his taste for "action" take precedence over everything else—and certainly over any work routine. He works only as he must to stay alive, and drifts from one unskilled job to another, taking no interest in the work. (p. 53.)

The poor are doomed by their hedonism. But, in the eyes of Banfield, the culture of poverty is such that it makes the slums actually desirable to the slum dwellers.

> The lower-class individual lives in the slum and sees little or no reason to complain. He does not care how dirty and dilapidated his housing is either inside or out, nor does he mind the inadequacy of such public facilities as schools, parks, and libraries: indeed where such things exist he destroys them by acts of vandalism if he can. Features that make the slum repellent to others actually please him. He finds it satisfying in several ways. First, it is a place of excitement—'where the action is.' Nothing happens there by plan and anything may happen by accident—a game, a fight, a tense confrontation with the police; feeling that something exciting

is about to happen is highly congenial to people who live for the present and for whom the present is often empty. Second, it is a place of opportunity. Just as some districts of the city are specialized as a market for, say jewelry or antiques, so the slum is specialized as one for vice and for illicit commodities generally. Dope peddlers, prostitutes, and receivers of stolen goods are all readily available there, within easy reach of each other and of their customers and victims. For "hustlers" like Malcolm Little (later Malcolm X) and the youthful Claude Brown, the slum is the natural headquarters. Third, it is a place of concealment. A criminal is less visible to the police in the slum than elsewhere and the lower-class individual, who in some parts of the city would attract attention, is one among many there. In the slum one can beat one's children, lie drunk in the gutter, or go to jail without attracting any special notice; these are things that most of the neighbors themselves have done and that they consider quite normal. (pp. 62–63.)

As Banfield sees it, the poor are the cause of urban problems:

So long as the city contains a sizeable lower class, nothing basic can be done about its most serious problems. Good jobs may be offered to all, but some will remain chronically unemployed. Slums may be demolished, but if the housing that replaces them is occupied by the lower class it will shortly be turned into a new slum. Welfare payments may be doubled or tripled and a negative income tax substituted, but some persons will continue to live in squalor and misery. New schools may be built, new curricula devised, and the teacher-pupil ratio cut in half, but if the children who attend these schools come from lower-class homes, they will be turned into blackboard jungles, and those who graduate or drop out from them will, in most cases, be functionally illiterate. The streets may be filled with armies of policemen, but violent crime and civil disorder will decrease very little. If, however, the lower classes were to disappear—if, say, its members were overnight to acquire the attitudes, motivations, and habits of the working class—the most serious and intractable problems of the city would all disappear with it. . . . The lower-class forms of all problems are at bottom a single problem: the existence of an outlook and style of life which is radically present-oriented and which therefore attaches no value to work, sacrifice, self-improvement, or service to family, friends, or community. (pp. 210–211.)

But most Americans do not believe this. They believe rather that the poor are poor because they have a deviant system of values that encourages behaviors that lead to poverty. We will review and attempt to refute each of these charges in the following section.

The most common belief is that the poor could escape poverty if they were not so lazy. This simply is not true. In the first place, according to the U.S. Department of Health, Education and Welfare, all but one percent of the persons receiving welfare in 1971 were in categories in which it was difficult to get jobs even if they wanted to:[6]

–24 percent were over 65 years of age
–50 percent were children (under age 18)
– 3 percent were incapacitated parents in the home
–13 percent were mothers (heads of households)
– 8 percent were permanently and totally disabled
– 1 percent were blind.

Despite these problems many of the poor do work. One-fourth of persons below the government's poverty line live in families headed by *fully employed* males who do not earn enough to rise above poverty. A job, for example, paying at the 1971 federal minimum wage rate of $1.60 an hour, brought in *less* than enough for the basic subsistence for a family of four. Commonly, the poor lack the education and training necessary for skilled jobs. They must work, then, at low paying jobs as dishwashers, janitors, laundry workers, migrant farm laborers, or other menial tasks.

The commonly held belief that the poor remain poor because they do not believe in hard work is refuted by several studies. Leonard Goodwin of the Brookings Institution compared 210 suburban Baltimore families with 307 welfare mothers to determine differences in attitudes. The results showed that welfare mothers believed in the work ethic just as strongly as the suburbanites did, and more strongly in some instances than the children of the affluent.[7] Leonard Reissman, in a study of 1,500 heads of households in New Orleans, found that the poor, particularly the black poor, were very willing to learn new routines, or to leave the city, or to give up leisure time, in order to take a better job. Reissman concluded that the poor people in his sample believed in the same kind of achievement values that characterize the more prosperous classes.[8]

Michael Harrington, whose book, *The Other America*, was instrumental in sparking the "War on Poverty" by the Federal Government has said, ". . . the real explanation of why the poor are where they are is that they made the mistake of being born to the wrong parents, in the wrong section of the country, in the wrong industry, or in the wrong racial or ethnic group."[9] This is another way of saying that the society is to blame for poverty, not the poor. The customary ways of doing things, the prevailing attitudes and expectations, and the accepted structural arrangements work to the disadvantage of the poor. Let us look at several examples of the way in which the poor are trapped.

Most good jobs require a college degree, but the poor cannot afford to send their children to college. Scholarships go to the best-performing students. Children of the poor most often do not perform well in school, largely because of the low expectations of teachers and administrators for them. This is reflected in the system of "tracking" by ability as measured on class-biased examinations. Further evidence is found in the disproportionately low amounts of money given to schools in impoverished neighborhoods. All of these acts result in a "self-fulfilling prophecy"—the poor are not expected to do well in school and they do not. Since they are "failures" as measured by "objective" indicators (e.g., disproportionately high number of "drop-outs" and discipline problems, and the very small proportion who desire to go to college), the school feels justified in its discrimination toward the children of the poor.

The poor are trapped in that condition also because they get sick more often and stay sick longer than the more well-to-do. The reasons, of course, are that they cannot afford preventive medicine, proper diets, and proper medical attention when ill. The high incidence of sickness prevalent among the poor means either that they will be fired from their jobs or that they will not receive money for the days missed from work (unlike the more well-to-do who usually have jobs with such fringe benefits as sick leave and paid-up medical insurance). No pay check for extended periods means that the poor will have even less money for proper health care—thereby insuring an even higher incidence of sickness. Thus, there is a vicious cycle of poverty. The poor will tend to remain poor, and their children also tend to perpetuate the same cycle.

The children of the poor are trapped in that condition in another way. A 1968–1970 study conducted by the Public Health Service noted that poor persons had about four times as much clear-cut iron deficiency anemia, and twice as many borderline cases, as the non-poor. The poor were also found to have about twice the incidence of clear-cut deficiency as the non-poor in the essential diet ingredients of vitamin A, vitamin C, and riboflavin.[10] Diet deficiencies are an important cause of infant mortality and disease. While pregnant, a mother's lack of essential vitamins and minerals often means her child will be born prematurely and with fewer brain cells, a smaller brain, and damaged nerve tissue. Infants receiving inadequate nutrition during their early years may suffer some irreversible physical or mental impairments. The inadequate diets of the poor, determined in larger measure by the economic necessity of buying the cheapest foods, may explain why many poor children do not perform well in school—they are more likely to be hungry, weak, sick, and even suffer from brain damage than the better-fed students.

The poor are branded as immoral. That is, they are believed to be unusually prone to criminal activity and sexual promiscuity. These beliefs have the effect of restricting jobs for the poor, since they are not considered trustworthy. The workings of the American social system ensure in blatant and subtle ways that the poor will be more immoral than the well-to-do in several ways. Let us take up each of these types of immorality in turn.

First, there is the popular notion that the poor are more apt to be criminals. The objective facts appear to substantiate this claim. Poor persons are arrested with greater frequency than the well-to-do. This leads to the conclusion that the poor commit more crimes. But is this so? Approximately 60 percent of all the arrests in the United States are for drunkenness, gambling, vagrancy, disorderly conduct, and breach of the peace. These are not crimes restricted to the poor, but the poor are the ones usually arrested for violation of them. Who gets arrested for drunkenness—the rich or the poor? Or, who gets arrested for gambling—the white collar men who play poker every Friday or those young persons playing craps in an abandoned house? If gambling or drunkenness were crimes that were enforced equally throughout the social structure, then most Americans would have a criminal record. Consider, for example, the gambling and occasional drunkenness by members of the upper and middle classes in country clubs, American Legion halls, Elks Clubs, or at football games.

Some crimes, such as vagrancy, are "crimes" that only the poor can commit. J. Skelly Wright, a judge in a large city, has said that it is a crime to be poor in public. And to make the condition of poverty criminal is futile and self defeating. "Instead of trying to find the vagrant a means of support, we brand him a criminal, throw him in jail, then release him. His criminal record makes it even more difficult for him to find a job, and he soon winds up in jail again. The cycle of oppression continues."[11]

What about stealing? The differential arrest rates by social class for burglary, larceny and theft seem to prove that the poor are more prone to steal. This may be true since they, by definition, do not have the necessities of life and may, when desperate enough, steal. But what about the amount stolen by the more well-to-do? What kinds of persons (by socioeconomic status) embezzle or make fraudulent statements on income tax returns, or conspire to perpetrate fraud? These crimes are committed overwhelmingly by others than the poor. Moreover, what of white collar crime? These figures are difficult to ascertain, but an educated estimate for 1971 was that "Employees in American businesses steal between 8.5- and 10-billion dollars a year. About four billion of this total is theft in cash and merchandise from retail establishments. The remainder is lost through kickbacks, bribery, theft of time, and loss of corporate secrets."[12] These crimes usually are not reported in the media, and very few persons are ever accused in court for these crimes. The courts, then, have full dockets of cases involving lower-class persons—leaving the impression that the poor are criminals. A more accurate conclusion would be, perhaps, that criminal behavior is found throughout the social structure—only the prosecution varies.

The system of justice, as was pointed out in Chapter 3, is inequitable. The poor, when compared to the more well-to-do accused of the same offense, are more likely to spend time in jail (because they cannot afford the bail), more likely to be convicted, and if convicted, more likely to serve longer sentences. The system of justice, from the policeman to the judge and even the law itself, is based on assumptions about the poor that lead to injustice. In the words of William Ryan, ". . . the judicial process does not seem to sort out the innocent from the guilty, so much as the well-to-do from the poor."[13]

Another aspect of immorality that is believed to center among the poor is sexual promiscuity. The assumption is that the poor are much more likely to engage in illicit sexual behavior than the more well-to-do. This is based upon the much higher rate of recorded illegitimate births among poor women (a ratio of about 8 to 1), the number of "common law" types of marriages, and the presumed rate of premarital promiscuity.

Reliable data are difficult to find about sexual behavior, but the notions just stated can be refuted. An important consideration is that the rate of illegitimate births is *not* an accurate index of promiscuity. The illegitimate status of a baby is concealed more easily in a private room in a private hospital than on a ward in a public hospital. Obviously, the poorer the woman, the more likely she will be in a ward in a public hospital. The same is true of abortion. The expense of abortion may preclude this method of reducing unwanted births for the poor. Another method of reducing the number of illegitimate births is through forced marriage. This

155

outcome is more likely to occur among the more well-to-do than with the poor, because they can afford marriage. Another factor, of course, is that the poor either have no information or no money for buying safe birth control techniques. The conclusion is that recorded illegitimate births are not reliable, and thus are not reliable indicators of promiscuity. They may, however, possibly indicate a tendency; if so, that tendency would be not nearly as great as conventional wisdom suggests for the poor.

But what of illicit sex itself? The poor are notorious for their promiscuity. Data in this area are impossible to document with any accuracy, but several points are worth noting. First, illicit sexual activities occur throughout the social structure. In 1971, for example, Gilbert Bartell, an anthropologist, noted that as many as two million middle-class Americans participate in the switching of married partners for impersonal extramarital intercourse.[14] The poor, however, have a more difficult time than the well-to-do in concealing their illicit behavior. The poor male cannot afford to finance a mistress in her own apartment, and he cannot afford to travel away from home for extended periods. Second, more and more young couples of the middle class are living together without legal sanction. Premarital and extramarital sexual behavior occurs frequently in all social classes.

Thus, the system often works to expose the poor as immoral when such immorality is found throughout the social structure. As a final example, many poor couples living together have not gone through the formality of divorce from their spouses because the procedure is too expensive. In Philadelphia the minimum cost for a divorce was $215 (in 1969). So, the poor structure new relationships without remarrying. Morality in this case is beyond their financial means.

The irony of this situation is that while the system (the customary, accepted ways of doing things) is to blame for the problems of the poor—we blame the victims. *They* are shiftless and lazy. *They* do not take care of their homes. *They* live in filth. *They* are immoral. In doing this, we blame the symptoms and not the disease.

The "Innate Inferiority" Thesis

The fundamental reason for poverty may still be considered to reside in the individual, if not in a culture of poverty, then perhaps in innate inferiority. Social Darwinism, a belief system prevalent around 1900, held that in the battle for economic survival the well-endowed succeed while the others fail. Thus, that system justified success as well as failure, since the recipients of both were seen as deserving of their fate.[15] Social Darwinism has not been held in high esteem in the scientific community for fifty years, although it has continued to provide a rationale for the thinking of many individuals. Recently, however, the work of two respected scientists has again raised this question. They both suggest that the poor are in that condition because they do not measure up to the more well-to-do in the most fundamental way—intellectual endowment.

Arthur Jensen, Professor of Educational Psychology at the University of California, has argued that there is a strong possibility that blacks are less endowed mentally than whites. From his review of the research on IQ, he found that approximately 80 percent of IQ is inherited, while the remaining 20 percent is attributable to environment. Since blacks differ significantly from whites in achievement on IQ tests and in school, Jensen believed that it is reasonable to hypothesize that the sources of these differences are genetic as well as environmental.[16]

Richard Herrnstein, a Harvard psychologist, agrees with Jensen that intelligence is largely inherited. His thesis goes one step further by positing the formation of hereditary castes based on intelligence.[17] For him, social stratification by inborn differences occurs because: (1) mental ability is inherited; and (2) success (prestige of job and earnings) depends on mental ability. Thus, a meritocracy develops through the sorting process (i.e., social classes by ability). Implied in this reasoning is that persons close in mental ability are more likely to marry and reproduce, thereby insuring castes by level of intelligence. In his words, ". . . in times to come, as technology advances, the tendency to be unemployed may run in the genes of a family about as certainly as bad teeth do now."[18] This is another way of saying that the bright people are in the upper classes and the dull dregs are at the bottom. Inequality is justified just as it was years ago by the Social Darwinists.

We will not critique the Jensen-Herrnstein argument here, although there are a number of flaws in the logic and evidence used. The important consideration at this point must be the implications of this thesis for dealing with the problem of poverty.

Implications of the Jensen and Herrnstein theses. Jensen and Herrnstein have argued that dispassionate study is required to determine whether intelligence is inherited to the degree that they state. Objectivity is the *sine qua non* of scientific inquiry, and one cannot argue with its merits. We should recognize, however, the important social consequences implied by the Jensen-Herrnstein argument. First, it is a classic example of blaming the victim. The individual poor person is blamed instead of the school, the culturally biased IQ tests, or the social barriers of race, religion, or nationality. By blaming the victim, this thesis claims a relationship between lack of success and lack of intelligence. This is a spurious relationship because it ignores the advantages and disadvantages of ascribed status. In the words of Ryan,

> Arthur Jensen and Richard Herrnstein confirm regretfully that black folks and poor folks are born stupid, that little rich kids grow up rich adults, not because they inherited Daddy's stock portfolio, but rather because they inherited his brains.[19]

A second implication is the belief that poverty is inevitable. The "survival of the fittest" capitalist ideology is reinforced with the result that discrimination against the poor is justified as well as privilege for the privileged. Inequality is rationalized so that little will be done to aid its victims. The acceptance of this thesis, then, has obvious consequences for what policy decisions will be made or not made in dealing with poverty.

This thesis divides Americans further by appealing to bigots. It provides scientific justification for their beliefs in the racial superiority of some groups and the inferiority of others. By implication, segregation of and unequal treatment toward "inferiors" is given scientific validity. The goal of integration and the fragile principle of egalitarianism are seriously threatened as this thesis is given credence or prominence by some in the scientific community.

Another serious implication of the Jensen-Herrnstein argument is the explicit validation of the IQ test as a legitimate measure of intelligence. The IQ test attempts to measure "innate potential," but this is impossible because the testing process must inevitably reflect some of the skills that develop during the individual's lifetime. For the most part, intelligence tests measure educability—i.e., the prediction of conventional school achievement. Achievement in school is, of course, also associated with a cluster of other social and motivational factors, as this writer observes.

> The test as a whole is usually validated, if at all, against the external criterion of school performance. It therefore comes as no surprise to find that IQ scores do in fact correlate highly with educational success. IQ scores are also found to correlate positively with socio-economic status, those in the upper social classes tending to have the highest IQs. Since social class, and all that this im-

plies, is both an important determinant and also an important consequence of educational performance, this association is to be expected.[20]

The Jensen-Herrnstein thesis, however, overlooks the important contribution of social class to achievement on IQ tests. This oversight is crucial, since most social scientists feel that these tests are biased in favor of those who have had a middle and upper-class environment and experience. IQ tests discriminate against the poor in many ways. They discriminate obviously in the language that is used, in the instructions that are given, and in the experiences they assume the subjects have had. The discrimination can also be more subtle. For minority group persons, the race of the person who administers the test influences the results. Another less well known fact about IQ tests is that they provide a self-fulfilling prophecy in many cases, as this observer notes.

> For example, IQ scores obtained at one age often determine how an individual is subsequently treated, and, in particular, what kind of education he receives as a consequence of IQ testing will in turn contribute to his future IQ, and it is notorious that those of low and high IQ do not get equally good education.[21]

The Jensen-Herrnstein thesis also provides justification for unequal schooling. Why should school boards allot comparable sums of money for similar programs in middle-class schools and lower-class schools if the natural endowments of the children in each type of school is so radically different? Why should teachers expect the same performance from poor children as children from the more well-to-do? The result of such beliefs is, of course, a self-fulfilling prophecy. Low expectations beget low achievement (as we will document further in Chapter 10).

The jury is still out on the Jensen-Herrnstein thesis. Clearly, unbiased research is needed before a definitive answer is known. Because of the discrimination that burdens the poor (and doubly, the black poor), an accurate understanding of the contribution of heredity to intelligence and socioeconomic status will be possible only when social conditions for all races and classes are equal and when this situation has existed for several generations.[22] Until such a time is reached, the Jensen-Herrnstein thesis must be assumed to be of questionable value for three reasons. In the first place, cultural and social differences explain so much of the variance between the social classes. Second, the ramifications of the Jensen-Herrnstein thesis have pernicious effects upon the victims of poverty. Finally, it encourages policy makers either to ignore poverty or to attack its effects rather than its causes in the structure of society itself.

THE CONSEQUENCES OF POVERTY

The psychological consequences of being poor are many. The poor person is rejected and despised by others in the society. He is looked down upon as lazy, shiftless, dirty, and immoral. Being poor is, therefore, degrading. The poor are not wanted by the more well-to-do as neighbors, friends, mates, or colleagues. Thus, many of the poor define themselves as failures. They are the rejects of society and they feel it.

Being poor also engenders feelings of hopelessness (thereby leading to apathy). The poor have virtually no power. They cannot afford lawyers or lobbyists. They cannot afford to go on strike against low wages or high rent. They tend, consequently, to feel that their fates are in the hands of powerful others.

There is also a great deal of anger among the poor. They pay higher interest rates (because they are poor credit risks—another vicious circle for the poor). They are the last to be hired and the first to be fired. They must live in poor housing and often filthy conditions. One of the most important sources of anger is that they see affluence all about them but they, no matter how hard they try, are unable to share in it.

Given the propensity for alienation, hostility, and lack of ego strength among the poor, there are three ways in which the individual poor cope with the conditions in which they find themselves.

One coping device is *accommodation,* i.e., trying to make it as best as possible by hard work and obeying the law. A second psychological mechanism is *avoidance*. This is escaping the harshness of reality through mental illness, alcohol, drugs, television, or religion. A variant of this mechanism is withdrawal in the form of total apathy (not working, and seeming to not care). A third possibility is *aggression*. Some individuals respond by openly attacking the system. This may take the form of participating in revolutionary or reform organizations, threats, complaints, destruction of property, or theft. In general, then, any repressed group (the poor in this case, but any minority group as we will note in the next chapter) has three basic responses. They can put up with the aversive situation, they can withdraw from it, or they can fight it.

But what of the consequences for the society if a significant proportion of the populace is poor? In economic terms, the cost is very high. In the first place, the poor constitute a relatively unproductive mass of people. In a sense these persons are wasted. Their work output is marginal. They pay little if any taxes (usually only sales tax since they have little property and low incomes). The cost to other taxpayers, however, is quite large because of welfare programs, urban renewal, and crime prevention. If the category of "poor" were eliminated through more better-paying jobs and more adequate monetary assistance to the permanently disabled or elderly, then the entire society would prosper because of the purchasing power and the larger tax base from those who were formerly poor.

Economic considerations, while important, are not as crucial as humanitarian reasons. A nation that can afford it must, if it calls itself civilized, eliminate the human misery (physical and psychological) associated with poverty.

THE ELIMINATION OF POVERTY

There is an oft-quoted verse from the Bible that says, "and the poor shall always be with us."[23] While this has been true, must it always be? Can Americans, living in the midst of plenty, eliminate the paradox of poverty? The answer is yes, if we mean by poverty that condition of life that is intolerable because the necessities of adequate health facilities, diet, clothing, and shelter are denied certain persons. The methods to accomplish this goal, however, are elusive. The remainder of this chapter will enumerate some of the assumptions that appear basic to such a goal and some of the general programs that adoption of these assumptions demand.

Assumption 1: Poverty can be eliminated in the United States. Michael Harrington has argued forcefully that poverty must be eliminated because America has the resources. "In a nation with a technology that could provide every citizen with a decent life, it is an outrage and a scandal that there should be such social misery."[24] This paradox—poverty in the midst of plenty—can be eliminated if the people wish to make such a commitment. The nation's priorities would need to be reordered in order for economic human misery to be eliminated. In the view of William Ryan, this would not even involve too much of a sacrifice. "A redistribution of about fifteen billion dollars a year (less than ten percent of our Gross National Product that is now pushing toward one trillion dollars annually) would bring every poor person above the present poverty line."[25]

Assumption 2: Poverty is caused by a lack of resources, not a deviant value system. Basic to a program designed to eliminate poverty is the decision on what keeps some people in a condition of poverty. Is it lack of money and power, or is it the holding of deviant values and life styles? This question is fundamental because the answer determines the method for eliminating poverty. The "culture of poverty" proponents would tackle these undesirable, non-middle-class traits. The target would be the poor themselves—making them more socially acceptable. Elimination of those pernicious traits would bring an end to poverty. The focus here is on developing the social competence of the poor—not changing the system. This approach places the blame on the victim rather than the source of the problem. Such attempts treat the symptom, not the disease. The disease can only be cured by attacking its sources within the society—the structural arrangements that maintain inequality. Thus the attack must be directed at the structural changes that will enable the lower-class person to earn a living to support his family adequately.

Assumption 3: Poverty is not simply a matter of deficient income for the poor; it results from other inequities in the society as well. Poverty involves a reinforcing pattern of restricted opportunities: deficient community services; powerful predators who profit from the poor; prejudiced attitudes; unequal distribution of resources. These can be eliminated through structural changes. These include, first of all, the enforcement of the laws regarding equal opportunity for jobs, advancement, and schooling. Second, power on the local and national levels must be redistributed. The present system works in such a way as to keep the poor powerless. What is needed, rather, is the organization of the poor into viable groups with power to determine or at least shape policy in the local communities. The poor need to have some power over school policies. They need to have a voice in the decisions about the distribution of resources within the community (e.g., money for parks and recreation, fire protection, street maintenance, refuse collection). The American system of representative democracy is one of "winner take all," and is therefore to blame for the powerlessness of all minorities. A system of proportional representation would guarantee a degree of power.

A third structural change involves an increasing reliance upon central planning and action at the national level to alleviate the causes of poverty. This shift from a relative *laissez faire* policy toward a relative socialism will be outlined in greater detail toward the end of this chapter.

Assumption 4: Poverty cannot be eliminated by the efforts of the poor themselves. The poor have neither the power nor the resources to bring about the structural changes necessary to eliminate poverty. A few of the individual poor by their own efforts may escape poverty, but poverty remains for the others unless the persons and groups with the power and the resources do change the system. This is not to say that the poor cannot have some effect. They can, but usually only indirectly through influential persons or groups who become concerned about the plight of the poor.

Assumption 5: Poverty cannot be eliminated by the efforts of the private sector of the economy. Assuming that private enterprises will not engage in unprofitable activities, we can assume also the private-enterprise efforts will never by themselves eliminate poverty. This is another way of saying that private profit will tend to subvert the human needs that are of public concern. This means that businesses will not provide jobs that they consider unnecessary or not immediately profitable. It also means that these businesses will not voluntarily stop activities that are profitable (e.g., persistence in renting deteriorated housing because the unimproved land may increase in value; lobbying to keep certain occupational categories outside of minimum wage restrictions).

Conventional wisdom, however, suggests that private business is the answer because it will generate new and better paying jobs. This simply is not the case, because the "new poor," as Harrington has referred to them, differ dramatically from the "old poor."[26] The "old poor"—i.e., the poor of other generations—had hopes of breaking out of poverty; if they did not break out themselves, then at least they believed their children would. This hope was based on the needs of a rapidly expanding economy. There were jobs for immigrants, farmers, and grade school dropouts because of the needs of mass production. The poor of the present generation, the "new poor," however, are much more trapped in poverty. There is now a much greater probability of poverty being "hereditary"—hence, a much greater pessimism by poor persons. The "new poor" could be called the "automation poor." They are workers (and their families) displaced by technological advancement. They left coal mining or the small farms, not because of the attraction .of the cities, but because they were forced out. Whereas immigrants years ago·without much skill were needed to supply muscle, these jobs are now done by machines.

The year 1956 marked a watershed, since it was the first time in history that there were more white-collar than blue-collar workers in the United States. The proportion of workers needed in blue-collar positions continues to decline. The less skillful white-collar jobs are also being replaced by computers and automated techniques. At the same time, however, the labor force grows at a rate of approximately 1.5 million a year. In other words, if the unemployment rate is to remain at the same level, 1.5 million new jobs must be generated annually. The private sector with its emphasis on profit (and therefore efficiency) will not generate the new jobs needed to meet this need, let alone reduce the unemployment rate.

Assumption 6: Poverty will not be eliminated by the efforts of state and local governments themselves. A basic tenet of political conservatism is decentralization of government. Relatively small and locally-based governmental units are believed to be best suited for meeting the needs of the people. This belief, although logical, has not always worked in practice. In fact, it has increased the problems of some localities.

A good deal of money is gathered and dispensed at the city, county, and state levels for the purpose of alleviating the misery associated with poverty. Some federal programs function only through the local units of government. The basic problem is that these local units differ so dramatically in their willingness to attack poverty. Let us look at some examples.

In 1971 ten counties in the United States refused the Department of Agriculture's food stamp plan for the needy. This plan gave low-income persons the chance to buy food stamps for cash. If a family of four had a net income of $110 to $199.99 a month they paid $28 and got enough stamps to buy $106 in food at a retail store. One of the ten counties that refused this plan (even though it did not cost the county anything), Seward County in Kansas, had in 1971, 13.2 percent of its labor force with incomes of less than $2,999 annually and 3.8 percent of the county's population were on welfare. Yet the county commissioners decided not to take this "hand out" from the federal government because, as one commissioner said, "We definitely don't feel we have any hungry people here."[27]

There are vast differences among state levels of welfare assistance. For example, the maximum monthly AFDC (Aid for Dependent Children) payment for a family of four in July, 1970, exceeded $300 a month in eight states but was less than $100 a month in four states. These widely varying rates contribute to the migration of the poor from the South (the ten states with the lowest AFDC payments were in order from the lowest: Mississippi, Alabama, Arkansas, South Carolina, Louisiana, Tennessee, Missouri, Georgia, Florida, and West Virginia) to the urban north. Most interstate migration of the jobless is probably based, however, on the hope of finding jobs—not increased welfare. Hence these heavily industrialized states and cities, which coincidentally provide higher welfare benefits, are faced with an increasingly intolerable burden. In 1971, for example, one out of five Boston residents was a welfare recipient; one out of seven in Baltimore, New York City (over 1,100,000 persons), St. Louis, and San Francisco; and one out of eight in Detroit, Los Angeles, and Philadelphia. Should these cities, which are all on shaky financial ground, give assistance to all who qualify and live within their boundaries? This is an unbearable situation, and the taxpayers have a legitimate reason to question the use of their money for aiding the poor who were forced to leave other localities where welfare payments and job opportunities were much less.

Assumption 7: Poverty is a national problem and must be attacked with massive, nation-wide programs financed largely and organized by the Federal Government. Poverty can be eliminated through the massive infusion of money and compensatory programs, coupled with centralized planning. This is a form of socialism, and therefore is suspect by many. Governmental control and government subsidies are not new phenomena in the United States. It is the curious fact, however, that subsidies for the poor are generally decried, while the others go unnoticed or even praised. The federal government has subsidized, for example, defense industries (loans), the oil industry (oil depletion allowance), all corporations (tax write-offs), students (government scholarships and interest-free loans), professors (research grants), home owners (the interest on mortgages is tax-deductible, usually saving homeowners hundreds of dollars a year), newspapers and magazines (through lower-cost postage), churches (no property tax or income tax), and farmers (farm subsidies). As an extreme example of government largesse to the well-to-do while the poor receive little, Texas farmers in 1966 shared $447.9 million in farm subsidies, with 1,916 farmers getting more than half of the state's total allocation. The more than 2.75 million persons in Texas below the poverty line received less than $8 million in all forms of food assistance in that year.[28]

What can the federal government do to achieve the goals of getting all persons permanently above the poverty line? Three quite different programs are needed, because there are three kinds of poverty: (1) the unemployed (or employed at jobs that pay below the minimum wage) because they lack the skills needed in an advanced technological society; (2) those who cannot work because they are too old, physically or mentally handicapped, or because they are mothers with dependent children; and (3) the children of the poor.

The poor who are able-bodied need three things: (1) adequate training; (2) guaranteed employment; and (3) guaranteed minimum income that provides the necessities of food, clothing, shelter, and medical care. An important need here is the creation of new jobs and even new occupational categories. Michael Harrington has suggested that these new jobs may involve working as "indigenous" neighborhood social workers, as teacher's aides, community organizers, or as research assistants. The new needs and opportunities would be in the service sector of the economy rather than in the goods-producing sector, which is where automation occurs.[29] Other jobs could be in such public-works areas as highway construction, mass transit, recycling waste materials, and park maintenance. An important component of such jobs is social usefulness. Jobs with high social productivity would also have some beneficial by-products (latent consequences) in less estrangement of the worker from his job and in overall improvements for the society itself.

All segments of society benefit under full employment. If the poor are paid adequately and therefore have more money to purchase products, the private sector of the economy will be stimulated, since more goods and services will be demanded. At the same time, full employment and decent pay will give power to the poor. The greater their resources, the greater their likelihood to organize for political and social power, to vote their interests, and to become respected by others.

The second type of poverty, involving the disabled and incapacitated who cannot or should not be employed, requires government subsidies to get these people above the poverty line. These subsidies may be in the form of money, food, housing, recreational facilities, or special care centers for the physically and mentally handicapped. An important need is adequate low-cost housing, since most of the poor currently live in deteriorated housing units. Whatever the cost,

there must be a nationwide commitment to provide a decent standard of living for these persons. In the words of an editorial in
Saturday Review, "One hallmark of a civilized society is its willingness to care for its poor, ill, elderly, dependent young, and permanently handicapped."[30]

About one-half of the poor are children. Present-day poverty
tends to be passed on to succeeding generations, since the poor
often drop out of school early because of the financial difficulties of
the home or because they do not perform well in school. Changing
this will require a crash program with massive investment of quality
education in the ghetto as well as in rural pockets of poverty.
Harrington has pointed to the need for compensatory programs:

> The poor, so to speak, cannot be given the same voucher as every-
> one else. Having been systematically deprived for so long, they re-
> quire the use of federal power to make the schooling market more
> favorable to them than to the children of affluent homes.[31]

PANEL 5–2

SOME WELFARE DILEMMAS

It is one thing to support government programs to aid the aged, the
mothers of dependent children, the handicapped, and the technologi-
cally unemployable. But what of those persons with an adequate education, with the skills to make it in American society, but who choose
to live on welfare? Although these able dropouts *are a tiny fraction of
the needy,* they are visible, defiant, and infuriating to mainstream Americans. They, therefore, endanger aid programs to the poor who are considered more deserving. Should these persons receive unemployment
insurance and food stamps? Should the taxpayers of a community or of
the nation support these persons in their quest for the good life?

To receive unemployment compensation, recipients must seek employment periodically. Since many prospective employers are "turned
off" by the hair and clothing styles of these "society dropouts," they
are not given employment. Does the local Welfare Board, then, have
the right to dictate life styles to those receiving unemployment compensation?

The fundamental problem associated with this phenomenon is that
welfare programs are dependent upon public support. Eliminating poverty will take a tremendous commitment and sacrifice by the public.
The more that skilled, able-bodied persons participate in the welfare
programs, the greater the difficulty in securing popular support for increased welfare programs.

PANEL 5–3

WHO BENEFITS FROM POVERTY?

Source: Herbert J. Gans, "The Uses of Power: The Poor Pay All," *Social Policy* 2 (July-August, 1971), pp. 20–24.

Herbert Gans, a sociologist, has some interesting insights about the benefits of poverty that are important to consider if this phenomenon is to be eliminated. He begins with the assumption (from the order perspective) that if some social arrangement persists, it must be accomplishing something important (at least in the view of the powerful in society). What, then, does the existence of a relatively large number of persons in a condition of poverty accomplish that is beneficial to the powerful?

1. Poverty functions to provide a low-wage labor pool that is willing (or unable to be unwilling) to do society's necessary "dirty work." The middle and upper classes are really subsidized by the existence of economic activities that depend on the poor (low wages to many workers in restaurants, hospitals, and in truck farming).

2. The poor also subsidize a variety of economic activities for the affluent by supporting, for example, innovations in medicine (as patients in research hospitals or as guinea pigs in medical experiments) and providing servants, gardeners, and house cleaners who make life easier for the more well-to-do.

3. The existence of poverty creates jobs for a number of occupations and professions that serve the poor or protect the rest of society from them (penologists, social workers, police, pawn shop owners, numbers racketeers, and liquor store owners). The presence of poor people also provides incomes for doctors, lawyers, teachers, and others who are too old, poorly trained, or incompetent to attract more affluent clients.

4. Poor people subsidize merchants by purchasing products that others do not want (seconds, dilapidated cars, deteriorated housing, day-old bread, fruit, and vegetables that otherwise would have little or no value).

5. The poor serve as a group to be punished in order to uphold the legitimacy of conventional values (hard work, thrift, honesty, and monogamy). *The poor provide living proof that moral deviance does not pay,* thus, an indirect rationale for blaming the victim.

6. Poverty guarantees the status of those who are not poor. The poor are at the bottom of the status hierarchy, therefore providing a reliable and relatively permanent measuring rod for status comparison, particularly by those just above them (i.e., the working class, whose politics, for example, are often influenced by the need to maintain social distance between themselves and the poor).

7. The poor aid in the upward mobility of others. A number of persons have entered the middle class through the profits earned from providing goods and services in the slums (pawn shops, second hand clothing and furniture stores, gambling, prostitution, and drugs).

8. The poor, being powerless, can be made to absorb the costs of change in our society. In the nineteenth century they did the backbreaking work that built the railroads and the cities. Today they are the ones pushed out of their homes by urban renewal, the building of expressways, parks, and stadia. Many economists assume that a degree of unemployment is necessary to fight inflation. Of course, the poor, since they are the ones who are "first to be fired and the last to be hired," are the ones who make the sacrifice for the economy.

In the words of Gans,

> This analysis is not intended to suggest that because it is often functional, poverty *should* exist, or that it *must* exist. For one thing, poverty has many more dysfunctions than functions; for another, it is possible to suggest functional alternatives. For example, society's dirty work could be done without poverty, either by automation or by paying "dirty workers" decent wages. Nor is it necessary for the poor to subsidize the many activities they support through their low-wage jobs. This would, however, drive up the costs of these activities, which would result in higher prices to their customers and clients. . . .
>
> In sum, then, many of the functions served by the poor could be replaced if poverty were eliminated, but almost always at higher costs to others, particularly more affluent others. Consequently a functional analysis [equivalent to the order model] must conclude that poverty persists not only because many of the functional alternatives to poverty would be quite dysfunctional for the affluent members of society. . . . poverty can be eliminated only when they become dysfunctional for the affluent or powerful, or when the powerless can obtain enough power to change society. (pg. 24.)

Or, as he argued in another article,

> . . . we should have a GI bill in the war against poverty and pay people to go to school, pay for their tuition, their books, and give them an additional living allowance if they have a family. The GI bill was one of the most successful social experiments this society ever had. Why does it require a shooting war for us to be so smart? Why can't we in the war on poverty say that the most productive thing a young person between ages 16 and 21 can do is go to school, and that this is an investment in the Great Society?[32]

The positive consequences of this plan would be, first of all, that a significant segment of the potential workers would be kept out of the labor force for a period of time, thereby reducing the number of jobs needed. Second, individuals would learn the skills needed in an automated society. Third, the educated workers could command greater wages and therefore pay more in taxes to the government. The lifetime earnings for the veterans who took advantage of the GI bill was significantly greater than for those who chose to bypass the plan—so much so that they will pay back to the government in taxes approximately six times more than the government invested in their education. This could work for the poor, too.

The problem with this emphasis on education (and with alleviating poverty in general) is the creation of enough socially useful jobs with a decent American standard of pay. Leon Keyserling, former Chairman of the Council of Economic Advisors, has said that, ". . . education and training as a conduit to a job is itself a travesty unless the jobs are created first: training for jobs can be meaningful only if the jobs are going to be available, and the training itself does not create jobs."[33] The creation of jobs, then, is the key to eliminating poverty. Since most of these jobs will no doubt be in the public sector of the economy, the government must divert its best minds to tackling this immense problem.

The general programs given above are indeed necessary if the United States is going to get everyone above the absolute minimum level of economic security. This goal is easily attainable because the productive capacity of the United States is great enough to make it possible without too great a strain. *These programs, however, will not solve the basic problem of inequality.* Thus, there is no insurance that these programs will eliminate urban riots, demonstrations, or crime. They will not eliminate the anger and bitterness that persons feel as they experience relative deprivation. They can, however, eliminate the human suffering associated with extreme deprivation.

170

SUGGESTED GENERAL READINGS

Harrington, Michael, *The Other America: Poverty in the United States* (Baltimore: Penguin Books, 1963). The classic statement on poverty in America.

Kotz, Nick, *Let Them Eat Promises: The Politics of Hunger in America* (Garden City, New York: Doubleday & Company, 1971). The problems of hunger and malnutrition are examined in this book with special emphasis on the political attempts to alleviate them.

Larner, Jeremy, and Irving Howe (eds.), *Poverty: Views from the Left* (New York: William Morrow and Company, 1965). A series of essays on poverty by socialists.

Miller, Herman P., *Rich Man, Poor Man* (New York: Thomas Y. Crowell, 1971). This book is by an economic statistician. It provides the authoritative data on the maldistribution of wealth in the United States.

Ryan, William, *Blaming the Victim* (New York: Pantheon Books, 1971). This important book is must reading for analysts of American social problems.

Valentine, Charles A., *Culture and Poverty: Critique and Counter-Proposals* (Chicago: University of Chicago Press, 1968). A survey of the culture of poverty controversy.

NOTES AND REFERENCES

1. For a survey of problems with missing census data see "The Census—What's Wrong With It, What Can Be Done," *Transaction* 5 (May, 1968), pp. 49–56. For a complete analysis see, Jacob S. Siegel, "Completeness of Coverage of the Nonwhite Population in the 1960 Census and Current Estimates, and Some Implications," *Social Statistics and the City*, David M. Heer (ed.), (Cambridge, Massachusetts: Harvard University Press, 1968), pp. 13–54.

2. Joe R. Feagin, "Poverty: We Still Believe That God Helps Those Who Help Themselves," *Psychology Today* 6 (November, 1972), pp. 101–110 and 129.

3. Shana Alexander, "The Crime of Poverty," *Newsweek* (October 30, 1972), p. 53.

4. For an especially ascerbic review of Banfield's book see, William Ryan, "Is Banfield Serious?" *Social Policy* 1 (November/December, 1970), pp. 74–76. For a series of papers on the culture of poverty see Eleanor Burke Leacock (ed.), *The Culture of Poverty: A Critique* (New York: Simon and Schuster, 1971).

5. Elliot Liebow, *Tally's Corner: A Study of Negro Streetcorner Men* (Boston: Little, Brown, 1967), p. 222. See also Hyman Rodman, "The Lower Class Value Stretch," *Social Forces* 42 (December, 1963), pp. 205–215; and Ulf Hannerz, "Roots of Black Manhood:

Sex, Socialization and Culture in the Ghettos of American Cities," *Trans-action* 6 (October, 1969), p. 20.

6. "Those Welfare Deadbeats," *St. Louis Post-Dispatch* (April 23, 1971).

7. Reported in "Viewing the Poor," *Trans-action* (May, 1971), p. 16.

8. Leonard Reissman, "Readiness to Succeed: Mobility Aspirations and Modernism Among the Poor," *Urban Affairs Quarterly* 4 (March, 1969), pp. 379–395.

9. Michael Harrington, *The Other America: Poverty in the United States* (Baltimore: Penguin Books, Inc., 1963), p. 21.

10. Associated Press release (April 30, 1971).

11. J. Skelly Wright, "The Courts Have Failed the Poor," *New York Times Magazine* (March 9, 1969), p. 26.

12. Lawrence R. Zeitlin, "A Little Larceny Can Do a Lot for Employee Morale," *Psychology Today* 5 (June, 1971), p. 22.

13. William Ryan, *Blaming the Victim* (New York: Pantheon Books, 1971), p. 203.

14. Gilbert Bartell, *Group Sex* (New York: Peter H. Wyden, Inc., 1971).

15. Richard Hofstadter, *Social Darwinism in American Thought*, Revised Edition (Boston: Beacon Press, 1955).

16. Arthur R. Jensen, "How Much Can We Boost IQ and Scholastic Achievement?" *Harvard Educational Review* 39 (Winter, 1969), pp. 1–123. The subsequent issues of the *Harvard Educational Review* include a large number of replies to Professor Jensen's article. See especially the articles appearing in the Spring 1969 and Summer 1969 issues.

17. Richard Herrnstein, "I.Q.," *Atlantic* 228 (September, 1971), pp. 43–64. For critiques, see Noam Chomsky, "The Fallacy of Richard Herrnstein's IQ," *Social Policy* 3 (May/June, 1972), pp. 19–25; and Karl W. Deutsch and Thomas Edsall, "The Meritocracy Scare," *Society* 9 (September/October, 1972), pp. 71–79.

18. Herrnstein, "I.Q.," p. 63. For an essay on what might occur in a meritocracy, see Michael Young, *The Rise of the Meritocracy 1870/2033: An Essay on Education and Equality* (Baltimore: Penguin Books, 1961).

19. William Ryan, "Postscript: A Call to Action," *Social Policy* 3 (May/June, 1972), p. 54.

20. Joanna Ryan, "IQ—The Illusion of Objectivity," *Race and Intelligence,* Ken Richardson and David Spears (eds.), (Baltimore: Penguin Books, 1972), p. 54.

21. Ryan, "IQ—The Illusion of Objectivity," p. 44.

22. From the official position of the Society for the Psychological Study of Social Issues, George W. Albee, *et al.*, "The SPSSI Statement," *Harvard Educational Review* 39 (Summer, 1969), pp. 625–627.

23. Matthew, 26:11.

24. Harrington, *The Other America,* p. 24.

172

25. Ryan, *Blaming the Victim*, pp. 117–118.

26. The following is taken largely from two sources: Michael Harrington, "The Politics of Poverty," *Poverty Views from the Left*, Jeremy Larner and Irving Howe (eds.), (New York: William Morrow and Company, Inc., 1965), pp. 13–38; and Michael Harrington, "Introduction," *Poverty in America: A Book of Readings*, Louis A. Ferman, Joyce L. Kornbluh, and Alan Haber (eds.), (Ann Arbor, Michigan: The University of Michigan Press, 1965), pp. vii–xiv.

27. David Arnold, "The County that Refused Food Stamps," *Topeka Daily Capital, Midway Magazine* (March 28, 1971), p. 11.

28. "Rich Farmers Get Huge Handouts While the Poor Go Hungry," *Rural Advance* 2 (Summer, 1968), p. 3.

29. Harrington, "The Politics of Poverty," p. 35.

30. "Welfare: Time for Reform," *Saturday Review* (May 23, 1970), p. 19.

31. Michael Harrington, "The Urgent Case for Social Investment," *Saturday Review* (November 23, 1968), p. 34.

32. Harrington, "Introduction," to *Poverty in America*, pp. xii–xiii.

33. Leon H. Keyserling, "Programs: Present and Future," *Dialogue on Poverty*, Paul Jacobs, *et al.* (eds.), (Indianapolis: The Bobbs-Merrill Company, Inc., 1966), p. 93.

CHAPTER 6

American Majority-Minority
Power Relations

The Characteristics of Minority Groups

The United States is a mosaic of different social groups and categories. These are not equal in power, resources, prestige, or presumed worth. They are differentially ranked on each of these dimensions. But why is one group alleged to be superior to another? The basic reason is differential power—power derived from superior numbers, technology, weapons, property, or economic resources. Those holding superior power in a society establish a system of inequality by successfully imposing their will upon less powerful groups, and this system of inequality is then maintained and perpetuated by power.[1] Inequality is maintained because the dominant group provides the standards (values and norms) by which individuals and groups are judged and the reward-punishment system; thus the dominant group's institutions systematically disadvantage some groups while favoring others.[2]

Because majority-minority relations is basically a power relationship, conflict or at least the potential for conflict is always present. Overt conflict is most likely when the subordinate group attempts to alter the distribution of power (as we established in Chapter 1).[3] Size is not crucial in determining whether or not a group is the most powerful. A numerical minority may in fact have more political representation than the majority, as is the case in the Union of

South Africa and in most colonial situations. Thus, the most important characteristic of a subordinate "minority" group is that it is dominated by a more powerful group.

A second characteristic of a minority group is that it is composed of persons with similar characteristics that differ significantly from the dominant group. These characteristics are salient—they are visible and they make a difference.

The behavior and/or characteristics of minority group members is stereotyped and systematically condemned by the dominant or majority group. Minority groups typically inspire stereotypes in the minds of the dominant group, presumably because these negative generalizations keep them "down." S. I. Hayakawa, in the following passage, has shown vividly how stereotyped ideas of minority groups are variable, irrational, and negative in their consequences (see also Panel 6–1).

> Mr. Miller is a Jew. If Mr. Miller succeeds in business that proves that "Jews are smart"; if he fails in business, it is alleged that he still has "money salted away somewhere." If Mr. Miller has different customs than ours, that proves that "Jews don't assimilate." If he is indistinguishable from other Americans he is "trying to pass himself off as one of us." If Mr. Miller fails to give to charity, that is because "Jews are tight"; if he gives generously, he is "trying to buy his way into society." If he lives in the Jewish section of town, that is because "Jews are so clannish"; if he moves to a locality where there are no other Jews, that is because "they try to horn in everywhere." In other words, because of our feelings towards Jews in general, Mr. Miller is automatically condemned, no matter who he is or what he does.[4]

A final characteristic that all minority groups have in common is that they are singled out for differential and unfair treatment. The discrimination may be subtle or blatant, but it is always detrimental to the minority group. A sizeable portion of this chapter will focus on the various manifestations of discrimination toward minority groups in the United States.

Using these criteria—relative powerlessness, visible differentiation from the majority, negative stereotyping, and unfair discrimination—six categories of people are commonly designated as "minority groups." *Race*, which refers to genetic and therefore immutable differences among individuals, is a typical basis for differential treatment in most societies. For some Americans, racial differences determine behavioral differences as well as skin color, shape of lips, and color of eyes. Although science belies this statement, the fact remains some segments within the society perceive

PANEL 6–1

IN-GROUP VIRTUE—OUT-GROUP VICE

Source: Robert K. Merton, Social Theory and Social Structure (Glencoe, Illinois: The Free Press, 1957), pp. 428–429.

Robert K. Merton, a distinguished sociologist, has provided an excellent illustration of how the very same behavior undergoes a complete change of evaluation in its transition from the in-group Abe Lincoln to the out-group Abe Cohen or Abe Kurokawa.

Did Lincoln work far into the night? This testifies that he was industrious, resolute, perseverant, and eager to realize his capacities to the full. Do the out-group Jews or Japanese keep these same hours? This only bears witness to their sweatshop mentality, their ruthless undercutting of American standards, their unfair competitive practices. Is the in-group hero frugal, thrifty, and sparing? Then the out-group villain is stingy, miserly, and penny-pinching. All honor is due the in-group Abe for his having been smart, shrewd, and intelligent and, by the same token, all contempt is owing the out-group Abes for their being sharp, cunning, crafty, and too clever by far. Did the indomitable Lincoln refuse to remain content with a life of work with the hands? Did he prefer to make use of his brain? Then, all praise for his plucky climb up the shaky ladder of opportunity. But, of course, the eschewing of manual work for brain work among the merchants and lawyers of the out-group deserves nothing but censure for a parasitic way of life. Was Abe Lincoln eager to learn the accumulated wisdom of the ages by unending study? The trouble with the Jew is that he's a greasy grind, with his head always in a book, when decent people are going to a show or a ball game. Was the resolute Lincoln unwilling to limit his standards to those of his provincial community? That is what we should expect of a man of vision. And if the out-groupers criticize the vulnerable areas in our society, then send 'em back where they came from. Did Lincoln, rising high above his origins, never forget the rights of the common man and applaud the rights of workers to strike? This testifies only that, like all real Americans, this greatest of Americans was deathlessly devoted to the cause of freedom. But, as you examine the statistics on strikes, remember that these un-American practices are the result of out-groupers pursuing their evil agitation among otherwise contented workers.

behavioral differences as racial, thereby justifying differential treatment.

A second category, *ethnicity,* is also a traditional basis for inequality. An ethnic group has a culture distinctive from the dominant one. An Amish rural community or an Italian neighborhood in Boston are examples of ethnic groups. Of course, racial groups may also differ culturally from the dominant group—e.g., the Chinese in San Francisco's Chinatown or any tribe of American Indians.

The third classification—*religion*—also places some categories in "inferior" positions. The Jews throughout most of their history have in one country after another been persecuted because of their religion (or assumed religious ties). Much of the unrest in Northern Ireland stems from religious differences. The Protestants in that country are dominant and the Catholics are the objects of discrimination.

Another category—the *impoverished*—comprise a minority group in all societies. As we found in the last chapter, the American poor are powerless and victims of varied forms of discrimination.

Certain *deviant* groups also have the characteristics of minority groups. Hippies, unmarried mothers, (and their offspring) and homosexuals are examples of deviant minority groups in the United States.

Finally, there is a basis for differentiation that has only recently been recognized as a basis for minority status—*sex*. Women in American society are relatively powerless, presumed to have stereotyped qualities (e.g., incapable of leadership because of being highly emotional), and are the victims of discrimination. See Panel 6–2 for the similarities between women and blacks in American society.

IS AMERICA A RACIST SOCIETY?

By way of introduction, we will describe the degree to which racism prevails in the United States. Although the concept refers specifically to race, the discrimination, hostility, and hatred implied in its usage also pertain to all other types of minorities. Racism is used here to refer to the dominant group members' feeling of superiority to the members of some other racial group, as well as to their harboring feelings of hatred, fear, and repulsion toward minorities. Included also in the concept of racism are conscious or unconscious forms of *discrimination,* all of which serve to keep the minority in a situation of relative powerlessness.

The evidence is that the United States historically has been a racist society. Charles Silberman in his excellent analysis, *Crisis in Black and White,* has suggested that the United States continues to be a racist society.

> What we are discovering, in short, is that the United States—all of it, North as well as South, West as well as East—is a racist society in a sense and to a degree that we have refused so far to admit, much less face. . . . The tragedy of race relations in the United

PANEL 6–2

CASTELIKE STATUS OF WOMEN AND BLACKS

Source: Adapted and updated from an original table by Helen Mayer Hacker, "Women as a Minority Group," *Social Forces* 30 (October, 1951), p. 65.

BLACKS	WOMEN
1. High Social Visibility	
a. Skin color, other "racial" characteristics	a. Secondary sex characteristics
2. Ascribed Attributes	
a. Inferior intelligence, smaller brain, less convoluted, scarity of geniuses	a. ditto
b. More free in instinctual gratifications. More emotional, "primitive" and childlike. Imagined sexual prowess envied.	b. Irresponsible, inconsistent, emotionally unstable. Lack strong super-ego. Women as "temptresses."
c. Common stereotype, "inferior"	c. "Weaker"
3. Rationalizations of Status	
a. Thought to be all right "in his place"	a. "Woman's place is in the home"
b. Myth of contented Negro	b. Myth of contented woman—"feminine" woman is happy in subordinate role

States is that there is no American Dilemma. White Americans are not torn and tortured by the conflict between their devotion to the American creed and their actual behavior. They are upset by the current state of race relations, to be sure. But what troubles them is not that justice is being desired but that their peace is being shattered and their business interrupted.[5]

The evidence is found in three sources—historical events, attitude surveys, and discrimination.

The historical record of American racism is clear. A few well known examples should suffice: (1) the legal existence of slavery;

BLACKS	WOMEN
4. Accommodation Attitudes	
a.　Deferential manner	a.　Flattering manner
b.　Concealment of real feelings	b.　"Feminine wiles"
c.　Fake appeals for directives; show of ignorance	c.　Appearance of helplessness
5. Discriminations	
a.　Limitations on education— should fit "place" in society	a.　ditto
b.　Confined to traditional jobs —barred from supervisory positions. Their competition feared.	b.　ditto
c.　Less pay for equal work	c.　ditto
d.　Deprived of political importance	d.　ditto
e.　Social and professional segregation	e.　ditto
f.　More vulnerable to criticism	f.　ditto (e.g., women drivers, conduct in bars)
6. Militancy	
a.　Rise of organizations that use various forms of protest for the goal of equality	a.　ditto

(2) the maltreatment of American Indians from broken treaties, policies of extermination, to the segregation of Indians on reservations; (3) immigration quotas that severely limited persons from certain parts of the world, particularly Asia; and (4) the forced internment of 110,000 Japanese Americans during World War II. A number of sources have recently documented the painfully shocking details of these developments in great detail.[6]

Racism remains in contemporary American life, although in somewhat more subtle forms than previously. For the moment, however, let us look at the evidence from attitude surveys.

The data from a number of sources show that there is a decline in the verbal expression of prejudice towards blacks by whites. The National Opinion Research Center, for example, asked the same questions to national samples in 1942, 1956, and 1968. The percentage of white Americans who favored school integration was 30 percent in 1942, 48 percent in 1956, and 60 percent in 1968. The percentage of white Americans giving a pro-integration response to the question, "If a Negro with the same income and education as you moved into your block, would it make any difference to you," was 35 percent in 1942, 51 percent in 1956, and 65 percent in 1968. Although the percentage of those admitting prejudice has declined significantly, more than one-third of the populace still expresses anti-integration attitudes.[7]

While approximately two-thirds of Americans claim to accept the goals of integration, there is rather widespread disagreement over the means to achieve it. More than half of Americans polled by Gallup in 1968 said that the federal government is pushing integration too fast.[8]

A poll of Minnesota residents in 1964 revealed that 58 percent believed that state and local governments, not the federal government, should have the main responsibility for seeing that blacks get fair treatment in jobs.[9] This seems like a logical belief, but it has racist consequences, since some states and localities have been notoriously resistant to changing the pattern of majority-minority relationships.

Finally, there is the remarkable finding by Gallup in 1968 that 54 percent of Americans (22 percent had no opinion) thought that blacks were more to blame for the conditions in which they find themselves than were whites—a classic example of blaming the victim.[10]

Skolnick has summarized it this way,

. . . during the 1960's assertive attempts to achieve political, social, and economic equality of opportunity for Negroes have met with the disfavor of a majority of white Americans. Only moderate legislation receives the approval of more than half of the whites in this country. At the same time, over the past twenty years, and despite some minor short-term fluctuation, there has been a steady increase in white support for the goals of integration and equality of opportunity for black Americans. Nevertheless it is abundantly clear that a great deal of resistance to racial change remains.[11]

Attitude surveys reflect rather accurately the official beliefs of a population. Individuals, however, may mask their true feelings. Beliefs may be inferred from action more reliably, but this method, too, may not be a true indicator of beliefs, since persons can also lie with behavior. A tolerant person may often discriminate, while an intolerant person perhaps may not because of economic gain or social pressure. The point is that discrimination occurs from several sources. Whatever the source, the extent of discrimination *is* an accurate barometer of majority-minority relations.

Discrimination in the United States

Discrimination is a complex phenomenon. The forms discrimination may take can vary from a Polish joke to mass murder. The discriminators may be individuals, groups, or even society itself. Moreover, the motivations of the discriminators, as we have seen, may include or lack malice toward those discriminated against. The analysis that follows will examine the modes of discrimination and the characteristics of the types of discriminators. The cross-classification of these two phenomena will provide a paradigm of discrimination.[12]

Throughout human history, dominant groups have used coercion, segregation, defamation and other techniques to keep the subjugated group "in its place"—i.e., powerless and disadvantaged. Of the many types of discrimination, three distinctive modes—derogation, denial, and violence—incorporate most of the means employed and show the breadth of the discriminatory spectrum.

At the least violent end of the continuum is *derogation*. This type of discrimination is in the form of words that put the minority group "down." These words may be common sayings that emphasize the stereotypes held such as "don't let him jew you down." Derogation is also found in jokes (Polish jokes, "Pat and Mike" stories, jokes about "Rastus") or stereotyped roles for minority group members in movies and plays. Epithets referring to minorities such as "nigger," "kike," or "greaser" are derogatory to those persons so labeled. Finally, derogation may occur in the form of the embittered oratory or writings by demagogues who focus on such things as the "mongrelization of the races" or the "international Jewish conspiracy."

A second type of discrimination, usually more direct than derogation, is *denial*. One form of denial—avoidance—is the practice of avoiding interaction with members of a minority group. Children are taught not to play with certain other children. Parents may take their children out of a newly integrated school to avoid the possibility of interaction with the minority group. Avoidance is also involved when whites move out of a neighborhood if a family of a minority group moves in.

Denial occurs when groups set up barriers limiting social interaction. Clubs, fraternities, and home owners' associations have on numerous occasions set up policies that explicitly denied access to members of other groups. All manner of segregation policies have occurred in the United States. The "Jim Crow" laws of the South prior to the 1960's are a good example. Under these laws the whites and blacks could not use the same drinking fountains, rest rooms, waiting rooms, or the same seating area in buses and trains.

The most extreme form of discrimination is *violence* or the threat of violence perpetrated upon minority group members. The destruction of the property and lives of minority group members have occurred throughout American history.

So much for the types of discriminatory acts. What about the sources of these acts? Robert Merton has developed a scheme by which he delineates four "types" of persons according to their consistency or inconsistency in prejudiced beliefs versus prejudiced actions.[13] Those whose actions and attitudes are consistent are the "active bigots" (whose beliefs *and* actions are bigoted) and the "allweather liberals" (always tolerant). The other two types are interesting in that they show inconsistencies that are present in the large portion of the American populace. In each case persons go against their feelings, whether basically bigoted or basically tolerant, when faced with countervailing social pressures. They conform to the wishes of their friends, reference groups, or the law, even though they would rather not. The "fair-weather liberal," while perhaps basically unprejudiced, refuses to serve blacks in his restaurant because he fears that he would lose customers. Similarly, an unprejudiced real estate salesman may nevertheless refuse to show certain homes to Mexican-Americans because it may affect his job.

This type of person presumably does not harbor feelings of malice toward minority groups, but the effects of his actions are no less discriminatory.

The "timid bigot" is also faced with social pressures, which in his case cause him to go against his true prejudiced feelings. He conforms to the laws or customs which demand that he serve black customers, sell homes to any persons who can afford them, and hire minority group members in his firm. *The social situation, then, is a powerful determinant of behavior regardless of personal feelings.* *

Merton's scheme, while useful, focuses on the individual. Only indirectly (in the cases of the "fair-weather liberal" and the "timid bigot") is the source of discrimination behavior found outside the individual. To focus only on the individual and his beliefs and acts is to ignore the direct and indirect ways that the institutions of society work to disadvantage minority group members systematically. This phenomenon has been labeled "institutional racism." It refers to the established, customary, and respected ways things are done in the society that keep the minority in a subordinate position. For Carmichael and Hamilton there are two types of racism—individual and institutional. Individual racism consists of overt acts by individuals that harm other individuals or their property. This type of action is usually publicly decried and is probably on the decline in the United States. Institutional racism is more injurious to more minority group members than individual racism, but it is not recognized by the dominant group members as racism. Carmichael and Hamilton illustrated the two types as follows:

> When a black family moves into a home in a white neighborhood and is stoned, burned or routed out, they are victims of an overt act of individual racism which many people will condemn—at least in words. But it is institutional racism that keeps black people locked in dilapidated slum tenements, subject to the daily prey of exploitative slumlords, merchants, loan sharks, and discriminatory real estate agents. . . . Respectable individuals can absolve themselves from individual blame: *they* would never plant a bomb in a church; *they* would never stone a black family. But they continue to support political officials and institutions that would and do perpetuate institutionally racist policies. Thus *acts* of overt, individual racism may not typify the society, but institutionalism racism does . . .[14]

* This is an important sociological truth. How else can one explain the existence of Kamakaze pilots or participants in lynch mobs? There is an enormous amount of sociological evidence for the power of the social situation upon individual actors.

For the sake of clarity, let us use the term *institutional discrimination* rather than institutional *racism*. The referent for racism is clearly race (and usually the black race). Institutional racism is present in American society, but this phenomenon is not limited to racial minority groups. The social system works to disadvantage *all* minority groups, thus suggesting the term institutional discrimination.

Discrimination can be subtle or blatant, covert as well as overt. As we have seen, it takes many forms as it comes from several sources. In order to describe discrimination in a systematic fashion, the types of discriminators and the types of discriminatory acts will be combined. Figure 6–1 provides the scheme that will be used. This paradigm is not exhaustive of all the possibilities since there are other types of motives for discrimination and other types of discriminatory behavior. However, the major ones are included, and these are sufficient to illustrate the complex and ubiquitous character of discrimination in American society.

The Active Bigot

The prejudiced person or group discriminates against individuals because of their membership in or identification with some hated group. The act is done consciously with malice.[15] Our interest here, however, is not so much the motivation of the discriminatory acts but the acts themselves, because they serve to keep the minority in a subordinate position.

Derogation by the "active bigot" (Type 1 from the paradigm in Figure 6–1) consciously puts the minority group "down" while

FIGURE 6–1   A Discrimination Paradigm

Types of Discriminators	Types of Discriminatory Acts		
	Derogation	Denial	Violence
The active bigot (individuals or groups)	1	2	3
The conformist to powerful social constraints (individuals or groups)	4	5	6
The social structure (institutional)	7	8	9

simultaneously elevating the majority. Panel 6–3 provides an example of this type.

The "active bigot" can also discriminate against those he hates by denial (Type 2). This may mean taking his children out of an integrated school, or on the job he may refuse a Puerto Rican service, or he may join organizations that deny membership to certain categories of persons.

Organizations as well as individuals may use denial. Many organizations by their nature are exclusive. Country clubs, lodges, fraternities and sororities are but a few examples of such organizations. In the summer of 1970, for example, the delegates of the national convention of the Benevolent and Protective Order of Elks voted 1550-22 to retain their whites-only membership requirement. Although the exclusiveness in college fraternities and sororities has been breaking down in recent years, they remain, by and large, exclusively white, Christian, and at least middle class. Ironically, some of these "Greek" organizations have gone so far as to even exclude Greeks.[16]

Another form of denial is to restrict neighborhoods to those of a certain ethnic category. In the recent past many neighborhoods remained exclusive through restrictive covenants and "gentlemen's agreements." Although their actions are formally unconstitutional, many neighborhoods manage to remain exclusive, barring minority group members by a variety of mechanisms. Perhaps the most famous (or infamous) case of neighborhood restrictive policies occurred in Grosse Pointe, Michigan, an exclusive suburb of Detroit, in 1960. The home owners had all prospective residents screened and evaluated by private detectives on the basis of race, ethnicity, religion, swarthiness of skin, accent, occupation, education, neatness of dress, grammar, and condition and neighborhood of present house. Points were awarded for each of these variables and persons were allowed to buy Grosse Pointe property if they met the criteria for inclusion. It was especially difficult for Jews to attain the required number of points. Panel 6–4 provides an example of just how formidable were the requirements for that minority group. Despite these hurdles some Jews did make it. Blacks and Orientals, however, were not allowed to buy property regardless of their points.

Acts of violence by the "active bigot" (Type 3) toward his enemies are numerous. These are overt acts by individuals or groups of the majority that cause death, injury or destruction of property for minority group members. Regrettably, minority group members have been physically abused throughout American history; blacks, Mexican-Americans, Indians, Irish immigrants, Chinese, Catholics, or Jews, depending upon the time or place, have been beaten, flogged, burned at the stake, hanged, or mutilated because they belonged to a hated group. Although violence of this sort has diminished, instances still occur with some regularity in American society. The homes of minority members are still bombed or damaged, some persons are threatened or beaten or even killed for "getting out of line." In the recent past black leaders (e.g., Martin Luther King, Jr., and Medgar Evers) have been assassinated, a black church was bombed in Birmingham killing five black children, and a black girl was shot and killed in the spring of 1971 a few hours after she graduated as an honor student from a high school in Mississippi. Violence against minority groups by individuals and collectivities

PANEL 6–3

BLACK "INFERIORITY"

Sources: "Scientists Say Negro Still in Ape Stage," *The Thunderbolt* (December-January, 1965). Also, Gordon W. Allport, *The Nature of Prejudice* (Garden City, New York: Doubleday Anchor Books, 1954), p. 110.

A series of statements, captioned "Scientists Say Negro Still in Ape Stage," appeared in *The Thunderbolt,* the newspaper of the National States Rights Party. Among these statements were the following:
   —The black skin of the Negro has nothing to do with climate, it is caused by animal coloring matter between the true and the scarf skins. It is proven the world over that black and yellow skins are signs of mental and spiritual inferiority and that no tinged race can create a civilization.
   —A few mulattoes may appear to be brilliant but this brilliance never allows them to invent or create, which shows they have not bridged the gap between the black and white, for no archaic form can become modern.
   —The Negro is much closer to the ape than any other race physically and consequently mentally, for form must determine mental and moral qualities and like must produce like. Every race is different physically and thereby mentally. With the Negro, the body —hence mind—is the lowest of all.
   —The Negro has had just as long as the white man to develop. Tens of thousands of years have passed by and the Negro has not produced a civilization. Where is his art, his science, his religion?

continues. The rate has declined, and when these acts occur more and more citizens are outraged. But even those persons who deplore such acts are often involved in keeping the minority groups "in their place" in much more subtle ways.

The Conforming Discriminator

This type of person discriminates against minority group members not because of prejudice or malice but because it is easiest to go along with the wishes of powerful others. Such persons feel constrained to discriminate because they need the approval of their family, friends, and work associates. They may feel the constraints of powerful reference groups such as customers, neighbors, or

What single aspect of civilization has he contributed to present day culture?
—The Negro has no morals. He is not immoral but non-moral. Without the white man to control him the Negro reverts to savagery and practices torture, cruelty and witchcraft. The Negro is a natural cannibal and on his native doorpost may be found choice cuts of human flesh. In Africa the Negro even sells his dead relatives and will eat human flesh after it has become decomposed.
—As the black genes of the Negro are more powerful than white genes—the Negro has thereby destroyed every white civilization that he has come in contact with or has left that civilization stagnant and rotting and dependent upon the last drop of white blood from outside to keep it going.

Other statements in this article give "evidence" that the Negro is apelike in many ways. Allport, in *The Nature of Prejudice,* has argued that this is untrue.

Anthropologists have found nothing conclusive to support the view that the white race is more "evolved" than any other. If cranial capacity were any indicator of "brain power" (which it is not) several groups on the average would exceed the white man, among them the Japanese, the Polynesians, and even the Neanderthal man. Although at first glance the facial features of the Negro and the ape may seem similar, actually the thin lips and plentiful body hair of the white are much closer to the ape than the corresponding features of Negroes. And underneath their fur most monkeys have white skin; even the great apes have a skin color lighter than the Negro, more resembling the white.

187

organizations to which they belong or would like to belong. For any of a variety of reasons, then, this type continues to discriminate even though there is no ideological or psychological basis for doing so. This type also participates in the discriminatory acts of derogation, denial, and violence.

PANEL 6–4

DISCRIMINATION IN GROSSE POINTE

Source: Benjamin R. Epstein and Arnold Forster, *"Some of My Best Friends . . ."* (New York: Farrar, Straus and Cudahy, 1962), pp. 111–112.

A letter mailed to the Attorney General of Michigan by Dr. Jean Braxton Rosenbaum of Detroit gives the details of a person who was denied the right to buy property in Grosse Pointe because of the point system employed by the homeowners of that area. The letter said:

My dealings were with Mrs. Irene Bledsoe and Mr. DeSantis of Johnstone & Johnstone, Grosse Pointe. When I asked to make a bid on a house, I was told by Mr. DeSantis that I must await being passed by the Grosse Pointe Property Owners Association. This took several weeks. I was told then by Mrs. Bledsoe that I could not buy or even look at a house in Grosse Pointe because I was Jewish and could not qualify. I will not belabor the point with needless detail, but I think some details of personal biography might be of interest in the light of my being disqualified.

First of all, I am half Jewish and my wife is not Jewish at all. I was told by Mr. DeSantis, incidentally, that she qualified and could move to Grosse Pointe. I forgot to ask them about my two-year-old son. We are all native-born citizens, light complexioned and without accent. My wife is a scholarship alumna of Cranbrook Academy. The half lineage which is not Jewish in myself is from my mother. She is a Braxton. She's a direct descendant of Carter Braxton who signed the Declaration of Independence. I was raised in Detroit and am a *cum laude* graduate of Wayne University. I am the inventor of the artificial electrical heart and have contributed this invention without recompense to the community. I am a member of Sigma Xi, the national honorary society. I am the author of many scientific articles in *Medicine* and am honored to be the recipient of four national medical awards. I am an Instructor at Wayne State University College of Medicine for which I accept no salary. . . . I hope my personal experience can be of some use to you. . . . I could go on but I think my point is clear. . . .

Derogation by the conforming discriminator (Type 4 from Figure 6–1) generally takes the form of telling jokes (or being amused by them) that "put down" a minority group and keep the negative stereotype alive. Jokes about Poles focus on their presumed qualities of strength, lack of sophistication, stupidity, and upper-lower-class tastes. Jokes about Jews often focus on their presumed clannishness and stinginess. The "pushy" Jewish mother is also a stereotype found in many jokes. Blacks are usually depicted as sexually promiscuous or lacking in proper grammar and other evidence of good taste.*

Another form of derogation is the use of common sayings that reinforce negative stereotypes of minority groups. A few examples will suffice: "I've been gypped," "Don't be an Indian-giver," "That's white of you," "Act like a white man," "Jew him down," "There's been a nigger in the woodpile," and "Two against one is nigger's fun." These sayings are sometimes used because one hates the specific minority group mentioned. Or, as is more common, persons learn and use them habitually without being aware of their consequences. They might also be said because the speaker wishes to cater to the presumed prejudices of his listeners.

Closely related to these sayings are the epithets persons use to refer directly to specific minorities: wop, spic, kike, greaser, nigger, chink, mackerel snapper, broad, queer, are but a few such epithets commonly used. They are utilized for the same reasons given above for the derogatory sayings.

The conforming discriminator also participates in subtle ways to *deny* minority group members equality (Type 5). Denial, as we have seen, can be a conscious act by the bigot. It may also be a conscious act by a non-bigot. The conforming discriminator may refuse to employ a qualified Chicano or refuse to sell a home to a Jewish family who can afford the price, or, if a coach, to refuse to start an all black team even if they are his best players. His discriminatory act results from external pressures—customers, neighbors, school constituency, and others who he feels may reject him if he did not discriminate. Resort owners, for example, may not personally harbor ill-feeling toward certain minority groups, but

---

* By studying the humor of a society, one can receive a great many insights into the life of that society. American humor, for example, is disproportionately attuned to minority groups, sexual inadequacy or promiscuity, and violence. William Bruce Cameron in an insightful and delightful essay entitled "The Sociology of Humor and Vice Versa," has said, "If you know what people joke about, you can guess what worries them."[17]

they may fear that their clientele do, and that their business might decrease in size or shift appreciably in composition. Rather than take such a chance they may discriminate. S. L. Wax demonstrated the denial that occurs in Canadian resorts in an interesting experiment (one that could be duplicated in the United States, not only with resorts but also with apartment rentals or real estate purchases). Wax wrote to 100 different resorts that advertised in two Toronto newspapers. To each of these hotels and resorts he wrote two almost identical letters. In each he asked for room reservations for exactly the same date. They were mailed at the same time. One letter was signed "Mr. Lockwood" and the other with "Mr. Greenberg." The results were as predicted. "Mr. Lockwood" received replies from 95 percent and 93 percent offered him accommodations. "Mr. Greenberg," however, received replies from only 52 percent and accommodations from 36 percent.[18]

Type 6 in the Discrimination Paradigm refers to the conforming discriminator who participates directly or indirectly in violence aimed at minority groups. At first glance, this combination does not seem possible, for surely only those who harbor deep seated resentments and hatreds do violence to minority groups. Consider, however, the jury members unwilling to convict the white slayer of blacks even though the evidence supports such a stand. There are also persons who, because of community pressures, fail to bring forth evidence that would lead to the conviction of the white. Such acts as these condone violence because they allow it to go unpunished. Research shows that many participants in race riots and lynchings did not harbor ill will toward the victims but were swept up in the emotions of the collective episode.

Apathetic citizens unwilling to take a stand or to vote for measures that would alleviate the poverty, inadequate medical services, and starvation of minority groups are partly responsible for their plight. The institutional discrimination (examined below) could be eliminated if changes in the structure were made. Those who favor the status quo, or who do not want to move decisively in solving social problems, are also guilty of contributing to the institutional violence that is directed against minority group members.

Institutional Discrimination

We have noted that some individuals and groups discriminate whether they are bigots or not. These individuals and groups operate within a social milieu that is also discriminatory. The social milieu includes laws, customs, religious beliefs, social stratification, the distribution of power, and the stable arrangements and practices through which things get done in society. These social arrangements and accepted ways of doing things may consciously or unconsciously disadvantage some social categories while benefitting others. The major sectors of society are all possible discriminators —e.g., the system of law and the administration of justice, the economic system, the formal educational structure, and health care. Thus, the term *institutional discrimination* is a useful one. As Knowles and Prewitt have said, the institutions of society

> . . . have great power to reward and penalize. They reward by providing career opportunities for some people and foreclosing them for others. They reward as well by the way social goods and services are distributed—by deciding who receives training and skills, medical care, formal education, political influence, moral support and self-respect, productive employment, fair treatment by the law, decent housing, self-confidence, and the promise of a secure future for self and children.[19]

The analyst of society, pursuing the phenomenon of discrimination needs to ask himself—how are things normally done in the society? Who gets preferential treatment under these normal arrangements? Who is automatically excluded because of these arrangements? The answers to these questions are not always easy because the arrangements are "natural" and the discrimination often unintentional or disguised. The task is especially difficult because the exact placement of responsibility is often impossible to pinpoint. Who is responsible for the low scores of ghetto children on standard IQ tests? Who is responsible for residential segregation? Who is responsible for the high unemployment rate of minority group members?

Let us examine some illustrations of how various aspects of the society work to put minority groups "down" (derogation), deny them equality, and even do them violence.

Institutional derogation (Type 7) occurs when minority groups and their members are made to seem inferior or possess negative stereotypes through legitimate means by the powerful in society. The way minority group members are portrayed in the media (movies, television, newspapers and magazines) are often derogating. Only recently has there been an effort to thwart the negative images of minorities in the media. The "Amos and Andy" radio program that was popular in the 40s and 50s used almost all the black stereotypes—and America laughed. The early Shirley Temple movies had an adult black by the name of Stepin Fetchit whose role was to be more childlike than Miss Temple. The traditional roles in movies, novels, and television by blacks, Indians, and women have typically focused on the negative stereotypes of these minority groups. Even advertising plays on this theme as evidenced by the Frito-Lay Company's use of Frito Bandito, a smiling, happy-go-

PANEL 6–5

"THE ENGLISH LANGUAGE IS MY ENEMY"

Source: Ossie Davis, "The English Language is My Enemy," *IRCD Bulletin* 5 (Summer, 1969), p. 13. (The following are Davis' words directly quoted.)

I stand before you, a little nervous, afflicted to some degree with stage fright. Not because I fear you, but because I fear the subject.

The title of my address is, "Racism in American Life—Broad Perspectives of the Problem," or, "The English Language is My Enemy."

In my speech I will define culture as the sum total of ways of living built up by a group of human beings and transmitted by one generation to another. I will define education as the act or process of imparting and communicating a culture, developing the powers of reasoning and judgment and generally preparing oneself and others intellectually for a mature life.

I will define communication as the primary means by which the process of education is carried out.

I will say that language is the primary medium of communication in the educational process and, in this case, the English language. I will indict the English language as one of the prime carriers of racism from one person to another in our society and discuss how the teacher and the student, especially the Negro student, are affected by this fact.

The English language is my enemy.

Racism is a belief that human races have distinctive characteristics, usually involving the idea that one's own race is superior and has a right to rule others. Racism.

The English language is my enemy.

But that was not my original topic—I said that English was my goddamn enemy. Now why do I use "goddamn" to illustrate this aspect of the English language? Because I want to illustrate the sheer gut power of words. Words which control our action. Words like "nigger," "kike," "sheeny," "Dago," "black power"—words like this. Words we don't use in ordinary decent conversation, one to the other. I choose these words deliberately, not to flaunt my freedom before you. If you are a normal human being these words will have assaulted your senses, may even have done you physical harm, and if you so choose, you could have me arrested.

lucky, dishonest character who speaks with a Mexican-American accent and wears a very large sombrero.*

A much more subtle instance of derogation within the way society

* A Chicano organization, Involvement of the Mexican American in Gainful Endeavor (IMAGE), has vigorously protested this gimmick and after four years won their battle to curb this slur on their heritage.[20]

Those words are attacks upon your physical and emotional well being; your pulse rate is possibly higher, your breath quicker; there is perhaps a tremor along the nerves of your arms and your legs; sweat begins in the palms of your hands, perhaps. With these few words I have assaulted you. I have damaged you, and there is nothing you can possibly do to control your reactions—to defend yourself against the brute force of these words.

These words have a power over us; a power that we cannot resist. For a moment you and I have had our deepest physical reactions controlled, not by our own wills, but by words in the English language.

A superficial examination of Roget's *Thesaurus of the English Language* reveals the following facts: The word "whiteness" has 134 synonyms, 44 of which are favorable and pleasing to contemplate. For example: "purity," "cleanness," "immaculateness," "bright," "shiny," "ivory," "fair," "blonde," "stainless," "clean," "clear," "chaste," "unblemished," "unsullied," "innocent," "honorable," "upright," "just," "straightforward," "genuine," "trustworthy,"—and only 10 synonyms of which I feel to have been negative and then only in the mildest sense, such as "gloss-over," "whitewash," "gray," "wan," "pale," "ashen," etc.

The word "blackness" has 120 synonyms, 60 of which are distinctly unfavorable, and none of them even mildly positive. Among the offending 60 were such words as "blot," "blotch," "smut," "smudge," "sullied," "begrime," "soot," "becloud," "obscure," "dingy," "murky," "low-toned," "threatening," "frowning," "foreboding," "forbidding," "sinister," "baneful," "dismal," "thundery," "wicked," "malignant," "deadly," "unclean," "dirty," "unwashed," "foul," etc. In addition, and this is what really hurts, 20 of those words—and I exclude the villainous 60 above—are related directly to race, such as "Negro," "Negress," "nigger," "darkey," "blackamoor," etc.

If you consider the fact that thinking itself is subvocal speech (in other words, one must use words in order to think at all), you will appreciate the enormous trap of racial prejudgment that works on any child who is born into the English language.

Any creature, good or bad, white or black, Jew or Gentile, who uses the English language for the purposes of communication is willing to force the Negro child into 60 ways to despise himself, and the white child, 60 ways to aid and abet him in the crime.

works is in the English language itself. Panel 6–5 reprints a portion of a speech by a distinguished black actor, dramatic artist, and writer, who shows how invidious the English language can be.

A second example of this subtle type of derogation is necessary if we are to be more attuned to the various ways we all participate in putting down minority groups. Panel 6–6 gives the editorial policy of an underground newspaper. It decries the male chauvinism so often found in all forms of publishing.

The system (customs, practices, expectations, laws, beliefs) also works to deny equality to minority group members (Type 8). Ironically, this most often occurs without malicious intent. Because it is the system that disadvantages, discrimination would continue even if tomorrow every American were to awake with all animosities toward minority groups erased from his "heart and mind." All that is needed for minorities to suffer is that the law continue to favor the owners of property over renters and debtors. All that is needed for job opportunities to remain unequal is for employers to hire those with the most conventional training and experience, and to use machines where they seem more immediately economical than manual labor. All that is needed to insure that poor children get an inferior education is to continue "tracking," using class-biased tests, making education irrelevant in their work, rewarding children that conform to the teachers' middle class concepts of the "good student," and disproportionately paying less for their education (buildings, supplies, teachers, counselors).[21] In other words, all that is needed to perpetuate discrimination in the United States is a philosophy of "business as usual."

Skolnick has put it this way with respect to blacks, but the same could be said for the treatment of other minority groups as well:

> . . . it is theoretically possible to have a racist society in which most of the individual members of that society do not express racist attitudes. A society in which most of the good jobs are held by one race, and the dirty jobs by the people of another color, is a society in which racism is institutionalized, no matter what the beliefs of its members are. For example, the universities of America are probably the least bigoted of American institutions. One would rarely, if ever, hear an openly bigoted expression at schools like Harvard, Yale, the University of Chicago, the University of California. At the same time, university faculties and students have usually been white, the custodians black. The universities have concerned themselves primarily with the needs and interests of the white upper middle and upper classes, and have viewed the lower classes, and especially blacks, as objects of study rather than of service. In this sense, they have, willy-nilly, been institutionally "white racist."[22]

PANEL 6–6

NO "CHICKS," "BROADS," OR "NIGGERS" FOR THIS PAPER

Source: Reprinted in part from the *Nickel Review,* Syracuse, New York (April 13, 1970), p. 3; quoting an editorial statement from an underground newspaper in the Boston area, The *Old Mole.*

The *Old Mole* announces that it will no longer accept manuscripts or letters that use language such as emasculation, castration, balls to mean courage, letters addressed "Dear Sir" or "Gentlemen" or other examples of male supremacist language.

Use of this language reflects values and patterns of thought that are oppressive to half the people in the world and harmful to all. To use the word balls to mean courage implies that (1) balls have something to do with courage and that (2) women, because they don't have balls, don't have courage. Similarly, the words castration and emasculation imply acceptance of the myth that man is superior to woman because of his strength that having a penis gives him.

These words reflect a power structure (men having power over women) that we want to change. One way we can work to change this is to challenge the use, conscious or unconscious, of words and phrases that go along with this power structure. In other words, we will not print letters that call women "broads" just as we would not print letters that call blacks "niggers". . . .

People have asked us to explain our policy of rejecting advertising which exploits women. These are ads everyone is familiar with: a movie ad illustrated with a picture of a girl in a bathing suit; a car, cigarette or record ad which implies that women will sleep with a guy if he buys the product; a cosmetics or deodorant ad which tries to make women feel inadequate or ugly without the "right" look; a classified ad in which men advertise for "chicks." These are all ads which use women as sex objects and play on stereotypes. . . .

Most people, especially men, still view women as secondary, different, mysterious, weak, stupid, decorative, sex objects—something less than real people (men). Those attitudes go so deep that even if they are not as blatant as in advertising they are still present to some degree in all of us. If we have any influence, as a newspaper, with anyone, we want to use it to say: male chauvinism is so intolerable to us that we refuse to print it for money.

People take it for granted that women are used this way in advertising. We are saying it is no longer something that people should take for granted. The use of women in advertising is one of the hammers beating against women's minds to keep them down.

Approximately one percent of American lawyers are black, Puerto Rican, Chicano, or members of other recognized minority groups. Six-tenths of one percent of American medical doctors are black. Racial minority groups are under-represented in the professions because they receive a "disadvantaged" education for the reasons given above. Individuals of the racial minorities have difficulty making it in grade school and high school. Educational deficiencies and lack of finances for most minority groups make colleges and graduate schools the almost exclusive havens of the majority group. Because the system discriminates, certain categories are victims. There is a "self-fulfilling prophecy" to all of this. Because such a small percentage of minority group members go on to college and graduate school, the school boards and legislatures justify not spending more for their education. This brings about the conditions that the dominant group consider proof of the minority's inferiority. As the great British playwright George Bernard Shaw is reported to have said—"The haughty American nation . . . makes the Negro clean its boots, and then proves the . . . inferiority of the Negro by the fact that he is a bootblack."

Women comprise one-third of the work force but only seven percent of the doctors, three percent of lawyers and one percent of the engineers. Women are under-represented in the professions for reasons different from those of most other minority groups. Women are expected to eschew careers in favor of raising families and making their husbands happy. Those in powerful positions (hiring, admission to graduate school) probably, all things being equal, accept males rather than females because females are not considered as "dependable" since they may interrupt their work to get married and become pregnant.

Women are denied equality in the job market because of blatant discrimination, but also from subtle attitudes that most persons acquire in the socialization process. For example, there is considerable evidence to suggest that even females believe women are inferior to men.[23]

The last type of discrimination (Type 9) is violence perpetrated on minorities by the way the system works. This type has occurred throughout American history, as we have noted before in the policy of exterminating the Indian, the relocation of Japanese during World War II, and of course, slavery. The law itself has helped to do violence to minority groups. One study of a lynching of a black man (in a Texas community of about 15,000 in the early 1930's) noted, for example, that in that community the customary penalty if a black man raped a black woman was a fine of $12.50. If, however, a black raped a white woman the penalty was death.[24] The administration of justice has also done harm to minority group members. Because they tend to be poor, they cannot afford bail, good attorneys, and other advantages the more well-to-do use to influence the judicial system. As an example, of the 3,859 persons executed from 1930 to 1971 in the United States, fully 53 percent have been black.[25]

The system also injures when reforms that would adequately house, clothe, feed, and provide medical attention are not instituted. A description by Carmichael and Hamilton (cited in Chapter 1) shows how this phenomenon does violence to minority members:

> When white terrorists bomb a black church and kill five black children, that is an act of individual racism, widely deplored by most segments of the society. But when in that same city—Birmingham, Alabama—five hundred black babies die each year because of the lack of proper food, shelter and medical facilities, and thousands more are destroyed and maimed physically, emotionally, and intellectually because of conditions of poverty and discrimination in the black community, that is a function of institutional racism.[26]

There is only about one doctor per 15,000 persons in the black ghettos of the large cities. This is reflected in the health statistics of blacks: the higher rates of infant and maternal deaths, and twice the national average in deaths from the diseases of poverty—pneumonia, tuberculosis, and influenza.[27] These blatant examples of institutional violence could be enumerated for any of the minority groups whose numbers are disproportionately poor.

All of this is not to say that minority group members are always unsuccessful in American society. Many have become wealthy and famous, particularly in the sports or entertainment fields, but also in education, science, business and politics. The solitary minority member, through unusual achievement, has been able to make it in the WASP world of middle class America. The point is, however, that these individuals made it as individuals *despite* the roadblocks provided by the system. Ironically, the system ("the American way") takes credit for these individuals' success. The even greater irony is that when individuals fail, they are blamed rather than the system—another example of blaming the victim.

THE BLACK REVOLUTION

American society has periodically experienced uprisings by minority groups who struck back at the source of their frustration. Currently the blacks present a widespread movement bent upon significant social, economic, and political changes in the social system (hence, the term "revolution" is appropriate). The focus here will be on the black revolution since: 1) it has a profound impact upon American life; (2) it is an excellent case study of a social movement (i.e., the collective attempt to bring about change in the social system); and (3) an understanding of it will also aid in understanding the rise of similar movements among the Chicanos, Indians, young Japanese, and other oppressed groups in the United States.

The tasks of this section are twofold: first, to explain the changes in goals and means within the movement, and second, to explain why the black revolution is occurring at this point in history.[28]

Chronology of Events Leading to Black Revolution

Throughout their history in the United States, blacks have engaged in militant action against oppression. There have been slave revolts, individual and group violence, and urban riots, all of which were protests against the inferior status to which blacks had been relegated.

Until the early 1960's the dominant thrust of black protest was aimed at attaining full social, economic, and political equality. The goal was the elimination of discrimination and full and equal inclusion in all aspects of American life. The key organization during this time was the National Association for the Advancement of Colored People. The primary technique employed by the NAACP was court actions. Court cases achieved legal equality by outlawing segregation in public schools, public accommodations, and in some forms of employment. One of the most significant events in the civil rights struggle occurred in Montgomery, Alabama, in 1955. Mrs. Rosa Parks, a black seamstress, refused to give her bus seat to a white man. This refusal started the year-long Montgomery bus boycott which culminated in an important victory for the blacks over discrimination. This boycott also brought a young (age 27) black minister to the forefront of the struggle—Martin Luther King, Jr. Under King's leadership the Southern Christian Leadership Conference was formed, and non-violent protest became the primary means of trying to get the white establishment to change its oppressive policies.

The activist strategy that was successful in Montgomery became more widely employed. Beginning in Greensboro, North Carolina, in 1960, young black students used the nonviolent protest tactic of "sit-ins," "kneel-ins," and "wade-ins" at segregated places to publicize the fact of discrimination and to upset the traditional patterns of race "etiquette." As these acts spread throughout the South, violent resistance—threats, physical harassment, beatings, and even murders—increased substantially. These acts by members of the majority were largely ignored by law enforcement officials, federal government agents (who claimed it was the state's responsibility), and the courts.

To this point the protest had occurred largely in the South. But the hostility of the northern ghettos surfaced in the Harlem riot of 1964 and the Watts riot of 1965. By this time many of the black activists were disillusioned with the nonviolent tactics of Martin Luther King, Jr. The Student Nonviolent Coordinating Committee (SNCC) renounced nonviolence under the leadership of Stokely Carmichael. His slogan of "Black Power" became a rallying cry for many suffering blacks, particularly the young, as it came to symbolize the shift that had occurred within the black movement. Whereas black activists were more or less unified in seeking integration and assimilation into the system, there was now the cry by many for cultural autonomy and a positive black consciousness. Additionally, (and these two points encompass what is really meant by "Black Power") there was a demand for meaningful participation at all governmental levels (national, state, and local), and for economic independence. "Black Power"—the new goal of blacks—is just that, power for black people, something they lack because of their status as a minority group. The goal of "Black Power" is at once moderate (not a cry for violence, and certainly within the intent of the Constitution), and yet revolutionary (seeking dramatic changes in American institutions). Carmichael and Hamilton have defined the goal of "Black Power" this way:

> . . . when black people have a majority, they will attempt to use power to exercise control. This is what they seek: control. When black people lack a majority, Black Power means proper representation and sharing of control. It means the creation of power bases, of strength, from which black people can press to change local or nationwide patterns of oppression—instead of from weakness.[29]

In addition to the goals of power and cultural autonomy, contemporary black militancy has stressed self-defense. By the mid 1960's the technique of passive resistance (non-violence) was considered by many to be a failure. White terrorists abused the black activists with very little interference from local or federal officials. It became clear to the activists that they must arm themselves against terrorist acts and even against police brutality. Defense groups formed in many black communities to protect blacks in the absence of police protection against white vigilantes. The Muslim leader Malcolm X, put it this way:

> . . . I'm for justice. I feel that if white people were attacked by Negroes—if the forces of law prove unable, or inadequate or re-luctant to protect those whites from those Negroes—then those white people should protect and defend themselves from those Negroes, using arms if necessary. And I feel that when the law fails to protect Negroes from whites' attack, then those Negroes should use arms, if necessary, to defend themselves.
>
> "Malcolm X Advocates Armed Negroes!"
>
> What was wrong with that? I'll tell you what was wrong. I was a black man talking about physical defense against the white man. The white man can lynch and burn and bomb and beat Negroes—that's all right! "Have patience" . . . "The customs are en-trenched" . . . "Things are getting better."
>
> Well, I believe it's a crime for anyone who is being brutalized to continue to accept that brutality without doing something to defend himself.[80]

It was the increasing acceptance of this stance, especially among the young, that spawned a number of more militant groups of blacks. Among the most prominent of these is the Black Panther Party, which began as a self-defense organization in 1966 in Oak-land, California. The use of the black panther symbolized self-defense: "The Panther never attacks first, but when he is backed into a corner, he will strike back viciously."[31] The black movement, as symbolized in the growth of the Black Panther and the decline of the NAACP, shifted from passive resistance (accepting the insults and physical abuse) to armed defense. They said, in effect, "all the violence of the past has been asymmetrical—it will at least be equal in the future."

In summary, from early 1960 to the latter part of that decade the black revolution shifted from an emphasis on civil rights to one of liberation. The early period was characterized by an order model perspective. The primary goal was integration into the mainstream of the dominant society. The problem was perceived as basically a southern phenomenon at the local level rather than societal-wide racism. Since the federal government and the courts were viewed basically as allies by blacks, change and progress against discrimi-natory laws and practices were to be mediated through them. Also nonviolent tactics were used in the hope that they would bring the moral force of the system upon the local racists.

The activists of the late 1960's, on the other hand, perceived society in conflict terms, and the arena was not limited to the South. They saw majority-minority relations as essentially an imbalance in power. The goal became the acquisition of power. This could be accomplished, they felt, through all manner of protest, including violence. Implicit in this view of society was the belief that the institutions of society—not just the local individual racists—were the real sources of structured inequality in the United States. This belief became widespread with the realization that democratic features such as the jury system, the Constitutional guarantees of States' rights, and the courts themselves actually worked in many instances to maintain racism rather than prosecuting and punishing it. Skolnick summed it up this way:

> The major American institutions had developed standards, procedures, and rigidities which served to inhibit the Negro's drive for equality. It was as if a cruel joke had been played; the most liberally enshrined features of democracy served to block the aspirations of equality—local rule, trade unionism, referendums, the jury system, the neighborhood school.[32]

The realization that the institutions were to blame for the maintenance and perpetuation of racism meant for many blacks that drastic change—a revolution—was the only cure. This could only result if the balance of power was shifted—thus, the cry for "Black Power."

Reasons for the Black Revolution Occurring Now

The compelling question is: why the shift from a "civil rights" perspective to a "liberation" perspective in such a short time? The answer, without the historian's "long look back" will be incomplete, since the forces are complex and interrelated. Moreover, some factors are not known presently. But to answer this question, even partially, is important, and it will help to answer the larger question: why is the black revolution occurring now? The remainder of this chapter will examine the historical, structural, and social-psychological bases for the social unrest among blacks now (and for many other minority groups as well). Some of these bases have always affected the way blacks have felt, but with the other variables they combine to explain much of the current unrest.

1. *The impact of historical events and forces on the contemporary black revolution.* Two facts of American history provide fuel for the black revolution: (1) the United States has always been racist; and

201

(2) oppressed minorities have invariably used protest and violence to achieve greater power (as majorities have used violence to suppress such efforts). Since this latter point was discussed at length in Chapter 1, we will not be redundant here except to say that the powerful do not willingly give any of their power to the relatively powerless. The first point is well known, especially with respect to the whites' treatment of blacks during and after slavery. But racist conceptions provided for many years the rationale for United States immigration laws, the impetus for the internment of the Japanese during World War II, and the justification for the mistreatment of the American Indians. Malcolm X has argued forcefully the blatant racism of Americans toward Indians in the following passage:

> Our Nation was born in genocide when it embraced the doctrine that the original American, the Indian, was an inferior race. Even before there were large numbers of Negroes on our shores, the scar of racial hatred had already disfigured colonial society. . . . even today we have not permitted ourselves to reject or to feel remorse for this shameful episode. Our literature, our films, our drama, our folklore all exalt it. Our children are still taught to respect the violence which reduced a red-skinned people of an earlier culture into a few fragmented groups herded into impoverished reservations.[33]

Another historical force that impinged upon blacks in the United States was the anti-colonial movement throughout the world during the 1950's and 1960's. This movement overthrew the white domination of nonwhites in much of the world. It served several functions to American blacks. First, it provided the recognition that racial oppression is a world-wide phenomenon. Second, the anti-colonial movement demonstrated that movements of liberation can be victorious against overwhelming odds. This success, especially the success of the African countries, served as a model for American blacks. It served as a model because the blacks began to think of themselves as constituting a colonized people. Eldridge Cleaver made this the basic definition for the Black Panther Party:

> We start with the basic definition: that black people in America are a colonized people in every sense of the term and that white America is an organized Imperialist force holding black people in colonial bondage.[34]

The liberated African countries also served as a model to the American blacks because they were whole societies, manned politically from top to bottom by blacks. The success of the African nations served to bring about a resurgence of pride in American blacks for their African heritage and culture. Instead of trying to resemble the white man, blacks took pride in their race and its African roots. This is evidenced in the shifts in behavior among young blacks in the last half of the 1960's (hair styles, clothing, speech). It is also seen in the demands for black history and other black studies in the nation's high schools and universities.

Blacks examined the policies of the federal government and found that they represented misplaced priorities. They noticed the billions of dollars spent on the space program and foreign aid and an unwillingness to spend funds to alleviate domestic problems. The typical interpretation was that the government wanted to keep the blacks in a subordinate role and therefore was unwilling to spend the resources necessary to alter the status quo.

The war in Southeast Asia provided another basis for the unrest among blacks. Coupled with the lack of clear reasons for American involvement was the perceived unfairness of the draft system itself. Because only a small proportion of blacks attend college, where deferments were easily obtained, blacks comprised a disproportionate number of the draftees for the Southeast Asian conflict. Additionally, since blacks often do not possess the skills that would keep them off "the firing line," the names of blacks accounted for a disproportionate number of the "killed in action" and "wounded in action" lists. Black servicemen must have wondered about the equitability of such things, particularly in the light of the lack of freedom that blacks have in the United States. Why is the United States, Martin Luther King, Jr., asked, ". . . taking the black young men who had been crippled by our society and sending them 8,000 miles away to guarantee liberties in Southeast Asia which they had not found in Georgia or East Harlem."[35] Some black spokesmen also perceived the war in Southeast Asia as a racist war—a war of whites against nonwhites.

The late 1960's was an era of awareness and action for many Americans, especially college students. There was a general feeling by many, white and nonwhite, that American actions were inconsistent with the humanitarian and equalitarian aims of national ideals and that American institutions were intransigent to change. The civil rights movement of the early 1960's was in many ways instrumental in generating the increased student protest. It was during the early sit-ins and marches that the students began to feel the oppressiveness of the system and the slowness of change. Consequently, many became allies of all oppressed minorities.

Another important historical factor impinging on the black revolution was the increased role of the mass media. The documentaries, exposés, and news stories found in newspapers, newsmagazines, and especially television made virtually all persons vicarious participants in the important events occurring around the world. Only in recent times could Americans witness assassinations, police brutality, the extreme poverty in the ghetto, and discriminatory acts virtually every day. Those who witnessed the interviews and actions of the Montgomery, Alabama, Chief of Police, Bull Conner, during the early days of the Civil Rights movement were either incensed or proud of him, depending upon their attitudes. It was impossible to be neutral about him. The mass media clearly exerted a tremendous amount of influence in the area of civil rights.

Finally, the election of Richard Nixon as President in 1968 and again in 1972 has had a significant impact on the direction of the black revolution. He ran on a so-called "southern strategy" that opposed busing and racial quotas, thereby ignoring the political potential of blacks and appealing instead to potential Wallace supporters. This strategy assumed that he would not get many black votes. He could, however, get the white votes in many areas, especially the southern states, by proclaiming that if elected he would protect the sovereignty of the individual states. The implication was that the federal government would not push for integration or actively support black demands for full equality.

While in office, President Nixon did three things to frustrate further the cause of blacks. His appointments to the Supreme Court caused a significant shift toward conservatism on civil rights issues. Second, the Justice Department under his appointees moved with glacial slowness in the prosecution of civil rights violators. Finally, he endorsed cuts in (or refused to spend money appropriated for) government programs aimed at aiding minorities (welfare, housing, job training). These policies by the Nixon administration are interpreted by many blacks as either indifferent or hostile to the aspirations of minorities, with the result that some former moderates are moved toward a more militant stance.

2. *The structural bases for the black revolution.* "Structure" refers to a number of sociological phenomena. In particular it refers to social behavior and arrangements that are *patterned* (i.e., relatively stable, expected, and legitimate). Thus, structure refers on one level to cultural phenomena. At another level it refers to the distribution of persons (where they are concentrated by age, sex, region, and race). Structure also refers to the distribution of the populace

in terms of social class (what categories of people are typically the recipients of the advantages of society—wealth, prestige, and power —and what categories are systematically left out).

Perhaps the most crucial structural variable is the distribution of power in the society. Whether a group has power or not determines majority or minority status. To be powerful means obtaining a disproportionate share of the available resources. Blacks and other minority groups have little political power. It was reported in 1970 that the number of black office holders, although the largest number in American history—1,469—represented only three-tenths of 1 percent of the more than 500,000 elected officials in the country. This represented a dramatic increase for blacks, especially in the South where there were 564 office holders in 1970 and only 75 in 1965. Yet three southern states with more than two million blacks—Alabama, Arkansas, and South Carolina—had no black as a member of the state legislature in 1970. And in Mississippi, where more than 42 percent of the population was black, only one served in the legislature.[36] This lack of representation for black interests in legislatures, city councils, county welfare boards, and school boards must be particularly irritating to blacks living in a so-called democracy. But changes are occurring. The Civil Rights Acts of the 1960's, the increase in voter registrations among blacks, and the ever greater concentrations of blacks in urban areas (to be discussed in detail below) is making "Black Power" a real possibility. This possibility increases the efforts of blacks to gain positions of power.

Another structural variable related to black unrest is the ever increasing concentration of blacks in the ghettos of the major cities. Throughout much of American history blacks were dispersed in rural areas mostly in the South. In 1900 only 22.7 percent of blacks lived in urban areas. In contrast, by 1960 this percentage had increased to 73.2 percent, a greater percentage than for whites. Most important is that one-third of all blacks by 1970 were concentrated in fifteen cities. New York City had 1,666,636 blacks and Chicago had 1,102,620 according to the 1970 Census. Thirteen other cities have black populations in excess of 200,000. Most blacks are concentrated (virtually segregated) within these urban areas. Most live in overcrowded and substandard housing. Their children go to schools that are inadequately staffed and poorly equipped. The cities, because of the lack of resources or misplaced priorities, do not provide adequate services for these areas (sanitation, recreation facilities, police and fire protection). The unemployment rate is unusually high because many of these people are unskilled and unhealthy. All of these conditions, coupled with the hopes that many had when they moved to the city, have fostered a great deal of anger among these people.

But rage is only one result of this structural variable. The other is that blacks are now concentrated rather than dispersed. This has political consequences, since there is greater possibility of mobilization for action than ever before. Six cities had, according to the 1970 Census, black majorities—Washington, D.C., and Compton, California, with 71 percent each; East St. Louis with 69 percent; Newark with 54 percent; Gary with 53 percent; and Atlanta with 51 percent. With mobilization of blacks, these cities and others have elected black officials.

Another structural variable is the distribution of the population by age. The number of black persons in the 14 to 19 age bracket is increasing. In 1950, 9.9 percent of blacks were in this age category. This decreased slightly to 9.7 percent in 1960, but then increased rather sharply to 11.2 in 1965.[37] The increase in this age bracket is significant, because young people tend to be the most militant. They are the most unwilling to "go slow!" This increase in the proportion of young people is especially significant if they are concentrated in one area. The probability of unified militant action then becomes much greater.

The return of hundreds of thousands of black veterans from service in Southeast Asia also aids in explaining social unrest among blacks. Upon return to the United States, black servicemen find that being black continues to mean "inferior." Surely this must raise serious questions, for those who recently risked their lives for the system, about the legitimacy of that system. Their rage is compounded by the difficulty in finding jobs upon their return. Although many of these servicemen learned useful skills while in the service, many have found unemployment as civilians. In 1971, the unemployment rate for black veterans was twice as high as that for white veterans.

Despite serious problems that remain, blacks are improving their absolute economic, educational, and occupational levels. James Geschwender compared the data from the 1940 Census with those from 1960 and found that blacks were improving their level of education more rapidly than have whites.[38] Gwartney, however, has stated that the changes in relative education have actually worked against nonwhites since World War II. The jobs requiring the most education showed the greatest racial disparities in income; therefore, he concluded that as blacks become better educated their comparative situation tends to deteriorate.[39] In occupation, blacks

206

moved more rapidly than whites from 1940 to 1960 into middle status occupations but were moving more slowly into the higher status occupations. The gap between white and black *income,* however, continued to widen—even though blacks were improving their material conditions of life. Blacks, then, remained behind whites in all three status areas and in some the gap is widening. The result is bitterness, anger, and frustration. Thus, structural variables cause psychological conditions—in this case by relative deprivation, a concept we will explain shortly.

Related to these structural changes—i.e., increasing proportions of blacks in higher educational categories and occupational statuses —is the phenomenon of status inconsistency. We have noted that generally the achieved statuses of blacks have improved. But ascribed status—i.e., classification by race as "inferior"—has not changed. In 1940 most blacks were low in racial status and low in education, occupation, and income—thus, they were status consistents. All blacks with relatively high income, education, and occupation would automatically become status inconsistents—and this was the case in 1960 and the proportion continues to rise. Status inconsistency is frustrating to the individual because of conflicting expectations and relative deprivation. Research has shown that the type of status inconsistency that blacks experience—low ascribed status combined with higher achieved status—is precisely the pattern most strongly associated with political activism.[40]

Economic factors provide some structural bases for racial unrest. Interest rates, the flow of money, and unemployment directly or indirectly affect the mood of individuals. For blacks, unemployment is always a factor, since their rate is disproportionately high. When the rate increased as it did from 1968 to 1971, the blacks (whose unemployment rates are typically twice those of whites) were the most adversely affected.

Finally, American values themselves are a source of racial unrest. Blacks find it difficult to believe in the concepts that "all men are equal before the law," or "anyone can be successful if he works at it," since these obviously do not apply to them. But the tremendous emphasis placed on materialism in America has been captured by most blacks. It is especially irritating and frustrating to be bombarded with advertising that says they can only be somebody if they own certain items—when these items cannot be purchased for lack of resources.

3. *The social psychological bases for racial unrest.* Historical and structural variables occur outside the individual. These objective

conditions have an impact upon individuals, however, in that they may produce psychological states which, in turn, produce rage and rebellion. As James Baldwin, the black writer, has said, "To be a Negro in this country and to be relatively conscious is to be in a rage almost all of the time."[41] Blacks may vary in income, degree of acceptance by whites, education, or religion, but one thing they probably all share is a resentment toward the system that allows whites to be superordinate over them. There are several psychological phenomena that can produce unrest and rebellion—frustration-aggression, rising expectations combined with declining satisfactions, alienation, and relative deprivation.

There is a good deal of evidence to indicate that when goal-directed behavior is blocked, hostile impulses are generated within the individual, i.e., frustration leads to aggression. Since minority group members are continually blocked in their pursuit of goals appropriate to the values of society, (such as getting a good education, securing a prestigious job, and achieving a good income) hostility often results. Although this hostility can be directed inward, it is also vented against the majority in a number of ways (e.g., withholding deference, limiting output, sabotage, indiscriminate destruction of property, looting, beatings, defiant gestures, demonstrations, and boycotts).*

Rising expectations combined with declining satisfactions is also a source of rage. This variant of frustration-aggression theory has been proposed by James C. Davies. Revolution is most likely to occur when a prolonged period of rising expectations and rising gratifications is followed by a sharp reversal during which the gap between expectations and gratification widens and becomes intolerable. Davies' theory is based on the assumption that human needs are never fully gratified. No matter how much we attain, we always want more. Improvement of conditions generates in individuals the expectation that improvements will continue. If these expectations are frustrated for many people, group conflict is likely to occur. Davies has put it this way:

> This is an assertion about the state of mind of individual people in a society who are likely to revolt. It says their state of mind, their mood, is one of high tension and rather generalized hostility, derived from the widening of the gap between what they want and what they get. They fear not just that things will no longer continue to get better but—even more crucially—that ground will be lost that they have already gained. The mood of rather generalized

* Ironically, frustration-aggression is also one explanation for the prejudice that some persons feel against minority groups.[42]

hostility, directed generally outward, begins to turn toward government.[43]

This theory seems to fit the facts of the black revolution of the
1960's. Blacks made significant gains in the 1950's and early 1960's
with Supreme Court decisions, legislation, executive orders, and the
sit-ins. This progress raised black expectations. There was reason to
believe that equality was possible soon. But the level of white
violence rose with the black gains. This violence was both unofficial
(private acts of individuals) and official (police dogs and fire
hoses). Moreover the federal government changed to a very slow
pace in enforcing the law (e.g., the goal of school desegregation
which was demanded by the 1954 Supreme Court decision was not
even approached 15 years later). By 1968, as we have already
observed, the election of Richard Nixon must have been perceived
by blacks as a step backward.

The concept of "alienation" refers to a state of feeling separated
or estranged from something. The individual does not feel a meaningful part of the relationship. He may feel alienated from his work,
his fellow men, or his society. He may even feel alienated from
himself. Melvin Seeman has shown that the concept "alienation"
actually has five different meanings, four of which have relevance
to majority-minority relations.[44]

The first usage, *powerlessness*, refers to the individual's sense of
being unable to influence socio-political events (elections, international affairs, economic decisions). This condition is especially
relevant to minority group members, since they are, by definition,
without power. Research has shown that blacks, especially those
from lower socioeconomic levels, were significantly more prone to
feel controlled by outside forces than were whites of the same
economic levels.[45]

The second usage, *normlessness*, denotes a situation where individuals are not sure how to behave because the norms regulating
conduct have broken down. This release from past norms can be
disconcerting to individuals because they are not sure what is
expected. How were individual blacks, for example, to act after the
breakdown of the Jim Crow system in the South? Confusion and ambivalence were common in both blacks and whites, since the old
rules no longer applied, yet the new ones were unacceptable for
some and "unnatural" for almost everyone. This type of alienation
(more commonly known as *anomie*) can result in individuals be-
lieving that socially unapproved behaviors are required to achieve
unusual goals (i.e., liberation).

A third type of alienation refers to individuals who are estranged from their society and its culture. This type—called *isolation*—is felt by many blacks. They reject American values and institutions. As Carmichael and Hamilton have said:

> The values of this society support a racist system; we find it incongruous to ask black people to adopt and support most of those values. We also reject the assumption that the basic institutions of this society must be preserved. The goal of black people must *not* be to assimilate into middle-class America, for that class—as a whole—is without a viable conscience as regards humanity. The values of the middle class permit the perpetuation of the ravages of the black community. The values of that class are based on material aggrandizement, not the expansion of humanity. The values of that class ultimately support cloistered little closed societies tucked away neatly in tree-lined suburbia. The values of that class do *not* lead to the creation of an open society. That class *mouths* its preference for a free, competitive society, while at the same time forcefully and even viciously denying to black people as a group the opportunity to compete.[46]

A fourth type of alienation—*self-estrangement*—refers to the inability of the individual to find the activities he engages in as rewarding. This means, for example, a lack of pride in work. Many blacks experience this type of alienation because they are relegated to the menial, unrewarding tasks in society. How can one feel pride in being a janitor or a dishwasher or a hospital orderly when he knows that these jobs lack prestige and that, because of his race, he is excluded from obtaining more prestigious ones.

All four of these types of alienation are present in individual blacks. Some experience more than one type of estrangement. Some individuals, on the other hand, are so much a part of the larger society that they do not experience alienation. But alienation is a psychological condition (or four different but related types of conditions) that is common among minority group members. The task of the sociologist is to determine (1) the social conditions that produce each of these four variants of alienation; and (2) their behavioral consequences.

Another social psychological phenomenon, *relative deprivation,* refers to an individual's comparing himself to some other person or group to which he feels he should be equal and perceiving that he comes up short. Commonly, individuals compare themselves with others who have similar backgrounds to see if they are getting equal incomes, or receiving equal prestige. If a number of persons in a social category perceive other social categories rising more rapidly than they, or having other advantages, the former category will experience dissatisfaction, hostility, and perhaps rebellion. When blacks find themselves consistently "shortchanged" when compared to whites, they must feel enraged, although many whites feel that blacks should be content since they have made such an improvement over the extreme poverty of their parents. But the present generation of blacks do not compare themselves with the preceding generation but rather with their more favored contemporaries. Table 6–1 compares educational and income levels by race. It shows vividly the relative deprivation most blacks experience.

The data in Table 6–1 show that the two races vary in income by as much as $2,500 for *the same educational level.* This, in a society where all persons are supposed to have an equal chance for success if they will but try. The facts show that trying (as measured by educational attainment) does not pay off for blacks to the degree it does for whites who make an equal investment in education. Thus,

TABLE 6–1. Percent Distribution of Families by Income Level, by Years of School Completed and Color of Head: 1966

Color of Head and Family Income Level	Elementary School		High School		College	
	Less than 8 years	8 years	1 to 3	4 yrs.	1 to 3	4+
White Families:						
Under $3,000	33.1	19.9	11.9	7.2	6.1	4.3
3,000 to 4,999	21.7	18.6	14.6	10.6	7.5	5.2
5,000 to 6,999	18.4	21.1	20.6	18.9	14.9	9.2
7,000 to 9,999	16.5	22.2	27.4	29.9	28.3	20.6
10,000 to 14,999	7.5	14.2	20.1	24.9	28.6	31.9
15,000 and over	2.7	4.0	5.4	8.4	14.6	28.9
Median income	$4,477	$6,103	$7,267	$8,217	$9,252	$11,697
Nonwhite Families:						
Under $3,000	45.2	31.9	29.8	18.1	11.0	7.6
3,000 to 4,999	26.1	26.0	27.4	21.7	16.2	5.5
5,000 to 6,999	14.4	15.8	16.8	21.3	22.5	13.6
7,000 to 9,999	9.6	18.3	15.9	21.2	27.5	28.5
10,000 to 14,999	3.9	6.9	7.6	14.4	21.1	29.4
15,000 and over	.9	1.0	2.6	3.4	1.8	15.3
Median income	$3,349	$4,399	$4,418	$5,886	$7,043	$9,510

Source: Dept. of Commerce, Bureau of the Census; *Current Population Reports,* Series P-60, No. 53; see also *Statistical Abstract of the United States: 1968,* p. 327.

211

objective conditions—the unequal way in which the system treats minority group members—produces feelings of relative deprivation, which in turn may yield rebellion.

Conclusion

What is perhaps most striking about the present black situation in the United States is not how angry and rebellious the blacks have become, but how reasonable they remain. The conditions of American society continue to be adverse toward blacks. The situation for blacks is better now than it was in 1800, 1900, or 1950, but as a group they are still relatively powerless and the objects of discrimination.

Will the majority of blacks continue to work within the system? If there is a dramatic shift toward greater revolutionary activity, blacks will meet resistance from many sectors of white society. The system itself may become even more repressive. These possibilities cause problems for black leaders. How fast should they proceed? Should the immediate demands be limited in scope or all-encompassing? Is the goal integration into white society or separation? What means should be used to achieve the goals? Some favor violence, others confrontation to dramatize the inequities of the present system. The more conservative leaders favor the slower route of exploiting traditional avenues to achieve power and equality (court action, passage of laws in Congress, election of blacks to positions of power). In the past ten or fifteen years most blacks were willing to proceed with some caution, but recently the pace seems to have quickened and moved in the direction of increasing confrontation.

Important historical, structural, and social-psychological forces seem to converge at this point in history, leading to the prediction that the black power movement will be successful within the next generation. Blacks have already been largely transformed psychologically into a group that is proud of being black. This is especially true for the young. As they grow older and replace the "old guard," blacks will uniformly be proud of their race. This will lead to an even greater cohesiveness among blacks.

Secondly, blacks are becoming an ever greater political force. Blacks form majorities in several major American cities. This number will increase. In cities where blacks remain a minority, they are gaining increased representation through the control of wards and districts. Blacks are only beginning to tap other political resources on the local level (e.g., school boards, welfare boards, and planning commissions). It is inevitable that blacks will organize—and organization means power.

Black economic power is also a distinct possibility, as those blacks who are successful are showing pride in the race by investing with the black community. This process presents a positive (as opposed to a "vicious") circle since it increases the economic opportunities of other blacks.

If the black power movement is successful—producing economic success, political power, and racial pride—then blacks will achieve some semblance of equality, and the institutions will become more equalitarian (ghetto schools, for example, with black leadership will be relevant for blacks, helping them to break out of their subordinate, colonial pattern). A reasonable guess would be that blacks will shift once again back to integration within the system. The basis for this prediction is that although much of the rhetoric is now militant and separatist, most blacks still have integration as their ultimate goal. A 1969 nationwide poll of blacks found 69 percent rejected the notion that blacks should have a separate nation in the United States.[47] Integration of blacks as equal partners in American society remains the dream of most blacks. However, broad societal changes must be made if this dream is to become a reality. The goal of the black revolution is to effect these changes.

SUMMARY FOR PART II

Part II of this book has been devoted to the analysis of social inequality. The thrust has been that much of American life is asymmetrical. Resources, prestige, and power are not randomly distributed, but tend to be concentrated in certain persons, families, and groups. Those persons with privileges tend to pass these benefits on to their offspring, perpetuating the inequality and leading to some ossification of the system. Moreover, those favored in the society tend to be unwilling to give up their beneficial position. This intransigence of the powerful leads to a good deal of disatisfaction among the not so well off. Let us review the recurring themes found in this section.

First, inequality appears to be a fact of social life. Man is a valuing creature, and apparently unavoidably ranks others in terms of society's (and his own) values. This ranking of individuals and groups takes place in a number of interrelated dimensions, but the three most crucial are property, prestige, and power. The system of ranking is patterned—that is, structured so that action is predictable, expectations are known, and one's placement in the structure is understood. Structured social inequality is therefore part of the social order. It governs much of human behavior—and consequently explains much of human behavior.

A second major theme of this section is the relationship of the system of social stratification to the distribution of national power. The wealthy have extraordinary power in American society. The members of the political elite come disproportionately from the upper social classes. The decision-making process, consequently, is heavily biased in favor of the interests of the wealthy. They determine the rightness of defense spending, economic expansion and the protection of American economic interests at home and abroad —interests which almost all Americans have come to feel are their interests as well. Moreover, legislation is passed that gives disproportionate privilege and advantage to the wealthy. As John Walton has expressed it,[48]

> The "pillars of society" who comprise less than 1 percent of the country own more than 70 percent of productive property, yet pay only 14 percent of federal taxes. Through a variety of legal devices such as depletion allowances, tax free bonds, capital gains tax, inheritance trust funds, tax exempt corporations, reinvested untaxable income, stock options, and expense accounts, the United States government grossly favors and subsidizes corporate wealth at

the expense of the wage earner: as incomes increase, so do legal tax exemptions—up to 100 percent.*

A third recurring theme in this section is the mistreatment of minority group members (including the poor). They tend to be ill-housed, ill-clothed, and ill-fed in a society that claims to be humanitarian and has the resources to alleviate these ills but does not.

Minority group members respond to being discriminated against by either acceptance of the adverse conditions, avoidance, or aggression. The net result of these responses is that the minority group members end up being blamed for their "inappropriate" behaviors. This "blaming of the victim" is prevalent in much of the conventional wisdom. But the victims are not to blame—they are symptoms of a "disease." The term "disease" is meant to refer to the unfairness of the institutions of society ("institutional discrimination")—a major theme of this section. It is the structure and not the individual that is basically at fault. The law is a source of injustice for the poor, blacks, and other minority group members. The maldistribution of wealth is integral to American society and as such usually benefits some persons and disadvantages others from generation to generation. The public schools are uncompromisingly "middle class." The private enterprise system rewards aggressive, even predatory, behavior which further disadvantages the disadvantaged. Since the remaining section of this book will focus on each of the major institutions, this theme—the bias of the system—will continue to be emphasized.

SELECTED READINGS

Carmichael, Stokely, and Charles V. Hamilton, *Black Power: The Politics of Liberation in America* (New York: Random House, 1967). The classic argument that black liberation will not come through traditional political processes.

Knowles, Louis L., and Kenneth Prewitt (eds.), *Institutional Racism in America* (Englewood Cliffs, New Jersey: Prentice Hall, 1969). An indictment of the American system backed by empirical data.

Malcolm X, *The Autobiography of Malcolm X* (New York: Grove Press, 1964). The autobiography of the famous black leader which provides valuable insights about the black revolution.

* This theme is elaborated more fully in the chapter on the economy (Chapter 11). Social stratification, power, poverty, and minority groups (the topics of Part II) are highly interrelated with each other and with economics.

Marx, Gary T., *Protest and Prejudice: A Study of Belief in the Black Community* (New York: Harper & Row, 1969). The report of a comprehensive 1964 study of the attitudes of black Americans.

Pettigrew, Thomas F., *Racially Separate or Together?* (New York: McGraw-Hill Book Company, 1971). A social psychologist explores the complexities of integration in the United States.

Roszak, Betty, and Theodore Roszak (eds.), *Masculine/Feminine: Readings in Sexual Mythology and the Liberation of Women* (New York: Harper & Row, 1969). A reader which provides an overview of women as a minority group.

Skolnick, Jerome H., *The Politics of Protest, A Staff Report to the National Commission on the Causes and Prevention of Violence* (New York: Ballantine Books, 1969). Chapters 4 and 5 provide excellent summaries of black militancy and the racial attitudes of white Americans.

Yetman, Norman R., and C. Hoy Steele (eds.), *Majority and Minority: The Dynamics of Racial and Ethnic Relations* (Boston: Allyn and Bacon, 1971). An excellent survey of the field that provides cross-cultural materials and studies of various American minorities.

NOTES AND REFERENCES

1. Norman R. Yetman and C. Hoy Steele, "Introduction," *Majority and Minority: The Dynamics of Racial and Ethnic Relations*, Norman R. Yetman and C. Hoy Steele (eds.), (Boston: Allyn and Bacon, Inc., 1971), p. 4.

2. Robert Bierstedt, "The Sociology of Majorities," *American Sociological Review* 13 (December, 1948), p. 709.

3. D. Stanley Eitzen, "A Conflict Model for the Analysis of Majority-Minority Relations," *Kansas Journal of Sociology* 3 (Spring, 1967), pp. 76–89.

4. S. I. Hayakawa, *Language in Thought and Action* (New York: Harcourt, Brace, 1949), pp. 190–191.

5. Charles Silberman, *Crisis in Black and White* (New York: Random House, 1964), pp. 9–12.

6. See especially Dee Brown, *Bury My Heart at Wounded Knee: An Indian History of the American West* (New York: Bantam Books, 1972); Winthrop D. Jordan, *White Over Black: American Attitudes Toward the Negro, 1550–1812* (Baltimore: Penguin Books, 1969); John Higham, *Strangers in the Land: Patterns of American Nativism, 1860–1925* (New Brunswick, New Jersey: Rutgers University Press, 1955); and Richard Bardolph (ed.), *The Civil Rights Record: Black Americans and the Law, 1849–1970* (New York: Thomas Y. Crowell Company, 1970).

7. Jerome H. Skolnick, *The Politics of Protest, A Staff Report to the*

National Commission on the Causes and Prevention of Violence (New York: Ballantine Books, 1969), pp. 181–182.

8.   Quoted in Skolnick, *The Politics of Protest*, p. 187.

9.   Hazel Erskine, "The Polls: Negro Employment," *Public Opinion Quarterly* 32 (Spring, 1968), p. 147.

10. Hazel Erskine, "The Polls: Recent Opinion on Racial Problems," *Public Opinion Quarterly* 32 (Winter, 1968–1969), p. 700.

11. Skolnick, *The Politics of Protest*, pp. 187–188.

12. The section that follows combines two different perspectives: — (1) the modes of discrimination as presented by Peter I. Rose, *They and We: Racial and Ethnic Relations in the United States* (New York: Random House, 1964), Chapter 5; and (2) the types of discriminators as presented in several works, including: by Norman R. Yetman and C. Hoy Steele (eds.), *Majority and Minority: The Dynamics of Racial and Ethnic Relations* (Boston: Allyn and Bacon, Inc., 1971), pp. 359–367; Robert K. Merton, "Discrimination and the American Creed," *Discrimination and National Welfare*, R. M. MacIver (ed.), (New York: Harper and Row, 1949), pp. 99–126; and Stokely Carmichael and Charles V. Hamilton, *Black Power: The Politics of Liberation in America* (New York: Vintage Books, 1967).

13. Merton, "Discrimination and the American Creed," p. 103.

14. Stokely Carmichael and Charles V. Hamilton, *Black Power: The Politics of Liberation in America* (New York: Vintage Books, 1967), pp. 4–5.

15. For a classic summary of what is known about prejudice see Gordon W. Allport, *The Nature of Prejudice* (Garden City, New York: Doubleday Anchor Books, 1956), especially Chapter 25, "The Prejudiced Personality."

16. Peter I. Rose, *They and We: Racial and Ethnic Relations in the United States* (New York: Random House, Inc., 1964), p. 109.

17. William Bruce Cameron, *Informal Sociology: A Casual Introduction to Sociological Thinking* (New York: Random House, Inc., 1963), p. 94.

18. Reported in Allport, *The Nature of Prejudice*, p. 5.

19. Louis L. Knowles and Kenneth Prewitt (eds.), *Institutional Racism in America* (Englewood Cliffs, New Jersey: Prentice Hall, Inc., Spectrum Books, 1969), p. 5.

20. "Chicanos Oppose Bad Media Images," *Race Relations Reporter* 2 (March 15, 1971), pp. 8–9.

21. David Steinberg, "Racism in America: Definition and Analysis," *People Against Racism* (Detroit, Michigan), p. 3.

22. Skolnick, *The Politics of Protest*, p. 180.

23. Philip Goldberg, "Are Women Prejudiced Against Women?" *Transaction* 5 (April, 1968), pp. 28–30.

24. Durward Pruden, "A Sociological Study of a Texas Lynching," *Studies in Sociology* 1 (1936), pp. 1–9.

25. "Death Row: A New Kind of Suspense," *Newsweek* (January 11, 1971), p. 24.

26. Carmichael and Hamilton, *Black Power*, p. 4.

27. "In the National Interest," a pamphlet about black medical care distributed by Meharry Medical College, Nashville, Tennessee.

28. A significant portion of the remainder of this chapter is taken from the source, Skolnick, *The Politics of Protest*, Chapter 4 "Black Militancy."

29. Carmichael and Hamilton, *Black Power*, p. 46.

30. Malcolm X, *The Autobiography of Malcolm X* (New York: Grove Press, Inc., 1964), p. 366.

31. From an interview with Black Panther leader, Huey Newton, reported in Skolnick, *The Politics of Protest*, p. 152.

32. Skolnick, *The Politics of Protest*, p. 133.

33. Malcolm X, *The Autobiography*, p. 368.

34. Eldridge Cleaver, *Revolution in the White Mother Country and National Liberation in the Black Colony* (Oakland, California, Ministry of Information Black Paper, Black Panther Party for Self-Defense, 1968), p. 1. See also Robert Blauner, "Internal Colonialism and Ghetto Revolt," *Social Problems* 16 (Spring, 1969), pp. 393–408; and Carmichael and Hamilton, *Black Power*, pp. 2–32.

35. Martin Luther King, Jr., "Beyond Vietnam," *Black Protest*, Joanne Grant (ed.), (Greenwich, Connecticut: Fawcett Premier, 1968), p. 419.

36. "Proportionately Few Blacks in Elected Offices," an Associated Press release of April 1, 1970.

37. U.S. Bureau of the Census, *Current Population Reports*, Series P-20, No. 155, "Negro Population: March, 1965," (Washington, D.C.: U.S. Government Printing Office, 1966), Table 2, p. 14.

38. James A. Geschwender, "Social Structure and the Negro Revolt: An Examination of Some Hypotheses," *Social Forces* 43 (December, 1964), pp. 248–256.

39. J. Gwartney, "Changes in the Non-white/White Income Ratio, 1939–67," *American Economic Review* 60 (December, 1970), p. 872.

40. Cf. Thomas F. Pettigrew, *Racially Separate or Together?* (New York: McGraw-Hill, Inc., 1971), p. 152; Gerhard E. Lenski, "Status Crystallization: A Non-Vertical Dimension of Social Status," *American Sociological Review* 19 (August, 1954), pp. 405–413; Elton F. Jackson, "Status Inconsistency and Symptoms of Stress," *American Sociological Review* 27 (August, 1962), pp. 469–480; and James A. Geschwender, "Continuities in Theories of Status Inconsistency and Cognitive Dissonance," *Social Forces* 46 (December, 1967), pp. 160–171.

41. Quoted by Charles E. Silberman, "Crisis in Black and White," *Analyses of Contemporary Society*, Bernard Rosenberg (ed.), (New York: Thomas Y. Crowell Company, 1966), p. 280.

42. John Dollard, *Caste and Class in a Southern Town* (Garden City, New York: Doubleday Anchor Books, 1949).

43. James C. Davies, "The J-Curve of Rising and Declining Satisfactions as a Cause of Some Great Revolutions and a Contained Rebellion," *Violence in America: Historical and Comparative Perspectives*, A Report Submitted to the National Commission on the Causes and Prevention of Violence, Hugh David Graham and Ted Robert Gurr (eds.), (New York: Bantam Books, 1969), p. 690. This article presents an intriguing analysis of the black rebellion of the 1960's in the light of this theory. See especially pp. 716–725.

44. Melvin Seeman, "On the Meaning of Alienation," *American Sociological Review* 24 (December, 1959), pp. 783–791.

45. Julian B. Rotter, "External Control and Internal Control," *Psychology Today* 5 (June, 1971), p. 58.

46. Carmichael and Hamilton, *Black Power*, p. 40.

47. "Angry—But They Still Have a Dream," *Newsweek* (June 30, 1969), p. 20.

48. John Walton, "Economic Order," *Society Today Resources Letter* (Del Mar, California: CRM Books, 1971), p. 8; see also Ferdinand Lundberg, *The Rich and the Super-Rich: A Study in the Power of Money Today* (New York: Bantam Books, 1968).

PART III

American Institutions: Stability and Instability

One distinguishing characteristic of societies is the existence of a set of institutions. The popular usages of this term are imprecise and omit some important sociological considerations. An institution is *not* anything that is established and traditional (e.g., a janitor who has worked at the same school for forty-five years). An institution is *not* limited to specific organizations such as a school or a prison or a hospital. An institution is much broader in scope and importance than a person, a custom, or a social organization. *Institutions are social arrangements that channel behavior in prescribed ways in the important areas of societal life.* They are interrelated sets of normative elements—norms, values, and role expectations—that the persons making up the society have devised and passed on to succeeding generations in order to provide "permanent" solutions for crucial societal problems.

Institutions are cultural imperatives. They serve as regulatory agencies, channeling behavior in culturally prescribed ways.

> . . . institutions provide procedures through which human conduct is patterned, compelled to go, in grooves deemed desirable by society. And this trick is performed by making the grooves appear to the individual as the only possible ones.[1]

221

For example, a society instills in its members predetermined channels for marriage. Instead of allowing the sexual partners a whole
host of options, it is expected in American society that they will
marry and set up a conjugal household. Although the actual options
are many, the partners choose what society demands. In fact, they
do not consider the other options as valid (e.g., polygyny, polyandry,
group marriage). The result is a patterned arrangement that regulates sexual behavior and insures a stable environment for the care
of dependent children.

Institutions arise from the uncoordinated actions of multitudes of
individuals over time. These actions, procedures, and rules evolve
into a set of expectations which appear to have a design, because
the consequences of these expectations provide solutions that help
maintain social stability. The design is accidental, however; it is a
product of cultural evolution.

All societies face problems in common. Although the variety of
solutions is almost infinite, there is a functional similarity in their
consequence, which is stability and maintenance of the system. The
list below gives a number of common societal problems and the
resulting institutions.

Societal Problems	*Institution*
Sexual regulation; maintenance of stable units that in-sure continued births and care of dependent children	Family
Socialization of the newcomers to the society	Education
Maintenance of order; the distribution of power	Polity
Production and distribution of goods and services; ownership of property	Economy
Understanding the transcendental; the search for the meaning of life and death and man's place in the world	Religion
Understanding the physical and social realms of nature	Science
Providing for physical and emotional health care	Medicine

This partial list of institutions shows the type of societal problems
for which solutions are continually sought. All societies, for instance, have some form of the family, education, polity, economy,
and religion. The variations on each of these themes that is found in
societies is almost beyond imagination. This variation, while most
interesting, is beyond the scope of this book. The thrust of Part III is
the examination of the major institutions in American society. By
looking at the interrelated norms, values, and role expectations that
provide "pat" solutions to fundamental societal problems, we will
begin to understand American society. A review of American institutions will not only have descriptive value, but will aid in under-

standing social change as well. In each instance we shall also examine how certain alternatives to these institutions are available for some segments of American society. These alternative life styles are often perceived by the majority not only as deviant but as a threat to the stability of American society. In this conflict of values lies an interesting dialectic leading to change. Contemporary American society provides an interesting case study of a small but significant proportion of a national populace lashing out at its social institutions, questioning the "rightness" of monogamy, marital fidelity, having children, capitalism, the legitimacy of government, the validity of organized religion, and existing modes of education. This protest typically provokes a reaction by the majority, the impetus of which (although not so intended) is itself responsible for the ensuing change.

The task of the remaining portion of the book is to examine closely five American institutions, all of which are troubled and under pressure. The description of each will be followed by an objective assessment of the positive and negative consequences of its traditional features. The alternatives will also be explored. In each instance we must ask: who benefits under the normal, expected way of doing things and who is disadvantaged? Is this the best alternative or should other alternatives be acceptable? We must not forget that institutions are made by men, and they can therefore be changed by men. We should be guided by the insight that while institutions appear to have the quality of being "sacred," they are not. They can be changed. But critical examination is imperative. Social scientists must look behind the facades. They must not accept the patterned ways as the only "correct" ways. This is in the American heritage—as found in the Declaration of Independence. As Skolnick and Currie have put it:

> Democratic conceptions of society have always held that institutions exist to serve man, and that, therefore, they must be accountable to men. Where they fail to meet the tests imposed on them, democratic theory holds that they ought to be changed. Authoritarian governments, religious regimes, and reformatories, among other social systems, hold the opposite: in case of misalignment between individuals or groups and the 'system', the individuals and groups are to be changed or otherwise made unproblematic.[2]

CHAPTER 7

The Sources of Contemporary Institutional Change

More and more Americans are criticizing their institutions. A few representative complaints are that: the government is unresponsive to public opinion, education no longer meets the needs of individuals, and private property is considered more important than human needs. What is the problem? Why are individuals and groups dissatisfied with the traditional ways of doing things? The answer, in brief, is that institutions as "pat" answers do not always meet the needs of persons in a rapidly changing society. Since social change is a constant property of societies, there will always be a gap between prescribed behaviors and the behaviors demanded by innovations. In a society characterized by accelerated change this gap becomes a gulf that many cannot bridge. Their actions are labeled by the more tradition bound as immoral, illegal, and illegitimate.

The traditional ways of 100 years ago or 20 years ago do not always fit today. American society is no longer a rural and agrarian economy. Societal power is now centralized rather than dispersed. Advanced technology has created a cornucopia of goods, instantaneous communication to all areas of the society, tremendous advances in transportation, and has brought affluence to many Americans. What have been the consequences of these changes for the society and its inhabitants? What have been the effects on the institutions of the family, religion, education, polity, and the economy?

FORCES FOR CHANGE

There are a number of important forces that converge in contemporary American society to heighten the questioning of the traditional behavior patterns (institutional demands) and which, therefore, ultimately bring institutional changes. These revolutionary forces— industrialization, urbanization, bureaucratization, and the rate of change—are the subject of the present chapter.

Industrialization

Technological change in the United States has been so rapid that it could be characterized as revolutionary. As Sykes has said, paraphrasing Michael Harrington,

> Our lives are becoming drastically transformed not by any self-conscious plan or the machinations of a few, but by the unanticipated consequences of economic and technological development in which we are all implicated. It is the man of business and industry, especially with his goal of productivity and his skillful allocation of resources, who has been the great revolutionary of our era. He has remade our existence far more than any ideologist, smashing institutions, shifting the landscape, stuffing some regions with people and depopulating others—all without a policy or overall purpose.[3]

Technological breakthroughs (e.g., the assembly line, computers, birth control pills) are indeed revolutionary since they create and destroy occupations. They may make some products obsolete and increase the demand for others. They alter behavior, and may even cause a shift in values. Thus, technology solves some problems but creates some new ones. As Charles Silberman has said,

> . . . economic growth reduces poverty, but it also produces congestion, noise, and pollution of the environment. Technological change widens the individual's range of choice and makes economic growth possible; it also dislocates workers from their jobs and their neighborhoods. Affluence plus new technology frees men from slavery to the struggle for existence, from the brutalizing labor that had been man's condition since Adam; it thereby forces them to confront the questions of life's meaning and purpose even while it destroys the faith that once provided answers.[4]

The industrial techniques of the early 1900's, for instance, had a number of profound effects. They created a need for a large working class of semi-skilled workers whose tasks were largely repetitive. They fostered the growth of cities (and conversely the decline of rural areas). They created products at a relatively low cost thereby causing the decline of many skilled craftsmen. The high influx of goods through mass production increased the probability of economic booms and depression, since production and distribution were not always synchronized.

As technology advances many of the jobs created in an earlier era are displaced. There is no longer the need for huge masses of semi-skilled workers. The present demand is for educated white collar workers with narrow specialties. In 1956, as mentioned in Chapter 5, there were for the first time more white collar workers than blue collar workers. The problem now is that having a narrow specialty insures obsolescence, since new techniques and knowledge undoubtedly will alter present arrangements very quickly.

Technological changes are the cause of many social problems as well as the source of varied blessings. The paradoxical nature of this trend is important to consider, because both aspects are real and have profound effects upon individuals, groups, and the society as a whole. Much of the current unrest is in reaction to the "bad" qualities engendered by these trends.

Contemporary technology has replaced tedious tasks and back-breaking tasks with labor-saving devices and more leisure time. Life without electricity, television, central heating, air conditioning, and other "necessities" would be difficult for most Americans to accept. For many Americans, however, man is viewed as a victim of technology. In the words of Philip Slater:

> We talk of technology as the servant of man, but it is a servant that now dominates the household, too powerful to fire, upon whom everyone is helplessly dependent. We tiptoe about and speculate upon his mood. What will be the effects of such-and-such an invention? How will it change our daily lives? We never ask, for example, if the trivial conveniences offered by the automobile could really offset the calamitous disruption and depersonalization of our lives that it brought about. We simply say "You can't stop progress" and shuffle back inside.[5]

Recent technological advances in communications and transportation have had profound liberating consequences for Americans. Transoceanic flights, space travel, instantaneous world-wide communications, color television from the moon or Rangoon have had the effects of emancipating man from the provinciality of his local community. He has seen alternatives. Dogma has less of a hold on his thinking. He has participated vicariously in historical events. The old customs, the status quo are brought into question as never before.

Television has had an especially important impact on American life. The exact nature of this impact is difficult to assess, however, since modern teenagers are the first generation to have been exposed to television from birth. The average American child by age 18 has watched 22,000 hours of television. This same average viewer has watched thousands of hours of inane situation comedy, fantasy, and soap opera (and an average of 4,286 separate acts of violence). He also has watched great drama, debates, music, and been educated to the wonders of nature. Additionally, the medium of television has been used to persuade him to "need" certain products, to form certain opinions, and to vote for particular candidates. But more important, television has forced persons to broaden their horizons. One's experience is no longer limited to the local community. Through television we participate vicariously in wars, riots, demonstrations, assassinations, coronations, United Nations debates, festivals, famines, summit meetings, the Olympic Games, national disasters, and international crises. Whereas persons once were exposed to a consistent set of expectations and constraints, television (as well as the modern means of transportation) presents modern man with a variety of life styles and ideologies.

We have seen that the technological revolution has an immense impact upon individuals and institutions since it is responsible for internal migration, changes in the occupational structure, and the freeing of individuals from the provinciality of localism. As a final demonstration of the magnitude of technological change let us look at the Gross National Product. The United States and the other "have" nations of the world (21 nations according to the Organization for Economic Cooperation and Development) are doubling their total output of goods and services (Gross National Product) about every fifteen years.

> This means, generally speaking, that the child reaching teen age in any of these societies is literally surrounded by twice as much of everything newly man-made as his parents were at the time he was an infant. It means that by the time today's teen-ager reaches age thirty, perhaps earlier, a second doubling will have occurred. Within a seventy-year lifetime, perhaps five such doublings will take place—meaning, since the increases are compounded, that by the time the individual reaches old age the society around him will be producing thirty-two times as much as when he was born.[6]

Urbanization

In 1790 only five percent of the American population lived in places with more than 2,500 persons. By 1960 the percentage had grown to 70 percent. The percentage living in areas of 50,000 or more was 54 in 1960. As evidence of the concentration of Americans in certain localities, about 20 percent of Americans live in five metropolitan areas: New York City, Chicago, Los Angeles, Philadelphia, and Detroit.

Aside from the obvious population shift from rural areas to the cities, these figures imply several additional trends. First, there is the growth of communities surrounding large cities as demand for space grows from rural migrants and city dwellers seeking the suburbs. A second and related trend is that more and more agricultural land is taken out of production and replaced by buildings, asphalt, concrete, and even artificial turf. A third trend implied in the process of urbanization is the birth of a new urban entity—the megalopolis—the growing together of very large cities until they are contiguous. For example, one-sixth of all the nation's people (1970) lived in a 450 mile strip running from Boston to Washington, D.C., along the Atlantic Ocean and stretching 150 miles inland—thus the megalopolis of "Boswash." Similar entities are taking shape elsewhere and might be called "Chipitts," (Chicago to Pittsburgh) and "San San," (San Francisco to San Diego).

While the cities grow and experience overcrowding, the rural areas of the United States have declined. Between 1950 and 1960 the urban population increased by 29 percent, while the rural population declined one percent. During that decade when the United States population grew by almost 28 million persons, 49 percent of the 3,134 counties actually lost population. One result of this trend is the decline and decay of the small town. Many of these areas are now economically depressed, a trend which in itself leads to greater migration.

Research has shown that migrants from the rural areas to the cities are by no means a cross section of the population. The rates of migration are especially high for young adults, since these are the very persons with the greatest productivity and reproductivity. Consequently, the rural areas suffer all the more.

Another category of persons disproportionately rural-to-urban migrant are blacks. In 1910 only 27 percent of blacks were classified as urban as against 48 percent of the white population. By 1960 the corresponding percentages had risen to 72 percent for blacks and 69 percent for whites. By 1970 the number of southern blacks migrating north to the cities was approximately 200,000 annually. This swelling of the proportion of blacks in urban places has profound ramifications. First, blacks (as well as all migrants) came to the cities because the economic and/or social advantages were believed to outweigh what they had. Although the migrants move to the cities with great hopes, these often are not realized, with resulting frustration and hostility. Because of the high unemployment rate among blacks, the tax base is not strengthened when blacks move in. A third outcome of the black influx in the cities is the subsequent flight of middle-class whites to the suburbs, leaving a racially segregated ghetto unable to afford the important services of education, recreation, and adequate police and fire protection. Finally, black power becomes a reality as blacks concentrate in given localities. The trend is clear that blacks will continue to be elected to office and have greater clout over urban political decisions.

The ever greater density of people in cities and the changing nature of cities have led to a number of problems that threaten to overwhelm urban man. Perhaps the greatest problem is money—money to provide adequate schools, water, electricity, waste disposal, mass transit, recreation facilities, low income housing, police and fire protection, and welfare. The cities receive some money from the federal and state governments, but the bulk must be obtained from the residents themselves. There are at least three reasons why the taxing of urban residents has not worked. First, great amounts of property are exempt from property taxes because they are owned by churches, the government, or philanthropic foundations. In 1971, for example, half of the real estate valuation in Boston and Washington, D.C., and one-third in New York City and Pittsburgh were exempt from real estate taxes.[7]

A second reason for the lack of money for the urban areas is the ever-increasing number of persons on welfare in the cities. New York City in 1970 had over 1 million persons on welfare (more than the entire population of Baltimore) at a cost of $1.7 billion a year. This situation is brought about by immigrants (often untrained and hard to employ) who come to American cities to live, as well as by internal migrants (rural to urban) who also often find employment difficult to obtain on a regular basis. Many of these migrants belong to racial minorities, and this compounds their problem with employment. Another reason (previously mentioned in Chapter 5) is that many states do not provide adequate support to persons needing welfare, thereby forcing these persons to move to cities and states where the payments may be three times as much. Thus, some cities provide welfare for citizens from other areas. This fact suggests that welfare is a national problem—not a local one—and should be supported by national funds.

A third basis for the lack of money in urban areas has been the middle class abandonment of the central city for the suburbs. The suburbs added 35 million persons from 1950 to 1970 while the cities added 10 million in that time period.* Concomitant with this has been the shift of factories and shopping areas from the central city to outlying areas. These trends reduce dramatically the tax base in the city (and raise it in the suburbs where the residents can afford the best of everything from schools to parks). As Gresham Sykes has said,

> We are becoming a society of people who live near big cities but not in them. In fact, the 1970 census showed that in the United States, for the first time, more people were living in the suburbs of big cities (74.2 million) than in the cities themselves (62.2 million).[8]

This exodus to the suburbs by the well-to-do overloads the remaining persons with the task of financing the city. In spite of this, suburbanites continue to use the cities' highways, shopping areas, recreational facilities, and police protection.

The flight of the relatively well-to-do also is a way of "copping out." Instead of facing the social problems of the city, the suburbanite flees, insulating himself from the harshness of urban life. As Sykes has lamented,

> . . . it is the social or moral distance between the two [urbanite and suburbanite] that concerns me at the moment, because the spatial distance results in a moral isolation of the suburbanite from the major social problems of his society. He can read about them in the newspapers or see them on TV, but that is not the same thing as living next door to them. The men and the women in the suburbs—and their children—are to a large extent shielded from direct, intimate, and continuing confrontation with the issues that are plaguing our era. . . . And one result is apt to be the loss of one of the major sources of political or social action.[9]

In many respects, the problems of the cities are self-perpetuating. The lack of money for adequate services insures that educational facilities will be substandard. Many urban residents, particularly

---

* See pages 424–425, Figure 31 and Figure 38 for the 1970 Census data on population by residence.

the slum dwellers, are trapped in their situation—without the skills or the other characteristics that make them employable. Their hopelessness is transmitted to their children. For them schooling is unimportant and deferred gratification makes no sense. Thus, the unemployment and welfare problems continue because poverty, discrimination, and illiteracy tend to be passed from generation to generation.

Crime is also concentrated among the urban poor. We have seen earlier (Chapter 5) that crime is centered among the poor because the laws and the courts discriminate against them. While this is true, the fact remains that the poor are the most likely to become heroin addicts. Primarily as a means to escape the harsh realities of slum life, many turn to alcohol and drugs. In New York City the estimated number of heroin addicts was over 100,000 in 1971. Each of these persons needs at least $40 a day to support this habit—a total of more than $1.5 billion annually for the addict population. Much of this money comes from stealing, selling narcotics, prostitution, and other crimes. Thus, it could be argued that New York City is gradually being killed by heroin. As the number of addicts grows and the number of robberies soars, more and more urban dwellers will leave—leaving the city an urban shell with its tax base wholly eroded, inhabited only by the very poor.[10]

Urbanization, as we have seen, is the process of city growth. Another concept, urbanism, refers to the kind of social life that urban residents experience. Most of the sociological literature has compared city life with a romantic notion of life in a small village. Urban social life was thus depicted as impersonal, void of close ties with friends or family, pragmatically oriented, and loosely controlled through formal means (the law and its enforcers).[11]

This pessimistic and depressing view of urban life has prevailed through much of the twentieth century. While it is true that social problems do center in the city, the ledger should be balanced. The city offers individuals more freedom than they would find in a small village where behavior, values, and attitudes are shaped in rather narrow corridors. Unquestionably, the city offers more work, entertainment, and recreation opportunities than the rural area. Whereas the small village offers a narrow range of associations, interest groups, and types of persons, the city offers great differentiation in terms of neighborhoods, social classes, religious groups, and organizations. Finally, contrary to the traditional view, city dwellers are not all isolated individuals. Although some urbanites are lonely, without primary group ties, there is great variation in life styles within the city, with some neighborhoods very family-centered and friendly while others are less so. While the traditional view of urbanism makes it appear as though all urbanites are lonely, isolated individuals, a more realistic view would take into account the variations within the city.

The process of urbanization has had a liberating effect on individuals. It, along with increased technology and the other forces noted in this chapter, has lessened the "sanctity" of the traditional ways. This has been accomplished through the diversity of life styles, ideologies, and behavior found in urban places. This freedom of choice, although not unlimited, is sufficiently greater than that found in rural places. Urbanization is a process, therefore, that tends to undermine the constraints of tradition (institutional demands).

Bureaucratization

The process of bureaucratization refers to the changes within organizations toward greater rationality—i.e., improved operating efficiency and more effective attainment of common goals. As the size and complexity of an organization grows, there is a greater need for coordination if efficiency is to be maintained or improved. Organizational efficiency would be maximized (ideally) under these conditions:

1. when there is a hierarchy of authority (chain of command) with each role in the chain having clearly defined duties and responsibilities;
2. when all decisions are made on the basis of technical knowledge, not personal considerations;
3. when the members are judged solely on the basis of proficiency, and discipline is impartially enforced.[12]

As one can see, the closer the organization approaches a pure bureaucracy, the more attitudes of sentiment and emotion are eschewed. There is a fundamental paradox, however, for in the quest for rationality lies irrationality. Or put another way, the quest for efficiency can lead to inefficiency. Blind obedience to rules and the following of orders means that new and unusual situations cannot be handled efficiently since the rules do not apply. Rigid adherence to the rules creates automatons. The organization's goal of efficiency is enhanced by member loyalty but in a pure bureaucracy the individual is appreciated only for his output. Any slackening in this output (regardless of the reason) may mean his job. So the individual participates more out of fear than loyalty.

The push toward increased bureaucratization prevades nearly all aspects of American life including the government (at all levels), the church (the Catholic Church, the Methodist Church), education (all school systems), sports (N.C.A.A., A.A.U., athletic departments at "big time" schools, professional teams), corporations (General Motors, IBM) and even crime ("mafia").

The majority of social scientists have viewed with alarm what they conceived to be the trend toward greater and greater bureaucratization. Individuals will, it is typically predicted, increasingly become small cogs in very big machines. Narrowly defined tasks, a rigid chain of command, and total impersonality in dealing with others will be man's organizational lot in the future. Man will be a rigid conformist—the prototype of the organization man.

This pessimistic view is countered by Warren Bennis, Alvin Toffler and others who have predicted the end of bureaucracy as we know it.[13] They feel that the pyramidal and impersonal type of organization—bureaucracy—is not capable of meeting the problems of a super-industrial ("post-industrial") society. Since bureaucracy was a social invention to meet certain kinds of problems, it will be replaced by another social invention—the ad-hocracy.

Bureaucracies, in this view, are no longer viable because they cannot adapt to the new conditions, dilemmas, and problems that result from the rapid changes in advanced technological societies. Several factors rule out the old bureaucratic forms. First there is a greater and greater turnover of personnel within organizations. Whereas there was once great loyalty to organizations, today's mobile society insures that many employees will move for faster advancement, more autonomy, and greater novelty.

A second factor is that organizations are no longer permanent arrangements with all members knowing exactly the rules and responsibilities of their roles. Changing conditions demand greater fluidity. Internal reorganizations are now fairly commonplace in organizations with jobs being given new responsibilities, departments added, deleted, or combined with others.

A most important factor in the break-up of bureaucracies is the need for flexibility to face temporary problems. Bureaucracies are efficient when tackling routine and predictable problems. But bureaucracies are incapable of responding effectively to situations not covered in the rules. There must be ways to meet these challenges if organizations are to attain their goals. Rules and tradition will not suffice in an age of dramatic change. The demise of bureaucracy is also accompanied by the break-up of the traditional chain-of-command. This is accomplished because of the necessity of relying on the advice of experts not in the traditional pyramid of power.

What, then, will be the characteristics of goal-oriented organizations in super-industrialized society? According to Bennis and Toffler:

1. They will be adaptive, rapidly changing *temporary* systems. Problems will be solved by task forces of relative strangers with diverse professional skills. These teams will not be bound by orthodoxy or the need to conform. They will be creative since they will be faced with novel problems.
2. Executives and managers will function as coordinators between these temporary work teams. They will put together teams to tackle specific tasks calling upon the specialties and expertise of various professionals. They will rely on the decisions made by these work teams. Leadership will also be responsible for the overall direction of the organization and its degree of goal attainment.
3. People will be differentiated according to skill, professional training, and expertise.
4. There will be little commitment to work groups because these will be temporary arrangements. Loyalty toward the organization will be replaced by loyalty to one's profession.

This new type of organization, while solving many of the problems of bureaucracy, is not a utopia. Just as bureaucracy produced social strains, so, too, will ad-hocracy, but they will be qualitatively different. Whereas bureaucracy caused problems of over-conformity, ad-hocracy will bring problems resulting from liberation. Social strains and psychological tensions will result from ambiguity, temporary relationships, and autonomy. The constant adaptation to new situations and role-partners will create severe stress in those persons unable to adapt.

The strain created by the organizational forms of the present (bureaucracy) and the future (ad-hocracy) affect the hold of institutional constraints. Persons unable to cope will seek alternatives. Ad-hocracy will encourage freedom from tradition. In either case, the traditional expectations for the family, education, economy, polity, and religion will increasingly be questioned.

The Rate of Change

Alvin Toffler's provocative book, *Future Shock,* illustrates vividly that in all the components of social experience change is accelerating at such a rapid pace that many individuals cannot cope psychologically.[14] His argument, in brief, is that the lives of most Americans only a few generations ago were relatively stable. Their relationships with others were permanent, with the extended family and life-long friendships. People remained in one locality for their lifetime. Even the objects they used (tools, furniture, toys, homes) were long-lasting. Ideas, too, were stable. Religious ideas were accepted, moral codes went unquestioned because virtually no one proposed alternatives. Additionally, few persons had a chance to view alternative ways of life.

Toffler contends that modern man, in sharp contrast, is faced with impermanence, a temporariness in all aspects of social life from the things he uses to the ideas he holds. Let us look at each of these various areas to illustrate the high rate of turnover.

1. *Things.* Man's relationships with man-made things are increasingly temporary. The United States is a "throw-away" society. Some products are produced for very short-term or even one-time use—paper towels, throw-away containers, disposable diapers, and even paper clothes. Many products become obsolete in a short time so consumers throw away or trade in the outmoded commodity. The average American, for instance, keeps his automobile three and one-half years. Television sets, computers, and other products typically undergo annual improvements making new purchases "necessary." The advertising industry with their sophisticated techniques does all it can to generate such "needs" in potential purchasers.

The temporariness of things is also evidenced by the increased rental (rather than ownership) of tools, cars, appliances, and homes. In 1969, for example, more building permits were issued in the United States for apartment construction than for private homes.

2. *Places.* Contemporary Americans are nomads. Toffler's thesis is that persons are no longer tied to a neighborhood or community. Consider, for example, that the average automobile owner today drives in excess of 10,000 miles annually while his counterpart in 1914 traveled about 340 miles with the aid of a horse or mechanical means. Many Americans commute relatively long distances to work. Vacations often take Americans long distances from home. Most important is that one out of five Americans moves to a new place of residence every year.

Although freedom from geographical location has some positive consequences (liberation from parochial ideas and constraints on behavior, new challenges), there are some important negative effects as well. In the first place, the novelty of the new place may mean that the migrants will differ from their new neighbors in ideology, speech, morality, and other customs. Being different is not always a pleasant experience. On the other hand, rapid conformity to new ways may lead to hypocrisy.

A second negative consequence is a loss of commitment to community. Thus, among frequent migrants, there is likely to be considerable apathy in elections (or voting with no concern for the long-range consequences), as well as little or no pride in the local community.

3. *People.* As persons in a society move more often from city to city or city to suburb, or as they change jobs more frequently, there is a decline in the average duration of human relationships. Long-term relationships continue among family members, but as mobility increases, the life relationships with friends, neighbors, job associates, and co-members in voluntary organizations shortens. This means that mobile persons (and their children) will not have the support of permanent friends. Although this is perhaps unfortunate, they have the advantage of selecting friends from a very large pool of acquaintances. There is also a higher probability that they will have friends that differ in ideas and customs, friends who will encourage a liberating effect from the constraints of tradition.

The rapid turnover ("transience") in things, places, and people so characteristic of American society is a consequence of the other forces we have mentioned—urbanization, technology, and bureaucratization. It highlights the increasing gap between the constraints of tradition and the alternative behaviors and values created by novel experiences, exposure to different ideas, and innovations.

THE CONSEQUENCES OF URBANIZATION, BUREAUCRATIZATION, INDUSTRIALIZATION AND THE RAPIDITY OF CHANGE

The conditions of modern society have led to two sometimes similar but often opposed predictions of what will be the characteristics of super-industrial society. To some observers American society will become a mass society; for others the trends imply even greater freedoms, hence a free society.

Possibility I: The United States as a Mass Society

A number of sociologists, social psychologists, and philosophers have compared traditional with modern societies.[15] They have noted that traditional societies were once small and close-knit.

Urbanization, industrialization and ever greater bureaucratization shattered these communities and replaced them with large, impersonal societies. Whereas men once lived comfortable lives with strong ties to individuals and small groups, their lives seem now isolated.* Modernization, therefore, was viewed with despair and the glories of the past romanticized.

No society exists presently that has a fully developed mass society. Many would argue, however, that the United States approaches this societal type. Let us examine the features of a mass society as they would be found in a hypothetical situation (ideal type).

A mass is an undifferentiated aggregate of people. Ethnic groups and religious groups have lost their distinctiveness. Social classes no longer are important sources of distinct values, styles of life, and social identity. The population is homogeneous in attitudes and behavior. They want the same thing; they superficially adhere to stereotyped values. In short, the masses are a glob of unrelated individuals.

A mass society results from the increased size of organizations and the revolution in communications, two conditions that prevail in the United States. Schools, churches, businesses, communities, and labor unions increase dramatically in size. The actual number of these entities diminishes (through mergers of corporations, the emergence of megalopolises) so that these entities become giants. Even voluntary associations (e.g. American Legion, Elks), often become so large that the individual has no voice in policy. These organizations had in the past served as mediators between individuals and the political elites. In a mass society, however, the elites and the non-elites are directly accessible to one another.

In a mass society political leadership is dependent on acceptance by the masses. Public opinion is the ultimate source of legitimation. Leaders, however, do not seek merely to respond to public opinion, but also try to control it. The tremendous advances in communication makes elite manipulation of the masses possible. The entire population can be presented simultaneously with the same stimuli (a speech, a news event, advertising), resulting in persons developing similar responses and becoming very much alike.

At the individual level, the primary characteristic of a mass society is social isolation. The individual interacts in a meaningful way only with members of the nuclear family. His remaining rela-

* For a summary of this tradition, focusing on the work of such sociological "giants" as Tonnies, Durkheim, Weber, Cooley, and Redfield, see an article by John C. McKinney and Charles P. Loomis, "The Typological Tradition."[16]

tives live, typically, in other parts of the country. He does not know his neighbors well, because either they move or he does. He works in an impersonal bureaucracy where personal feelings and compassion are believed to lead to inefficiency. The "mass man," therefore, is without secure social roots. He has no sense of community.

Individuals are also without power. Communication is asymmetrical—toward individuals and from the power elite, or from their superiors in the job, church, or other organization. They feel powerless. Things happen to them rather than their having any direct influence. Individuals are thus manipulated by the elite, by the media, and by the social constraints of situations in the bureaucracies to which they belong.

The result of the felt social isolation and powerlessness of mass man is alienation—individuals feel estrangement or separation from their jobs, from others, and even from themselves.

What effects do the conditions of a mass society have on individuals and on the society as a whole? There are several very important consequences. First, the masses are vulnerable to elite control, resulting in a relatively closed elite that authoritatively rules the society. Since individuals are alone (not members of viable groups) they are much more susceptible to manipulation by the powerful. The mass media, particularly television, is an important tool for manipulation of the masses.* Elite control is also accomplished because individuals in a mass society tend to be apathetic, since they feel they have no control over political decisions.

A second consequence of a mass society is the vulnerability of the individual to the appeals of mass social movements. These may be fads or crazes, or they may be political or religious movements. Individuals will be inundated with pressures to conform to whatever is popular at the moment. Political extremist movements that promote revolution are always a possibility in a mass society (for reasons that will be enumerated shortly). Thus, the power elite will act in either of two ways: (1) increased reliance on force to control the masses (including surveillance, taking political prisoners, etc.); or (2) manipulating the people through popular action ("bread and circuses") and staying away from unpopular actions that might foment revolt.

The anxiety and despair that accompany the typical individual in a mass society because of his atomization often result in a search for meaning in a meaningless world and roots in a rootless world.

* The book by Joseph McGinnis, *The Selling of the President 1968*, is an account of how media experts "packaged and sold" Richard Nixon in his successful quest for the Presidency in 1968.[17]

Where individuals feel powerlessness and separation they seek purpose and a cause to believe in and be part of. Thus, another significant consequence of mass society is the rise of a plethora of social movements with charismatic leaders. Religious cults, "Jesus Freaks," "the God Squad," astrology, mysticism, radical political groups of the left (Weathermen, Father Berrigan and his followers) or the right (The Minutemen, American Nazi Party). As Eric Hoffer has said, "When people are ripe for a mass movement, they are usually ripe for any effective movement, and not solely for one with a particular doctrine or program."[18]

Part of the isolation that individuals feel in a mass society is brought about by the formalness of social relations. In the job, in church, or in the neighborhood there is little sense of community, but rather an impersonal "look out only for yourself" and "don't rock the boat" approach. The strict adherence to rules, impersonal justice, segmental relationships (i.e., knowing someone only in one role such as waitress or clerk or foreman rather than the whole person) may result in organizational efficiency (although this is debatable) but they omit some vital elements in human lives— meaningful social relationships, the expression of emotions, the caring for others and being cared for. This explains the paradox of contemporary American life where on the one hand we strive for greater rationality by using computers, impersonal rules, and organizational flow charts, while on the other hand there is a great emphasis on feeling (drug culture, philosophy, music, emotional types of religion, receiving good "vibes") and caring for others (helping the needy, sharing one's resources with a group). The growth of communes is an important trend and signifies the need that many individuals in a mass society have for a sense of community.

Possibility II: The United States as a Free Society

The super-industrial society of the future, unlike mass society, will not restrict people, according to Toffler's analysis.[19] They will be faced with a surfeit of alternatives in the material goods they purchase and the services they may use. Even art, education, and the mass media will offer fantastic diversity. In art, for instance, contemporary man is bombarded with abstract impressionism, surrealism, representationalism, hardedge, pop, op, and even kinetic. In education, we are witnessing the decentralization of universities and an increased use of specialized programs to meet the needs of individuals at all educational levels. The mass media, from radio stations that specialize by type of music (rock, soul, country, or classical) to 30,000 books published annually, appeal to varied and distinctive tastes. Magazines, too, are becoming more and more specialized. This may have been the reason for the death of *Life* magazine in 1972. As one of their writers put it,

> We didn't know who we were writing to. We continued to try to put out a mass magazine when America was not "mass" any more but divergent groups of specialized interests.[20]

Even television, although currently homogenizing taste, will, with the greater use of cable TV and cassette TV, open many more options to viewers.

As the society moves toward greater specialization, there will be an increased variety of groups from which to choose. There will be specialties within disciplines. There will be special interest groups of infinite variety—e.g., hippies, skin divers, homosexuals, vegetarians, philatelists, flat earthers, and surfers. Sheer size of organizations will partly explain the persistence of diversity, for groups will tend to splinter as they approach a certain size. This occurrence is common whether the organization is a church, a publishing house, or a commune.

The problem facing mankind of the future will not be conformity, nor will it be regimentation. To the contrary, individuals will be burdened by too many options—where to live, choice of friends, how to spend leisure time, which of the blinding array of new goods and services to acquire, which social groups to join, and how to cope with colliding value systems.

The primary problem of such a society will be to maintain integration. The more differentiated the society, the greater the problem of social integration. Consensus on values will no longer be the integrative force because such a consensus will not be a characteristic of such a society. The challenge of this type of society will be to find new types of integrative mechanisms.

Many individuals in the super-industrial society will be unable to cope with the diversity, and the rapid turnover in things, places, and social relations. There are several forms of individual maladaptation in such a society. One form is outright denial. This person refuses to accept change. He finds solace in such clichés as "the more things change, the more they stay the same." A second maladaptive response is specialism. This person attempts to keep pace with change in a narrow sector of life while denying the realities of change in other areas.

A third possibility is to be a reactionary. This individual reverts back to the comfortable ways of the past that are now irrelevant and inappropriate. His solutions to social problems are rigid—do what worked in some past "Golden Age." This response is found among many conservatives and liberals alike. Right-wingers may glory in force to maintain order, authoritarian modes or socialization, or States Rights because these solutions worked at one time. Left-wingers, too, may glory in the past. Exaggerated veneration of pre-technological societies, contempt for science and technology, Marxism, anarchy, communal living, are all attempts to revive the ways of the past to cope with the demands of the present.

Another form of adaptation, closely related to the previous one, is to oversimplify the explanations and solutions to complex problems. Thus, the Communist conspiracy is believed by some to explain race riots and student riots; the international Jewish conspiracy explains America's foreign policy; permissiveness is the cause of racial strife, the youth rebellion, and the lack of respect for authority, or capitalism is the cause of America's social problems.

The problem of overchoice may also "force" individuals to join social movements. Groups with an ideology, a set of guidelines, "pat answers," may attract and influence individuals who need to organize their life, explain events, and reduce the complexity of their choices. Astrology, Zen Buddhism, fundamentalist Christianity, The American Nazi Party, Black Muslims, all serve to provide simple answers to complex problems. Such groups also provide individuals a niche, a place where they belong, where they can be part of something that will bring about significant social change.

A final form of maladaptive behavior is withdrawal. The affluent can withdraw by living in the suburbs with others like themselves. Others among the affluent may withdraw with other insulating mechanisms—alcohol, drugs, television. Some young people, and a few adults, have dropped out of society altogether. Their withdrawal is total.

The new (post industrial) society, whether it resembles a mass society or a free society, will offer few roots to individuals. Enduring relationships with people, organizations, or places will be missing for the most part. The wisdom of the past, customs, and ideologies will be questioned all the more. These facts of the future will serve to shake up and change society's institutions. Many individuals will not "feel at home" in either of the societal types described here, but for different reasons. Many persons in a mass society will react against the homogenization of life and the demands for conformity. Many individuals in a free society, on the other hand, will react negatively to freedom itself. Regardless of the direction of the future society, then, masses of persons will be unable to adapt. They will feel alienated (powerless, estranged from self, community, and others) and anomic (unsure of the norms). Unquestionably there will be an intense search for meaning, fulfillment, commitment, and community by many. Some will drop out and become totally apathetic. Others will search for viable alternatives to the institutional demands. Some will work for reform within the system and others will seek revolution of that system. The future will doubtless be characterized by social unrest and social change.

Conclusion

Societies are, paradoxically, stable yet changing. There is always a dialectic between the institutional push toward stability and the desire on the part of individuals and groups to find better ways of doing things. This chapter has focused largely on the forces which have liberated modern man from the constraints of his institutions. This freedom is far from absolute, since man is still torn by conflicting demands. It is important to note that modern man is the most liberated in history. This freedom, however, is a mixed blessing, as Silberman has noted in the following quote:

> In the past men inherited their occupations, their status, their religion, and their life style; their wives were selected for them, and their struggle to survive gave them little time to question anything. Today, by contrast, they are presented with a bewildering range of options; they are forced to choose their occupations, jobs, places to live, marital partners, number of children, religion, political allegiance and affiliation, friendships, allocation of income, and life style. This widening of the range of choice and enhancement of individuality have had the effect of reducing the authority of tradition, which in turn requires still more choices to be exercised.
>
> The burden is heavy. The choices are frightening, for they require the individual, perhaps for the first time in history, to choose, and in a sense to create, his own identity.[21]

This mixed blessing, as we have noted throughout this chapter, is a result of the combined forces of urbanization, bureaucratization, technology, and the rate of change. These factors are most important for the understanding of stability and change in American society. They do not explain all change, however. Let us examine briefly some additional sources that also undermine the legitimacy of American institutions.

Externally, there are events and forces throughout the world that cause many to doubt the legitimacy of the American political system, economic system, or the educational system. Russia's early lead in the space race (in the late 1950's) brought about some swift changes in the American educational system. Economic crises always lead to a questioning of current practices. Involvement in a war such as that in Indo-China, where no side wins and the cost of lives and resources is great, is a cinch to provoke dissent. The United States, obviously, is not a closed system. It affects others and is affected, in turn, by their actions. When important international events are perceived by a segment of Americans as having deleterious effects for the United States, then the legitimacy of some part of the system is questioned, since proper action, presumably, could have prevented it.

There are also some internal reasons for the questioning of institutions. One is the inability of the institutional network to solve social problems such as poverty, racism, crime, and pollution. There is obvious room for improvement.

Despite their lack of success in alleviating some social problems, certain persons and groups (those who benefit under the existing arrangements) defend the institutions and even stifle dissent. It is the nature of institutions (and their spokesmen) to be relatively inflexible. Not only is the system not geared for change but it actually represses dissent and innovation.

Another internal source for questioning is the increased awareness by some that the system is at fault. The traditional ways often work to give advantage to some and disadvantage to others. As we have seen in earlier chapters, such established traditions as the law, the jury system, the draft, college admission policies, and IQ tests work in such a way as to maldistribute society's benefits. With increasing frequency critics are pointing out the flaws in the system to the public in books, articles, and television documentaries. Although it is becoming fashionable to attack American institutions, we should not forget that individuals depend on them for stability and guarantees against chaos. Therein lies the basic dilemma—institutions are necessary, yet because they are based on rooted permanence they do not keep up with change and inequities result.

The remainder of this book deals with each of several specific American institutions. In each case, we will describe the accepted social arrangements that serve to channel behavior in prescribed ways as well as the alternatives posed by those who question tradition. This clash between the old (thesis) and the new (antithesis) with the resulting synthesis will provide us with a basis from which to understand the fundamental social changes that are occurring in contemporary American society.

SUGGESTED FURTHER READING

Banfield, Edward C., *The Unheavenly City: The Nature and Future of Our Urban Crisis* (Boston: Little, Brown and Company, 1968). Interpretations and solutions of urban problems are presented that are opposite those found in Ryan's *Blaming the Victim.*

Hoffer, Eric, *The True Believer* (New York: A Mentor Book, 1951). This lively book looks at social movements and what types of persons are predisposed to join them. If Hoffer is correct, then their number will increase disproportionately as the United States moves in the direction of either a mass or a free society.

Knowles, Louis L. and Kenneth Prewitt, editors, *Institutional Racism in America* (Englewood Cliffs, New Jersey: Prentice-Hall, Inc., 1969). This book documents the inequities inherent in American institutions.

Kornhauser, William, *The Politics of Mass Society* (New York: The Free Press, 1959). A classic statement of the antecedents, conditions, and consequences of mass society.

Skolnick, Jerome H. and Elliott Currie, editors, *Crisis in American Institutions* (Boston: Little, Brown and Company, 1970). This reader provides a framework and a series of articles that examine social problems from an institutional perspective.

Toffler, Alvin, *Future Shock* (New York: Bantam Books, 1970). A popular book that looks at the future implications of ever accelerating change in society.

Williams, Robin M., Jr., *American Society: A Sociological Interpretation,* third edition (New York: Alfred A. Knopf, 1970). A thorough treatment of American institutions from the order perspective.

NOTES AND REFERENCES

1. Peter L. Berger, *Invitation to Sociology: A Humanistic Perspective* (Garden City, New York: Doubleday Anchor Books, 1963), p. 87.

2. Jerome H. Skolnick and Elliott Currie, "Approaches to Social Problems," *Crisis in American Institutions,* Jerome H. Skolnick and Elliott Currie (eds.), (Boston: Little, Brown and Company, 1970), p. 15.

3. Gresham M. Sykes, *Social Problems in America* (Glenview, Illinois: Scott, Foresman and Company, 1971), p. 30; see also

245

Michael Harrington, *The Accidental Century* (Baltimore: Penguin Books, Inc., 1965).

4.   Charles E. Silberman, *Crisis in the Classroom: The Remaking of American Education* (New York: Random House, 1970), p. 22.

5.   Philip Slater, *The Pursuit of Loneliness: American Culture at the Breaking Point* (Boston: Beacon Press, 1970), pp. 44–45.

6.   Alvin Toffler, *Future Shock* (New York: Bantam Books, 1970), p. 24.

7.   Alfred Balk, *The Free List: Property Without Taxes* (New York: Russell Sage Foundation, 1971).

8.   Sykes, *Social Problems in America*, p. 38.

9.   Sykes, *Social Problems in America*, p. 62.

10. Stewart Alsop, "The Smell of Death," *Newsweek* (February 1, 1971), p. 76.

11. See especially Louis Wirth, "Urbanism as a Way of Life," *American Journal of Sociology* 44 (July, 1938), pp. 1–24.

12. For a more complete list of bureaucratic characteristics see Max Weber, *The Theory of Social and Economic Organization,* trans. A. M. Henderson and Talcott Parsons (New York: The Free Press, 1947), pp. 329–341.

13. The following is taken from Warren Bennis, "Beyond Bureaucracy," *Trans-action* 2 (July–August, 1965), pp. 31–35; Warren Bennis, "Post-Industrial Leadership," *Trans-action* 6 (July–August 1969), pp. 44–51 and 61; and Alvin Toffler, *Future Shock* (New York: Bantam Books, 1970), Chapter 7, "Organization: The Coming Ad-Hocracy."

14. This section is largely dependent on Alvin Toffler, *Future Shock,* Chapters 4–8.

15. William Kornhauser, *The Politics of Mass Society* (New York: The Free Press, 1959); and summaries in Marvin E. Olsen, *The Process of Social Organization* (New York: Holt, Rinehart and Winston, 1968), pp. 326–330; and William Kornhauser, "Mass Society," *International Encyclopedia of the Social Sciences,* Volume 10, David L. Sills (ed.), (New York: The Macmillan Company, 1968), pp. 58–64.

16. John C. McKinney and Charles P. Loomis, "The Typological Tradition," *Contemporary Sociology,* Joseph S. Roucek (ed.), (New York: Philosophical Library, 1958), pp. 557–582.

17. Joseph McGinnis, *The Selling of the President 1968* (New York: Trident Press, 1969).

18. Eric Hoffer, *The True Believer* (New York: A Mentor Book, 1951), p. 25.

19. Toffler, *Future Shock,* especially Chapters 12, 13, 14 and 16.

20. Quoted in *Newsweek* (December 18, 1972), p. 110.

21. Silberman, *Crisis in the Classroom,* pp. 22–23.

CHAPTER 8

The American Family

We have seen that institutions are conservative. They serve to maintain society by clinging to proven patterns which insure that certain important goals of the society are accomplished. The institution of the family (the stable arrangements of marriage, child rearing, and kinship relations) is foremost among the institutions in meeting the basic societal problems of stability and continuity. The family, for example, provides a regular input of new members to the society, who are physically and emotionally cared for in a stable environment. Most important, these new members will learn the society's culture primarily through the family. Family members act as a primary source of pressure on individuals to keep them within the behavioral limits prescribed by society, thus performing an important social control function.

Another function of the family, which serves to perpetuate the status quo, is that it is the primary agent of social location. Membership in a family, involuntary though it may be, automatically confers the family's social status to each offspring. Not only is status transmitted, but also wealth and property and the benefits that they can purchase ("life chances," see Chapter 3). The family, then, is a primary source for the perpetuation of social inequality. From the standpoint of the society this is useful because it prevents chaos. People will automatically know their place, hence, stability will tend to prevail.

All known societies have rules (formal and informal) regarding the family to regulate and determine morality, responsibility for children, accessibility of marriage partners, type of marriages, line of descent, and other functions. The range of variation found around the world in each of these areas is staggering. For instance, some societies allow a plurality of wives while others favor a plurality of husbands. Most commonly, the biological parents are responsible for the nurture of their children, but some societies demand that the biological mother and the maternal uncle will raise the child while the biological father cares for the children of his sister. Some societies forbid marriage partners from visiting or even seeing each other from a distance until the actual wedding ceremony. While these customs may seem weird to Americans, they are normal to those practicing them. The important factor is not the variation, but rather that all societies have found it necessary to have rules regarding marriage and the raising of children. The primary task of this chapter will be to describe the typical American family patterns. This will be followed by a discussion of the American family of the future.

There is great risk in attempting to describe any American institution, since there is so much diversity. With respect to the family, there are regional, social-class, religious, and ethnic differences. Additionally, each family unit may have its own idiosyncratic role expectations, mode of socialization, and rules. Thus, the reader should remember that the description of the American family presented here is of the typical family. By necessity, such a description must be done with "broad brush strokes." Although subject to oversimplification, the description of the American family is important, because it will help us understand why Americans are the way they are and why they differ from persons in other societies.

American family customs, when compared with the family customs of other societies, are characterized by considerable freedom.[1] One instance of relative autonomy is that the American family is unusually equalitarian. Although there is a tendency for the male parent to be considered the head of the household, most families are relatively democratic. Certainly there is a wide variation by family unit in type of power arrangement.

An important source of freedom in American society is that Americans leave their families when they reach adulthood and set up their own nuclear family. Often there is a great distance from one's own home and that of his parents. Thus, grown children are no longer under the direct influence of their parents as is the case in many societies where there are extended families.

Characteristic of the American system is the free choice of mates. Unlike most societies where marriage is arranged by parents on practical grounds, Americans are free to "fall in love" with whomever they please. This freedom is, in part, illusory because there are social pressures that guide the selection process. Persons tend to marry individuals similar to themselves in social class, religion, race, and level of education (this tendency for like to marry like is called homogamy). This freedom is also illusory because what individuals perceive as desirable characteristics in the opposite sex are affected greatly by the values of one's parents, peers, and the influence of the media. Despite these constraints on mate-selection, the individual is considered "free" to marry his or her choice, providing that party is also willing.

Finally, there is relative freedom of choice within each American family in the exact arrangements (rights, duties, obligations, spheres of authority, division of labor) between the husband and wife. The lack of the formalized and detailed blueprint for family roles found in some other societies is a source of strain in many marriages. With each change in family situation (e.g., moving to a new neighborhood, working a different shift, the arrival of children) there must be decisions about allocation of duties and expectations. While many of these decisions occur automatically, others create conflicts.

The relative freedom of choice that occurs in most American families is a mixed blessing. It can create ambiguities, strain, and conflict. Much of this freedom results from the relative isolation of each family unit from any larger kin group. This autonomy, while refreshing at times, means that many of society's most basic burdens (economic, emotional, and physical) must be borne by the nuclear family. The result is a relatively high rate of family instability (a topic to be covered later in the chapter), mental illness, and alienation (see Panel 8–1).

AGE AND SEX ROLES OF FAMILY MEMBERS

In the chapter on culture (Chapter 2) we mentioned briefly the concept of role. This concept is borrowed directly from the theatre and is a metaphor intended to convey the idea that conduct adheres to positions (statuses) in a system. This is to say that because of one's position in an organization (e.g., family, corporation, community) one has certain rights and privileges as well as duties and obligations to persons occupying other positions in that social structure. In occupying a specific position, a person experiences a num-

249

ber of normative expectations, and these expectations are the role. They specify what one should, ought, and must do, and usually how to do it. In this section we are especially concerned with the specific roles (i.e., specific behavioral expectations) of American husbands, wives, and children. The sociological significance of this concept is that although millions of different persons occupy these family roles, the behaviors in each are so routinized that they are duplicated (varying somewhat by social class, region, and ethnicity, but within a given range of tolerance) throughout American society. Because roles provide guidelines for social actions and they are followed, they give regularity and predictability to our social interactions. Finally, with respect to family roles, they provide the social mechanism that insures a continuous supply of adequately socialized new members.

PANEL 8–1

THE HAZARDS OF THE NUCLEAR FAMILY

Source: Margaret Mead, "Future Family," *Trans-action* 8 (September, 1971), p. 52.

The Nuclear Family is a family consisting of one adult man and one adult woman, married to each other, and minor children. The presence of any other person in the household is an insult. The only people that can come in are cleaning women and sitters. In-laws become sitters—which means that when they come in, you go out, and you never have to see them. Furthermore, today, mothers are very uncomfortable with adolescent daughters in the house. So they push them out as rapidly as possible. If they're rich, they send them to Barnard, and if they're poor, they get them married, and they work at it, very hard, because there isn't room in the kind of kitchens we've had since 1945 for two women.

We have put on the Nuclear Family an appalling burden, because young couples were expected to move as far from both sets of relatives as they could, and they had to move, a great deal of the time.

Millions and millions of Americans move every year, moving miles from relatives or anybody that they know. We know now that the chances of a post-partum depression for a woman are directly proportional to the distance she is from any female relative or friend. When we put her in a new suburb all by herself, her chances of getting a post-partum depression go way up. There are millions of young families living in such suburbs, knowing nobody, with no friends, no support of any kind.

Furthermore, each spouse is supposed to be all things to the other. They're supposed to be good in bed, and good out of it. Women are

The Roles of Women and Men

The masculine and feminine roles are basically cultural, not physiological phenomena. Slater has summarized it as follows:

> We know by now . . . that there is virtually nothing in the way of personal characteristics or behavior that is defined in every culture as masculine or feminine. In some societies women are assumed to be stronger, and carry all the heavy burdens. In some societies women are supposed to be impractical and intuitive, in others men are. In most societies women are seen as earthy, men as spiritual, but Victorian England reversed this order. Even within our own society there are odd contradictions: activity is seen as a masculine characteristic, passivity as feminine. Yet men are supposed to move and talk slowly, while women are expected to be birdlike in body movement—constantly moving their hands, using

supposed to be good cooks, good mothers, good wives, good skiers, good conversationalists, good accountants. Neither person is supposed to find any sustenance from anybody else.

Young people from Europe who wanted to come to the United States had to bring their spouses with them, and leave their parents behind or they'd never have gotten here. In India or Africa, when you have a great mass of very traditional relatives, the thing to do is to take your girl and leave, and go a long way off if you want to live the way you want to live.

So it's a good style of family for change, but it's a hazardous kind of family, nonetheless. And if it is hazardous enough in the city, it's a hundred percent more hazardous in the suburbs. There's a special kind of isolation that occurs in the suburbs. So the attack on the Nuclear Family is, I think, thoroughly justified.

There is a need to have more people around: more people to hold the baby, more people to pitch in in emergencies, more people to help when the child is sick, when the mother is sick, more children for other children to play with so you don't have to spend a thousand dollars sending them to nursery school, more kinds of adults around for the children to pick models from in case father or mother can't do the things they want to do. The communes aim to supply these. Real communes, of course, are more extreme—this country was founded by many forms of communes, and it's been so with them ever since—but the bulk of people don't live in communes. One of the things the communes are emphasizing is a lot of people sharing child-care, sharing bringing up the children again, so the children have more security, and don't have to think every day, "What if something happens to Mommy; what if something happens to Daddy? Will there be anyone at all?" I think we're going to have a trend toward different kinds of living.

many more facial muscles, talking rapidly. Paradoxically, a man who is too active in the most physical sense of using many muscles from moment to moment is considered "effeminate." It should be emphasized, then, that when we talk of "masculine" and "feminine" we are referring only to the ways in which these are customarily defined in our culture, and since sex role definitions change from time to time there is ample room for confusion.[2]

Masculine and feminine roles, then, are cultural. The defining characteristics of masculinity in American society are assumed to be dominance, aggressiveness, competitiveness, and independence. To have these traits in American society is rewarding in the American system of values; that women lack these traits is a major explanation for their secondary status. If, on the other hand, a woman possesses these traits then she is "put down" for not being feminine. Consequently, it is a situation of being damned if you do and damned if you don't—typical of the dilemma all minority groups face.* Thus, one basis for the current women's liberation movement is the drive for women to develop their own potential. They stress that the traditional masculine-feminine roles are archaic and of benefit only to the male.

To be "feminine" in American society is to have a role that is conforming, passive, and dependent. A crucial element, however, is self-sacrifice. The female in American society is taught to sacrifice her own wishes for those of her husband and children. The self-sacrifice of being a wife and mother may have benefits for some women as their husbands climb to the top occupationally or economically or as their children successfully reach maturity. Unfortunately, many self-sacrificing women have problems later in life because they find they have lost much of their sexual attractiveness and their children no longer need them. For them, their *raison d'être* has evaporated with the passage of time. Menopause thus becomes a special problem for American women, not only because of the hormone changes taking place, but because it represents symbolically their decline into "uselessness" or perhaps their wasted life potential.[4]

Although the women's liberation movement has made some headway, the adult female role in American society is now what it always has been. She has the fundamental responsibility for the home and the rearing of the children. It is now common for married women to work outside the home (31 percent in 1960 and 37 percent in 1968). It is not common, however, for men to stay home

* For an interesting account of the mental problems women face because of sex-role stereotypes in American society see Phyllis Chesler's article, "Men Drive Women Crazy."[3]

and care for the home and raise the children. For the male in American society the key life role is his occupation.

Sexism in American society

Sexism is the term that refers to the exploitative way in which men and women are related in social, economic, and sexual contexts. It refers, further, to the second-class status of women. Finally, it refers to the institutional mechanisms (the media, education, religion, laws, customs) that keep women in this servile position. Although a few women have fought sexism throughout American history, there is now a frontal assault on male power privilege by ever increasing numbers of females. The methods advocated and the rhetoric used vary from mild to radical, but the target is the same—male supremacy. Let us briefly review the ways in which male supremacy is perpetuated in American society.

   A. Females are forced through the socialization process to accept an inferior role in society (as well as in the community, church, family, or other social arrangement) and to believe in their own inferiority. In the toys given them, the stories read to them, the admonitions addressed to them, girls learn to be docile, fragile, and dependent. They aspire to the jobs of social worker, teacher, or nurse, rather than doctor, minister, judge, engineer, or President. They run for class secretary rather than class president; these are examples of the suppression of choice by cultural tyranny. The literature for children is a common mode by which traditional masculine and feminine roles are taught and reinforced. One book, for example, is devoted to the appropriate occupational roles of women. The entire list of possible jobs was as follows: nurse, stewardess, ballerina, owner of a candy shop, model, movie star, secretary, artist, singer, nursery school teacher, dress designer, housewife, and mother.[5] Clearly omitted from this list are jobs that women are as capable of doing as men but traditionally denied them (e.g., pilot, doctor, engineer, lawyer, plumber, electrician, and professor). Another book designed for children lists the differences between boys and girls in another way that implies the limited abilities of females. Two examples will suffice:

   Boys fix things.   Girls need things fixed.
   Boys invent things.   Girls use what boys invent.[6]

   B. Females have an identity problem forced on them by the system. Whereas leadership, intelligence, and aggressiveness are

253

traits by which American males are judged competent or not, these are not relevant for the female. Her appearance is judged by many males to be more important in the business world than her intelligence or personality. Thus, she is considered a sexual object, not a person. Her achievements also make little difference, for her social status depends on the achievements of her husband. As if in reinforcement of this, the prefix to the female's name indicates her married status, whereas the form of address for men is constant in American society. Moreover, women will most often be addressed as Mrs. Fred Smith, losing in marriage both first and last names. Society relates to the married woman, not as an individual, but as a part of someone else.

C. *According to the 1970 Census the vast majority of women* (over 14) have been married (78 percent), and of these many have no occupation other than housewife. Those that work outside the home do the housewife chores also. Although many consider the role of housewife important (because of the way they have been socialized), the duties imply for the most part being a domestic servant. Thus, menial housework is apportioned in the United States on the basis of sex.

D. *Women are treated unequally in the occupational world.* They are overrepresented in some jobs (secretary, teacher, nurse, sales clerks) and underrepresented in others. Compare, for example, the predominant sex in each of the following pairs: airline pilot—stewardess; dentist—dental hygienist; elementary school principal —elementary teacher; doctor—nurse; corporation president—secretary. Clearly there is job discrimination in American society. This results from differences in expectations (from the socialization process), from parental guidance, from sex-role models, from the sex-roles found in movies, television, and novels, from requirements of the professions, and from quota systems. Unquestionably women are underpaid for equal work. Moreover, they find fewer opportunities for promotion. The occupational structure is clearly male-oriented.

E. *Women lack social power.* Only men are allowed to take the initiative with women. They ask for dates while women must remain at home waiting for the phone to ring. Men pay the way on dates, giving the impression of "renting" the girl for the evening. Second, males rule females in all aspects of social life—in the family, on the job, in churches (women are Sunday School teachers while men are deacons, elders, trustees, and ministers).

F. *Even the English language is sexist.* The words "man" and "mankind" are terms for the whole human race. God is a male. There is a joke that points to the way we typically picture God:

"Did you hear the news about God?"
"No, what?"
"She's black."[7]

Division of Labor in Marriage

Evidence for cultural prescriptions for the masculine and feminine roles is seen clearly in the way duties are divided in American families. Blood and Wolfe studied some 731 Detroit families in 1955 and found a good deal of role specialization in household tasks. Table 8–1 shows their findings.

The division of labor noted in Table 8–1 indicates that men and women tend to do those tasks for which they have been culturally trained. Males are expected to be more mechanical and muscular while females are trained to know more about cooking and cleaning. Clearly, there is a strong tendency for the division of labor to be along these lines, but there is variation. Each family unit must work out the particulars of its own division of labor.

Each family must also decide who will make decisions in the key areas. Whether the male or the female predominates in a particular decision-making area is culturally assigned, but as with division of labor, there is some variation. Blood and Wolfe present data that show how decision-making is allocated for their sample of Detroit families (Table 8–2).

Blood and Wolfe concluded that the old patriarchal system is no longer part of American society. Their data can be interpreted differently, however. Since the male in Amercian society tends to make decisions in those areas that are culturally defined as more vital, it remains the dominant role.

Parent Roles

The primary responsibility of parents is to teach their children the attitudes, values, and behaviors considered appropriate by the parents (and society). This insures that most children will be reared to take acceptable niches in the society when they reach adulthood. Parents, therefore, are the most important societal agents of sociali-

TABLE 8–1. Division of Labor, by Household Tasks[a] (731 Detroit Families)

Who does it?				Task (in Percentages)				
	Repairs	Lawn	Walk	Bills	Groceries	Breakfast	Living Room	Dishes
1. Husband always	73	66	61	19	7	16	1	1
2. Husband more than wife	11	9	13	6	7	5	1	2
3. Husband and wife exactly the same	6	6	8	34	29	4	17	13
4. Wife more than husband	3	6	7	11	20	7	15	12
5. Wife always	3	7	7	30	36	66	65	70
No Answer	4	6	4		1	2	1	2
Total	100	100	100	100	100	100	100	100
Wife's mean task performance	1.46	1.71	1.81	3.27	3.72	4.04	4.44	4.52

[a] The questions asked about these eight tasks follow:

1. Who repairs things around the house?
2. Who mows the lawn?
3. Who shovels the sidewalk?
4. Who keeps track of the money and the bills?
5. Who does the grocery shopping?
6. Who gets the husband's breakfast on work days?
7. Who straightens up the living room when company is coming?
8. Who does the evening dishes?

Source: Robert O. Blood, Jr., and Donald M. Wolfe, Husbands and Wives (New York: The Free Press, 1960), p. 50.

TABLE 8–2. Allocation of Power in Decision-Making Areas[a] (731 Detroit Families)

Who Decides?	Decision (in Percentages)							
	Husband's Job	Car	Insurance	Vacation	House	Wife's Work	Doctor	Food
1. Husband always	90	56	31	12	12	26	7	10
2. Husband more than wife	4	12	11	6	6	5	3	2
3. Husband and wife exactly the same	3	25	41	68	58	18	45	32
4. Wife more than husband	0	2	4	4	10	9	11	11
5. Wife always	1	3	10	7	13	39	31	41
No Answer	2	1	2	3	1	3	3	3
Total	100	100	100	100	100	100	100	100
Husband's mean power[b]	4.86	4.18	3.50	3.12	2.94	2.69	2.53	2.26

[a] The eight questions on marital power are listed below:

1. What job the husband should take
2. What car to get
3. Whether to buy life insurance or not
4. Where to go on a vacation
5. What house or apartment to take
6. Whether or not the wife should go to work or quit work
7. What doctor to have when someone is sick
8. How much money the family can afford to spend per week on food

[b] The mean for each column is computed on the basis of the weights shown, e.g., "husband always" = 5.

Source: Robert O. Blood, Jr., and Donald M. Wolfe, Husbands and Wives (New York, The Free Press, 1960), pp. 19–21.

zation in the child's formative years. There is a wide latitude, however, in the mode of socialization.

There are two broad patterns of socialization that can be identified in American society. One stresses punishment for wrong behavior while the other emphasizes rewards for good behavior. One demands obedience of the child to adults. The other allows the child freedom to explore and find things out for himself. Thus, one is adult-centered while the other is child-centered. One is much more strict when it comes to thumb sucking, toilet training, cleanliness, and aggression control, while the other is more tolerant. The first mode of socialization for each of the above comparisons is called "repressive socialization" while the second has been named "participatory socialization." Repressive socialization is based on the premise that children can and should be molded to conform, to be obedient. Participatory socialization, on the other hand, assumes that children should be given freedom to explore and develop their own unique potentialities.

Although few parents are consistent in the manner by which they interact with their children, there appear to be discernible patterns by social class. The empirical evidence is that working-class parents tend toward repressive socialization while middle-class parents are more likely to practice participatory socialization.

Social class appears to make a difference in socialization modes because of the variance in life experience among the classes. The members of the middle class, for example, tend to have a good deal of autonomy in their occupations, while working-class persons are more likely to take orders under strict supervision. Parents, apparently, use the mode of socialization that they are comfortable with and the one that makes adjustment to life the easiest. The patterns continue over time because the social class behaviors are reinforced. Children live in relatively homogeneous neighborhoods by social class, thereby giving the impression that a particular mode is the most natural because almost everyone does it. Persons also tend to marry within their social class. This, too, reinforces one type of socialization practice as the typical one for a particular social class.[8]

Participatory socialization has not always been the primary mode of the middle classes. Child rearing practices, especially among the middle and upper classes, have vacillated according to the prevailing views of experts. The bulletin *Infant Care*, published by the United States Children's Bureau, has gone through a number of editions and has changed significantly since its inception in 1914. In that year the views of psychologist John B. Watson were enunciated. He believed that the development of the child was shaped entirely by the habits he acquired. Thus, mothers were instructed to: never rock their baby, begin toilet training by the third month, and never let the child suck his thumb. In the 1930's the philosophy of Sigmund Freud prevailed. The concern then was with the emotional damage that could occur from unfavorable experiences during the first years of life. Parents were enjoined to make the environment of the child supportive and loving.[9]

Participatory socialization, so prevalent in the contemporary American middle class, is in large measure due to the persuasive influences of Dr. Benjamin Spock, whose book *Child and Baby Care* had sold more than 21 million copies from 1947 to 1970.[10] Most parents (at least middle-class parents) were greatly influenced by the child-rearing philosophy of Spock. He argued that young children should be treated with kindness in a relaxed atmosphere. Babies should not be fed on a rigid time schedule, but when they want it. Children should be taught to love rather than fear their parents. In later editions (1957 and 1968) Spock was less permissive but the basic philosophy remained—that children should be raised in a relaxed, loving environment. Although accused by many of advocating wanton permissiveness, Spock, especially in his later editions, placed great emphasis on the child's need for parental control and the importance of not letting the child become a tyrant in the home.

Participatory socialization, with its overall emphasis on the child "doing his thing," has been under attack from various sides. A *Life* magazine editorial, for instance, has stated, "When it comes to parental authority, the U.S. may well be the loosest ship in history."[11] This may be a cause, the editorial goes on to say, of the rising tide of vandalism. Dr. Norman Vincent Peale, the popular minister, has criticized Dr. Spock for his child-raising doctrines. These add up to, in Peale's words: "Feed 'em whatever they want; don't let them cry; instant gratification of needs. The result is a student generation that thinks it can get whatever it yells for."[12]

What are the consequences of most middle-class parents adopting the participatory socialization philosophy of Spock since the 1940's? The jury is still out on this question, but there is some evidence for evaluation. To begin with, Spock's ideas have reinforced feminine domesticity (thereby incurring the wrath of Women's Liberationists). He has been quite explicit in his belief that a woman's place is in the home. The task of child rearing is considered to be so important and difficult that it has priority over all other possible activities. This follows from his belief that the child is unique and has great potential. Therefore, the Spock-oriented mother has the opportunity to turn out a really outstanding product. The results of this belief, aside from reinforcing feminine domesticity, are: (1)

millions of housewives living lives of emotional and intellectual poverty; and (2) a large number of women who are failures (i.e., they either do not devote full time to their children or their children do not turn out as envisioned by the mother).[13]

A second result of an entire generation of "Spock-marked" children was the student revoluton of the late 1960's. This is not to say that mode of socialization was *the* cause of the youth rebellion, but it has been demonstrated that it was a prominent contributor. Richard Flacks, a sociologist, made a comparison of student activists with student nonactivists and found some interesting differences: (1) activists were more likely to come from upper-status families; (2) their fathers were overwhelmingly professionals (college faculty, lawyers, doctors) rather than businessmen, white collar employees or blue collar workers; (3) the parents of the activists were more politically liberal than were the parents of the nonactivists; and (4) activists' parents were more "permissive" than were the parents of nonactivists.[14]

There are at least two reasons why persons raised in a "permissive" family are more likely to participate actively in student rebellions than are persons raised in a "strict" family. First, there is an incongruence between the environment in a permissive family and the bureaucratization found in American high schools and universities. The democratic, egalitarian, interpersonal relations found in many upper-middle class, professional homes is in sharp contrast with the impersonality, competitiveness, strict adherence to rules and chains of command found in bureaucracies. This incongruity added to the second reason—a questioning attitude—explains why some fight the system. Kenneth Keniston has put it this way:

> Given what we know about the general characteristics of the families of protest-prone students, it also seems probable that the dominant ethos of their families is unusually equalitarian, permissive, "democratic," and highly individuated. More specifically, we might expect that these will be families where children talk back to their parents at the dinner table, where free dialogue and discussion of feelings is encouraged, and where "rational" solutions are sought to everyday family problems and conflicts. We would also expect that such families would place a high premium on self-expression and intellectual independence, encouraging their children to make up their own minds and to stand firm against group pressures.[15]

It would seem probable that youngsters encouraged to be independent thinkers and dissenters in the home would continue with those actions outside the family.

While Reverend Peale's attack may appear to describe this group accurately as spoiled brats crying until they get their way, these youngsters turn out in actuality to be more idealistic, responsive, and humanitarian than were children raised in strict homes. Philip Slater even claims that "The product of child-centered, Spockian child rearing is the most socially conscious youth America has ever known."[16] If this is the case, then Spock and the mode of socialization he inspired are to be praised rather than condemned.

There is another mode of socialization that characterizes a sizeable minority of lower-class families (but is found in some families in the other social classes as well), and that is excessive freedom. This freedom is different from that found in participatory socialization, because in this case the freedom is not because of adherence to a particular philosophy of child-raising, but because of either neglect by the parents or rebellion by the children. Either of these may prevail in the lower class as the result of several factors: (1) the chance of two parents present in the home is reduced because of the conditions of lower-class life; (2) children living in an achievement-oriented society may not have any respect for their parents and therefore disobey their wishes; (3) for the minority-group families that are so predominant in this stratum there is a huge "generation gap" because the youngsters consider their parents "uncle toms" for not fighting the system that keeps them in such a lowly state.

Adolescence

According to the 1970 census there were over 27 million American teenagers (13 through 19)—about 13 percent of the total population. This is a very significant category in American society for several reasons. First, they are a strong economic force. For example, they account for more than one-fourth of the record sales and more than one-third of the movie audiences. They spend collectively an enormous amount of money on clothes and toiletries. As they shift from fad to fad, fortunes are made and lost in the clothing and entertainment industries. Second, adolescents are a financial burden to society. Most adolescents are in school and not in the labor market. They are furnished with an education that they did not earn. Within each family, adolescents and the younger children are economic liabilities. They do not earn their way. The United States is probably the first nation to transform children from a family asset as labor to a family liability as student-consumer. A third basis for this category being important is that many adolescents are disenchanted and alienated. This results in withdrawal, apathy, or rebellion.

For some of the young, their disenchantment is brought about by a moral gap—not a generation gap. They see older people as mainly interested in making money and oblivious to the social ills of the society. They want to put into practice what the Constitution says but the government does not enforce. Furthermore, they feel that young people are forced to fight in wars brought about by the older generation. Many young people become disenchanted because they are unsure of their identity. Unlike adults who find identity in their vocations or avocations, adolescents must find their identity elsewhere—in a cause, in religion, in sports, in sexual promiscuity, in being "tough." Adolescence is an age of "self" discovery. For many young persons, this is a difficult task.[17]

Why is the stage of adolescence in American society a period of stress and strain for so many? The most important reason is that it is an age of transition from one social status to another. There is no clear line of demarcation between adolescence and adulthood. Are people considered adult when they can get a full-time job, when they are physically capable of producing children, or when they can be drafted for military service? There is no clear distinction. Most primitive societies, by contrast, have "rites of passage" that seem cruel and barbaric but do serve the function of clearly identifying the individual as a child or an adult. Adulthood in American society is unclear. As Stephens has said, "The postponement of sociological adulthood produces a social status which is filled, somewhat uncertainly, by millions of our society's members. This is adolescence; the state of being physically mature but not working, sexually mature but not married, 'grown-up' but still dependent on parents."[18] Surely much of the acting out by adolescents in the United States can be explained partially at least by these status ambiguities.

These status ambiguities are probably unavoidable in a society where the state of technological development demands an extended period of education. Full-time schooling for a college degree or beyond tends to defer marriage well beyond the age of full biological maturity. This presents special problems for the adolescent. Young men and women are permitted and encouraged to date without chaperons. They are sexually mature and are members of a society that places a good deal of emphasis on sex (movies, novels, magazines, advertising). Ira Reiss, the acknowledged expert on premarital sexual behavior in the United States, made a study of sexual attitudes in 1963. His study involved a representative national sample of about 1500 adults (single and married) and about 1200 high school and college students (all single) from three different states. Table 8–3 presents these data. Especially interesting are the differences between adults and students.

Examination of Table 8–3 reveals that (1) there is a sexual double standard in American society—substantially more persons

TABLE 8–3.   Percentage Agreeing With Selected Statements

Statement	Adult Sample	Student Sample
1. I believe that full sexual relations are acceptable for the male before marriage when he is engaged to be married.	19.5	52.2
2. I believe that full sexual relations are acceptable for the female before marriage when she is engaged to be married.	16.9	44.0
3. I believe that full sexual relations are acceptable for the male before marriage when he is in love.	17.6	47.6
4. I believe that full sexual relations are acceptable for the female before marriage when she is in love.	14.2	38.7
5. I believe that full sexual relations are acceptable for the male before marriage when he feels strong affection for his partner.	16.3	36.9
6. I believe that full sexual relations are acceptable for the female before marriage when she feels strong affection for her partner.	12.5	27.2
7. I believe that full sexual relations are acceptable for the male before marriage even if he does not feel particularly affectionate toward his partner.	11.7	20.8
8. I believe that full sexual relations are acceptable for the female before marriage even if she does not feel particularly affectionate toward her partner.	7.4	10.8

Source: Adapted from Ira L. Reiss, *The Family System in America* (New York: Holt, Rinehart and Winston, Inc., 1971), pp. 153–154.

accept premarital sexual behavior by males than females; (2) adults are much less permissive on sexual behavior than are students; (3) love between the partners is an important component if premarital sexual behavior is to be accepted; and (4) premarital chastity is the ideal under most conditions. While all of these present problems to the adolescent, the second is of special interest to our understanding of the conflicts the adolescents face—the clash between parents and their children on sexual attitudes and behaviors. Reiss commenting on his findings from several studies has said: "Thus a generational clash of some sort is almost inevitable. When children reach their late teens or early 20's, they also reach the peak of their permissiveness; their parents, at the same time, reach the nadir of theirs."[19]

Another source of difficulty for adolescents has been noted by Urie Bronfenbrenner, the famous researcher of family relationships.[20] The *de facto* responsibility of raising children has shifted away from the family to other societal settings. The family still has the primary moral and legal responsibility for raising children, but other influences are becoming more important. The reasons for this shift are many and stem from the changes occurring within American society. To begin with, the nuclear family that moves (once every five years on the average) is bereft of relatives other than father, mother, and sibs who take an active interest in the upbringing of the children.

Second, the members of most nuclear families do not spend very much time together. The father most commonly works at some distance from his home. He may work evenings, weekends, and be away from home for extended periods. The mother may work (more than one-third do) and thus also be away from home. If not working, she may be away from home anyway because of social obligations, errands, and other activities. Consequently, many adolescents do not have adequate adult-role models.

Children, too, are away from home a good deal at school activities, club meetings, on dates, and being with their friends. The time children spend with others tends to be more with peers than with adults (especially as the child becomes a teenager). The typical peer group of children tends to be homogeneous. This results from seeking friends who share the same interests. A less obvious reason is that young people are restricted in choice of friends by propinquity. The typical urban or suburban neighborhood is noted for its sameness—in architecture and age of homes, but more importantly in the characteristics of the inhabitants. The individuals tend to be of the same race, socioeconomic level, and even age. Thus the relationships that children form tend to be limited to persons who are similar in important ways.

The typical American youngster at some point in time turns away from parents to peers for opinion, advice, or companionship. The impact of the peer group on the child is great. A study by James Coleman of youngsters in ten high schools is especially instructive on this point. He found that although approximately three-fourths of the boys' parents wanted their youngsters to be remembered as brilliant students, only 31 percent of the boys wanted to be so remembered (44 percent wanted to be remembered as athletic stars). Apparently the attitudes of the students were not only anti-intellectual but antithetical to those of their parents.[21]

Adolescents have a tremendous need to be popular, to be acceptable, to belong. They are "other-directed," which means that their peer groups become so important that they are the sources of direction for the individual.[22] Thus the sources for attitudes, clothing styles, hairstyle, slang, for most teenagers are their close friends.

The Aged

The age distribution of the population has shifted in recent years, with more and more Americans living past the arbitrary dividing line of 65 years of age. In 1940, for example, 9 million persons (6.8 percent) were 65 or older whereas more than 20 million Americans (9.8 percent) were in that category according to the 1970 census. This change in the composition of the population has important effects upon family life and the society in general.

The elderly in American society are somewhat analogous to adolescents in the ambivalence they face, because they are in a transition stage (in this case between work and death). As a category they are neither self-sufficient nor productive. As a category, the elderly are accorded low status, unlike many societies where they are believed to be especially wise and therefore hold the power. In a sense they constitute a minority group for they are subject to unfavorable treatment (forced retirement, difficulty in finding employment). They are believed by many to be inflexible, cantankerous, and unreliable—all false stereotypes.[23] These negative stereotypes are held by many Americans. They probably stem from the fear of old age that is prevalent in the youth-oriented American society.

Stereotypes of the aged are difficult to dispel, largely because research on aging is a recent development in both the biological and the social sciences and research findings reach the public at a snail's pace. Many widely held but inaccurate images, inadvertently repeated through the mass media, come from social workers who serve the poor, the lonely and the isolated, and from physicians and psychiatrists who see the physically ill and the mentally ill. Thus we base many of our current stereotypes on a picture of the needy rather than on a picture of the typical older person.

Studies of large and representative samples of older persons are now appearing, however, and they go far toward exploding some of our outmoded images. For example, old persons do not become isolated and neglected by their families, although both generations prefer separate households. Old persons are not dumped into mental hospitals by cruel or indifferent children. They are not necessarily lonely or desolate if they live alone. Few of them ever show overt signs of mental deterioration or senility, and only a small proportion ever become mentally ill. For those who do, psychological and psychiatric treatment is by no means futile.

Retirement and widowhood do not lead to mental illness, nor does social isolation. Retirement is not necessarily bad; some men and women want to keep on working, but more and more choose to retire earlier and earlier. Increasing proportions of the population evidently value leisure more than they value work. Nor do retired persons sicken physically from idleness and feelings of worthlessness. Three-fourths of the persons questioned in a recent national sample reported that they were satisfied or very satisfied with their lives since retirement. This is in line with earlier surveys. Most persons over 65 think of themselves as being in good health and they act accordingly, no matter what their physicians think.

But the most insidious stereotype of all, in many ways, puts the old (or, for that matter, the young or the middle-aged) into a distinct category or a distinct group. There is, in truth, no such thing as "the" young, or "the" old. People *do* differ; they also become increasingly different over time, as each person accumulates an idiosyncratic set of experiences and becomes committed to a unique set of people, things, interests, and activities. One has only to recall, for instance, the range of differences among the members of one's high school graduating class and then to see these persons at a class reunion 25 years later. They are much more varied as 40-year-olds than they were as 18-year-olds. In a society as complex as the United States, with increasing social permissiveness for people to follow their own bents, a good case can be made that—despite the counterpressures that create conformity—increased differentiation occurs over the life cycle.[24]

Despite the disclaimers just presented, the elderly in American society often are lonely. This is a consequence of the nuclear family system which separates the aged from their chidren. Often the children of the elderly live a great distance from their parents. Added to this spatial separation is the social separation that occurs through social mobility. Many children surpass their parents in social status. Concomitant with a widening gap in social status but also a result of age differences are discrepancies in life styles, behaviors, and attitudes between parents and their adult children.

Another way in which the elderly tend to be isolated from kinship ties is through the death of one's mate—widowhood. There are about 11 million widowed persons with the present ratio of widows to widowers being more than 4 to 1. This dramatic difference results from a variance in life expectancy (in 1967 males had a life expectancy of 67.0 years while females had one of 74.2 years—a difference of over seven years) and the tendency for males to marry someone younger than themselves (usually about a two year differential). Thus, the average married female can expect nine years of widowhood—and, therefore, dependency upon social security, insurance, savings or help from her family.[25]

Isolation of the elderly also occurs from a break in occupational ties. In the past when many persons farmed or owned small businesses, work was a lifetime process. In an industrial, bureaucratized society, however, retirement is usually abrupt. Many firms have established policy that makes retirement compulsory at a given age (regardless of the individual's willingness to continue, expertise, and experience). Since one's work is the source of income, social status, and identity, to be cut off against one's will may be a traumatic experience from which it is difficult to recover.

A final source of isolation is the breakup of community ties. A relatively recent trend has been the creation of entire communities for the aged in Florida, California, and Arizona (14.5 percent of Florida's population, for instance, is 65 years of age or older). Many old people are enticed to leave their home communities and live in these age-segregated communities. Another way in which the elderly may be separated from community life is by living in nursing homes or confined in mental hospitals.

Talcott Parsons, a highly esteemed sociologist, has wondered if two alleged behavioral consequences of old age are the result of the high probability of being isolated from kinship ties, occupational ties, and community ties. These may explain, at least partially, the increased political agitation among the elderly, on the one hand, or it may manifest itself in the high incidence of psychosomatic illnesses and at least partly in the well known disabilities of older people.[26]

FAMILY STABILITY AND INSTABILITY

A family can, for a variety of reasons, dissolve. Marriage partners can agree to separate or formally sever the marriage through divorce. Although this section is entitled stability and instability there is no way of knowing the number of unstable homes (where the partners remain together in a high state of tension). Thus, we will devote our discussion solely to divorce, which is just the visible portion of the iceberg. Although some societies have a higher rate of family dissolution, the family in American society is especially vulnerable. A primary reason is that the most important bond in American marriages is romantic love, a feeling that may change as the partners age, or as they are upwardly or downwardly mobile.

One often hears from ministers, politicians, and editorial writers, the assertion that about one out of four marriages ends up in divorce. This statistic is misleading because it is based on dividing the number of marriages that occur in a given year by the number of divorces in that same year. Thus, in 1968 there were 2,059,000 marriages and 582,000 divorces and annulments or a "divorce rate" of 28 percent. This rate is unreliable because the number of divorces occurs from the entire pool of married couples (47 million in 1968), not just those married in one year. The matter is complicated further by those persons who get divorced more than once.

The best method to arrive at a fairly accurate rate would be to keep track of one marriage cohort (those persons married in a given year) throughout their married lives.* Since this has not yet been done satisfactorily, the best approximation we have is to determine the number of divorces that occur annually per 1000 married women fifteen years of age and over. Using this statistic the rates for selected years are as follows:

1920	8 divorces per 1000 couples
1947	18 divorces per 1000 couples
1970	14 divorces per 1000 couples[28]

* A preliminary study of this kind has been done. The data gathered from interviews of 50,000 households by the Bureau of the Census predict that about 25 to 29 percent of women in their late twenties and thirties will end their first marriage by divorce. This prediction is tentative because it is based on the divorce experience of older cohorts, but it does lend some support to the "one divorce out of four marriages" contention.[27]

268

The year 1947 was selected because it represents the highest divorce rate in American history—the result, no doubt, of the hasty marriages and/or long separations caused by World War II. The rate stabilized during the decade of the 1950's at about 10 divorces per 1000 couples. Since about 1965, however, the rate has slowly increased. One expert, Ira Reiss, predicts the rate will level off at about 14 per 1000 couples.

We can make some generalizations about divorce in the United States based on accurate data.[29]

1. The average duration of marriages that end in divorce is seven years. In other words, after seven years of marriage 50 percent of those couples who are going to divorce will have actually divorced.
2. The divorce rate is related to economic conditions. The rate increases during prosperity. Apparently this is due to unwillingness to break up a marriage when wives and children will need greater support.
3. The younger the age at marriage of the partners, the greater the likelihood of divorce. About 27 percent of the women married 20 years earlier as teenagers were divorced by 1967, while only 14 percent of those who were married in their twenties were divorced by that year.[30]
4. The higher the income the less the likelihood of divorce. A 1971 study conducted by the Census Bureau found that in 71 percent of households where the family income was less than $5,000 both partners had been married only once. The rate increased to 77 percent in households with incomes ranging from $5,000 to $10,000. For those families with incomes between $10,000 and $15,000, the figure was 81 percent, and with income of $15,000 or more, it was 83 percent. This same relationship holds for education as well. The greater the educational attainment, the greater the chance of a marriage surviving.[31]
5. Twenty-five percent of all marriages in a given year involve at least one person who has been previously married (three-fourths of whom were divorced). Well over 90 percent of those who lose a spouse by death or divorce between the ages of 20 and 35 will eventually remarry.[32]

The Black Family in Contemporary American Society

The alleged family instability among minority groups, especially blacks, has been used as the explanation for their problems. This is best exemplified by the 1965 governmental report authored by Daniel P. Moynihan, a sociologist.[33] This controversial document can be summarized as follows:

> The fundamental source of weakness in the black community is an unstable family structure caused by the experience of slavery, the absence of husbands and a high rate of illegitimacy. The modal family type, then, is a matriarchy. A matriarchal form of family is detrimental because it is at variance with the standard pattern in American society. It is especially harmful to boys who will be denied adequate sex role models. Thus, the institution of the black family is assumed to be defective. Black culture produces a weak and disorganized form of family life, which, because it is self-perpetuating, is the obstacle to full realization of equality.

There are a number of criticisms of the Moynihan Report. They are important, because by itself the Moynihan Report indicts blacks rather than society (the racism that perpetuates unequal opportunities and the massive over-representation of blacks among the poor) and masks the relationship between poverty and family stability regardless of race.

An initial criticism is directed at the common practice of over-generalization. To speak of "the" black family is a fiction. There is a wide diversity of family forms in different geographic regions, at different income levels, and at different social status levels throughout American society. Blacks are not a homogeneous group.

A related criticism is the contention that black family structure, when contrasted with white family structure, is highly unstable. Overall, this is correct but it incorrectly implies that the crucial difference in family structure is race. The more important differences, however, are the relative economic positions of the two categories. Poor families are disproportionately unstable when compared to the more well-to-do, regardless of race. Since nearly half of all black families are poor, compared to 10 to 15 percent of white families, the higher instability rates for blacks are explained not by race itself, but by the racism that systematically disadvantages blacks and advantages whites. Moynihan bases his claim on the breakup of the black family on data from the early 1960's. These data show: (a) 23 percent of all nonwhite homes were headed by a woman; (b) 24 percent of all black births were illegitimate; and (c) 36 percent of black children live in broken homes. Although these figures reflect marital instability, they do not have sufficient strength for the claim that black families are unstable. To the contrary, these same figures show: (a) 77 percent of all nonwhite homes are headed by a male; (b) 76 percent of all black babies are born to a man and wife who are legally married; and (c) 64 percent of black children are living with both parents. Thus, these same statistics show that *the overwhelming majority of black families are stable.*

The majority of black families being stable belies the contention of Moynihan that deviant family forms are part of black culture. Matriarchy and husband desertion are believed to result from the continual humiliaton of the black male under slavery and the Jim Crow laws of the South. Without question these practices were humiliating, but these occurrences do not prove a black culture that transmits a peculiar family form (as well as mode of socialization, power relations, family roles) from generation to generation.

Several writers have mentioned two factors other than divorce and separation that help to explain a high rate of family breakup among blacks—premature death and illegitimate birth. Both of these factors are closely linked to economic factors.[34] One-fourth of all non-white female heads of household with children under 18 are widows. Twice as many black men between the ages of 20 and 40 will die as whites (one out of every 12). These statistics do not reflect cultural differences between whites and non-whites, but differences in health services (the poor are deprived of health services either because of discrimination or because of inability to afford necessary services).

Illegitimacy, too, occurs disproportionately in black births. The rate of 24 percent among blacks is about eight times greater than among whites. Why the vast difference? The cultural explanation is that black girls are more promiscuous because of their "background." Such an explanation is spurious, as Ryan has argued:

> Young black women do not engage in premarital intercourse eight times more frequently than white women. All the evidence points to the conclusion that differences in the amount of premarital sexual activity between lower class and middle class females, or between white and Negro ones, is relatively small. Vast differences in recorded illegitimate births—and consequently the formation of mother-child family units—are accounted for by: poor access to contraception and abortion, few forced marriages, little concealment, and low availability of adoption services. White middle-class women are no more committed to virginity, in practice or in theory, than poor women and Negro women are. It is simply that they can get and can afford Enovid; if they get pregnant, they are more able to obtain an abortion; if they have a baby, they are more able to conceal the absence of a husband, and they have a much greater chance to give up a baby for adoption. The differences are due, then, not to culture, or values or a racial habit of promiscuity cultivated on the old plantation; the differences are due to the effect of social and economic forces, and to the discriminatory withholding of information, resources and services *today*.[35]

The strong relationship between income level and illegitimacy rates can also be found among blacks. One study in New York compared high and low income tracts and found that the proportion of births out-of-wedlock in relation to total nonwhite births varied from a high of 38 percent in the Central Harlem district to a comparative low of 9 percent in the Pelham Bay district.[36] We must conclude that the differences found between blacks and whites result from social-class phenomena, not racial differences.

A final objection to the Moynihan Report is that it is a classic case of "blaming the victim." According to this thesis, the pathology lies within black Americans, especially black males, not in social institutions. Thus, Moynihan's solution was ". . . a national effort towards the problems of Negro Americans must be directed towards the question of family structure. The object should be to strengthen the Negro family so as to enable it to raise and support its members as do other families."[37]

But the problem lies not in the black family but in the oppressive white racist society. The target should not be the black family but discrimination in the schools, and on the jobs. Furthermore, power and wealth need to be more equally distributed. Then, the "problem" black family will cease being a problem for whatever problem it presents is an artifact of economic and social inequality.[38]

THE FUTURE FAMILY

As with all institutions, the family changes very slowly. It is important to recognize, however, that changes occur. As the United States changed from a rural, agrarian society to an urban, industrial one, the family has been affected. Before we look to the future prospects of the family, let us examine the changes that have taken place. These will provide some clues about the future.

Trends of the Recent Past that Affect the Family

In a rural environment with little geographical mobility the family of the past consisted of three or four generations living together or adjacent to one another.[39] The present family is comprised of two generations—parents and their dependent children. The nuclear family of today allows for a good deal of freedom but lacks the emotional and physical supports of the extended family.

A second trend has been the loss of many functions of the family. The family of the past was a production unit (family farm or business). It was the primary socialization agent for the youngsters. The family provided the leisure time activities for all members. Finally, the family provided for the affectional needs of its members. Actually, in the present family, all of the functions but affectional have been lost or attenuated. Economically, the family is fragmented, as the family members tend to have various and often unrelated jobs. The family is now far less important as an instrument in the socialization of children. Pre-school children often go to nursery schools or are raised in the daytime hours by baby-sitters. The school itself has taken over many chores once the prerogative of the family (vocational training, citizenship training, sex education). Older children are away from home so much (school, leisure-time activities) that the peer group replaces the parents as the primary source for approval and belonging as well as attitudes and values.

The family is less stable today in at least two respects. First, the family members are apart a good deal and are increasingly under the influence of constraints from other sectors (organizations, professions, peer groups). Second, and often related to the first, is the instability of marriage itself. Earlier we mentioned the divorce rate and the number of remarriages. A significant minority of Americans practice serial monogamy. This is not to say that the marriages of the past were happier than those of the present. The constraints (religious, family, community) precluded divorce in the past. Divorce is accepted to a greater extent today. An important reason for the higher divorce rate today, moreover, is the increased longevity of the marriage partners. In 1890 the average wife was a widow when her last child left home for marriage. By 1960 the average couple lived 15 years together in an "empty nest" after the last child left home. By 1970 they lived closer to 30 years together (increases in life expectancy and tendency for women to have all their children before age 30). This long time together with the concomitant shift in roles (especially for the female) places increased burdens on the marriage bond.

The relationship between the spouses is increasingly egalitarian in American society. In the past most families were patriarchal. Most homes today are relatively democratic. A good case can be made for a *de facto* matriarchy occurring in many homes because the father is absent so much of the time—in the well-to-do suburbs or the slums.

The increasing egalitarianism in the family is related to another trend—the changing role of women. Instead of always having subserviant roles, women are now elected to political office and are

273

making inroads in the professions. Women are organizing to fight male oppression. This liberation from the old ways will have a profound impact on the family of the future.

There are some demographic trends that affect the family cycle. There is an increase in the proportion of persons married (nuptiality). In a reversal from the previous decade, there was by 1970 an increase in the age of partners at the time of marriage and an increase in age at which childbearing begins. At the same time, however, women tended to concentrate all their childbearing before age 30.

The most important demographic trend is the decrease in family size. In 1800 the average family had six children. This decreased to 4.7 children in 1900 and to 2.5 children by 1971. This decline is a result of several factors: (1) in an urban setting children are a liability rather than the asset they would represent in a rural setting. The average cost of raising children to age 18 is about $30,000 each—a serious constraint on large families; (2) the almost universal employment of family planning techniques insures that families can have just the number of children they want. The liberalization of abortion laws also limits family size.

Some persons have predicted that the rapid decline in births will bring about zero population growth in the near future. Philip Hauser, an expert on demography, however, has stated that we are a long way from that goal.[40] In the first place, it is impossible to predict the future birth rates. Shifts in attitudes, economic booms and depressions, and other factors affect birth rates. Second, ZPG will be achieved when the birth rate reaches 2.11 children per couple and remains at that rate for about 70 years. It will take that long for the age structure of the United States to change so that each age level would produce a replacement level of children. For instance, even assuming the ZPG rate of 2.11 was achieved in 1973 (and it continued at that level) the population of the United States would increase to 247.7 million by 1990 and 266.3 million by 2000.

Another trend has been an enhanced tolerance for and recognition of a wide variety of life styles. This tolerance is not widespread, but it is increasing, especially among college students. The liberated female, the homosexual, the interracial couple, the couple living together without legal sanction, the individuals uniting in a commune—all probably face intolerance, even hostility from some segments of the American population, but the intensity and the numbers of the conservatives have been diminishing in the past few years.

Trends of the Near Future that Will Affect the Family

There will be a change in the age distribution in the next two decades.[41] The late 1960's were dominated by the children born during the "baby boom" between 1948 and 1953. During those years the number of babies born rose by almost 50 percent. By 1960, however, the total number of babies had begun to drop. For instance, the absolute number of babies born in 1967 was 20 percent less than the number in 1960. What are the consequences of these demographic facts?

First of all, this has meant a shift in what Peter Drucker has called the "center of population gravity"—i.e., the largest single age group in the population over 15. In 1960 the center of population gravity in the United States was in the 35 to 40 group. Five years later (1964) the center shifted to age 17 and remained there until 1971. Thus, the period from 1964 to 1971 was dominated by teenagers,* a category of persons who naturally rebel against authority, who take opinions, attitudes, and concerns principally from their peers rather than from their family, and who are addicted to causes. No wonder, then, that the late 1960's was a time of turmoil—student riots, demonstrations, rapid growth of social movements, and new life styles. The youth culture that "spawned" these attacks on the establishment would appear the wave of the future. Drucker, for one, disagrees. He says the age structure will continue to change. The center of population gravity from 1971 on is shifting steadily upward. By 1975 the dominant age year will be 21 or 22. Whereas the late 1960's was the teenage era, the late 1970's and 1980's will be the era of young marrieds. The number of men and women between age 24 and 34 will increase 60 percent while those between 15 and 24 will increase only 10 percent. For Drucker, the years from 17 to age 21 are the true generation gap. The individual must shift from irresponsibility to responsibility, from dependency to independency. Young adults from 21 to 35 tend to become very conventional. This is the age of child-bearing and raising, the time when one assumes a home mortgage. It is also the time of concern with job and career advancement. This age group during the 1970's will be especially concerned about jobs. The babies of the baby

---

* The use of the word "dominate" is Drucker's. It is meant to imply power through size alone—i.e., the largest age category will through the sheer force of its numbers have a major impact on the society. But size alone is not the only determinant of social power as was demonstrated in Chapter 6. Societies in the early stages of modernization have very young populations but are dominated by a small elite of much older persons of great economic wealth.

boom will force a glut in the job market. Each year of this decade 40 percent more jobs will be needed than in each year of the 1960's. This does not include the increased numbers of women who want careers outside the home. Job scarcity will be a potent force for conventional behavior—those with jobs will not want to jeopardize them and those without will not want to alienate their potential employers.*

Four additional societal trends are mentioned by Lee Rainwater that will particularly have an effect on the family. On the basis of current facts he predicts first of all, a continuation of the trend toward suburbanization (with the subsequent decline of the cities). This will increase the likelihood of families living in homogeneous environments. Second, by the mid-1980's the median educational attainment will reach 12.6 years (in 1960 the median was 10.6 years and in 1969 it was 12.1). One result of more persons attending school longer will be a trend toward marrying at a later age. Related to older age at marriage is being older at the time when the first child is born, and this tends to mean that fewer children will be born to the family unit. A third prediction is that the bulk of American families will become even more affluent than they are presently. By the mid-1980's the median family income will grow from $10,000 to $16,000 (in dollars of 1970 purchasing power). Thus half of the population will have a level of living enjoyed by only the top three percent in 1947 or the top 15 percent in 1971. This affluence will likely not mean redistribution of the income, however; the poorest 20 percent will probably still receive less than five percent of the money income. But the vast majority will enjoy affluence. With greater affluence the family can better insulate itself from those categories of people deemed undesirable (the poor and other minority group members). It also means that children will grow up in a world surrounded by "things" that are considered important. Affluence also means that the children will have many advantages (schooling, medical care, diet, and educational trips). It will also add to the problem of "overchoice" mentioned by Toffler in the last chapter. Another possible byproduct of affluence might be the greater tendency to change life styles. Rainwater has argued this point as follows:

> The ability to pursue a life style more tailored to individual choice (and less constrained by standards as to what a respectable con-

* Just how conventional this group will be is an empirical question. One could argue that this is the first generation in history raised from infancy on a steady diet of television. Moreover, many were raised in homes where they were allowed to question rather than accept the "pat" answers. These two factors may produce a generation very much different than any other.

forming person should be like) is tremendously enhanced by the increases in material affluence and cultural sophistication. Because of higher incomes one can afford to take up and put aside different styles of living without regretting the capital investment that each may take. The security about the future which goes with steady increases in prosperity allows for the deferral of more permanent life style choices to the future; without this kind of security individuals feel they must make the permanent commitments relatively early in life.[42]

Greater affluence by the majority will allow more and more persons to increase their commitment (psychological, financial, and temporal) to leisure time activities. Coupled with shorter work weeks or the compression of 40 working hours into four days, leisure time will become a boon to some and a burden to others. A safe prediction is that a greater proportion of families will devote a greater proportion of their time to family-centered leisure activities (camping, boating, skiing, swimming, vacationing).

The Family of the Future

The popular press are fond of pointing to the crises that face the family. They see many unmarried couples living together, young people living in communes, the high divorce rate, and the 1970 annual estimate of 500,000 teenage runaways and they wonder if the nuclear family structure is losing its effectiveness.[43]

Is the family near death? It seems we can safely say that the nuclear family, despite its problems, is actually working fairly well. In 1970, for example, 87 percent of Americans lived in families that included both parents. Furthermore, we can safely predict that the nuclear family will continue to be the dominant type of family in the foreseeable future. The turbulence of the future may even drive people deeper into their families rather than otherwise, since families may become *the* source of roots in a highly transient world.[44]

It could be argued that the family has gone through a great deal of turmoil because of being in the "shake down" phase between agrarian life and the industrial world, between rural life and urban life, between frugality and affluence. Perhaps the family is now adapted to the modern world. This is not to say that the family will no longer change. As Ira Reiss has said,

Change is inevitable, but the radical changes are behind us and not ahead of us. We now possess a family system congruent in many ways with our urban-industrial society . . . a number of indices point to the fact that the essentials of our current family system

277

were formed in the early decades of this century and that they now come to be established in several relatively stable patterns. I expect mostly modest changes in the remaining three decades of this century. Nothing on the scale of the family system changes of the first three decades of this century should occur during the last three decades. . . .[45]

Alternative Possibility I: Pluralism

Although the nuclear family will remain the choice of the majority, there will continue to be experimentation with alternative family forms. The future will be characterized by pluralism and freedom. Rainwater has predicted:

> Life styles will increasingly be built out of a rapidly expanding multiplicity of choices—choices made possible by the interaction of affluence and cosmopolitanism. One of the most striking things about American society since World War II (or longer than that) has been the extent to which the lives of most Americans involve what they put together out of the choices available to them rather than to what they are constrained to do by their socioeconomic situation. Much of the conflict and turmoil in the society probably has as much to do with anxiety and uncertainty engendered by continuing massive increases in the range of choices available to people as with more frequently cited factors. Indeed the 'oppression' that many of those who 'protest' feel (aside from blacks and other minorities) is probably more the oppression of having many choices and not knowing how to choose among them than of being 'forced' to do things one does not wish to do.
>
> Out of the current ferment about life styles is very likely to come the institutionalization of a set of pluralistic standards which legitimate a far wider range of ways of living in American society than has previously been the case. From the various liberation movements (black, brown, red, women, gay men, gay women, youth) will probably come a more widespread ethic of pluralism in life styles. (And this will be more than toleration in that it will involve recognition of the legitimacy of different kinds of identities and life styles.)[46]

The acceptance of a wide diversity of life styles will enhance the probability of a greater proportion of interfaith and interracial marriages. Homosexuals will no longer hide their identities. More and more married couples will choose to remain childless.

One current alternative to the nuclear family that will be accepted more in the future will be communes. Communes are, generally speaking, conscious efforts on the part of several persons to recapture the warmth and intimacy of extended families.* They result from the feelings of isolation and alienation that some persons feel in a depersonalized, segmentalized, bureaucratic, and mobile society. The establishment of communes is not new in American history.[47] Some persons have always sought alternatives to the predominant arrangement for family living. What is especially interesting about communes to the sociologist is that here the extended family is a chosen one (instead of one imposed by the accident of birth), by persons who share cultural, social, and/or political outlooks. They will be especially important phenomena of the future because they are havens for those persons who consciously choose an alternative life style and/or to those who cannot cope with the pressures of a rapidly changing society. A commune is by definition composed of people who want stability and security— two qualities missing in contemporary American society.

Another alternative to the present monogamous form of marriage has been mentioned by several observers.[48] They feel that the conditions of the future will augur against life-long monogamy. Life expectancy rates are rising, which means people will be forced to live together for a longer time. As the rate of change in society accelerates and as the individual family moves geographically and socially, the interests and values of husband and wife will change, often away from the supports they had when the marriage was formed. These changes may not develop at comparable rates or perhaps not even in the same direction. Thus, the odds against the success of the life-long marriage may become overwhelming. If this occurs, then we can anticipate a somewhat more open public acceptance of serial monogamy (or temporary marriage).

Toffler predicts a three-step marriage career that departs radically from the present norms as the typical pattern of the future. At each stage the couple would sign a marriage contract. At the end of the contracted period they could decide whether to renew it or not. The first stage occurs in the late youth or early adult years. It is a probationary marriage ("trial marriage") with or without the benefit of the ceremony. This stage is a romantic one without children, where couples practice at cohabitational living. The second stage in the process is the time of child-raising and career advancement. The couple at the end of stage one must decide if they want to terminate their arrangement and seek new partners or not for this very different part of the life cycle. The third stage occurs when the children

---

* A commune in Lawrence, Kansas, for example, is called "Ujaama," a Swahili word meaning "extended family."

leave home. It will probably last thirty years or so. The requirements of the partners are different than before. The persons are
mature. They have only themselves and their career(s) to consider.
By this time the interests, attitudes, and values are stable. The
marriage partners at this stage can match their interests and psychological needs. The chances of this relationship enduring are
quite good, although the time of retirement is a difficult stage for
many and may necessitate one final change in marriage partners.

Alternative Possibility II: Societal Constraints

The first set of future alternatives was essentially optimistic, since it
envisioned a tolerance for different life styles. There is always the
possibility, however, that individual choices will be curtailed by the
government meeting some crisis. For example, the present low
fertility rate may shift upward. The resulting population pressures
may become so great that the government would have to impose a
limit on family size (for pregnancies beyond the prescribed limit the
government could demand abortion or an exorbitant fine).

If unemployment becomes a serious problem, the government
may be forced to limit the number of "breadwinners" to one per
family unit. High unemployment rates may also bring about lower
mandatory retirement ages and government imposed limits on the
number of hours worked.

The limitation on individual freedoms may also occur because the
values of Americans demand a change. Individuals and organizations may organize to pressure the legislatures and courts to curb
communes, trial marriages, abortions, and easy divorces simply
because they are convinced that these arrangements are wrong.
Similarly, they may also attempt to pressure those in power to
protect morals by a rigid censorship of movies, plays, magazines,
and literature. Religious groups are the most likely to make such
demands, but the pressure may become more widespread in reaction against the permissiveness that many believe pervades in the
family, school, church, and courts.

Conclusion

There will be more variation and more experimentation in family
life of the future. While this means more communal living, more
trial marriages, and a higher divorce rate, the nuclear family will

remain. The family will be smaller, more egalitarian and even more nuclear than at present. The family will continue because it will be the one source of stability, of primary relations, and of irrationality in a shifting, secondary, and overly rational social world.

SUGGESTED FURTHER READING

Bronfenbrenner, Urie, *Two Worlds of Childhood: U.S. and U.S.S.R.* (New York: Basic Books, 1970). An important study of the contrasting child rearing patterns in two societies.

O'Neill, Nena, and George O'Neill, *Open Marriage: A New Life Style for Couples* (New York: M. Evans and Company, 1972). A controversial book that presents alternatives to the prevailing norms regarding marriage.

Reiss, Ira L., *The Social Context of Premarital Sexual Permissiveness* (New York: Holt, Rinehart and Winston, 1967). This book presents a systematic sociological study of a national sample on premarital sexual attitudes.

Reiss, Ira L., *The Family System in America* (New York: Holt, Rinehart, and Winston, 1971). A comprehensive textbook on the American family by an expert in the field.

Scanzoni, John H., *The Black Family in Modern Society* (Boston: Allyn and Bacon, 1971). This book focuses on the two thirds of black households headed by a man with a wife present. It, therefore, destroys many of the stereotypes whites hold about blacks.

NOTES AND REFERENCES

1. This theme is elaborated in William N. Stephens, "Family and Kinships," *Sociology: An Introduction*, Neil J. Smelser (ed.), (New York: John Wiley and Sons, Inc., 1967), pp. 535–543.

2. Philip Slater, *The Pursuit of Loneliness* (Boston: Beacon Press, 1970), p. 71.

3. Phyllis Chesler, "Men Drive Women Crazy," *Psychology Today* 5, (July, 1971), p. 18–22, 26–27, 97–98.

4. For a survey of the studies noting sex differences see the articles in Eleanor E. Maccoby (ed.), *The Development of Sex Differences* (Stanford, California: Stanford University Press, 1966). This volume also includes an annotated bibliography and a summary of research in sex differences. See also the entire issue of *Merrill-Palmer Quarterly* 10 (January, 1964), which is devoted to sex-role identification.

5. Dean Walley, *What Girls Can Be* (Kansas City, Missouri: Hallmark Cards, Inc.), no date given.

6. Whitney Darrow, Jr., *I'm Glad I'm a Boy! I'm Glad I'm a Girl!* (New York: Windmill Books/Simon and Schuster, 1970). For an extended analysis of the impact of sexual stereotypes in children's literature, see Lenore J. Weitzman, Deborah Eifler, Elizabeth Hokado, and Catherine Ross, "Sex-Role Socialization in Picture Books for Preschool Children," *American Journal of Sociology* 77 (May, 1972), pp. 1125–1150.

7. There is a vast literature on women's liberation. The following are especially helpful: Betty Roszak and Theodore Roszak (eds.) *Masculine/Feminine* (New York: Harper & Row, Publishers, 1969); Kate Millett, *Sexual Politics* (New York: Doubleday & Company, 1969).

8. There are a number of sources that document the differences in mode of socialization by social class. Especially important is the article that summarizes twenty-five years of studies of parent-child relationships by Urie Bronfenbrenner, "Socialization and Social Class Through Time and Space," in E. E. Maccoby, T. M. Newcomb, and E. L. Hartley (eds.), *Readings in Social Psychology* (New York: Holt, Rinehart and Winston, 1958), pp. 400–425. See also Melvin L. Kohn, "Social Class and Parental Values," *American Journal of Sociology* 64 (January, 1959), pp. 337–351.

9. For an historical review of child rearing patterns see Robert R. Sears, Eleanor E. Maccoby, Harry Levin, *et al.*, *Patterns of Child Rearing* (Evanston, Illinois: Row, Peterson, 1957).

10. Benjamin Spock, *Child and Baby Care* (New York: Pocket Books, 1947).

11. "The Young Defacers," *Life Magazine* (April 9, 1971), p. 34.

12. Quoted in "What's a Mother To Do?", *Newsweek* (September 23, 1968), p. 68.

13. This discussion is taken from the critique of Spock by Slater, *The Pursuit of Loneliness*, pp. 62–70.

14. Richard Flacks, "The Liberated Generation: An Exploration of the Roots of Student Protest," *Journal of Social Issues* 23 (July, 1967), pp. 52–75. This issue is entitled "Stirrings Out of Apathy: Student Activism and the Decade of Protest" and is highly recommended to the interested student.

15. Kenneth Keniston, "The Sources of Student Dissent," *Journal of Social Issues* 23 (July, 1967), p. 120.

16. Slater, *The Pursuit of Loneliness*, pp. 63–64.

17. David Matza, "Position and Behavior Patterns of Youth," *Handbook on Modern Sociology*, Robert E. L. Faris (ed.), (Chicago: Rand McNally and Company, 1964), pp. 200–216.

18. Stephens, "Family and Kinship," p. 542.

19. Ira L. Reiss, "How and Why America's Sex Standards are Changing," *Trans-action* 5 (March, 1968), p. 21.

20. Urie Bronfenbrenner, "The Split-Level American Family," *Saturday Review* (October 7, 1967), pp. 60–66.

21. James S. Coleman, *The Adolescent Society* (New York: The Free Press, 1961).

22. For a discussion of "other-directedness" in American society, see David Riesman, *The Lonely Crowd* (New Haven, Connecticut: Yale University Press, 1950).

23. Milton L. Barron, *The Aging American* (New York: Thomas Y. Crowell Co., 1961), chapter 4, "The Aged as a Quasi-Minority Group."

24. Bernice L. Neugarten, "Grow Old Along With Me! The Best is Yet to Be," *Psychology Today* 5 (December, 1971), pp. 46 and 48.

25. Felix M. Berardo, "Widowhood Status in the United States: Perspective on a Neglected Aspect of the Family Life Cycle," *The Family Coordinator* 17 (July, 1968), pp. 191–203.

26. Talcott Parsons, "Age and Sex Structure of the United States," *Essays in Sociological Theory*, Talcott Parsons (ed.), (New York: The Free Press, 1949), pp. 102–103.

27. Paul C. Glick and Arthur J. Norton, "Perspectives on the Recent Upturn in Divorce and Remarriage," paper presented at the annual meeting of the Population Association of America, Toronto, Canada (April 15, 1972).

28. Ira L. Reiss, *The Family System in America* (New York: Holt, Rinehart and Winston, Inc., 1971), p. 282.

29. Unless otherwise noted the source used for the information below is Reiss, *The Family System in America,* chapter 17.

30. U.S. Bureau of the Census, *Current Population Reports,* Series P–20, No. 223, "Social and Economic Variations in Marriage, Divorce, and Remarriage: 1967," U.S. Government Printing Office, Washington, D.C., 1971, p. 1.

31. Quoted in Associated Press release (September 23, 1972). See also U.S. Bureau of the Census, *Current Population Reports,* Series P–20, No. 223, "Social and Economic Variations in Marriage, Divorce, and Remarriage: 1967," U.S. Government Printing Office, Washington, D.C., 1971, p. 3; Paul C. Glick and Arthur J. Norton, "Frequency, Duration, and Probability of Marriage and Divorce," *Journal of Marriage and the Family* 33 (May, 1971), pp. 307–317.

32. William J. Goode, *The Family* (Englewood Cliffs, New Jersey: Prentice-Hall, Inc., 1964), p. 100.

33. *The Negro Family: The Case for National Action* (Washington, D.C.: Office of Policy Planning and Research, United States Department of Labor, 1965).

34. William Ryan, *Blaming the Victim* (New York: Pantheon Books, 1971), pp. 71–73; Elizabeth Herzog, "Is There a 'Breakdown' of the Negro Family?" *Social Work* 11 (January, 1966), pp. 3–10.

35. Ryan, *Blaming the Victim,* pp. 72–73.

36. Jean Parker, Henry J. Rosner, Harold Jacobzinger and Grieda

Greenstein, "Out-of-Wedlock Births in New York City, I—Sociologic Aspects," *American Journal of Public Health* 51 (May, 1961), pp. 683–696.

37. *The Negro Family*, p. 47.

38. Several sources will be especially helpful to the student wishing to delve into this problem more deeply. See especially: Lee Rainwater and William L. Yancey, *The Moynihan Report and the Politics of Controversy* (Cambridge, Mass.: M.I.T. Press, 1967); Charles V. Willie (ed.), *The Family Life of Black People* (Columbus, Ohio: Charles E. Merrill Publishing Company, 1970); Clyde V. Kiser (ed.), "Demographic Aspects of the Black Community," *The Milbank Memorial Fund Quarterly* 48 (April, 1970); Herbert H. Hyman and John Shelton Reed, " 'Black Matriarchy' Reconsidered: Evidence from Secondary Analysis of Sample Surveys," *Public Opinion Quarterly* 33 (Fall, 1969), pp. 346–354; Reynolds Farley and Albert I. Hermalin, "Family Stability: A Comparison of Trends Between Blacks and Whites," *American Sociological Review* 36 (February, 1971), pp. 1–17.

39. Much of this section is taken from Philip M. Hauser, "Social Science Predicts and Projects," *The Future of the Family*, Richard E. Farson, Philip M. Hauser, Herbert Stroup, and Anthony J. Wiener (New York: Family Service Association of America, 1969), pp. 21–38.

40. "Hauser Testifies on Demographic Realities," testimony before Special Sub-Committee on Human Resources, United States Senate, Committee on Labor and Public Welfare, October 14, 1971, *ZPG Reporter* 3 (November/December, 1971), p. 1.

41. The following section depends to a large extent on the insights of: Lee Rainwater, "Post-1984 America," *Society* 9 (February, 1972), pp. 18–27; and Peter F. Drucker, "The Surprising Seventies," *Harper's Magazine* 243 (July, 1971), pp. 35–39.

42. Rainwater, "Post-1984 America," p. 20.

43. "The American Family: Future Uncertain," *Time* (December 28, 1970), pp. 34–39.

44. Alvin Toffler, *Future Shock* (New York: Bantam Books, 1970), p. 239.

45. Reiss, *The Family System in America*, p. 414.

46. Rainwater, "Post-1984 America," p. 20.

47. For a comparison of successful and unsuccessful communes of the past, see: Rosabeth Moss Kanter, "Communes," *Change* (Del Mar, California: Communications Research Machines, Inc., 1972), pp. 367–372.

48. Margaret Mead, "Future Family," *Trans-action* 8 (September, 1971), pp. 50–53; and Toffler, *Future Shock*, Chapter 11.

CHAPTER 9

Religion in America

Religion is a ubiquitous phenomenon that has a tremendous impact on any society and its members. It is part of a large social system, affected by and affecting the other institutions of the society—i.e., patterns of the family, the economy, education, and the polity. Since religious trends may be responses to fundamental changes in society, and some religious ideas may constrain social behaviors in a narrowly prescribed manner, the understanding of any society is incomplete unless one comprehends the religion of that society.

But, what is religion? The variety of activities and belief systems that have fallen under this rubric is almost infinite. There are some essential elements to religion, however, that allow us to distinguish it from other phenomena.[1] A starting point is that religion is man-made (i.e., it is a part of culture). It is an integrated set of ideas by which a group attempts to explain the meaning of life and death. Religion is also a normative system, defining immorality and sin as well as morality and righteousness. Let us amplify some of these statements further.

1. Religion deals with the ultimate of human concerns—the meaning of life and death. It provides answers as to man's place in society and in the universe.

2. There is an emphasis on man's conduct. There are prescriptions for what one ought to do as well as the consequences for one's misconduct.

3. There is a distinction between the sacred and the secular. Some objects and entities are believed to have supernatural powers

and are therefore treated with respect, reverence, and awe. What is sacred and what is not is a matter of belief. The range of items believed to be sacred is limitless. They may be man-made objects (idols, altars, or amulets), animals or animal totems, parts of the natural world (mountains, volcanos, or rivers), transcendental beings (gods, angels, devils), or persons (living or dead, such as prophets, messiahs, or saints).

4. Because the sacred is held in awe, there are beliefs (theologies, cosmologies) and practices (rituals) to express and reinforce proper attitudes among believers about the sacred. The set of beliefs attempts to explain the meaning of life. Moreover, these beliefs present a set of guidelines for action toward the sacred, and toward one's fellow men. Ritual, with its symbolism and action, evokes common feelings among the believers (awe, reverence, ecstasy, fear) which lead to group unity.

5. An essential ingredient of religion is the existence of a community of believers. There must be a social group that share a set of beliefs and practices, moral values, and a sense of community (a unique identity).

One important consequence of a group of persons having the same religious heritage and beliefs is unity. All believers, whether of high or low status, young or old, are united through the sharing of religious beliefs. Thus, religion, through the holding of common values to be cherished, sins to be avoided, rules to be followed, and symbols to be revered, integrates. Group unity is also accomplished through the universal feeling that God or the Gods look upon this particular group with special favor (the ethnocentric notion that "God is on our side"). An example of this is found in a verse of the national anthem of Great Britain:

> O lord our God, arise
> Scatter our enemies
> And make them fall.
> Confound their politics,
> Frustrate their knavish tricks,
> On thee our hopes we fix,
> God save us all.

Another consequence of religion is that it constrains the behavior of the community of believers thus providing a social control function. This is accomplished in two ways. First, there are explicit rules to obey which if violated will be punished. Second, in the process of socialization, children internalize the religious beliefs and rules. In other words, they each develop a conscience which keeps them in line through guilt and fear.

286

A final positive consequence of religion—positive in the sense that it aids in uniting persons—is the legitimation of social structures that have profane origins.[2] There is a strong tendency for religious beliefs to become intertwined with secular beliefs, thereby providing religious blessings to the values and institutions of society. In American society, for example, private property and free enterprise have become almost sacred. Democracy, too, is believed to be ordained by God.

The very same religious bases that promote group integration also divide. Religious groups tend to emphasize separateness and superiority, thereby defining others as inferior ("infidels," "heathens," "heretics," or "nonbelievers"). This occurs because each religious group tends to feel it has the way (and perhaps the only way) to achieve salvation or reach nirvana or whatever the goal.

Religious differences accentuate the differences among societies, denominations, and even within local churches. Since religious groups have feelings of superiority, there may be conflict brought about by discrimination, competition for converts, or feelings of hatred. Also because religious ideas tend to be strongly held, groups may split rather than compromise. Liberals and fundamentalists, even within the same religion, denomination or local church, will, doubtless, disagree on numerous issues. A common result, of course, is division.

A major divisive characteristic of religion is its tendency, through established churches, to accept the acts of the state. American churches, for example, have condoned such things as slavery, segregation, white supremacy, and war.* Within the church, there have always been those who spoke out against the church's cohabitation with the secular. This ability of the church to rationalize the activities of the state no matter how onerous has split many churches and denominations. The slavery issue, for example, split Baptists into American Baptists and Southern Baptists.

Conflict itself can occur between religious groups (with the sanction of each religion). Recent world history gives bloody evidence of this occurrence (e.g., Moslems vs. Hindus in India and Pakistan, Moslems vs. Jews in the Middle East, Catholics vs. Protestants in Northern Ireland). Religious conflict has also occurred within the United States at various times. Confrontations between Catholics and Protestants, between warring sects of Muslims (Black Muslims

---

* Actually the Church has sometimes actively pursued some of these policies. The Puritan Church of the early settlers condoned witch hunts. The defeat of the Indians was justified by most Christian groups on the grounds that they were heathens and in need of white man's religion. Finally, most religious denominations sought Biblical rationalizations for slavery.[3]

vs. Sunni Muslims), as well as Protestants and Jews, have been fairly commonplace.[4] Clearly, religious values are reason enough for individuals and groups to clash.

SOME DISTINCTIVE FEATURES OF AMERICAN RELIGION

Civil religion. One feature of American religion, traditionally, has been the separation of Church and State (established by the first amendment to the Constitution). This is both a consequence and the cause of the religious diversity found in the United States. There is a relationship between religion and the state in America, but it differs from the usual conception of one dominant church that is inseparable from the state. In many respects, God and Country are conceived by most Americans as one. This has been labelled the civil religion of the United States.[5]

America's civil religion is seemingly antithetical to the Constitutional demand for separation of Church and State. The paradox is that on the one hand the government sanctions God (the Pledge of Allegiance has the phrase, "one nation, under God," the phrase, "In God We Trust," is stamped on all money, every Presidential inaugural address except Washington's second has mentioned God, and present-day Presidents have regularly scheduled prayer breakfasts), while at the same time declaring it illegal to have prayer and/or religious instruction in the public schools. The basis for the paradox is that the civil religion is not a specific creed. It is a set of beliefs, symbols and rituals that is broad enough for all citizens to accept. The God of the civil religion is all things to all people. One thing is certain—politicians, if they want to be successful, must show some semblance of piety by occasionally invoking the blessings of this non-denominational, non-sectarian God.

There are several central themes of the civil religion that are important for the understanding of American society. First, there is the belief that God has a special destiny for the United States. This implies that God is actively involved in history and most important that America has a holy mission to carry out God's will on earth. John F. Kennedy said this message well in the conclusion to his inauguration address: "With a good conscience our only sure reward, with history the final judge of our deeds, let us go forth to lead the land we love, asking His blessing and His help, but knowing that here on earth God's work must truly be our own."[6] This belief has been the source of self-righteousness in foreign relations.

It has allowed Americans to subdue the "pagan" Indians, win the frontier, follow a policy of manifest destiny, and defeat fascism. Currently, the defeat of communism is seen as a holy crusade.

A second aspect of the civil religion is maintenance of the status quo. The God of civil religion is more closely allied to law and order than to changing the system. Thus civil religion tends strongly toward uncritical endorsement of American values and the system of stratification. Order and unity are the traditional ways of God, not change and dissent. Thus, public policy tends to receive religious sanction.

At the same time, however, the civil religion enjoins Americans to stand up for certain principles—freedom, individualism, equal opportunity. Consequently, there are occasions when current governmental policy or the policy of some group is criticized because it does not measure up to certain ideals. The civil religion of America, then, accomplishes both the priestly (acceptance of what is) and the prophetic (challenging the existing system) roles of traditional religion, with emphasis, however, on the former.

The variety of religious belief. Some societies are unified by religion. All persons in such societies believe the same religious ideas, worship the same deities, obey the same moral commandments, and identify strongly with each other. Superficially, through its civil religion, the United States appears to be homogeneous along religious lines. Moreover, two-thirds of Americans are Protestants and another one-fourth are Catholics—a total of 92 percent being Christian (the remaining eight percent are Jewish, Muslim, atheists or other religious preference). But the range of attitudes and beliefs among Christians is fantastic. Among Catholics, for example, there are radical priests who disobey the instructions of bishops, cardinals, and even the Pope. At the same time, however, there are priests who rigidly adhere to all the rules set down by the church authorities. If anything, the range within Protestantism is even greater. For some individuals and groups the Bible is an accurate portrayal of history; for others, the Bible is purely allegorical. Some have so much faith in the healing power of religion that they will not go to physicians under any circumstances. Within Protestantism are Amish, Quakers, high church Episcopalians, Pentecostal Holiness groups, Congregationalists, and even snake handlers.[7]

Further evidence for the diversity of religious expression in the United States is found in the variance of beliefs concerning basic tenets of Christianity. Glock and Stark have demonstrated this in their study of a random sample of church members in four metro-

289

politan counties in northern California (see Table 9–1). These data show clearly the wide disagreement among the various denominations, Protestant and Catholic, on a number of presumably central tenets of Christianity. They demonstrate, moreover, that with few exceptions there is considerable within-denomination variation on each of these articles of faith.

Religious organization. Very broadly, American religious organizations can be divided according to their secular commitments into two categories—churches and sects.[8]

Religious groups have a choice—to reject and withdraw from the

TABLE 9–1.   Percent of Members in 11 Religious Groups Holding Specified Beliefs: Four Metropolitan Counties in Northern California, 1964 (in percentages)

	N	(1)	(2)	(3)	(4)	(5)	(6)	(7)	(8)
					Beliefs in				
Congregationalists	151	41	40	21	36	6	2	38	58
Methodists	415	60	54	34	49	13	7	45	57
Episcopalians	416	63	59	39	53	17	18	47	54
Disciples of Christ	50	76	74	62	64	18	6	78	64
Presbyterians	495	75	72	57	69	31	21	66	48
American Lutherans	208	73	74	66	70	49	49	77	47
American Baptists	141	78	76	69	72	49	23	78	45
Missouri Lutherans	116	81	93	92	84	77	86	97	38
Southern Baptists	79	99	99	99	97	92	43	97	29
Sects[a]	255	96	97	96	94	90	47	96	61
Catholics	545	81	86	81	75	66	68	51	57

The full statement of beliefs, by column above, are as follows:

(1)   "I know God really exists and I have no doubts about it."
(2)   "Jesus is the Divine Son of God and I have no doubts about it."
(3)   "Jesus was born of a virgin" (response checked: "Completely true").
(4)   "There is a life beyond death" (response checked: "Completely true").
(5)   "The devil actually exists" (response checked: "Completely true").
(6)   "A child is born into the world already guilty of sin" (response checked: "Completely true").
(7)   For salvation: "Belief in Jesus Christ as Saviour is absolutely necessary."
(8)   For salvation: "Doing good for others is absolutely necessary."

[a] Included are: The Assemblies of God, The Church of God, The Church of Christ, The Church of the Nazarene, The Foursquare Gospel Church, and one independent Tabernacle.

Source: Based on data in Charles Y. Glock and Rodney Stark, *Religion and Society in Tension* (Chicago: Rand McNally and Company, 1965), adapted from Tables 5–1, 5–2, 5–3, 5–5, 5–6, 5–7, and 5–9.

secular society, or to accommodate to it. The basis for a decision to reject the social environment is maintenance of spiritual and ethical purity. Such a choice, by definition, entails withdrawal from the world, thereby consciously avoiding any chance to change it. The opposite choice—accommodation—requires compromise and the loss of distinctive ideals but it also means that the group can influence the larger society. The accommodation or resistance to the secular world is the fundamental difference between a church and a sect.

The *church*, as an ideal type, has the following attributes:

1. The tendency to compromise with the larger society and its values and institutions.
2. Membership tends to occur by being born to parents who belong. Membership, moreover, takes place through infant baptism, which implies that all members are "saved."
3. A hierarchy of authority, with those at the top being trained for their vocation.
4. Acceptance of a diversity of beliefs, since the membership is large, and for many the scriptures are interpreted metaphorically rather than literally.
5. There is a tolerance of the popular vices.

A *sect* in its perfect form is exactly opposite a church in every way.

1. There is a fundamental withdrawal from and rejection of the world. A sect is a moral community separate from and in many ways hostile toward the secular world.
2. Membership is only through a "conversion" experience. Membership is therefore voluntary and limited to adults. Hence, adult baptism is the only accepted form of baptism.
3. Organization is informal and unstructured. Ministers are untrained. They became ministers by being "called" from the group.
4. The belief system is rigid. The Bible is the source and it is interpreted literally. The goal of the membership is spiritual purity as found in the Early Christian Church.
5. There are rigid ethical requirements restraining the members from the popular vices of drinking, smoking, card playing, dancing, and cursing.

The church-sect dichotomy does not exhaust all of the possibilities. Some religious groups would fit somewhere in between—as institutionalized sects. These groups (e.g., Mormons, Disciples of Christ, and Southern Baptists) incorporate features of both a church (trained leadership, some accommodation to the larger society) with the sect-like attributes of adult baptism, and an unwillingness to compromise on some theological questions.*

For our purposes, however, the church-sect dichotomy, while oversimplifying the situation, is useful in two ways: to depict a form of social change, and to show why certain categories of persons are attracted to one type and not the other.

The church-sect dichotomy illustrates an important sociological phenomenon—the very process of organization deflects away from the original goal of the group. A group may form to pursue a goal such as religious purity, but in so doing it creates a new organization, which means that some of the group's energies will be spent in organizational maintenance. Consequently, a sect may form with the explicit intention of eliminating a hierarchy and a codification of beliefs. Patterns of behavior emerge, however, as certain practices are found to be more effective. In particular, the selection of ministers tends to become routinized, and a system of religious instruction for children is developed so that they will learn the catechism in the proper sequence. Sects, then, tend to become churches. This is illustrated by the type of leader found in each. Often a sect is formed by a charismatic person and his followers. This person is followed because he is believed to possess extraordinary qualities of leadership, saintliness, gifts of prophecy, or ability to heal. What happens to such an organization when this leadership is gone? The organization is faced with a crisis of succession. Groups typically find ways to pass on the charisma ("routinization of charisma") by either: (1) selection of the successor by the original charismatic leader; (2) designation of a successor by the group closest to the original leader ("disciples"); (3) hereditary transmission; or (4) transmission of charisma by ritual ("laying on of hands").[10] In this last instance there is the recognition of a charisma of office—i.e., whoever holds the position possesses charisma. When this occurs, the organizational machinery is advanced enough to move the group away from its sect-like qualities toward a church. The important sociological point here is that organizations seldom remain the same. The simple tends to become complex. But the process does not stop at complexity; as the original goal of the sect (religious purity with the necessity of separation from the world) is superseded when the organization gets larger and more bureaucratic, some persons will become dissatisfied enough to break away and form a new sect. Thus, the process tends to be cyclical.

* Other classification schemes make further analytical distinctions. Bryan Wilson, for example, has distinguished four types of sects—adventist, introversionist, conversionist, and gnostic.[9]

Increased bureaucratization (and subsequent splintering) is characteristic of modern urban society. This leads us to a final consideration relative to the church-sect dichotomy—the motivation to join sects. At the risk of oversimplification, we can identify two important features of sects that help explain why some categories of persons are especially prone to join sects rather than churches. The first is that a sect (more so than a church) may provide a total world of meaning and social identity, and a close circle of persons to whom members can turn when troubled. The sect provides precisely those things missing in the lives of many urban dwellers. They find meaning in a meaningless world. They find friends in a sea of strangers. They find stability in a setting that is rapidly undergoing change. Thus, the alienated are especially attracted to sects. So, too, are new migrants to the city. In the city, they are confronted with a variety of new and difficult problems—industrialized work, work insecurity, loss of kinship ties, and disruption of other primary group ties. The sects, unlike the established city churches, appeal to such persons by their form of worship, emphasis on individual attention, and lack of formal organization appeal.[11]

A second variable affecting attraction to a sect or church is social class. Generally, low-status persons tend to be attracted to sects rather than churches because religious status is substituted for social status (or as the Bible puts it, "and the last shall be first"). It makes sense for persons of low social or economic status to reject this world and the religious bodies that accommodate to it. Such persons would be especially attracted to a religious group that rejects this world and assures its followers that in the next world "true believers"—those who are religiously pure—will have the highest status. The sect represents to its followers a reaction against or escape from the dominant religious and economic systems in society. It is a protest against the failure of established churches to meet the needs of marginal groups.[12] The sect, moreover, rejects the social class system as irrelevant and in fact a system of rewards that is in exact reverse order from God's will.*

Churches, on the other hand, attract the middle and upper classes. Since these persons are successful, they obviously would not turn to a religious organization that rejects their world. As Max Weber said over fifty years ago:

---

* It is incorrect to say, however, that all lower class persons who are alienated will join religious sects in order to attack the establishment. Their estrangement may lead them to join other kinds of social movements (e.g., labor or political) or toward social isolation.

> Other things being equal, classes with high social and economic
> privilege will scarcely be prone to evolve the ideas of salvation.
> Rather, they assign to religion the primary function of legitimizing
> their own life pattern and situation in this world.[13]

Both the sect and the church, consequently, have well developed
theodicies.[14] A *theodicy* is a religious legitimation for a situation
that otherwise might cause guilt or anger (such as defeat in a war
or the existence of poverty among affluence). Sects tend to have a
theodicy of suffering—i.e., a religious explanation for their lack of
power and privilege. Churches must explain the inequalities of
society, too, but their emphasis is on legitimation of possessing
power and privilege. This tendency to develop theodicies has the
important social function of preserving the status quo. They convince their adherents that all is well, that one should accept his fate
as God-given. This makes their situation less intolerable and the
possibility of revolution remote—the suffering know they will be
rewarded, while the guilt of the well-off is assuaged. Consequently,
there is no reason to change the system.

The relationship between socioeconomic status and religion. The
dominant religion in the United States, Christianity, stresses the
equality of all men in the sight of God. All persons, regardless of
socioeconomic status, are welcomed in Christianity. We might expect, therefore, that the distribution of members by socioeconomic
status within any denomination would be randomly distributed. We
might also assume that the organization of any local congregation
would ignore status distinctions. Although these two assumptions
seem to have surface validity, the empirical situation refutes them.

We have seen that sects and churches tend to have a social class
bias—the lower the socioeconomic status, the greater the probability of belonging to a sect. There also seems to be a ranking of
denominations in terms of the socioeconomic status of their members. Although there is always a range of the social classes within
any one denomination, there is a modal status that characterizes
each. The reasons for this are varied: the proportion of members
living in rural or urban areas, which immigrant groups brought the
religion to the United States and during what historical period, the
appeal of the religious experience (ritual, evangelism, close personal ties, salvation, legitimation of the social system or attacks on
the establishment). This last point is especially important because
"Life conditions affect men's religious propensities, and life conditions are significantly correlated with the facts of stratification in all
societies."[15]

294

There is a relationship between socioeconomic status and denominational affiliation. Table 9–2 presents data from a national sample that orders the major United States denominations by decreasing status. Although the data are from the early 1950's, they are representative of the many studies of local communities as well as of large national samples.

Even though Table 9–2 shows that the denominations can be ranked by socioeconomic status, it is clear that each denomination includes persons of high, middle, and lower status. As Demerath, after presenting this same table, has stated, "Episcopalians may be *relatively* upper class, but more than 40 percent are from the lower class. Baptists may be *relatively* lower class, but they claim their Rockefellers as well."[16]

Local churches, even more so than denominations, tend to be homogeneous in socioeconomic status. This is partly the result of residential patterns—i.e., neighborhoods are relatively homogeneous by socioeconomic status and the local churches are attended mostly by persons living nearby. Another reason, and perhaps just as important, is the tendency for persons to want to belong to organizations composed of persons like themselves. They do not want to feel out of place, so they are attracted to churches where

TABLE 9–2   Social Class Profiles of American Religious Groups (in percentages)

	Socioeconomic Status			Number of Cases
Denomination	Upper	Middle	Low	
Episcopal	24.1%	33.7%	42.2%	(590)
Congregational	23.9	42.6	33.5	(376)
Presbyterian	21.9	40.0	38.1	(961)
Methodist	12.7	35.6	51.7	(2100)
Lutheran	10.9	36.1	53.0	(723)
Roman Catholic	8.7	24.7	66.6	(2390)
Baptist	8.0	24.0	68.0	(1381)

Source: Adapted from Herbert Schneider, *Religion in 20th Century America* (Cambridge, Massachusetts: Harvard University Press, 1952), Appendix, p. 288.*

* This exact order is also noted by Liston Pope in his analysis of four polls taken in 1945–46 covering a total of approximately 12,000 cases. See Liston Pope, "Religion and the Class Structure," *The Annals* 256 (March, 1948), pp. 84–91.

the members have the same life style (e.g., speech patterns, clothing tastes, and educational background). The result, then, is that persons belonging to a particular denomination will often seek out the local congregation in the city where they feel most comfortable. To paraphrase Broom and Selznick, "although rich and poor, educated and uneducated are members of one denomination, they tend to worship under different roofs."[17]

There is some range, however, in every local church. Probably no one congregation is comprised totally of persons from exactly the same status niche. Although the status differentials may be minimal within a local congregation, they are evidently important to the parishioners. The rule is that the higher the socioeconomic status of the member, the greater his or her influence in the running of the local church. There is greater likelihood that such persons will be elected or appointed to office (elder, deacon, trustee, Sunday School Superintendent) and that their opinions will carry greater weight than persons of lower social status. This may be partly a function of the disproportionately large financial contributions by the more well-to-do, but the important point here is that the secular world intrudes in the organization of each local congregation.

The common indicators of religious involvement—church membership, attendance at church services, and participation in the church's activities—all demonstrate a relationship to socioeconomic status. On each of these measures, persons of high status are more involved than those of low status.[18] Table 9–3 gives the data for attendance at Sunday church for a representative cross-section of American adults 18 years of age and over (2,783 personal interviews).

The data from Table 9–3 indicate clearly that upper-status persons are more likely to attend church than lower-status persons. This finding is similar to what we would find if we examined church membership or participation in church activities. Unfortunately these are not very good measures of religiosity, although often assumed to be. The problem is that upper-class persons are much more likely to join and actively participate in all sorts of organizations. The joining of churches and attending services are but the manifestations of a more general phenomenon—the tendency for middle- and upper-class persons to be "joiners" while lower-class individuals tend to isolate themselves from all types of organizations. The spuriousness of the relationship between socioeconomic status and "religiosity" is more clearly seen when we analyze the importance of religion to persons of varying socioeconomic circumstances, as well as differences in religious beliefs and the degree to which church activities are secular by social class.

Goode, after comparing white-collar church members with working-class church members, found that while the former were more likely to belong and participate in formal activities of the church, the latter were in fact more religious.

> They participate less in formal church activities, but their religious activity does not appear to be nearly so secularized. It is more specifically religious in character. This is indicated by the fact that on a number of other religious dimensions, dimensions not dependent on extraneous nonreligious variables, individuals of manual-status levels appear to display a considerably higher level of religious response. This is true particularly of psychological variables, such as religious "salience," the greater feeling that the church and religion are great forces in the lives of respondents. It is also true for "religiosity" as measured by a higher level of religious concern, and for religious "involvement," the extent to which the individual is psychologically dependent on some sort of specifically religious sociation in his life.[19]

TABLE 9–3.   Attendance at Sunday Church, 1965 (in percentages)

| Status Variable | ATTENDANCE | | | | |
	Don't Attend	Once a Month or Less	About Twice a Month	About 3 Times a Month	Every Sunday
Race:					
White	30%	14%	7%	10%	39%
Non-white	41	10	10	9	30
Education:					
College grad	26	17	6	10	41
1–3 yrs. coll.	24	17	6	8	45
H.S. grad	28	13	8	11	40
1–3 yrs. H.S.	37	13	8	9	33
0–8 grades	42	9	7	9	33
Income:					
Upper	26	13	9	11	41
Middle	30	14	7	9	40
Lower	38	12	8	9	33

Source: Adapted from Martin E. Marty, Stuart E. Rosenberg, and Andrew M. Greeley, *What Do We Believe? The Stance of Religion in America* (New York: Meredith Press, 1968), pp. 212, 214.

Table 9–4 presents evidence for the "secularization of religion" by the upper classes and the difference by socioeconomic status of religious beliefs.

Examination of Table 9–4 reveals that the higher the socioeconomic status of the respondent, the more likely to hold liberal religious beliefs. This means, in effect, that the middle- and upper-status categories have tended to abandon the bases of Christianity.

In summary, there is a rather complex relationship between socioeconomic status and religion. Although the relatively poor and uneducated are more likely to be indifferent to religion than the better educated and financially well-off, those who are religious tend to make religion a more integral part of their lives than better off persons. They go to church more for religious than secular reasons. They believe much more strongly than the well-to-do in the fundamental beliefs as expressed in the Bible. Thus we have the paradox that on many objective measures of religious involvement—church attendance and participation in formal church activities—the middle- and upper-status persons exceed those of lesser status, whereas if importance of religion in the lives of the individual is considered, the poor who go to church outstrip their more economically favored brethren.

TABLE 9–4. Religious Attitudes for a Sample of American Adults, 1965 (in percentages)

	Absolutely Believe in God	Bible is Revealed Word of God	There is a Heaven
Income:			
Upper	73%	70%	62%
Middle	83	79	68
Lower	84	85	71
Education:			
College Graduate	66	55	51
1–3 years college	78	71	67
H.S. graduate	82	82	68
1–3 H.S.	85	85	72
0–8 years	87	88	74

Source: Adapted from Martin E. Marty, Stuart E. Rosenberg, and Andrew M. Greeley, What Do We Believe: The Stance of Religion in America (New York: Meredith Press, 1968), pp. 216, 218, 228, 229, 248, 249.

TRENDS, PROBLEMS, AND PROSPECTS IN CONTEMPORARY AMERICAN RELIGION

Is there a religious revival? Will Herberg, writing in 1960, noted that religion was enjoying a boom of unprecedented proportions in America. As evidence, he cited the facts that over 95 percent of Americans identify themselves as either Protestants, Catholics, or Jews; that the number of church members had nearly doubled in the past half century; and church attendance had risen.[20] Lipset, however, has argued that little change has occurred. He shows that Americans have always almost universally identified with some religious group; that church membership figures are subject to errors of such magnitude as to leave them useless; and that church attendance has remained the same during the past ten years (he wrote this article in 1959). He concluded that "By far the most striking aspect of religious life in America is not the changes which have occurred in it—but the continuities it retains."[21]

Both Herberg and Lipset were writing around 1960. What is the case in the 1970's? The evidence is conflicting but very important. First, there appears to be a trend toward less and less religious participation by a series of Gallup polls (see Table 9–5). Each year since 1940 a sample of persons have been interviewed and asked, "Did you, yourself, happen to attend church in the last seven days?" (During 1970, for example, the Gallup pollsters interviewed 15,738 persons in more than 300 scientifically selected sample points at ten different weeks during the year to account for seasonal fluctuations.)

TABLE 9–5.   Percentage Attending Church During Average Week

1955	49%	1964	45
1956	46	1965	44
1957	47	1966	44
1958	49	1967	45
1959	47	1968	43
1960	47	1969	42
1961	47	1970	42
1962	46	1971	40
1963	46	1972	40

Source: George Gallup, Jr., and John O. Davis III (eds.), *Religion in America, 1971* (Princeton, New Jersey: Gallup International, Inc., 1971), p. 43. The data for 1971 and 1972 are from George Gallup, "Churchgoing Maintains Status," (Princeton, New Jersey: Field Enterprises, Inc., 1972).

299

The data in Table 9–5 show a clear downward trend. The reader will note that for the years around 1960, when Herberg and Lipset were making their assessments, the percentages were relatively stable. And, if the data from the tables earlier in this chapter are any indication of the future, the trend will continue downward. This is based on the empirically based probability that the more affluent and educated people become, the less seriously they take religion.

As the decline in church-going continues downward, the early 1970's have witnessed, paradoxically, a revival in religion. Whether this revival is a short-term phenomenon or not remains to be seen, but the fact remains that, especially among young people, there has been a return to religion and fundamental religion at that. In addition to the so-called "Jesus freaks" there is a rise of the occult, Satan worshippers, scientism, Zen, Yoga, transcendental meditation, and astrology among various segments of American society, and not just among the young.

The Jesus movement with its rigid fundamentalism (without the strings of organized religion) is an especially interesting phenomenon. Almost overnight thousands of persons have shifted from drugs to religion, from political activism to religious fanaticism, from immorality to morality. Jesus is everywhere on sweatshirts, on "honk if you love Jesus" bumper stickers, and in popular music ("Jesus Christ Superstar"). The possible reasons for the upsurge and appeal of this type of fundamentalistic religion are many.[22] One assertion is that the motivation of the Jesus movement for teenage youth is the need to resolve the adolescent identity crisis. The Jesus trip preserves childhood morality (absolute definitions of right and wrong). Furthermore, it resolves the crisis of the onset of sexuality by denying sexual feelings. According to this view then, the Jesus trip is taken in part to avoid the anxieties related to identity and adulthood.

Others joined the Jesus movement because of the need for answers—the authority of the scriptures and/or a charismatic leader —was desired by those unable to cope with the dramatic changes occurring in society. Dogma is but another form of escape, since it reduces complexity to a manageable form.

Yet another possible reason for immersion in the Jesus movement is the search for community in a lonely world. A group of believers living a righteous life not only gives a lonely person meaning and a social identity, but also an "extended family" for social and psychological support.

Related to these reasons is the attraction of religion for persons living in an overly rational world. They react against the technology, materialism, efficiency, and bureaucracy that characterize American life. They prefer, rather, to live by faith. They seek out irrational substitutes such as religious fundamentalism, the occult, astrology, numerology or scientology.*

Another possibility concerns the appeal of the apolitical nature of fundamentalist Christianity to many who had participated in the frustrating and unfulfilling days of political activism in the 1960's. For many of the activists who had participated in marches, demonstrations, boycotts, and door-to-door campaigns designed to bring about fundamental changes, the continuation of institutional racism, poverty, injustice, and war, was too much. They switched dramatically to a movement where the goal was inner peace and the goal of changing society was perceived as irrelevant.

Finally, juxtaposed from the reason just given is the appeal of Christianity as a force for change. The message of these persons is that Jesus was a revolutionary. He came to overthrow the injustices of his day and he calls upon followers in this day to do the same. Some clergymen, obeying this call, have been imprisoned for their radical activities (e.g., Martin Luther King, Jr., in the 1960's and the Catholic priests Daniel and Philip Berrigan in the early 1970's).

Trouble in the churches. We have already noted two indicators of trouble in the churches—the sliding attendance figures, and the search by persons who are "turned off" traditional religion but who seek solace outside the church organizations, in various movements from the "God squad" to the occult. There are other indicators of the crises facing contemporary churches. First is the growing phenomenon of underground churches (i.e., persons of like mind gathering wherever they can, to do what they feel called to do—outside the traditional channels). This is related to the second indicator of trouble in the churches—the continued splintering of local congregations (internal conflict leading to sect formation and/or underground churches). Third, there is a growing number of clergymen who are "dropping out." At least 3,000 Protestant clergymen left the ministry annually in 1968 through 1970 (about one percent each year). Even more dramatic was the 4 percent dropout rate of Catholic clergymen during those years (2,500 annually).[24]

These indicators of trouble in the churches point to a basic question as to the fundamental function of the church. The dilemma is

* Peter Rowley says that adherents to new, unconventional religion in America have increased from 100,000 to 2.5 million from 1960 to 1970. Most of these are odd, esoteric varieties often dealing with some form of mysticism.[23]

that the Christian church has two contradictory roles (analogous to order and conflict approaches to the social order)—to comfort the afflicted and to afflict the comforted (or to comfort and to challenge). It is the church's commitment to both of these functions that has generated much of the trouble in the contemporary church.[25] The comforting role is one of aiding individuals in surmounting of trials and tribulations of sickness, the death of loved ones, financial woes, social interaction with family, neighbors, colleagues, or enemies. The church aids by such means as pastoral counseling and collecting and distributing food and clothing to the needy. Another way the church comforts the afflicted is through providing a rationale for suffering (theodicy), the consequence of which is sanctification of the status quo.

Three related criticisms of the comforting function are immediately apparent. First, some would say that the church (and the clergy) have allowed this function to supersede the other role of challenger. Second, if the church would do more challenging and less comforting, evils such as poverty would be eliminated. By helping people to accept an imperfect society, the church preserves the status quo—i.e., the injustice and inequality that caused the problems in the first place. In this way, religion *is* an opiate of the masses because it convinces them to accept an unjust situation rather than working to change it from below. Third, the comfortable will not feel guilty, thereby preventing them from working to change the system from above.

The other function of the church—to challenge—is the injunction to be an agent of social protest and social reform. The church, through its pronouncements and leadership, seeks to lead in the fight to right the inequities of the society. A fundamental problem is in winning the support of the members. Change is almost by definition controversial, since some persons benefit under the existing social arrangements. When the church takes a stand against racial segregation, abortion, war, the abuses of business or labor, some members will become alienated. They may withdraw their financial support or even leave the church. The church, of course, has a commitment to its members. Since it cannot afford to lose it membership, the church may compromise its principles. Such an action, however, may make others angry at the church because of its hypocrisy. Consequently, the church is in the unenviable position of trying to keep a very precarious balance between compromise and purity.

The evidence is that, in general, the contemporary Christian church has opted in favor of the comforting function. The most popular preacher of the 1960's and 1970's has been Billy Graham. His theology is an excellent example of the prevailing "comforting" view. He has said, for example, "We should work for peace but all we can really do is patch things up, because the real war is in man's own heart. Only when Christ comes again will the lion lie down with the lamb and the little white children of Alabama walk hand in hand with the little black children."[26] This philosophy is anti-interventionist. One does not attack society. One either waits until the Second Coming or one changes the hearts and minds of individuals. Social problems, by this philosophy, are a result of man's sinful nature and are to be dealt with on that level rather than on the level of changing the law or the social structure. Religion in this light is essentially a private transaction between an individual and God, and not a force for overcoming social ills.

Of course, clergymen vary in their interpretation of the role of the church. They are truly men in conflict. There are conflicting expectations on clergymen from all sides (resulting in role conflict). The church hierarchy expects the clergyman to behave in a particular way (consider the rules issued by the Catholic hierarchy, for example). Most parishioners will doubtless favor the comforting role. Most joined the church to be comforted (if poor, to know they will be rewarded later; if rich, to have their wealth and power legitimized). There will, however, be some parishioners who wish the clergyman to take a stand on controversial issues and work for social change. A final source of the clergyman's role conflict is his own definition of the role. These various expectations, and the resulting role conflict on the clergyman, amount to one reason why he may drop out. Another is that if he takes a stand (or does not), he may automatically alienate a segment of his parish and perhaps the church hierarchy. He may, consequently, be forced to resign.

Those who do not resign may solve their dilemma by being non-controversial. This non-boat-rocking stance is all too familiar and results in another problem—irrelevancy. By not talking about social problems, one in fact legitimates the status quo. Hence, the inequities of the society continue, since the moral force of the churches is mainly quiet. For an examination of the tendency for certain kinds of clergymen toward this type of silence see Panel 9–1.

Not all clergymen are content with the emphasis on "comfort." There is a "new breed" of clergymen who are not content to let the church continue to perpetuate injustice by not speaking out. They are committed to a socially relevant church, one which seeks social solutions to social problems. They speak out, they participate in marches, work for integrated housing, and demonstrate against the war. Such activities, however, are not acceptable to the bulk of American Protestants. Hadden in a 1967 national survey found 72 percent answered "yes" to the question, "I would be upset if my (minister/priest/rabbi) were to participate in a picket line or demonstration."[27] As a result, the socially active clergymen often become the object of discrimination by their parishioners.[28] Another consequence is that the laity trust their clergymen less and less. As behavior in one area is questioned—e.g., social activism—church members are likely to withdraw confidence in others as well. Finally, churches have divided on this issue. Some want social action instead of just pious talk. Others want to preserve the status

PANEL 9-1

"THE SOUNDS OF SILENCE"

Source: Rodney Stark, Bruce D. Foster, Charles Y. Glock, and Harold Quinley, "Sounds of Silence," *Psychology Today,* 3 (April, 1970), pp. 38–41; 60–61.

Four sociologists analyzed questionnaires from a random sample of 1,580 California clergymen in 1968 to determine whether clergymen were including controversial subjects in their sermons. They assumed that this would be determined in part from their religious convictions. A Doctrine Index was constructed, scoring for a minister whenever he expressed unwavering faith in any of the five traditional beliefs: the existence of a personal God; the divinity of Jesus; life beyond death; the literal existence of the devil; and the necessity to believe in Jesus in order to be saved. The scores ranged from zero ("modernists") to four ("traditionalists"). The respondents were then asked if they had delivered a sermon in the past year that dealt mainly with a controversial topic (a list of topics was provided). The results classified by Doctrine Index Score were as shown in the adjoining table.

These findings indicate clearly that the more theologically conservative (and they far outnumber the more liberal clergy) the respondent, the more likely his sermon content will ignore social issues. Not indicated in the above data is the startling finding that one-third of the clergymen had *never* said a word in their sermons about the Vietnam war.

quo. The hypocrisy found in many churches forces splits, the formation of underground churches, or total rejection of Christianity as the source of social action. Others may leave because they feel the church has wandered too far from the beliefs upon which the faith was founded. This dilemma accelerates the current dropout problem—by parishioners and clergy alike. The problem (—if the author may here interject his bias—) seems to be that for the most part those who drop out are the social activists who leave the church with a residue of "comforters." If this is the case, the future of the church is bleak unless there is a reversal and prophets of social action ascend—an unlikely possibility given the propensity by most parishioners for the message of "comfort" over the message of "challenge."

Percent who gave a sermon during the previous year which dealt mainly with:	Doctrine Index				
	Modernists		Traditionalists		
	0 (N=28)	1 (N=134)	2 (N=296)	3 (N=437)	4 (N=568)
Open housing	95%	80%	74%	65%	29%
Vietnam war	89	80	75	69	49
Racial problems	78	66	63	53	25
National poverty	68	36	25	29	12
Capital punishment	19	18	10	8	4
Black Power	22	18	12	7	3
Conduct of public officials	15	6	4	5	5
Birth control	19	2	5	2	1

The authors concluded that,
   ". . . a major reason that clergymen high on doctrinalism are so unlikely to preach about the problems of race, war and poverty is that they see such problems as mundane in contrast to the joys of the world to come, and besides, they believe these social ills would take care of themselves if enough men were brought to Christ. Thus it is because of their religious convictions that many Protestant clergymen do not speak out on social issues. If the majority are silent, it is because they believe that is best."

SUGGESTED FURTHER READING

Glock, Charles Y., Benjamin B. Ringer and Earl R. Babbie, *To Comfort and to Challenge: A Dilemma of the Contemporary Church* (Berkeley, California: University of California Press, 1967). This book deals with the essential dilemma facing clergymen and churches—whether to comfort the afflicted or afflict the comforted.

Hadden, Jeffrey K., *The Gathering Storm in the Churches* (Garden City, New York: Doubleday & Company, Inc., 1969). A sociologist examines the crises facing contemporary Protestant churches. These are shown to have emerged from a conflict among clergymen and laymen over the basic theological doctrines of Christianity.

Rowley, Peter, *New Gods in America* (New York: David McKay Company, 1971). A book dealing with the rise of new, unconventional religious activity in the United States.

Selznick, Gertrude J., and Stephen Steinberg, *The Tenacity of Prejudice: Anti-Semitism in Contemporary America* (New York: Harper and Row, 1969). This book reports the findings of a cross-section of Americans on anti-semitic attitudes. It assesses the extent and the sources of this form of religious bigotry.

NOTES AND REFERENCES

1. These elements are taken primarily from Elizabeth K. Nottingham, *Religion and Society* (New York: Random House, 1954), pp. 1–11.

2. Peter L. Berger, "Religious Institutions," *Sociology*, Neil J. Smelser (ed), (New York: John Wiley and Sons, Inc., 1967), pp. 343–344.

3. Pierre L. van den Berghe, *Race and Racism: A Comparative Perspective* (New York: John Wiley & Sons, Inc., 1967), p. 82.

4. Earl Raab (ed.), *Religious Conflict in America* (Garden City, New York: Doubleday Anchor Books, 1964); see also Robert Lee and Martin E. Marty, *Religion and Social Conflict* (New York: Oxford University Press, 1964).

5. The following account is taken largely from Robert N. Bellah, "Civil Religion in America," *Daedalus* 96 (Winter, 1967), pp. 1–21; and Conrad Cherry, "American Sacred Ceremonies," *American Mosaic: Social Patterns of Religion in the United States*, Phillip E. Hammond and Benton Johnson (eds.), (New York: Random House, 1970), pp. 303–316.

6. Bellah, "Civil Religion in America," pp. 1–2.

7. For an interesting account of serpent handlers see, Nathan L. Gerrard, "The Serpent-Handling Religions of West Virginia," *Transaction* 5 (May, 1968), pp. 22–28.

8. Ernst Troeltsch, *The Social Teaching of the Christian Churches*, Olive Wyon (trans.), (New York: The Macmillan Company,

1931); and Liston Pope, *Millhands and Preachers* (New Haven, Connecticut, Yale University Press, 1942), pp. 117–140.

9. Bryan Wilson, "An Analysis of Sect Development," *American Sociological Review* 24 (February, 1959), pp. 3–15.

10. *Max Weber, The Theory of Social and Economic Organization,* A. M. Henderson and Talcott Parsons (trans.), (Glencoe, Illinois: The Free Press, 1947), pp. 358–366.

11. J. Milton Yinger, *Sociology Looks At Religion* (New York: The Macmillan Company, 1961), pp. 21–25.

12. This is the conclusion of Liston Pope after his study of the rise of sects in a small town in North Carolina. Liston Pope, *Millhands and Preachers* (New Haven, Connecticut: Yale University Press, 1942), p. 140.

13. Max Weber, *The Sociology of Religion*, Ephraim Fischoff (trans.), (Boston: Beacon Press, 1963), p. 107.

14. Peter L. Berger, *The Sacred Canopy: Elements of a Sociological Theory of Religion* (Garden City, New York: Doubleday & Company, Inc., 1967), pp. 53–80.

15. Thomas O'Dea, *The Sociology of Religion* (Englewood Cliffs, New Jersey: Prentice-Hall, Inc., 1966), p. 60. For an elaboration of this point see the insightful discussion by Weber in *The Sociology of Religion.*

16. N. J. Demerath III, *Social Class in American Protestantism* (Chicago: Rand McNally & Company, 1965), p. 3.

17. Leonard Broom and Philip Selznick, *Sociology,* fourth edition, (New York: Harper and Row, Publishers, 1968), p. 321.

18. This relationship does not always hold, however, if other dimensions of religious involvement are examined. See especially Demerath, *Social Class in American Protestantism,* pp. 1–124.

19. Erich Goode, "Social Class and Church Participation," *American Journal of Sociology* 72 (July, 1966), p. 111.

20. Will Herberg, "Religion and Culture in Present-Day America," *Anatomies of America,* Philip Ehrensaft and Amitai Etzioni (eds.), (New York: The Macmillan Company, 1969), p. 255. Herberg also acknowledged that this upsurge in religion was curious since most Americans recognize that religion is quite peripheral to their everyday lives.

21. Seymour Martin Lipset, "Religion in America: What Religious Revival?" *Anatomies of America,* Philip Ehrensaft and Amitai Etzioni (eds.), (New York: The Macmillan Company, 1969), p. 271.

22. James Nolan, "Jesus Now: Hogwash and Holy Water," *Ramparts* 10 (August, 1971), pp. 20–26; Robert Lynn Adams and Robert Jon Fox, "Mainlining Jesus: The New Trip," *Trans-action* 9 (February, 1972), pp. 50–56; and Peter Marin, "Children of Yearning," *Saturday Review* (May, 1972), pp. 58–63.

23. Peter Rowley, *New Gods in America* (New York: David McKay Company, 1971).

24. Associated Press release (February 14, 1970):

25. Much of the following discussion is taken from Charles Y. Glock, Benjamin B. Ringer, and Earl R. Babbie, *To Comfort and To Challenge: A Dilemma of the Contemporary Church* (Berkeley, California: University of California Press, 1967), especially chapter 9; and Jeffrey K. Hadden, *The Gathering Storm in the Churches* (Garden City, New York: Doubleday & Company, Inc., 1969).

26. "The Preaching and the Power," *Newsweek* (July 20, 1970), p. 52.

27. Jeffrey K. Hadden, "Clergy Involvement in Civil Rights," *The Annals* 387 (January, 1970), p. 122.

28. Dora Jane Hamblin, "Crunch in the Churches," *Life* 65 (October 4, 1968), pp. 79–84, for a series of examples of the reaction of the laity to the social activism of their pastors.

CHAPTER 10

American Education

Few Americans are neutral about their schools. While almost everyone recognizes the necessity of a formal system of education,* many complain about the cost, the inequality, the impersonality, the techniques, the curriculum, the coercive (or permissive) environment, the rules, or other presumed weaknesses.

Despite these problems, the schools perform several vital functions for the maintenance of society. Education, along with the institutions of the family and religion, has a primary responsibility for the socialization of newcomers to the society. A second function of education is the shaping of personalities so that they are in basic congruence with the demands of the culture. In other words, one goal of the educational system of any society is to produce persons with desired personality traits (e.g., competitiveness, altruism, bravery, conformity, or industriousness, depending upon the culture of the society). A third function is to prepare individuals for their adult roles. In American society this means the preparation of individuals for the specialized roles of a highly complex division of labor. It also means the preparation of youngsters for life in a rapidly changing world. In early American history the primary aims of schooling were teaching the basics of reading, writing, spelling, and arithmetic. These were needed to read the Bible, write correspondence, and do simple accounting—the required skills for adults in an agrarian society. Modern society, on the other hand, de-

---

* A notable exception is Ivan Illich, in *Deschooling Society*. We will briefly consider Illich's radical proposals at the end of this chapter.[1]

mands persons with specialized occupational skills, with expertise in narrow areas. The educational system is saddled with providing these skills in addition to the basics. Moreover, the schools have taken over the teaching of citizenship skills, cooking, sewing, and even sex education—skills and knowledge that were once the explicit duty of each family to transmit to its offspring.

These three functions provide the rationale for the way education is conducted in American society. In this chapter our first section will describe the characteristics of American education. The second section will focus on several crises facing American education. Finally, we will present several alternative models for education in the future.

THE CHARACTERISTICS OF AMERICAN EDUCATION

Education as a conserving force. The formal system of education in American society (and in all societies, for that matter) is conservative. This must be the case, since the avowed function of the schools is to teach to newcomers the attitudes, values, roles, specialties, and training necessary to the maintenance of society. In other words, the special task of the schools is to preserve the culture, not to transform it. Thus, the schools indoctrinate their pupils in the culturally prescribed ways. Children are taught to be patriotic. They learn the myths, the superiority of their nation's heritage, who are the heroes and who are the villains. Jules Henry has put it this way:

> Since education is always against some things and for others, it bears the burden of the cultural obsessions. While the Old Testament extols without cease the glory of the One God, it speaks with equal emphasis against the gods of the Philistines; while the children of the Dakota Indians learned loyalty to their own tribe, they learned to hate the Crow; and while our children are taught to love American democracy, they are taught contempt for totalitarian regimes.[2]

There is always the explicit or implicit assumption in American schools that the American way is the one really right way. When this assumption is violated on the primary and secondary school level by the rare teacher who asks students to consider the viability of world government, or who proposes a class on the life and teachings of Karl Marx or about world religions, then strong enough

310

pressures usually occur from within the school (administrators, school board) or from without (parents, the American Legion, and the Daughters of the American Revolution) to quell the disturbance. The consequence is that creativity and a questioning attitude are curtailed in school. But the school really has no choice, as Jules Henry has argued so forcefully in Panel 10–1.

Mass education. Americans have a basic faith in education. This faith is based on the assumption that a democratic society requires an educated citizenry so that individuals may participate in the decisions of public policy. It is for this reason that they not only provide education for all citizens, but they compel children to go at least to the eighth grade or until age 16 (although this varies somewhat from state to state).

It is hard to quarrel with the emphasis that all children should be compelled to attend school, since it should be for their own good. After all, the greater the educational attainment, the greater the likelihood of greater economic rewards and upward social mobility. However, to compel a child to attend school for six hours a day, five days a week, forty weeks a year, for at least ten years, is quite a demand. The result, of course, is that many students are in school for the wrong reason. The motivation is compulsion, not interest in acquiring skills or curiosity about their world. This involuntary feature of American schools is unfortunate since so many school problems are related to the lack of student interest.

Local control of education. Although the state and federal governments finance and control education in part, the bulk of the money and control for education comes from local communities. There is a general fear of centralization of education—into a statewide educational system or even worse federal control. Local school boards (and the communities themselves) jealously guard their autonomy. Since, as it is commonly argued, local people know best the special needs of their children, local boards control how money will be allocated, the curriculum, the rules for running the schools, as well as the hiring and firing of personnel.

There are several problems with this emphasis on local control. First, tax money from the local area traditionally finances the schools. Whether the tax base is strong or weak has a pronounced effect on the quality of education received (a point we will return to later in this chapter). Second, since the democratic ideal requires that if schools be locally controlled, the ruling body (school board) should represent all segments of that community. Typically, however, the composition of school boards has overrepresented the business and professional sectors and overwhelmingly underrepresented blue collar workers and the various minority groups. This results in a governing body that is typically conservative in outlook and unresponsive to the wishes of persons unlike themselves. A final problem with local control is the lack of curriculum standardization across school districts. Since families move on the average of once every five years (and the rate is probably higher for families with school-age children), the large number of children moving from district to district often find a wide variation in curriculum and graduation requirements.

The competitive nature of American education. It is not surprising that the schools in a highly competitive society are competitive. Competition is found in virtually all school activities. The composition of athletic teams, cheerleading squads, "pom pon squads,"

PANEL 10–1

"THE SCHOOLS AND CREATIVITY"

Source: Jules Henry, *Culture Against Man* (New York: Vintage Books, 1963), pp. 286–288. The following is directly quoted from these pages.

The function of education has never been to free the mind and the spirit of man, but to bind them; and to the end that the mind and spirit of his children should never escape, *Homo sapiens* has employed praise, ridicule, admonition, accusation, mutilation, and even torture to chain them to the culture pattern. Throughout most of his historic course *Homo sapiens* has wanted from his children acquiescence, not originality. It is natural that this should be so, for where every man is unique there is no society, and where there is no society there can be no man. Contemporary American educators think they want creative children, yet it is an open question as to what they expect these children to create. And certainly the classrooms—from kindergarten to graduate school—in which they expect it to happen are not crucibles of creative activity and thought. It stands to reason that were young people truly creative the culture would fall apart, for originality, by definition, is different from what is given, and what is given is the culture itself. From the endless, pathetic, "creative hours" of kindergarten to the most abstruse problems in sociology and anthropology, the function of education is to prevent the truly creative intellect from getting out of hand. Only in the exact and the biological sciences do we permit unlimited freedom, for we have (but only since the Renaissance, since Galileo

debate teams, choruses, drill teams, bands, and dramatic play casts are almost always determined by competing with one's classmates. Grading in courses, too, is often done by comparing the individuals with each other ("grading on a curve") rather than against some standard. To relieve boredom in the classroom, teachers often invent competitive games such as "spelling baseball," or "hangman." In all of these cases, the individual learns at least two lessons: (1) one's classmates are "enemies" for if they succeed, they do so at the expense of others, (2) fear of failure is the great motivator, not intellectual curiosity or love of knowledge. Jules Henry has provided an incident from a fifth grade arithmetic lesson that speaks to both of these points in Panel 10–2.

The "sifting and sorting" function of schools. Schools play a considerable part in choosing those youth who come to occupy the higher status positions in society. Conversely, school performance

and Bruno underwent the Inquisition) found a way—or *thought* we found a way—to bind the explosive powers of science in the containing vessel of the social system.

American classrooms, like educational institutions anywhere, express the values, preoccupations, and fears found in the culture as a whole. School has no choice; it must train the children to fit the culture as it is. School can give training in skills; it cannot teach creativity. All the American school can conceivably do is nurture creativity when it appears. And who has the eyes to see it? Since the creativity that is conserved and encouraged will always be that which seems to do the most for the culture, which seems at the moment to do the most for the obsessions and the brutal preoccupations and anxieties from which we all suffer, schools nowadays encourage the child with gifts in mathematics and the exact sciences. But the child who has the intellectual strength to see through social shams is of no consequence to the educational system. The schools have therefore never been places for the stimulation of young minds. If all through school the young were provoked to question the Ten Commandments, the sanctity of revealed religion, the foundations of patriotism, the profit motive, the two-party system, monogamy, the laws of incest, and so on, we would have more creativity than we could handle. In teaching our children to accept fundamentals of social relationships and religious beliefs without question we follow the ancient highways of the human race, which extend backward into the dawn of the species, and indefinitely into the future. There must therefore be more of the caveman than of the spaceman about our teachers.

PANEL 10–2

"THE SCHOOLS AND COMPETITION"

Source: Jules Henry, *Culture Against Man* (New York: Vintage Books, 1963), pp. 295–296. The following is directly quoted from these pages.

Boris had trouble reducing "$12/16$" to the lowest terms, and could only get as far as "$6/8$." The teacher asked him quietly if that was as far as he could reduce it. She suggested he "think." Much heaving up and down and waving of hands by the other children, all frantic to correct him. Boris pretty unhappy, probably mentally paralyzed. The teacher, quiet, patient, ignores the others and concentrates with looks and voice on Boris. She says, "Is there a bigger number than two you can divide into the two parts of the fraction?" After a minute or two, she becomes more urgent, but there is no response from Boris. She then turns to the class and says, "Well, who can tell Boris what the number is?" A forest of hands appears, and the teacher calls Peggy. Peggy says that four may be divided into the numerator and denominator. Thus Boris' failure has made it possible for Peggy to succeed; his depression is the price of her exhilaration; his misery the occasion for her rejoicing. This is the standard condition of the American elementary school, and is why so many of us feel a contraction of the heart even if someone we never knew succeeds merely at garnering plankton in the Thames: because so often somebody's success has been bought at the cost of our failure. To a Zuni, Hopi, or Dakota Indian, Peggy's performance would seem cruel beyond belief, for competition, the wringing of success from somebody's failure, is a form of torture foreign to those noncompetitive redskins. Yet Peggy's action seems natural to us, and so it is. How else would you run our world? And since all but the brightest children have the constant experience that others succeed at their expense they cannot but develop an inherent tendency to hate—to hate the success of others, to hate others who are successful, and to be determined to prevent it. Along with this, naturally, goes the hope that others will fail. This hatred masquerades under the euphemistic name of "envy."

Looked at from Boris' point of view, the nightmare at the blackboard was, perhaps, a lesson in controlling himself so that he would not fly shrieking from the room under the enormous public pressure. Such experiences imprint on the mind of every man in our culture the *Dream of Failure,* so that over and over again, night in, night out, even at the pinnacle of success, a man will dream not of success, but of failure. *The external nightmare is internalized for life.* It is this dream that, above all other things, provides the fierce human energy required by technological driveness [sic]. It was not so much that Boris was learning arithmetic, but that he was learning *the essential nightmare. To be successful in our culture one must learn to dream of failure* [italics in the original].

also sorts out those who will occupy the lower rungs in the occupational prestige ladder. Education is, therefore, a selection process. The sorting is done with respect to two different criteria: the child's ability and his/her social class background. Although the goal of education is to select on ability alone, ascribed social status (the status of one's family, race, and religion) has a pronounced effect on the degree of success in the educational system. The school is analogous to a conveyor belt with persons of all social classes getting on at the same time but leaving the belt in accordance with social class—the lower the class, the shorter the ride. We will examine the reasons for this relationship in detail later in this chapter. Suffice it to say at this point that school performance and social class are closely related.

The preoccupation with order and control.[3] There is a fundamental assumption shared by most administrators and teachers that school is a collective experience requiring subordination of individual needs to those of the school. American schools are characterized, then, by constraints on individual freedom. The school day is regimented by the dictates of the clock. Activities begin and cease on a timetable, not by the degree of interest shown or whether the students have mastered the subject. Silberman characterizes this as the "tyranny of the lesson plan" where teachers too often see the lesson plan as the end rather than as a means to an end. Another indicator of order is the preoccupation with discipline (i.e., absence of unwarranted noise and movement as well as the following of orders).

Schools in their quest for order also demand conformity in clothing and hair styles. Dress codes are infamous for their constraints upon the freedom to dress as one pleases. School athletic teams also restrict freedom (see Panel 10–3) and these restrictions are condoned by the school authorities. Conformity is also demanded in what to read, where to set the margins on the typewriter, and how to give the answers the teacher wants. The brilliant poet E. E. Cummings, because he did not follow the rules on capitalization, would doubtless fail English composition in a vast majority of American schools.

The many rules and regulations found in our schools are a result of a number of factors. The belief in order by the school authorities is one reason. They, in fact, rate teachers not on ability to get pupils to learn but rather on the degree to which their classroom is quiet and orderly. The community also wants order. A survey of high school students' parents in 1969 found that nearly two-thirds believe that "maintaining discipline is more important than student self-inquiry."[4] Another reason is that so many students are bored in school—the school is not meeting their needs. An important reason is that schools operate on the assumption of distrust. As Christopher Jencks has observed, "The school board has no faith in the central administration, the central administration has no faith in the principals, the principals have no faith in the teachers, and the teachers

PANEL 10–3

"RULES"

Source: Adapted from an actual list of team rules furnished to the author from a high school in Kansas.

The following list of rules was provided by one coach for his high school basketball team in 1971. We have selected from a longer list those rules that appear particularly restrictive of individual freedom.

1. You are expected to be a gentleman off the court as well as on the court. If you cannot behave in the halls and classrooms you will be suspended from the team.
2. Hair will be cut short enough to look neat and trim. Sideburns will be no longer than the middle of the ear.
3. Every basketball player will address the coaches as Mr. or Coach.
4. We do not want a boy out for basketball that we would not be glad to have visit us in our homes. If you have not been taught by your parents or guardians how to act, then we can't use you out here, unless you are willing to learn how.
5. If you find it necessary to miss practice because of illness—call your coach ahead of time. Failure to do this will result in immediate suspension from the team.
6. No one will drink water during practice.
7. There will be no loud talking in the dressing room at any time (except after victories).
8. No horseplay will be tolerated.
9. Holding hands or displaying affections for girls in the halls will result in a one game suspension.
10. Visiting with anyone in the halls outside the gym between 3:00 and 3:20 will result in a one game suspension.
11. During game days you are requested not to be with a girl outside of school hours until after the game.
12. We practice on Saturdays and during Christmas vacation. If you have a valid excuse to miss practice, notify your coach ahead of time. You will be required to run one mile for every hour of practice you miss. (Varsity under 6:00 minutes and Sophomores under 7:00 minutes.)
13. No one will sit down or lean against anything during practice.

have no faith in the students."[5] The consequence of this distrust is a self-fulfilling prophecy. When teachers are not treated as professionals (not consulted on matters that concern them most, having to punch time clocks) they do not act as professionals. When students are treated as slaves they do not develop into self-reliant, self-motivated individuals. An excerpt from a famous (or infamous) essay entitled "The Student as Nigger" dramatizes the demands for order in American schools.

> [Students] haven't gone through twelve years of public school for nothing. They've learned one thing and perhaps only one thing during those twelve years. They've forgotten their algebra. They've grown to fear and resent literature. They write like they've been lobotomized. But Jesus, can they follow orders! . . . Students don't ask that orders make sense. They give up expecting things to make sense long before they leave elementary school. Things are true because the teacher says they're true. At a very early age we all learn to accept "two truths," as did certain medieval churchmen. Outside of class, things are true to your tongue, your fingers, your stomach, your heart. Inside class things are true by reason of authority. And that's just fine because you don't care anyway. Miss Wiedemeyer tells you a noun is a person, place or thing. So let it be. You don't give a rat's ass; she doesn't give a rat's ass. The important thing is to please her. Back in kindergarten, you found out that teachers only love children who stand in nice straight lines. And that's where it's been at ever since.[6]

The emphasis on interschool sports competition. The importance of competitive athletics in the life of the American school cannot be questioned. The practice time allotted to athletes, bands, cheerleaders, pep club members, drill teams; the time devoted to talking about sports inside and outside of class; the amount of space devoted to sports in school papers and yearbooks; and the disproportionate amount of honors given to athletes as evidenced by the number of sports trophies in the school trophy case—all this attests to the important role of sports in American education. This emphasis is encouraged by school authorities who believe sports to build good citizenship and other valued character traits such as hard work and learning to cope with victory and defeat. They also believe sports to exemplify the value of the democratic process, since individuals on the playing field are supposedly judged for what they can do, not on the basis of the social, ethnic, or economic group to which their families belong.[7] Interschool sports are also encouraged because they provide a major source of entertainment for the school and the community. They are seen as an effective means for school and community unity.

The one important negative consequence of this emphasis on

sports is that the rewards from the school, community, and peer group for success in sports is a deterrent to academic achievement.[8] Coleman found, for example, that in response to the question, "how would you most like to be remembered here at high school?" 44 percent wished to be remembered as an athletic star, while only 31 percent wanted to be remembered as a brilliant student (three-fourths of the parents of these boys, on the other hand, wanted their boys to be remembered as brilliant students). Coleman concluded that persons with the greatest talent divert their energies away from scholarship to athletics where the rewards are. Those adolescents who are labelled "scholars" are, therefore, not necessarily those persons with the highest intelligence, but are only the ones who are willing to work hard at a relatively unrewarding activity. Thus, with the blessing of the community and the school authorities, the schools engage in activities that actually work against the objectives of the school.

Let us summarize how this section has characterized American education by listing a series of paradoxes. These paradoxes indicate the many profound dilemmas in American education. They set the foundation for the remaining sections of this chapter, which deal with the crises facing education and with some alternative modes.

1. Formal education encourages creativity, but it curbs the truly creative individual from being too disruptive to society.
2. Formal education encourages the open mind, but teaches dogma.
3. Formal education has the goal of turning out mature students, but does not give them the freedom essential to foster maturity.
4. Formal education pays lip service to meeting individual needs of the students, but in actuality encourages conformity at every turn.
5. Formal education has the goal of allowing all students to reach their potential, yet fosters all kinds of competition which continually cause some persons to be defined as "failures."
6. Formal education is designed to allow persons of the greatest talent to reach the top, but it systematically benefits certain categories of persons regardless of their talent—the middle- and upper-class students who are white.

THE CRISES IN AMERICAN EDUCATION

Most observers of American education will attest to the fact that there are severe problems in the system. We will examine two representative problems here—inequality of educational opportunity, and the inadequacies of higher education. In contrast to the way many persons interpret these and other problems, we will focus on the system as the generator of the problem, rather than on the victims. Typically, Americans see the problem as the minority group members dropping out of school, rather than as the system operating to push them out. Or Americans see student protestors as the problem, not the reasons for the protest. Somehow the blame is shifted from the source to the object. This section will attempt to overcome this prevalent and fallacious form of fault-finding.*

Education and Inequality

Education is presumed by many to be the great equalizer—the process by which the disadvantaged get their chance to be upwardly mobile. Unfortunately, the schools have served to aid in the perpetuation of social and economic differences. *There is no question that children of low socioeconomic background do not perform in school as well as children of the more well to do.* Let us first examine the evidence for this assertion and then turn to the reasons for the inequality.

The evidence that educational performance is linked to socioeconomic background is clear and irrefutable. In Cleveland, for example, an inverse relationship was found between the proportion of persons on welfare and reading level for the school. In the sixth grade the top one-third of schools in reading level had but 8 percent of students from welfare homes. For schools rated in the lowest third, however, 43 percent of the children came from families living on welfare. This same relationship was found in every elementary grade level.[9]

A similar relationship has also been found in Chicago (see Table 10–1). In addition to two measures of reading, these data show that socioeconomic status is related to the proportion who believe they will enter college.

Since college attendance is so important as a mobility escalator, we should examine carefully who enters by social class origin. Table 10–2 shows clearly the strong relationship between socioeconomic status and entering college. Moreover, these data show that the relationship has remained relatively stable since 1920.

---

* This section, in keeping with the tone of the chapter, is critical of American education. Of course, there are exceptions to the criticisms being made. There are schools which have instituted black studies programs, modular courses, mini-courses, and other curricular innovations. The relatively small number of schools that are truly innovative, however, proves the rule that schools are basically conservative and do not meet the needs of children.

The sorting accomplished by the education system culminates in who makes it into the graduate and professional schools. Obviously, because social class background affects who drops out and who remains all along the educational process, the residue who are left for the highest educational achievements are most likely to be above

TABLE 10–1.   Socioeconomic Factors in School Achievement in High Schools of Chicago

School number	SER[a]	Achievement[b]	Low reading level[c]	Say will enter college[d]
1	290	52	0	94
3	199	54	0	91
5	123	40	12	71
7	97	36	0	74
9	82	29	22	55
11	79	36	5	74
13	74	41	0	49
15	68	33	14	52
17	66	28	4	48
19	54	11	16	46
21	53	21	15	76
23	53	25	12	42
25	50	23	0	41
27	39	22	4	38
29	27	27	0	44
31	23	11	16	36
33	22	4	56	53
35	20	14	29	39
37	17	4	37	51
39	11	6	41	53

[a] Socioeconomic ratio of adults in the school's attendance area in 1960. The higher the ratio, the higher the socioeconomic status of the area.
[b] Percent of ninth and eleventh graders in top three stanines on standard tests of reading. (For city as a whole, 23 percent are in the top three stanines.)
[c] Percent of ninth-grade English classes in Basic English. Pupils are below sixth-grade level in such classes. In some high schools there are too few such pupils to form a class, though almost every high school has at least a handful of such pupils.
[d] Students who will graduate in June are asked in the spring whether they expect to go to college. (Composite of data from 1962, 1963, and 1964).

Source: Adapted from Robert J. Havighurst, The Public Schools of Chicago (Chicago: The Board of Education of the City of Chicago, 1964), pp. 208–209.

average in socioeconomic status. This is true even if one holds ability constant, since in America's open class system persons with ability are assumed to be able to make it to the top. Colin Greer, however, has cited a research finding that explodes this myth.

. . . of high school graduates who rank in the top fifth in ability among their classmates, those whose parents are in the top socio-

TABLE 10–2.   Social Class Origins of College Entrants

Social Class	1920	1940	1950	1960	1965 Males	1965 Females
Upper and upper-middle	40	70	75	80	90	80
Lower-middle	8	20	38	50	62	45
Upper-working	2	5	12	25	35	24
Lower-working	0	0	2	4	8	4
Percent of total age group entering college	6	16	22	33	43*	32*

* When 1965 figures for males and females are averaged, the percent of the total age group who enter college is approximately 37.

Source: Robert J. Havighurst and Bernice L. Neugarten, *Society and Education,* Third Edition (Boston: Allyn and Bacon, Inc., 1967) p. 98.

TABLE 10–3.   Overall Differences in Achievement Between White, Puerto Rican, and Black Students in the Metropolitan Northeast

Test	Group	6th Grade	9th Grade	12th Grade
Verbal Ability	White	6.0	9.0	12.0
	Puerto Rican	3.3	6.1	8.4
	Black	4.4	6.6	8.7
Reading Comprehension	White	6.0	9.0	12.0
	Puerto Rican	2.9	5.7	8.3
	Black	4.2	6.4	9.1
Mathematics	White	6.0	9.0	12.0
	Puerto Rican	3.2	5.6	7.2
	Black	4.0	6.2	6.8

Source: Robert A. Dentler, "Equality of Educational Opportunity: A Special Review," *The Urban Review* 1 (December, 1966), p. 27. These data are from James S. Coleman, *Equality of Educational Opportunity* (Washington, D.C.: U.S. Government Printing Office, 1966).

economic status quartile are five times more likely to enter graduate or professional schools than those of comparable ability whose parents fall in the bottom quartile.[10]

Inequality in education occurs also along racial lines (which, of course, is closely related to socioeconomic status). The Coleman Report, an analysis of all third, sixth, ninth, and twelfth grade pupils in 4,000 schools, noted, for example, remarkable differences by race in various achievement areas. Table 10–3 summarizes these data, comparing white, Puerto Rican, and black students in the metropolitan Northeast.

These data demonstrate vividly, not only the wide gaps between whites and various minority groups in educational achievement, but also that these intervals increase the longer they remain in school. Clearly the school is to blame, for in no instance is the initial gap narrowed with the school experience. Moreover, the increasing gaps are *understated*, since there is a greater tendency for the persons of lowest aptitude among the minority groups to drop out of school.

William Ryan has summarized the situation as follows:

> The school is better prepared for the middle-class child than for the lower-class child. Indeed, we could be tempted to say further that the school experience is tailored for, and stacked in favor of, the middle-class child. The cause-and-effect relationship between the lack of skills and experiences found among lower-class children and the conditions of lower-class life has yet to be delineated. So far, explanations of this relationship have been, at best, sketchy, and have been based on casual observation. We know poor and middle-class children exhibit certain differences in styles of talking and thinking, but we do not know yet why or how these differences occur.
>
> We do know, however, that these differences—really differences in *style* rather than ability—are not handicaps or disabilities (unlike barriers to learning as poor vision, mild brain damage, emotional disturbance or orthopedic handicap). They do represent inadequate *preparation* for the reality of the modern urban school. They are, in no sense, cultural or intellectual defects.[11]

How is the educational system stacked in favor of the middle and upper class child and stacked against children from the lowest classes?* There are at least four interrelated factors that explain

---

* Note that we have phrased the question so as to focus on the system, not the victims. This is contrary to the typical response, which is to focus on the "cultural deprivation" of the poor. That approach attacks the home and culture of poor people. It assumes that these persons perform inadequately because they are handicapped by their culture. To the contrary, however, we cannot make the value judgment that their culture is "deprived." We can

why the educational system tends to reinforce the socioeconomic status differentials in the United States—finances, curriculum, segregation, and personnel. Let us examine each in turn.

1. *Finances and facilities.* Almost every American community pays for its public schools by taxing real estate. In 1971, however, the California Supreme Court ruled that it is discriminatory and hence unconstitutional to base public school financing on widely divergent property values, since rich school districts can spend more money on each student at a lower taxing rate than poor ones. In 1973, however, the Supreme Court ruled that the federal government *cannot* interfere with the system of local property taxation (although it left open the possibility that states may do so in the future). Thus, the Court permitted the many glaring disparities to continue as before. In Kansas, for example, property owners in the Moscow school district paid in 1972 a tax levy of $7.53 for every $1,000 of assessed valuation to finance their schools. This raised enough money to spend $1,742 per pupil. In Galena, Kansas, a community not blessed like Moscow with oil and gas fields, the tax rate is $36.68 for every $1,000 of assessed valuation. Although this rate is five times greater than in Moscow, it raises only enough to spend $509 per pupil (less than one third the money spent for pupils in Moscow).[12] These variations can also be observed on the state level. The President's Commission on School Finances noted that educational spending among the states in 1970 ranged from $1,237 per pupil in New York to $438 in Alabama.[13]

Wealthy districts and states can afford to provide equipment, buildings, libraries, audio-visual materials, and to attract better teachers through higher pay scales. But there is within-district variation as well. Patricia Sexton found in her study of a large city school system that

> . . . money spent on schools there, and the quality of education offered, varied in direct proportion to the income of families in the school neighborhood. Inequalities were found in: quality and adequacy of school buildings and facilities, school and class overcrowding, quality of teaching staff, methods of testing and estimating pupil performance, methods of selecting and segregating children, quality of the secondary curriculum, vocational and educational counseling of students, opportunities for completion of

only note that this does not prepare children to perform in schools geared for the middle class. In other words, children of the poor and/or minority groups are not nonverbal—they are very verbal but not in the language of the middle class.

secondary school and admission to college, use of school buildings by communities, enrollments in pre-first grade programs, health, recreation, and food service facilities, total costs of educating students. All of these had their correlates in the poorer school performance of lower-income students.[14]

These devastating findings by Sexton for a large metropolitan school system are, unfortunately, typical. In an analysis of a similar report, a study of 490 schools in 41 cities showed that

> . . . both teachers and principals in low socioeconomic status schools were less experienced and less satisfied in their jobs than in high-status areas. School principals in the highest status areas were considerably more satisfied with their teachers. In the highest status areas, 17 percent of principals wanted a principalship of "more prestige," compared to 43 percent in the lowest. Forty-two percent of teachers in the lowest and 18 percent in highest status schools wanted a transfer to a school "in a better neighborhood." Teachers in the lowest status schools were on the average younger, less experienced, newer to the school and getting less pay. "Teaching performance, whether in respect to competence in subject matter, innovation, interest in pupils, cooperation with school personnel, teaching methods, or the maintenance of discipline, was found to be somewhat poorer in schools of lowest than of highest socioeconomic status."[15]

Summarizing the famous Coleman Report, Dentler has noted this same relationship along racial lines (of course, race is closely related to socioeconomic status):

> The basic findings of the Coleman Report in this regard are these: in the metropolitan North Negro and Puerto Rican pupils, as compared to white pupils, attend school in older, larger, more crowded buildings. They have access to fewer laboratories and library books, auditoriums and gymnasiums. Their elementary teachers show a slightly lower score on a short vocabulary test. Even their cafeterias and athletic playing fields are in shorter supply. . . . The Coleman data are comprehensive enough and the findings distinct enough to release us from endless cycling on questions of equality of public educational services. *Facilities, staffs, and services are distributed unequally.* Without exception, on the factors catalogued, the pattern of the inequality uniformly reinforces handicaps brought to the school by the low-income, minority-group learner.[16]

Just as important in the cataloguing of differences in lower-class and middle-class schools is the conclusion of Coleman that these differences have an especially detrimental effect upon minority group youngsters.

The average white student's achievement is less affected by the strength or weakness of his school's facilities, curricula, and teachers than is the average minority pupil's. To put it another way, the achievement of minority pupils depends more on the schools they attend than does the achievement of majority pupils. . . . The conclusion can then be drawn that improving the school of a minority pupil will increase his achievement more than will improving the school of a white child increase his. Similarly, the average minority pupil's achievement will suffer more in a school of low quality than will the average white pupil's. In short, whites . . . are less affected one way or the other by the quality of their schools than are minority pupils. This indicates that it is for the most disadvantaged children that improvement in school quality will make the most difference in achievement.[17]

On a different level, finances also go disproportionately to the well-off. Colleges, even low-tuition public colleges, cost a good deal, and therefore are often prohibitive to the able and willing but poor student. Sexton, quoting an American Council on Education Survey Report, found that even scholarships and student loans favor the well-off. "Of 8,000 scholarship winners in 65 leading institutions, only 1,200 went to students from families with incomes below $5,000."[18] Even the National Merit Scholarships, a program initiated to help provide educational opportunities for able youth from lower socioeconomic strata, give their primary benefits to the well-to-do. The data in Table 10–4 demonstrate this, using occupation as an indicator of socioeconomic status.

The table data show that the selection of the academically elite for scholarships is essentially based on status factors. This does not prove that scholastic ability is skewed in favor of the children of white collar workers, but that the educational opportunities for poorer children are poorer.

2. *Curriculum.* American schools are essentially middle or upper class. The written and spoken language in the schools, for example, is expected to be middle class. For children of the poor, however, English (at least middle-class English) may be a second language.*

* Marvin Loflin, a linguist, has argued that the language spoken by millions of American blacks, regardless of region, should be considered a separate language from standard English, rather than as a dialect. He points to some basic differences in syntax between the two forms of English which have usually created a gap between the teacher's ability to teach and the child's ability to learn about what constitutes "good English." Since most teachers have defined "good English" in an ethnocentric fashion, strictly in relation to their own standard of white middle-class dialect, they are poorly equipped to cope with the basic differences of another dialect or language. He feels the schools must change their curriculum and teachers must change their attitude

The problem is that the curriculum of the schools does not bend. The schools do not adapt and accommodate themselves to the special needs of the poor. To the contrary, the schools assume that the language and behaviors of the poor are not only alien but wrong—things to be changed. This assumption denigrates the ways of the poor and leads to the loss of ego strength (a trait already in short supply for the poor in a middle-class world).

The curriculum also is not very germane to the poor child's world. What is the relevance of conjugating a verb when you are hungry? What is the relevance of being able to trace the path of how a bill becomes a law when your family and neighbors are powerless? Irrelevancy for the poor is also seen in the traditional children's primers which picture "nice" surroundings and well-behaved blond children. There is little effort at any educational level to bring to bear the experience of slum children on realistic life situations of any kind. Schools also have a way of ignoring real-life problems and controversial issues. Schools are irrelevant if they disregard topics

TABLE 10–4.   Father's Occupation and Production of National Merit Scholars, 1956

Father's Occupation	Number of National Merit Scholars	Index of Productivity of Scholars —how many workers required to produce one scholar
Professional, technical & kindred workers	234	12,672
Manager, officials, and proprietors	115	37,153
Sales workers	34	77,632
Clerical & kindred workers	28	95,380
Craftsmen, foremen, and kindred workers	56	140,112
Operatives and kindred workers	27	313,731
Service workers	7	366,270
Farmers and farm managers & farm laborers	16	389,643
Laborers, except farm & mine	1	3,581,370

Source: Horace Mann Bond, "The Productivity of National Merit Scholars by Occupational Class," *School and Society* 85 (September 28, 1957), p. 268.

to meet the challenges of teaching that English exists in more than one form, that language "standards" are arbitrary, and that there is no single "standard" or "original" that has been "corrupted" by those who speak different forms.[19]

such as race relations, poverty, and the distribution of community power.

The typical teaching methods, placement tests, and curricula are misplaced when applied to children from poor families. This, along with the other factors mentioned in this chapter, results in failure for a large proportion of these youngsters. They perceive themselves (as do others in the system) as incompetents. As Silberman has put it,

> . . . students are not likely to develop self-respect if they are unable to master the reading, verbal, and computational skills that the schools are trying to teach. Children must have a sense of competence if they are to regard themselves as people of worth; the failure that minority-group children, in particular, experience from the beginning can only reinforce the sense of worthlessness that the dominant culture conveys in an almost infinite variety of ways, and so feed the self-hatred that prejudice and discrimination produce. Chronic failure makes self-discipline equally hard to come by; it is these children's failure to learn that produces the behavior problems of the slum school . . . and not the behavior problems that produce the failure to learn.[20]

Although Silberman has addressed himself to the problems of minority-group children, the list should be broadened to include all of the poor children (who are, after all, also a minority group). The poor of all races experience prejudice and discrimination. They learn very quickly that they are considered by the middle class (teacher, administrator, man-on-the-street) as misfits.

3. *Segregation.* American schools tend to be segregated by social class. This is accomplished in two ways: neighborhood segregation and within-school segregation by ability grouping. The first instance is that schools are based in neighborhoods that tend to be relatively homogeneous by socioeconomic status. In 1972, for example, nearly one-third of the schools in Cleveland were 90 percent black. In Cincinnati, about two-thirds of the black students attended 90 percent black schools. In Oakland, 72 of the 91 schools were considered racially imbalanced.[21] Racial and economic segregation is especially true at the elementary school level but it carries over to a lesser degree in the secondary schools. Colleges and universities, as we have seen, are peopled by a middle- and upper-class clientele. Thus, at every level, children tend to attend a school with others like themselves in socioeconomic status and race. This results most often in unequal facilities, since rich districts provide more for their pupils than poor districts. Also within districts, the schools labelled as "lower class" tend to get a disproportionately smaller slice of the economic pie than "middle-class" schools.

But even if schools were equal in economic outlay, would the education be equal? Put another way, can schools be "separate but equal?" This has been and continues to be an important issue. Southerners have proclaimed that segregated schools can be equal. President Nixon in 1972 made the same declaration when he used his powers as President to eliminate the practice of busing children across neighborhood boundaries, which had been the primary means to integrate the schools more fully (racially and indirectly economically). The courts, on the other hand, have demanded that segregation must be eliminated if the ideal of equal education is ever to be realized.

But is quality education possible with racial and economic segregation? The overwhelming evidence is that the answer is no!

Item: The United States Senate's Select Committee on Equal Educational Opportunity, after two years of hearings and study concluded that "disadvantaged" children perform better in schools that have a majority of "advantaged" children.[22]

Item: In Evanston, Illinois, a three-year study of the city's total integration plan demonstrated improved achievement by black children and normal performance by white children.

Item: Hartford, Connecticut, began in 1966 to send children from its ghetto schools to five surrounding suburbs. A recent study showed that black fourth-graders bused to the suburbs were reading at a level four months behind their white classmates, but nine months ahead of their counterparts in the city.[23]

Item: A two-year study in New Haven, Connecticut, compared three groups of second graders. The first was a group bused from the inner city to suburban school districts. A second group consisted of children from inner-city schools whose schools were the recipient of a large federal grant intended to improve inner-city education by purchasing equipment, books, and hiring specially trained teachers. The third group (a control group) was composed of inner-city children whose school was not involved in the special federal funding. The findings were that the children bused did significantly better in reading than the children in a "typical" ghetto school or the children in the compensatory program.[24]

Item: The Coleman Report found that the educational disadvantages of black children were substantially reduced by racial and economic integration. The analysis indicated

> . . . that children from a given family background, when put in schools of different social composition, will achieve at quite different levels. This effect is again less for white pupils than for any minority group other than Orientals. Thus, if a white pupil from a

home that is strongly and effectively supportive of education is put in a school where most pupils do not come from such homes, his achievement will be little different than if he were in a school composed of others like himself. But if a minority pupil from a home without much educational strength is put with schoolmates with strong educational backgrounds, his achievement is likely to increase. This general result . . . has important implications for opportunity. . . . the principal way in which the school environments of Negroes and whites differ is in the composition of their student bodies, and it turns out that the composition of the student bodies has a strong relationship to the achievement of Negro and other minority pupils.[25]

4. *Tracking and teachers' expectations.* Even though schools are more or less segregated by the socioeconomic composition of local neighborhoods, the correlation is by no means perfect. Almost total segregation by socioeconomic status is realized within the schools, however, by the tracking system. This system, employed by about half of the high schools in the United States, divides the entire student body into two or more distinct career lines, or tracks such as college preparatory, vocational, business, general, or remedial. The major rationale for tracking is that it makes possible a better fit between the needs and capabilities of the student and the demands and opportunities of the curriculum. Slower students do not retard the progress of brighter students, and the teacher can adapt his teaching to the exact level of his class. The special problems of the different ability groups from "gifted" to "retarded," can be dealt with more efficiently when groups of students share the same or similar problems.

While these benefits may occur, there are some very serious criticisms of this practice. First, those in lower tracks are discouraged from producing up to their potential. Second, college-bound students develop feelings of superiority while others may define themselves as inferior. Third, and most important, the tracking system is closely linked to the stratification system—i.e., students from low-income families are disproportionately placed in the lowest track, resulting in a reinforcement of the social class structure. If this criticism is correct, the tracking system so prevalent in American schools denies equality of educational opportunity. This, of course, is contrary to the ideal of the school system as open and democratic.

Since this last criticism is one that, if correct, is very damning of current educational practices, let us examine one study of this question in detail.[26] Data were collected in 1964 of the graduating classes in two midwestern high schools (one of 753 students and the other 404). Both schools had two tracks—college prep and a general track. Table 10–5 summarizes what Schafer and his associates found to be the difference between the two tracks.

The basic conclusion from this study is that children from low-income and minority-group families are found disproportionally in the non-college track. Social class is an important indicator of placement in a track, since lower-class children do not perform well on middle-class-biased IQ tests.[27] The social class basis noted here is not unusual. Using race as a guide, the U.S. Civil Rights Commission found that in St. Louis ". . . a disproportionate percentage of students in Track I (the highest track) have been white and a similar disproportion in Track III (lowest) have been Negro."[28]

Another conclusion from the study by Schafer and his associates is that the system is virtually irreversible. Only seven percent of the college track moved down in their high school careers, and only seven percent of those persons in the general track moved up. Once placement is made at the beginning of the sophomore year, the "die is cast."

TABLE 10–5. Characteristics and Behavior of Persons Placed in College and Non-College Tracks (in percentages)

	College	General
Background		
Social Class:		
White collar	83%	17%
Blue collar	48	52
Race:		
Whites	71	29
Blacks	30	70
Effects		
Graduated in upper quarter of class	37	2
Graduated in lowest quarter of class	12	50
Drop out rate	4	36
Non-participants in extra-curricular activities	21	58
Participant in 3 or more activities	44	11
Committed 3 or more violations of school rules	19	70
Have a court record for juvenile delinquency in high school	6	16

Source: Adapted from Walter E. Schafer, Carol Olexa, and Kenneth Polk, "Programmed for Social Class: Tracking in High School," *Trans-action* 7 (October, 1970), pp. 40–42.

The tracking system itself has several pernicious effects on those placed in the lower track. There is a stigma to being "second class." Also operating is a self-fulfilling prophecy where teachers, administrators, and parents do not expect much, and that is what they get (we will return shortly to this phenomenon because it is extremely important). Finally non-college students tend to lack enthusiasm for school because they do not perceive it as having much payoff in the future. All of these add up to the consequence that non-college track students do not do well in school. Since it has been argued that this is the case because lower-class homes do not prepare persons for school performance, the researchers controlled for the effects of social class, IQ (which they admit is not a good measure of ability), and school performance before high school. They found that track position had an *independent effect* on academic achievement that is greater than the effect of each of these other factors. For example, whereas 37 percent of the college track students graduated in the top one-fourth of their class and only two percent of the students in the general track did, these rates change only slightly, to 30 percent and four percent respectively, when the influence of IQ, social class, and previous school performance are eliminated.

Academic performance is also affected by informal grading policies. There are grading ceilings for non-college students and grade floors for college-bound students. This is based on the assumption that noncollege students are less bright and do not perform as well. These policies have an obvious effect on motivation and commitment to the system. The result is that there is a tendency for college-prep students to improve in their grades as they move through high school, while a large proportion of the non-college students show a declining grade-point average.

These findings, coupled with the knowledge that those placed in the non-college track also exhibited a greater tendency to drop out of school, to participate less in extracurricular activities, to misbehave more in school and out, led the researchers to suggest that at least in part these behaviors are caused by the tracking system. They label this phenomenon "when the forecasters make the weather."

How is the tracking system itself guilty of these charges? There are several reasons why the tracking system encourages antischool attitudes and otherwise stunts academic performance.

1. *Stigma effects of tracking.* Assignment to a lower track carries a strong stigma. The individual is labelled as an intellectual inferior. His self-esteem wanes as he sees himself in the way others perceive him and behave toward him. Charles Horton Cooley, an early

American sociologist, made the observation that throughout our lives, our sense of self-esteem arises from the perceived reactions of others. In essence we see ourselves as others see us. Cooley called this the "looking-glass self."[29] Thus, the individual assigned to a track other than college prep perceives himself as "second class," as unworthy, stupid, and in the way. Clearly, assignment to a low track is destructive to the student's self-concept.

2. *The self-fulfilling prophecy effect.*[30] This explanation is closely related to stigma. If placed in the college-prep track, the student is likely to receive better instructions, to have access to better facilities, and be pushed to his capacity, more than those assigned to the other tracks. The reason is clear: the teachers and the administration *expect* great things from the one group and lesser things from the other. These expectations, moreover, are fulfilled. Those in the higher track do better and those in the lower track do not. These behaviors justify the greater expenditures of time, faculties, experimental curricula for those in the higher track —thus perpetuation of what Merton has called a "reign of error."

An illustration of how this works comes from Scotland where "an IBM computer was incorrectly programmed, sending the 'slow' students into a high track and the 'bright' ones into the low track. About one year later, when the mistake was uncovered, authorities found that the 'slow' pupils were behaving as though they were bright and the 'bright' pupils were behaving as though they were stupid."[31]

Another example comes from the controversial study by Rosenthal and Jacobson. Although this study has been criticized for a number of methodological shortcomings, the findings are consistent with theories of interpersonal influence and with the labelling view of deviant behavior. In the spring of 1964 all students in an elementary school in San Francisco were given an IQ test. The following fall the teachers were given the names of those children identified by the test as potential academic spurters. There were five such children assigned to each classroom. Actually the names of the "spurters" were chosen by means of a table of random numbers. The only difference between the "experimental group" (those labelled as "spurters") and the "control group" (the rest of the class) was in the imaginations of the teachers. At the end of the year all the children were again tested and the children from whom the teachers expected greater intellectual gains showed such gains (in IQ and grades). Moreover, they were rated by their teachers as being more curious, interesting, happy, and more likely to succeed than the children in the control group.[32]

The "self-fulfilling prophecy" is also demonstrated by a study conducted by Beez. Sixty master's level students in a teacher-training program were each asked to tutor a five-year-old child from a "disadvantaged" background. Each tutor was given a faked psychological report on the child before the tutoring session. These reports labelled one-half of the children, selected randomly, as having high potential while the others indicated that the children had low potential for success in school. Each tutor was given 20 cards, each having a reading-lesson word such as "men" or "stop," and the task was to give the child as many words as he thought he could get the child to recognize in ten minutes. Following the session, the child was tested to see how much he had learned. The results were striking: regardless of actual IQ, the "high potential" pupils gave twice as many correct answers as the "low potential" pupils. Moreover, the teachers who thought the child had high potential covered twice as many words in the ten minutes as did those who believed the student had low potential. Apparently, tutors of those with "low potential" spent more time reviewing the same words and explaining the meaning of words than was necessary.[33]

The implications of these three illustrations are clear. Teachers' expectations have a profound effect on the performance of their students. When students are over-rated, they tend to over-produce; when they are under-rated, they under-achieve. The tracking system is a labelling process which in turn affects the expectations of the teachers (and we should include fellow students and parents). The limits of these expectations are crucial in the educational process. These insights provide a solution to the problem. The self-fulfilling prophecy can work in a positive direction. Therefore, teachers must have an unshakable conviction that their students *can* learn. Concomitant with this belief, the teachers should hold *themselves*, not the students, accountable if the latter should fail.[34] Employed in this manner the self-fulfilling prophecy can work to the benefit of *all* students.*

* This question of responsibility was raised in a 1972 court case involving a suit against the San Francisco school district for $1 million. The 18-year-old plaintiff, although rated as normal in IQ and a regular class attender, graduated from high school, but with only a fifth grade reading ability. The suit charged the school district with negligence, misrepresentation, and breach of statutory duty. In other words, *the school system* not the pupil was responsible for the latter's near-illiteracy. As this is written, the court has not made a judgment in this case. "This case," says James W. Guthrie, professor of educational policy planning at the University of California, "has more potential to affect what actually goes on in the classroom than any other case I have ever heard of. This could really come to grips with what gets taught—and how."[35]

3. *Future payoff.* School is perceived as relevant for those students going to college. Grades are a means to qualify for college. For the non-college-bound student, however, school and grades are far less important for entry into a job. At most they need a high school diploma, and grades really do not matter as long as one does not flunk out. Thus, non-college-bound students often develop negative attitudes toward school, grades, and teachers. These attitudes for students in the lower tracks are summed up by sociologist Arthur Stinchcombe,

> . . . rebellious behavior is largely a reaction to the school itself and to its promises, not a failure of the family or community. High school students can be motivated to conform by paying them in the realistic coin of future advantage. Except perhaps for pathological cases, any student can be motivated to conform if the school can realistically promise something valuable to him as a reward for working hard. But for a large part of the population, especially the adolescent who will enter the male working class or the female candidates for early marriage, the school has nothing to offer. . . . In order to secure conformity from students, a high school must articulate academic work with careers of students.[36]

As we have seen, being on the lower track has negative consequences. These students are more rebellious in school and out and they do not participate as much in school activities. Finally, what is being taught is often not relevant to their world. Thus, we are led to conclude that many of these students tend to feel that they are not only "second class citizens" but perhaps even "pariahs." A pariah is someone who is so low as to not be part of the system. What other interpretation is plausible in a system that disadvantages them, shuns them, and makes demands of them that are irrelevant?

4. *The student subculture.* The reasons given above suggest that a natural reaction of persons in the lower track would be to band together in a subculture that is antagonistic toward school. This subculture would quite naturally develop its own system of rewards, since those of the school are inaccessible. David Hargreaves' *Social Relations in a Secondary School* shows this to be the case in an English secondary school that incorporated tracks (or "streams" as they are called in England). He found boys in the high stream were drawn to the values of the teachers, while lower-stream boys accorded each other high status for doing the opposite of what the teacher wanted. To quote Hargreaves,

> The informal pressures within the low streams tend to work indirectly against the assumption of the teachers that boys will regard

promotion into a higher stream as a desirable goal. The boys from the low streams were very reluctant to ascend to higher streams because their stereotypes of 'A' and 'B' stream boys were defined in terms of values alien to their own, and because promotion would involve rejection by their low-stream friends. The teachers were not fully aware that this unwillingness to be promoted to a higher stream led the high informal status boys to depress their performance in examinations.[37]

The above factors show how the tracking system is at least partly responsible for some categories of persons (those in the lower tracks) being relatively low achievers, unmotivated, uninvolved in school activities, more prone to drop out of school, and to break school or community rules. To segregate students, by ability or by future plans, is detrimental to the students labelled as lower. It is an elitist system that needs, in light of the evidence presented here and elsewhere, to be re-evaluated and changed. We should not lose sight of our original purpose in presenting the issue of tracking—that this practice segregates primarily on the basis of social class background. Tracking is a barrier to equal educational opportunity for lower-income and other minority students who are disproportionately assigned to the lowest track. It is an elitist system that for the most part takes the children of the elite and educates them to take the elite positions of society. Conversely, the children of the non-elite are trained to recapitulate experiences of their parents. In a presumably democratic system that prides itself in providing avenues of upward social mobility, such a system borders on immorality.

Let us conclude this section on inequality in the educational system by reiterating the basis of the critique—many persons fail in the American school, but this is the fault of the school and not of the children who fail. To focus on these victims is to divert attention away from the inadequacies of the schools. The blame needs to be shifted, as Patricia Sexton has advocated in the following paragraph.

> The doctor-patient relationship is not present in the school. If a patient is sick and does not get well, it is assumed that the doctor or the state of medical knowledge has failed. The patient or his family culture is rarely blamed; nor is the patient told to leave the hospital because he refused to get well. The school, on the other hand, often assumes that the child, or his parents, have failed and that this is a normal feature of statistical law. Educators who assume that one out of ten or so must fail are surprised when they meet resistance or rebellion. Doctors who assumed that one out of ten must die on the operating table might arouse similar responses

in patients. It would be equally foolish of course, for doctors to assume that there were *no* differences between their patients and the normal population. Their patients are sick and the doctor's job is to cure them.[38]

Or phrased another way, this time by Ryan,

We are dealing, it would seem, not so much with culturally deprived children as with culturally depriving schools. And the task to be accomplished is not to revise, and amend, and repair deficient children but to alter and transform the atmosphere and operations of the schools to which we commit these children. Only by changing the nature of the educational experience can we change its product.[39]

The Crises in Higher Education

Higher education, through its advanced degrees, is a very significant gatekeeper for society. Unfortunately, these "gates" are relatively closed for the lower socioeconomic groups and open for the middle and upper groups. Thus, the system of higher education is basically an elite institution that perpetrates the system of stratification in the larger society. The elitist nature of higher education justifiably makes it a target of the disadvantaged groups in American society. This problem, however, results mainly from the educational system that precedes college—the lack of fit between lower socioeconomic children and the schools. It is reflected at the higher level, however, in the admission standards, the granting of scholarships to those who do exceedingly well in high school, and the skills needed to succeed.*

We will focus our attention here, however, on the internal problems specific to higher education. In general, we can say that American colleges and universities are faced with a confidence crisis. Three important groups have tended to lose confidence in these schools. At the forefront are many students who find the experience especially alienating. In addition to the sources of student alienation to be enumerated shortly, there are two related ones that deserve note. The nature of the job market has become such that virtually all jobs providing an entrée into the middle class require a college education. Thus we have the paradox that a higher

---

* We will not take the time to document this generalization further. The interested student may wish to examine the excellent chapter entitled, "Social Stratification and Mass Higher Education," in Christopher Jencks and David Riesman, *The Academic Revolution.*[40]

education is compulsory for anyone with mobility aspirations, yet a higher education, for the most part, does not actually train one to do any specific job. Many students, then, are in school because they must be, yet the experience is not perceived as having any real benefit. Many of these persons rebel against the schools and/or society by either protest or withdrawal. A second distrustful group is the faculty. Faculty members disagree often on the goals of the university. Moreover, many have become alienated from the university because they are not part of the decision-making process. Consequently, many give their primary allegiance to their profession or to a granting agency. A final group that has become discontented with the university is the constituency—parents, alumni, and former friends. This is reflected in the money crisis that almost all public and private colleges and universities face. The sources of money (legislative appropriations, gifts) have dried up because the citizens have been upset over student unrest, by the university losing its political neutrality, over the presumed permissiveness by administrators, and the activities by some faculty members (e.g., radical political behavior, research activities taking precedence over teaching, and lenient grading policies). There are three major interrelated sources for the loss of confidence by these groups in higher education:—increased size, changing philosophy, and the structure of universities. Let us examine each of these in turn.

1. *Size.* It is not uncommon for universities to have more than 20,000 students. Some even exceed 50,000. This has occurred because of a rapid expansion during the 1960's when the war babies reached adulthood and when an increased proportion of the population started attending colleges and universities. The number of persons enrolled in college, for example, increased from 4,643,000 to 7,413,000 in but seven years (from October, 1964 to October, 1970).[41] This dramatic increase resulted in larger faculties, larger classes, more administrators—in short, a larger impersonal bureaucracy. Students and faculty alike feel treated like so many cogs in a machine, each cog known only by its IBM number.*

Particularly alienating are the large classes that freshmen and sophomores must take. At the very time when these individuals need to find themselves and make important decisions affecting their future, they are thrust into extremely impersonal situations.

* College attendance levelled off in the early 1970s, however, as the last remnants of the post-war baby bulge graduated. While the problem of impersonality in the universities remained, the levelling of enrollments (and sometimes declining enrollments) brought other problems, the most important of which was a monetary crisis.

Objective tests graded by machines determine their success or failure. Teacher-student dialogues are almost impossible. Teachers and students, even the students themselves, do not get to know each other. The university, however, has been forced through a lack of resources (plus the reluctance of many professors to teach beginning classes) to utilize large classes. One alternative selected by many universities is to use graduate students as the teachers in smaller sections (e.g., 45 instead of 450). This practice, too, is often unsatisfactory. Graduate students not only lack experience as teachers but are relatively new to the field and therefore cannot offer much depth. Two structural reasons in particular, however, account for the negative valence usually associated with the usage of graduate students as teachers. First, graduate students are notoriously underpaid (receiving typically one-fifth the wage of an assis-. tant professor). Second, graduate students are primarily interested in getting their own degree. Teaching is only a means to that end. Hence, preparation for teaching is often slighted. This is not to say that professors are immune from such neglect, as we will note further below.

2. *Guiding philosophy.* Traditionally the university has remained aloof from society. In its ivory tower the members of the university produced knowledge for its own sake, which in turn was taught to students. This aloofness meant, furthermore, that the university was not involved in the direct solution of the problems of labor, business, poverty, the city, or foreign policy. The basis for this detachment was a goal of scientific objectivity. To get involved, to be active in bringing about changes, was considered unscientific. More and more students, along with small segments of faculty, have questioned these assumptions, however, in recent years. They contend that to be neutral, in fact, takes a stand since it allows certain things to take place—creation of bombs or propaganda techniques or urban renewal. We must, they assert, be concerned with the effects of newly created knowledge. What is more, we should be actively engaged in the direct solution of problems from the humanitarian perspective. While it is difficult to quarrel with pleas to be humanitarian, many academics do not see that as the role of the university.[42] Involvement in the solution of social problems is anathema to the "pure" scientist. Others, particularly students, disagree. They want involvement, not detachment; they see the necessity of change to make society more humanitarian; yet many professors resist this kind of engagement. Thus a dilemma has developed:—what is the purpose of the University? The answer is

unclear, with segments of the university community torn over the alternatives.

Another dilemma concerning the role of the university involves the relationship between teaching and research. Universities have always wanted to strike a balance between the two. The university was to be at the cutting edge of new knowledge and to transmit knowledge to students. In many schools the balance has shifted, however, to favor research over teaching. This change is supported by those who benefit most directly (university administrators and trustees, since the university budget typically receives about one half of research grants from granting agencies; professors who get money to do the research, which in turn becomes translated into books, articles, and increased professional status; and student assistants who receive stipends for working on these projects). The university, therefore, has placed extraordinary emphasis on the attainment of research grants. Evidence for this is seen in the reward system of the universities since "grant-getters" receive the rewards (speedy promotions, large salary raises). The irony is that the university rewards those activities that have little to do with students. As a general rule, the higher the professor's status, the less he has to do with students. Distinguished professors are a case in point. Many faculty members are not particularly interested in students; in fact, students are viewed by some as "in the way"—i.e. taking time away from research. Of course, students and some faculty resent such attitudes and demand that good teaching be acknowledged as having an equal status with research in the reward system.

Both "ivory tower" research and the overemphasis on research are part of the fuel for student unrest. Another aspect to the research problem that especially galls some students is the type of research that some professors do. They accept grants from agencies to do projects that support the establishment, especially the military-industrial complex. Thus, the university which prides itself on detachment really is involved, often in promoting the status quo.

3. *University structure.* There are several aspects of the university structure that also create tension within the university community. The first involves the system of university governance. There is a clash between those who favor the democratic and those who prefer the elitist models. Traditionally universities have been very elitist. Rules came down from the administration. Decisions concerning hiring, firing, and promotions were done only by high-ranking professors. For example, tenure decisions were typically made by those

with tenure in a department. Their decision, if favorable, was then passed upon by a university-wide committee or a dean. Many faculty members felt left out of this process. Certainly students were left out of decisions that directly affected them. Their input in the system consisted, typically, of complaints by isolated individuals. The student government that existed did not make decisions except over matters of little consequence, such as homecoming arrangements. The student rebellions of the late 1960's however, have brought about changes in many universities. Students serve and vote on important committees, even those who consider hiring, firing, tenure, and promotion.

Most schools have not let this movement get "out-of-hand." They have limited student participation to a rather insignificant proportion (typically 20 percent of a committee's composition). This has led to the charge of cooptation—allowing a small percentage of a potentially dissident group to enter the decision-making body, a technique designed to give the appearance of power transfer to the weak when in actuality nothing has changed.*

Another structural problem of the university is typical of most bureaucracies. The university is divided into schools which are subdivided into departments. Just as in any social system, these parts are interdependent. But since they are also separate entities, they must justify their continued existence. Each unit must compete with the others for scarce resources (teaching positions, salaries, graduate students, supplies). Since the amount of resources is finite, what one segment gets is achieved at the expense of the other segments. Thus, the organization of the university (just as is the case in other organizations) promotes competition rather than cooperation. A sense of community is therefore difficult to achieve across disciplinary lines. Since this problem is insoluble in a large organization, efforts must continually be expended to at least minimize it.

CHANGING THE EDUCATIONAL SYSTEM: REFORM OR REVOLUTION?

No one would deny that the system of American education has problems. Virtually everyone is aware that the system needs better financing and equality of opportunity from the ghetto to suburbia.

---

* Philip Selznick defines cooptation as ". . . the process of absorbing new elements into the leadership or policy-determining structure of an organization as a means of averting threats to its stability or existence." (p. 13).[43]

But most persons do not question the structure and philosophy of the system. There is a minority view, however, that the system itself is wrong and the generator of many profound problems. These persons desire that the entire educational enterprise be reconstructed along very different lines. This demand for change is based on three related assumptions. The first is that the school is a microcosm of the larger society. Since, as they assert, society is sick (competitive, repressive, inhumane, materialistic, racist, and imperialist) so, too, are the schools. If society is to be changed, one must change the schools.

The second assumption of the radical critics of education is that the process of public education as it is presently constructed damages, thwarts, and stifles children. The schools somehow manage to suppress the natural curiosity of children. The school begins with inquisitive children and molds them into acquisitive children with little desire to learn.

Third, the educational system is a product of society and hence shapes its products to meet the requirements of society. The present system is predicated on the needs of an industrial society where citizens must follow orders, do assigned tasks in the appropriate order and time span, and not "rock the boat."* But these behaviors will not be appropriate for life in the future (even the near future or perhaps even the present). The future will likely require persons who can cope with rapid turnover—changes in occupations, human relationships, and community ties. Moreover, the citizens of the future (present?) must be able to cope with a complex of choices. Does an educational system built on order, a rigid time schedule, and the lecture method adequately prepare youngsters for life as it is and will be (see Panel 10–4)?

The remainder of this chapter will consist of the brief presentation of three alternatives to the present system of American public education. Each meets the criticisms of the present system in a unique manner. While all are radical, the first two are revolutionary: The third alternative (the open classroom approach) is more of a reformation (albeit a substantial one) of the present system.

Alternative I: Deschooling Society

Ivan Illich is opposed to schools, not education.[44] For him, schools are coercive (e.g., obligatory curriculum, forced sequence of events, and requirements for certification) which is counterproductive.

* My colleague, Kenneth C. W. Kammeyer, has put it another way, "The job of education in America is to provide workers for I.B.M.; workers who will not bend, fold, or mutilate on command."

PANEL 10-4

"EDUCATION: PRESENT AND FUTURE"

Source: Alvin Toffler, *Future Shock* (New York: Bantam Books, 1971), selections from Chapter 18, "Education in the Future Tense," pp. 398–427.

Young Americans are exhorted from all sides to stay in school. Education is believed to be more important now than ever before. "Yet for all this rhetoric about the future, our schools face backwards toward a dying system, rather than forward to the emerging new society. Their vast energies are applied to cranking out industrial men—people tooled for survival in a system that will be dead before they are." (p. 399)

Mass education in the United States was fashioned after an industrial model to fit persons for an industrial society. ". . . the whole idea of assembling masses of students (raw material) to be processed by teachers (workers) in a centrally located school (factory) . . . followed the model of industrial bureaucracy. The very organization of knowledge into permanent disciplines was grounded on industrial assumptions. Children marched from place to place and sat in assigned stations. Bells rang to announce changes of time. The inner life of the school thus became an anticipatory mirror, a perfect introduction to industrial society. The most criticized features of education today— the regimentation, lack of individualization, the rigid systems of seating, grouping, grading, and marking, the authoritarian role of the teacher— are precisely those that made mass public education so effective an instrument of adaptation for its place and time. Young people passing through this educational machine emerged into an adult society whose structure of jobs, roles and institutions resembled that of the school itself." (pp. 400–401)

While mass education based on industrial principles was appropriate until the recent past, fundamental changes must occur so that the educational systems can meet the needs of students of a super-industrial society. Men to perform endlessly repetitious jobs will no longer be needed. Men who take orders in unblinking fashion will no longer be needed. The schools will have to turn out persons who can make critical judgments, who can cope with an ever increasing hectic pace of change. "For education the lesson is clear: its prime objective must be to increase the individual's 'cope-ability'—the speed and economy with which he can adapt to continual change. And the faster the rate of change, the more attention must be devoted to discerning the pattern of future events. It is no longer sufficient for Johnny to understand the past. It is not even enough for him to understand the present, for the here-and-now environment will soon vanish. Johnny must learn to anticipate the directions and rate of change. He must, to put it technically, learn to make repeated, probabilistic, increasingly long-range assumptions about the future. And so must Johnny's teachers." (p. 403)

In Toffler's vision of the future we will face ever-accelerated change and overchoice. What must the educational system do to prepare children for such a world? The most obvious necessity is to prepare them to be adaptive. Today most classrooms are dominated by teachers who lecture (after the old top-down, hierarchical structure of industry). The teacher-led class must give way to the training for role versatility. This can be accomplished through techniques such as role playing, gaming, participation in community activities, work in numerous settings, and the like. The schools can also facilitate adaptation by experimenting with varied arrangements. "Classes with several teachers and a single student; classes with several teachers and a group of students; students organized into temporary task forces and project teams; students shifting from group work to individual or independent work and back— all these and their permutations will need to be employed to give the student some advance taste of the experience he will face later on when he begins to move through the impermanent organizational geography of super-industrialism." (p. 409)

The current curriculum is obsolete because it imposes standardization and does not prepare for the future. Toffler says, "Instead of a standardized elementary and secondary school curriculum in which all students are essentially exposed to the same data base—the same history, math, biology, literature, grammar, foreign languages, etc.—the futurist movement in education must attempt to create widely diversified data offerings. Children should be permitted far greater choice than at present; they should be encouraged to taste a wide variety of short-term courses (perhaps two or three weeks in length) before making longer-term commitments. Each school should provide scores of optional subjects, all based on identifiable assumptions about future needs." (p. 412) All students, however, should be well grounded in certain skills needed for human communication and social integration. Each student must learn how to learn, since knowledge will grow increasingly perishable and must be replaced. The increased turnover in social relationships will also require new skills in relating. We will have less time to develop friendships in the future. Therefore, ". . . education must help people to accept the absence of deep friendships, to accept loneliness and mistrust—or it must find new ways to accelerate friendship formation. Whether by more imaginative groupings of students, or by organizing new kinds of work-teams, or through variations of the techniques discussed above, education will have to teach us to relate." (p. 416)

Finally, education will have to prepare us for making choices in situations of overchoice. "Super-industrial educators must not attempt to impose a rigid set of values on the student; but they must systematically organize formal and informal activities that help the student define, explicate and test his values, whatever they are. Our schools will continue to turn out industrial men until we teach young people the skills necessary to identify and clarify, if not reconcile, conflicts in their own value systems." (pp. 417–418)

Schools also have a hidden curriculum that perpetuates the myths of society (e.g., that bureaucracies are efficient and benevolent, that increased production will provide a better life, and that individuals in society need to be ranked). He has stated, moreover, that schools encourage dependence upon them when they are in fact unnecessary.

> Schools are designed on the assumption that there is a secret to everything in life; that the quality of life depends on knowing that secret; that secrets can be known only in orderly successions; and that only teachers can properly reveal these secrets. An individual with a schooled mind conceives of the world as a pyramid of classified packages accessible only to those who carry the proper tags.[45]

Finally, the school is guilty of undermining "learner sovereignty"— the free determination by each learner of his own research for living and learning. In other words, every individual should be free to decide throughout his life what sorts of skills and knowledge he wishes to acquire and when. The result will be individual freedom and uniqueness.

But how is this freedom and uniqueness of the individual to be accomplished? According to Illich, schools should be replaced by "learning webs." The important difference between Illich's approach and that of traditional schooling is that the latter labels educational resources according to the curricular goals of educators. Illich, on the other hand, provides four avenues by which the student may gain access to any educational resource which helps him to define and achieve his own goals:

1. Reference Services to Educational Objects—which facilitate access to things or processes used for formal learning. These may be stored in libraries, laboratories, museums, or theaters or they may be found in factories, airports, or on farms. All of these resources should be available to persons upon request.
2. Skill Exchanges—which permit persons to list their skills and the conditions under which they would be willing to serve as models for others who want to learn these skills.
3. Peer-Matching—a communications network which permits persons to designate the learning activities they are interested in so that they might team with others who are interested in the same activities.
4. Reference Services to Educators-at-Large—who can be listed in a directory with self-descriptions of professionals, para-professionals, and free-lancers, along with conditions of access to their services.[46]

The basic assumption of Illich is that man is curious. Free of the constraints of schools, individuals will use available resources to learn what they feel is important to their goals. Thus, the educational path of each person is a lifelong process for each to follow individually.

Alternative II: Summerhill

In 1921 A. S. Neill founded a school in England named "Summerhill." Based on a radical approach to education, it has become the most famous experimental school in the world. In sharp contrast to the autocracy and coerciveness of traditional schools, the philosophy of Summerhill is democratic and in no way coercive. The goal is a happy and creative child, not a child molded to fit a coercive society. Thus, the child is free—free to explore, free to read or not read, free to go to school or stay away. But freedom is not total, since there is a rule that the child may not infringe on the rights of others. The following principles summarize the bases for Neill's system: [47]

1. The child is innately good and wise. If left to himself he will develop as far as he is capable of developing.
2. The aim of education is to work joyfully and find happiness.
3. Happiness now takes precedence over efforts to prepare for the future.
4. Education must be geared to the needs of the child. In other words, make the school fit the child, not the child fit the school.
5. Dogmatically imposed discipline and punishment create fear, which, in turn, creates hostility.
6. Fear, hostility, and hypocrisy result from guilt feelings, which are a by-product of authority. Guilt is primarily an awareness of disobedience against authority and fear of reprisal.
7. Freedom is necessary for only under freedom can the child grow in his natural (good) way.
8. Freedom does not mean license. The child must respect the rights of others.
9. It is natural for children to want to learn. Thus, learning is self-motivated rather than imposed.
10. A school should be education for creativity.
11. A school should be a democratic community with every member—student, teacher, or A. S. Neill—having one vote. The rules of the community are made by a legislative process in which the whole group participates.

Alternative III: The Open Classroom

One criticism of Neill's radical approach to education is that schools based on a child-centered, open-structured, individualized, and unoppressive environment do not teach the hard skills.[48] A common occurrence is that skills such as reading and mathematics are not acquired in a purposeful and sequential manner. In fact, these skills are not taught until the child asks someone to teach him. The result is that some children never ask for these skills.

An alternative method that is based on some of the principles of Summerhill but presents more structure is the open classroom approach (called "informal schools" in England where by 1971 about two-thirds of the primary schools adhered to this model).[49]

The open classroom approach is opposed to the traditional American school, which seems preoccupied with order and control, repressive, teacher-dominated, and group rather than individual centered. The assumptions of this alternative approach are:

1. Children learn from their environment, peers, and adults.
2. Childhood and school are to be enjoyed.
3. Learning is most effective when it grows out of the interests of the learner rather than the interests of the teacher.
4. Teachers have the responsibility to teach and guide the children. This is done chiefly by structuring the environment so that it meets each child's evolving interests and needs.
5. The goal is to transmit, create, and evoke the skills, values, attitudes, and knowledge that will help children grow into mature and creative adults. In other words, the teachers and the school are active agents—not repressive as in traditional schools and not so free as to turn the children loose to do their own thing—in each child's achievement of certain skills and knowledge.
6. There is an emphasis on the student doing rather than the teacher telling. Teaching means creating situations where ideas, principles, concepts, and structures can be discovered by the student. Since children learn at different rates and at different ages, the teacher must arrange the classroom environment in such a way as to permit each child to learn at his own pace. Thus, activity groups may be large or small groups (and often at the individual level).

The alternatives mentioned above are all radical. Illich's proposal is the most radical, since he would abolish compulsory education and replace it with a system geared to individual initiative. Neill's solution is also radical. Although keeping schools, he advocates the elimination of all coercion. Children do what they want to do. The other alternative presented, the open classroom, is radical too, but

PANEL 10–5

"A Description of the English Informal School"

Source: Charles E. Silberman, *Crisis in the Classroom: The Remaking of American Education* (New York: Random House, 1970), pp. 221–225. The following is directly quoted from these pages.

To enter an informal classroom for the first time is a disorienting experience for an American (or for that matter, an Englishman) accustomed to traditional formal schooling. To begin with, the classroom does not *look* like a classroom. It is, rather, a workshop in which "interest areas" take the place of the familiar rows of desks and chairs, and in which individualized learning takes the place of what informal English educators now disparagingly call "the talk and chalk" method, i.e.,—the teacher conducting a lesson for all the children simultaneously from her vantage point at one of the "chalkboards" lining the front and side of the room. . . .

The reading corner, for example, typically is an inviting place, with a rug or piece of old carpet on which children may sprawl, a couple of easy chairs or perhaps a cot or old couch for additional comfort, and a large and tempting display of books at child's height. The arithmetic (or "maths," as the English call it) area most likely will have several tables pushed together to form a large working space. On the tables, in addition to a variety of math texts and workbooks, will be a box containing rulers, measuring tapes and sticks, yardsticks, string, and the like; other boxes, containing pebbles, shells, stones, rocks, acorns, conkers (the acorn of a chestnut tree), bottle tops, pine cones, and anything else that can be used for counting, along with more formal arithmetic and mathematical materials, such as Cuisenaire rods, Dienes blocks, Stern rods, and Unifisc cubes. There will be several balance scales, too, with boxes of weights, as well as more pebbles, stones, rocks, feathers, and anything else that can be used for weighing.

Near the maths area is an infant school room, and frequently in the lower grades of a junior school, there is likely to be a large table-height sandbox and a specially constructed table, at about the same height, for water play. The water table comes "equipped" with an assortment of empty milk cartons and bottles, plastic detergent bottles, pitchers, plastic containers, and the like, all with their volume (⅓ pint, ½ pint, quart, gallon) marked on them, for practice in maths. There may also be an oven; following a recipe for muffins or cookies provides still another application of simple mathematical notions, along with practice in reading.

Nearby will be a table, or perhaps several cartons on the floor, some with blocks, tinkertoys, and the like, some containing "junk" (so marked), i.e., empty cereal and soap boxes, egg cartons, toilet paper and paper towel rollers, cardboard, pieces of wood, scraps of wallpaper and fabric, oaktag, cigar boxes—anything children might use for constructing things (airplanes, trucks, cars, steamrollers, robots, spaceships, houses, office buildings, bridges) or for making collages or murals. Somewhere in the room, or perhaps in the hall outside, there will be some large easels with jars of paints and large brushes. In one corner, or perhaps in a converted closet, will be a "Wendy House," a child-size play house, furnished with dolls, furniture, dishes, kitchenware, and a pile of cast-off adult clothing for children to dress up in.

To complete the general picture, and without allowing for the idio-syncratic arrangements that distinguish one teacher's classroom from another even in the same school, there typically is a music area with xylophones, drums, cymbals, castanets, recorders, and other (some-times homemade) instruments. Somewhere or other too, there is a sci-ence area, with rocks and shells, leaves and other local flora, candles and jars, perhaps some small motors, batteries, bulbs, and wire, and in all probability, an animal or two or three, be it rabbit, turtle, hamster, or kitten. And this in classrooms which more often than not contain as many as forty children.

How do they find room? In good measure by replacing the desks and chairs with a small number of tables and chairs. There is no need to have a seat and desk for each child: the teacher seldom instructs the class as a whole, and when she does, the children simply gather around her, pulling up chairs or sitting on the floor. But teachers also create space for the various interest areas and activities by using closets, cloakrooms, indeed, every conceivable nook and cranny, and by spilling over into the halls, lobbies, playgrounds, and other common space. "An infant school classroom is too small and too confined for all the things children need to do," the Plowden Committee observed. "They overflow into the open air where there are no walls to shut off one class from another; they stray into corridors which are not marked out into pens like sheep folds."

Indeed, a visitor accustomed only to formal classrooms is likely to be disoriented by the sound and movement of an informal classroom even more than by its physical arrangements. To photograph a formal classroom in action, one needs only a still camera with a wide-angle lens; to photograph an informal classroom for infant and younger junior school children, one needs a motion-picture camera with sound, for the initial impression is that the children are all in motion. At any one moment, some children may be hammering and sawing at a work-bench, some may be playing musical instruments or painting, others may be reading aloud to the teacher or to a friend, still others may be curled up on a cot or a piece of carpet, reading in solitary absorption, oblivious to the sounds around them. (They belong to a generation, after all, that does its homework with the "telly" or a transistor radio blaring away.)

Elsewhere in the room, moreover, there are likely to be children seated at a table or sprawled on the floor, writing a story. Other chil-dren are in the maths area, counting or weighing acorns, bottle caps, pebbles, cones, shells, and what have you, or measuring the perimeter of the room, or the teacher's desk, or the length of a visitor's shoes, or one another's height, and writing it all down; others are measuring the ingredients of a cookie recipe, getting them ready for the oven. There are children playing in the sandbox, and others at the water table, filling the various-sized containers and enjoying the feel of the water, and there are children acting out various roles as they play at being grown-ups. And always there is the sound of children talking—to themselves, to their friends, to the teacher, to the headmistress as she walks around, to the visitors from America, in sharp contrast to the United States (or to formal classrooms in England), where children and visitors usually are carefully segregated from each other.

The sound and movement are not limited to the classroom itself. There is a continuous ebb and flow of children into and out of the room —into the halls and corridors, the stairs, the cloakrooms, the library, the hall, the head's office, other classrooms, the lobby or entrance hall; and in halfway decent weather (half-way decent, that is to say, by English rather than American standards), out of doors, as well; into the playground, if it is a city school, and perhaps even into the surrounding fields, if it is a rural school. In the seventy- and eighty-year-old build-ings that seem almost standard in London, for example, the corridors are almost always used, not just as a passageway, but as part of the classroom, as part of the total learning environment. They contain easels, workbenches, water tables, and displays and activities of every sort. . . .

Understandably, in view of all the sound and motion, the first impres-sion may be one of chaos. In most schools, it is a false impression. "You always have to assess the nature of the noise," the headmis-tress of the first school the writer visited helpfully explained. "Is it just aimless chatter, or does it reflect purposeful activity?" And as the visi-tor becomes acclimated, it becomes clear that the activity usually is purposeful; it does not take very long to be able to assess the nature of the noise, and to distinguish classes where the children's play is lead-ing to learning from those where it is pleasant but aimless.

As the strangeness wears off, one becomes aware of many things. One becomes aware, for example, of the teacher's presence: in con-trast to the first moments of wondering where she is, or whether she is even there at all, the visitor begins to see that the teacher is very much there and very much in charge. She seems always to be in motion, and always to be in contact with the children—talking, listening, watching, comforting, chiding, suggesting, encouraging—although from time to time she stops for a moment to jot down a comment in the record book she keeps for each child. (Peter is trying to write his name for the first time, Evelyn is making much brighter pictures, John seems to be resisting maths, Susan has learned to multiply by two, James is coming out of his shell—he talked more easily and played with others for the first time. . . .)

less so than others. It seeks to transform the existing system, not abolish it totally. Classrooms with teachers teaching remain, but freedom and joy are also ingredients.

The proponents of these alternatives (and others) are critical of American education. They all conclude that American schools are failing not only children from the ghettos of large cities, but also suburban and small-town youngsters as well.* They fail because they treat children as miniature adults; because they treat children as a group rather than individuals; because they stifle creativity; because they are repressive. The important questions we must ask (and answer) are these: What will American society be like in the next two generations? How should the educational system be changed to meet the demands of that society? If the society of the near future will be highly structured and we will all work at mindless, repetitive tasks, then we need to retain the present system of education.

If, on the other hand, the future society will be characterized by freedom, transitory friendships, and workteams, the educational system must be transformed to turn out products who will be prepared for such a life. If we do not, then the proportion of individuals unable to cope with increasing change will increase dramatically.

SUGGESTED FURTHER READING

Farber, Jerry, *The Student as Nigger* (New York: Pocket Books, 1970). A critique of education that focuses on the consequences for students when they attend authoritarian, teacher-centered, tradition-bound schools.

Hart, Harold H., editor, *Summerhill: For and Against* (New York: Hart Publishing Company, 1970). This volume presents a series of laudatory and negative essays on A. S. Neill's revolutionary philosophy and practice of education.

Holt, John, *The Under-Achieving School* (New York: A Delta Book, 1969). Holt indicts public schools as places that prevent learning. He

---

* It is important to recognize that the present educational crisis is not a result of the schools suddenly doing worse. As Peter Drucker has stated:

"Today's school does no poorer a job than it did yesterday; the school has simply done a terribly poor job all along. But what we tolerated in the past we no longer can tolerate. . . . the school has suddenly assumed such importance for the individual, for the community, for the economy and for society, that we cannot suffer the traditional, time-honored incompetence of the educational system."[50]

presents a number of alternatives that if adopted would truly revolutionize education.

Illich, Ivan, *Deschooling Society* (New York: Harper and Row, 1971). This book presents a radical proposal for education—the total elimination of formal schooling.

Jencks, Christopher, *Inequality: A Reassessment of the Effect of Family and Schooling in America* (New York: Basic Books, 1972). A provacative and controversial book which concludes that neither family background, cognitive skill, educational attainment, nor occupational status explains much of the variation in men's incomes. In other words, school reform will not likely have any significant effect on the degree of inequality among adults.

Nyquist, Ewald B., and Gene R. Hawes, editors, *Open Education: A Sourcebook for Parents and Teachers* (New York: Bantam Books, 1972). This reader presents the philosophy and principles of the "open classroom" approach as well as how it works in practice.

Silberman, Charles E., *Crisis in the Classroom: The Remaking of American Education* (New York: Random House, 1970). The book is divided into two parts: (1) a critique of American education; and (2) the case for the "open classroom" approach.

NOTES AND REFERENCES

1. Ivan Illich, *Deschooling Society* (New York: Harper and Row, 1971).

2. Jules Henry, *Culture Against Man* (New York: Vintage Books, 1963), pp. 285–286.

3. The following is especially dependent on Charles E. Silberman, *Crisis in the Classroom* (New York: Random House, 1970), pp. 122–157.

4. Silberman, *Crisis in the Classroom*, p. 145.

5. Quoted in Silberman, *Crisis in the Classroom*, p. 133. As a former high school teacher, the author of this textbook can attest to the validity of Jencks' statement.

6. Jerry Farber, *The Student as Nigger* (New York: Pocket Books, 1970), p. 92.

7. This assumption happens to be a myth, however. See Norman R. Yetman and D. Stanley Eitzen, "Unequal Opportunity for Equal Ability: Black Americans in Basketball." *Civil Rights Digest* 5 (August, 1972), pp. 21–34.

8. The following is taken primarily from the important study of ten high schools by James S. Coleman, *The Adolescent Society: The Social Life of the Teenager and Its Impact on Education* (New York: The Free Press, 1961).

9. *Cleveland Plain Dealer* (April 23, 1971).

10. Colin Greer, "Public Schools: The Myth of the Melting Pot," *Saturday Review* (November 15, 1969), p. 85.

11. William Ryan, *Blaming the Victim* (New York: Pantheon Books, 1971), pp. 35–36.

12. *Lawrence Daily Journal World* (February 21, 1972).

13. Quoted in "The Schools Go Begging," *Newsweek* (June 7, 1971), p. 101.

14. Patricia Cayo Sexton, *The American School: A Sociological Analysis* (Englewood Cliffs, New Jersey: Prentice-Hall, Inc., 1967), p. 54.

15. Sexton, *The American School*, p. 55, summarizing and quoting from Robert E. Herriott and Nancy Hoyt St. John, *Social Class and the Urban School* (New York: John Wiley, 1966), p. 207.

16. Robert A. Dentler, "Equality of Educational Opportunity: A Special Review," *The Urban Review* 1 (December, 1966), p. 27–28.

17. *Equality of Educational Opportunity* (Washington, D.C.: U.S. Department of Health, Education and Welfare, 1966), p. 21.

18. Sexton, *The American School*, p. 52.

19. Marvin D. Loflin, "Black American English: Independent Motivation for the Auxiliary Hypothesis," Technical Report No. 2 (Milwaukee: Institute for the Study of Urban Linguistics, April, 1972).

20. Silberman, *Crisis in the Classroom*, p. 67.

21. "Busing: An American Dilemma," *Newsweek* (March 13, 1972), p. 20.

22. Tom Wicker, "A Substitute for Busing," *New York Times News Service* (February 28, 1972).

23. The above two "items" were taken from "Busing: An American Dilemma," p. 23.

24. "Ghetto Children Benefit from Suburban Busing," Associated Press Release (April 13, 1972).

25. *Equality of Educational Opportunity*, p. 22.

26. The following is taken from Walter E. Schafer, Carol Olexa and Kenneth Polk, "Programmed for Social Class: Tracking in High School," *Trans-action* 7 (October, 1970), pp. 39–46 and 63.

27. Louis K. Knowles and Kenneth Prewitt (eds.), *Institutional Racism in America* (Englewood Cliffs, New Jersey: Prentice-Hall, Inc. 1969), pp. 35–37.

28. U.S. Civil Rights Commission, *Civil Rights U.S.A., Public Schools Cities in the North and West* (Washington, D.C.: Government Printing Office, 1962), p. 292.

29. Charles Horton Cooley, *Human Nature and the Social Order* (New York: Charles Scribner's Sons, 1903), pp. 151–153.

30. For an extensive treatment on this phenomenon in other contexts see Robert K. Merton, *Social Theory and Social Structure* (Glencoe, Illinois, The Free Press, 1957), pp. 421–436.

31. Arthur Pearl, *Educational Change: Why—How—For Whom* (compiled from his speeches by the San Francisco Human Rights Com-

mission), p. 5, quoted in Knowles and Prewitt (eds.), *Institutional Racism in America*, p. 39.

32. Robert Rosenthal and Lenore Jacobson, *Pygmalion in the Classroom: Teacher Expectations and Pupils Intellectual Development* (New York: Holt, Rinehart and Winston, 1968). For a critique of the methodology see Richard E. Snow, "Unfinished Pygmalion," *Contemporary Psychology* 14 (April, 1969), pp. 197–199.

33. W. V. Beez, "Influence of Biased Psychological Reports on Teacher Behavior and Pupil Performance," *Proceedings of the 76th APA Annual Convention* (Washington, D.C.: American Psychological Association, 1968, pp. 605–606; quoted in Alan Edward Guskin and Samuel Louis Guskin, *A Social Psychology of Education* (Reading, Massachusetts: Addison-Wesley Publishing Company, 1970), pp. 12–13.

34. Silberman, *Crisis in the Classroom*, p. 98.

35. Quoted in "Why Johnny Can't Read," *Newsweek* (December 11, 1972), p. 122.

36. Quoted in Schafer, Olexa and Polk, "Programmed for Social Class," p. 44.

37. Quoted in Schafer, Olexa and Polk, "Programmed for Social Class," p. 46.

38. Sexton, *The American School*, p. 61.

39. Ryan, *Blaming the Victim*, p. 60.

40. Christopher Jencks and David Riesman, *The Academic Revolution* (Garden City, New York: Doubleday and Company, Inc., 1968), pp. 61–154.

41. U.S. Bureau of the Census, *Characteristics of American Youth: 1971* (Washington, D.C.: U.S. Government Printing Office, 1972), p. 17.

42. Robert A. Nisbet, "The University Had Better Mind Its Own Business," *Psychology Today* 4 (March 1971), pp. 22, 28, 30, 32, 34, 37.

43. Philip Selznick, *TVA and the Grass Roots* (New York: Harper Torchbooks, 1966).

44. Ivan Illich, *Celebration of Awareness* (Garden City, New York: Doubleday, 1970); and Ivan Illich, *Deschooling Society* (New York: Harper and Row, 1971); and Ivan Illich, "The Alternative to Schooling," *Saturday Review* 54 (June 19, 1971), pp. 44–48; 59–60. For a critique of this alternative see Manfred Stanley, "Illich Defrocked," *Society* 9 (March, 1972), pp. 50–52. For arguments pro and con, see the three articles in the special section entitled, "Illich, Pro and Con," *Social Policy* 2 (January/February, 1972), pp. 32–41.

45. Illich, *Deschooling Society*, p. 76.

46. Illich, *Deschooling Society*, pp. 78–79. See pp. 79–104 for a full description of the way in which these things and persons can be used to facilitate individual learning.

47. A. S. Neill, *Summerhill: A Radical Approach to Child Rearing* (New York: Hart Publishing Company, 1960); see especially the

introduction by Erich Fromm, pp. xii–xv. For a summary of the pros and cons on Summerhill see Harold H. Hart (ed.), *Summerhill: For and Against* (New York: Hart Publishing Co., Inc., 1970); for a scathing critique see especially the article by Max Rafferty, pp. 11–25; for a sympathetic appraisal see the paper by Goodwin Watson, pp. 175–192.

48. Jonathan Kozol, "Free Schools Fail Because They Don't Teach," *Psychology Today* 5 (April, 1972), pp. 30, 34, 36, 114.

49. Silberman, *Crisis in the Classroom*, pp. 207–369. See also Joseph D. Hassett and Arline Weisberg, *Open Education: Alternatives Within Our Tradition* (Englewood Cliffs, New Jersey: Prentice-Hall, Inc., 1972).

50. Peter F. Drucker, "School Around the Bend," *Psychology Today* 6 (June, 1972), p. 49.

CHAPTER 11

The American Economy

Economic activity involves the production and distribution of scarce goods and services. An urban and industrialized society such as the United States requires a complex network to transform raw materials into finished products, to transport these products, to merchandise these products. Services, too, are varied. People need things repaired, they want advice, they desire credit, they seek investments. The list is endless but the point is clear—American society is composed of persons doing highly specialized tasks which, because of the interdependence of the parts, result in the production and distribution of the material goods and the services that people want.

The task of this chapter is to describe the American economy—the rules and customs that govern the production and allocation of scarce goods and services. Because many of the concepts underlying this chapter have already been covered in preceding chapters, especially the entire unit on inequality, this chapter can be briefer than the subject itself deserves. Such brevity should not be construed as suggesting that the economy is relatively unimportant. To the contrary, the economy can be considered the primary determinant of the social structure, since it can determine the system of stratification and hence, the distribution of power and material rewards.[1]

The Division of Labor in American Society

An essential ingredient of the economy is a divison of labor. Virtually everyone who is not too young, too old, or disabled is employed.* The importance of a person's occupation cannot be overemphasized, for it provides him or her with a certain level of monetary rewards, power, and prestige. The rewards for particular jobs are neither distributed equally nor randomly in American society (as noted in Chapter 3).

The vast majority of Americans work at highly specialized occupations. According to Wilensky there are roughly 30,000 occupations in the United States. The degree of specialization is almost infinite as the following illustration demonstrates:

> In the baking industry one can make a living as a cracker breaker, meringue spreader, a pie stripper, or pan dumper. In the slaughter and meat-packing industry one can specialize as: a large stock scalper, belly shaver, crotch buster, gut snatcher, gut sorter, snout puller, ear cutter, eyelid remover, stomach washer (sometimes called belly pumper), hindleg toenail puller, frontleg toenail puller and oxtail washer.[2]

The individual's actual choice of a particular job depends on a number of factors: (1) degree of success in school (which is the great "sifter and sorter" of society); (2) native abilities and acquired skills; (3) interest; and (4) availability of jobs. This last point is of special interest because societal-wide forces impinge upon individual decision-making. Some occupations are relatively closed to new members because of race or sex. Some occupations are closed because the current members keep the standards high (e.g., the professions). Some occupations have few openings because the industry itself is dying (e.g., harness making, strip mining, small scale farming). Some have few openings because there is a surplus of workers (as this is written two occupations in particular share this problem—teaching and aeronautical engineering). Others have limited openings because automation is replacing semi-skilled and unskilled labor. At the same time technological change encourages persons to work at new types of occupations (e.g., computer programming, waste material recycling, nuclear engineering).

* The exceptions in American society are the young (about 25 percent of all Americans are in school), adult women where only about 40 percent work fulltime outside the home, and the approximately five percent (1972) who are unemployed because they cannot find work.

We have witnessed within the past few decades some dramatic societal-wide occupational shifts—from farming to non-farming, from unskilled to skilled, from blue-collar to white-collar. As technology changes, the division of labor is altered. There are two types of occupational shifts—intergenerational (where, for example, sons of blue-collar workers became teachers) and intragenerational (where individuals change occupations). Both types occur with greater frequency as the demands of the economy affect the desirability of occupations.

The division of labor has two very important consequences for society. First and most obvious is that it insures that the necessary tasks of producing and distributing goods and services are accomplished. Second and much more subtle is its role in accomplishing societal integration in complex societies.

The great French sociologist, Emile Durkheim, spent his professional life analyzing the mysteries of group and societal integration. In his classic, *The Division of Labor in Society*, he suggested that there are two fundamentally different types of societies, one type where integration is based on similarity of custom, beliefs, and ideas, and the other type where solidarity is maintained not by similarities but by differences. This latter type is found in large, complex societies such as the United States. In an urban, industrial society every individual must depend upon farmers, merchandizers, bankers, teachers, policemen, etc., in order to survive.[3] A highly developed monetary and credit system especially leads to a complex interdependence of the parts in the economic system.

One important consequence of a highly interdependent system is the greater likelihood of booms and depressions. For example, a depression comes about (in overly simplistic terms) when the flow of money is restricted by high taxes, high interest rates, high unemployment, and restricted buying practices by individuals. When large numbers of persons delay buying items such as a new car or refrigerator because they are uncertain of the future, the sales of these decline dramatically. This decrease itself is a source of further pessimism, thereby dampening sales. The price of stocks in these companies will of course plummet under these conditions, causing further alarm. Moreover, many workers in these industries will be laid off. These newly unemployed persons, in turn, will purchase only the necessities, thereby throwing other industries into panic as their sales decline. A depression, then, is the result of actions by individual consumers, boards of directors of corporations, banks, savings and loan associations, individual and institutional investors, and the government. Additionally, the actions of this nation and the actions of other nations greatly affect the economic conditions of each other because they, too, form an interdependent network.

As a result of the interdependence that characterizes the American economy, individuals tend to feel powerless. Jobs may be lost and businesses may fail as an outcome of decisions made by a legislature, by the President, by a corporation board of directors, by a union, or even by a foreign government. Thus, the individual is at the mercy of forces in the economy beyond his control.

The fact that cooperation and interdependence is a function of labor division does not mean that conflict is absent. To the contrary, conflict is the direct result of the differences between occupational groups, because the groups are not equal. The division of labor quite naturally results in conflicts of interest. Owners of enterprises desire to maximize profits, while their workers want greater material rewards and more power over their destiny. This has resulted in the rise of labor unions. By combining into one organization, individuals have created power where it was absent. Although the workers have the right to strike and conduct boycotts in their battle with owners, their power is blunted by the right of the President and Congress to curtail or even eliminate these activities if they are interpreted as harmful to the national interest.

The American Economy Is a Mixture of Capitalism and Socialism

Capitalism, according to classical economists such as Adam Smith, is based on a market free of governmental interference. As individuals seek to serve their own self-interest, supply and demand will lead to the production and distribution of the best products at the lowest possible cost. Thus, through the profit motive, private enterprise, and competition, the greatest good for the greatest number is achieved. This "greatest good" is translated into individual self-fulfillment and general material progress of the society.

A trend of this century has been the steady erosion of this classic form of "laissez-faire" capitalism. Several problems with capitalism have led to an increased role of government in market activities—thereby leading to a mixture of capitalism and socialism.[4] First, laissez-faire capitalism did not meet the challenge of the Great Depression. Capitalist thought offered no solution to getting the economy out of the Depression, because it assumed that the economy would correct itself without governmental interference. They had no answers for the ever-descending spiral except patience. It became evident to most experts that a laissez-faire economy inevitably results in drastic economic cycles. Since these are injurious to individuals, corporations, and the society, governmental inputs to direct the economy were deemed desirable by those in power.

Second, it has been generally recognized that laissez-faire capitalism has not achieved the greatest good for the greatest number. Left only to the competitive market, some entrepreneurs have taken advantage of their competition and customers with unfair business practices. Additionally, an unfettered economy seems to widen the gap between the haves and the have-nots.

Similarly, entrepreneurs without governmental constraints have often disregarded the welfare of their employees. Because of the demands from workers, unions, and the government, laws have been passed which provide for minimum safety standards, minimum wages, social security, unemployment insurance, workmen's compensation, and other benefits to workers which would not be present to such a degree if left to the wishes of employers.

The decades of the 1960's and 1970's will probably be remembered by historians as an era of revolt against inequality.[5] Students, women, homosexuals, blacks, chicanos, consumers, and other groups were increasingly impatient about not getting their share. They demanded that government guarantee greater equality by forcing employers, schools, the military, and others to cease discrimination in hiring, firing, salaries, and promotions. In particular, they insisted that wealth be distributed more equitably, a goal that requires drastic shifts in policies regarding taxes, welfare, and other subsidies.

Another reason for the loss of confidence in an economy based on unrestrained capitalism is the existence of giant corporations that have dominated major industries, actually stifling competition. The growth of corporations to giant size was the undoing of a free and competitive market.

Finally, the huge costs of fighting World War II and the Cold War afterward meant profits for business, jobs for labor, and a steady source of demand for products. The tremendous impact of the government on the economy is only of relatively recent origin. In 1929 only about eight percent of all economic activity was from federal, state, and local governments, whereas approximately one-fourth is now generated from the various governmental levels.[6] Since the gross national product in 1972 approximated $1 trillion, the governmental impact on the economy was in the neighborhood of $250 billion. The number of jobs, the fortunes made by individuals and corporations, and the services provided vitally affect the economy. Clearly, the economy is dependent upon the government for much of its growth and vitality. Thus, the government in this century has become a vital source of economic stability (smoothing economic cycles, regulating abuses), and profit.

Let us briefly note how the current mixture of capitalism and socialism has developed some interesting characteristics. First, there is the paradox that although the labor force is made up of a number of profit-oriented persons, fully one-fourth of the labor market works in non-profit organizations (e.g., government, schools, hospitals, churches, and foundations).[7] Similarly, over 20 million American workers belong to labor unions, whose avowed primary goal is equality rather than inequality.

A second paradox is that the economy is free yet controlled. Prices are determined, for the most part, by supply and demand. Occasionally, however, the government artifically supports prices at a higher level than would be the case in a free market. Conversely, the government has at times also placed a ceiling on prices to keep them down in periods of inflation. The government also places constraints on the freedoms of businesses in order to curb abuses. Many private corporations are regulated (prices, markets, growth) by the government. This occurs especially in the public utilities, transportation and communication fields.

Another paradox is that the economy is competitive yet uncompetitive. There is the widespread belief, spoken at Chamber of Commerce banquets, that "competition is the lifeblood of the American economy." Yet the numerous exceptions to this principle of the "survival of the fittest" seem to make it irrelevant. For example, special interest groups continually lobby in Congress for favorable legislation that will give them special advantages (such as the oil depletion allowance, and the anti-trust provisions allowed owners of professional sports teams). Moreover, businesses seek governmental contracts because they often limit competitive bidding (see Chapter 4). Finally, competition is restricted by the existence of various forms of collusion as well as by government monopolies. The government monopolies are obvious forms of socialism (post office, schools, public utilities, public transportation). Meanwhile, the private corporations of the United States often combine to restrict competition. This is accomplished typically by "fixing of prices" by the few large firms that dominate a given field. Imperfect competition also occurs from the inability of small corporations to compete with the huge ones. Smaller businesses often cannot afford the enormous capital investment (including the cost of advertising campaigns) necessary to enter an established field. They may also be kept from these areas because the large firms control the strategic raw materials, personnel, and patents.[8]

Finally, there is a widespread belief in "rugged individualism" —that the individual is responsible for his actions and his place in society. Although such beliefs hinder efforts to aid the needy, there are governmental programs to ease the burden of poverty (and, some critics would say, destroy individual initiative). At any rate, the government does provide several forms of welfare—unemployment compensation, pensions, and aid for dependent children.

The Corporation-Dominated Economy

Although there are countless corporations and proprietorships in the United States, a relatively small number of business enterprises dominate the economy.

> Of the almost two million corporations in America, one-tenth of 1 per cent controls 55 per cent of the total assets; 1.1 per cent controls 82 per cent. At the other end of the spectrum, 94 per cent of the corporations own only 9 per cent of the total assets.[9]

The largest corporations dominate sales, influence Congress, and transform the buying habits of consumers through massive advertising. Table 11–1 provides a glimpse at the enormity of these enterprises.

Several important points can be drawn from the data of which Table 11–1 is constructed. First, 186 American corporations exceeded $1 billion in revenues (20 companies generated $4 billion in sales). Clearly, these are huge corporations. Even the company ranked 500th sold $399 million in goods, a not too modest sum.

Second, when it comes to assets the "big are getting bigger." *Forbes* noted that in 1968 only eight companies had assets of over $10 billion while the number was 17 for 1971. If all the 500 largest companies were ". . . lumped together into a gargantuan multicompany, its assets would total $1,149 billion. The 500 listed in 1968 were worth $851 billion. That amounts to a 35% increase in *three years*."[10] This increase is the result of two factors—inflation and mergers. Mergers are important because they suggest that the smaller enterprises are being "swallowed up" by the larger ones. From 1968 to 1971 approximately 20,000 mergers took place.[11] This results, of course, in the actual number of business enterprises declining while the largest continue to expand.

As another example of how large these corporations are, Table 11–1 shows that Airco ranked 500th with a net worth of better than one-half billion dollars. Although Airco is very large indeed, it is but a dwarf alongside AT&T whose assets approximated $55 billion in 1971. As a public utility, this corporation has a virtual monopoly. Its rates are therefore regulated. In 1965 when that company's gross

TABLE 11–1.   America's Largest Corporations, 1971

Rank	Revenues	($000,000)	Assets	($000,000)
1	Gen. Motors	28,264	AT&T	54,548
2	Standard Oil (N.J.)	18,701	Bank America Corp.	33,986
3	AT&T	18,511	First Nat'l City	29,302
4	Ford	16,433	Chase Manhattan	24,509
5	Sears	10,006	Standard Oil (N.J.)	20,315
6	G.E.	9,425	Fed. Nat'l Mtge.	18,591
7	IT&T	8,811	Gen. Motors	18,137
8	IBM	8,274	Mfrs. Hanover	14,277
9	Mobil	8,243	J. P. Morgan	13,616
10	Chrysler	7,999	Western Bancorp	13,281
.	.	.	.	.
.	.	.	.	.
.	.	.	.	.
.	.	.	.	.
500	Cyclops	339	Airco	583

Rank	Profits	($000,000)
1	AT&T	2,240
2	Gen. Motors	1,936
3	Standard Oil (N.J.)	1,462
4	IBM	1,079
5	Texaco	904
6	Ford	657
7	Gulf Oil	561
8	Sears	551
9	Mobil	541
10	Standard Oil	511
.	.	.
.	.	.
.	.	.
.	.	.
500	Mercantile Bancorp	16

Source: Adapted from a series of tables appearing in Forbes 109 (May 15, 1972).

revenues were only $11 billion (7½ billion less than in 1971), it grossed more money than the three largest state governments combined (California, New York, and Pennsylvania).[12]

Turning to the profits these corporations generated in 1971, Table 11–1 shows that the lowliest corporation on the list (number 500) cleared $16 million, which means it was a very large concern indeed. One hundred eighty-three corporations had profits in excess of $50 million and 64 surpassed $100 million. Four companies exceeded $1 billion in profits. Clearly the huge corporations turn a nice profit. There are several possible reasons why these profits may be excessive, since they occurred because of special concessions. There are a number of tax loopholes that allow corporations to make huge profits. For example, corporation profits are taxed at a lower rate than are wages for individuals; the oil depletion allowance omits 20 percent of the profits from oil from being taxed (note that five of the top ten companies in profits have a primary interest in oil). The size of these corporations also limits competition—the smaller companies often cannot compete successfully because they cannot afford price cutting, massive advertising, and the costs of retooling.

1. *The concentration of corporate power.* The owners of a corporation are its holders of stock. For most American corporations, stock is widely held, giving the impression of dispersed, therefore democratic, power. For example, in 1970 some 31 million persons owned shares of stock. Since 83 percent of these persons had incomes of less than $25,000,[13] one might conclude that the ownership of American corporations is widely scattered among the not so wealthy. To the contrary, however, *stocks are actually highly concentrated among a relatively few wealthy persons.*

> In 150 of the largest 500 firms, ownership large enough to give control rests in the hands of an individual or members of a single family. Names such as Ford, Mellon, Pew, Rockefeller, Duke, Firestone, Kaiser, McDonnell, Hughes and Fairchild are heard frequently enough by most Americans. But there are at least 140 more such family names in the largest 500 corporations. . . . Now taking the *directors* of the dominant corporations as a group, we find that their share of ownership *in their own companies* is sufficient to give them financial control of at least two-thirds of the 250 largest corporations.[14]

Or put another way, "Although many Americans now own some stocks, 2 percent of all individual stockholders own about two-thirds of stocks held by individuals."[15]

Financial control (and control over the corporation's policies) is possible with less than 50 percent of a corporation's stock. This is because corporations are not democratic. They hold annual meetings for shareholders, but these are for the most part a sham. The widely dispersed shareholders, each owning a relatively small number of shares, usually cannot attend these meetings, and they have no opportunity to band together with other shareholders. Their function is to accept, usually by proxy votes, the wishes of the dominant group (who may control as little as 5 or 10 percent of a company).

The power of a corporation is, however, not as monolithic as it might appear. Of course, ultimate decisions are made by majority stockholders who dominate the Board of Directors. But another source of power is also very important—the group called the "technostructure" by Galbraith. This body is composed of persons who have the information and expertise required to plan, coordinate, and utilize modern technology. As Galbraith has said,

> . . . nearly all powers—initiation, character of development, rejection or acceptance—are exercised deep in the company. It is not the managers who decide. Effective power of decision is lodged deeply in the technical, planning and other specialized staff.[16]

Thus, Galbraith has contended that the modern corporation and the demands of modern technology serve to divorce the owner of capital (the stockholders) from actual control of the enterprise.

2. *The degree of social responsibility by corporations.* The thrust of corporations is the pursuit of profit. Corporate decisions are always made in the hope of increasing profit. Although this goal has resulted in the fantastic growth of individual businesses and the economy, it also has a number of unfortunate consequences. First, the quest for efficiency means replacing people with machines. It means paying the work force as little as possible. It has meant that minority group members were not hired for responsible positions, since such actions might be thought to hurt sales or the morale within the organization. It has meant, furthermore, that corporations continue to pollute the air and water, since it is cheaper to dump wastes than to recycle them.

The primacy of money making has also led corporations to minimize competition as much as possible through mergers, price fixing, and other techniques. Also some corporations have used misleading advertising, deceptive packaging, inferior merchandise, and other schemes to bilk consumers. Occasionally corporations have even endangered the physical well-being of consumers in the name of profit, as the cases in Panel 11–1 attest.

All of the above instances should not obscure the fact that many corporations have made socially useful contributions to their workers, consumers, and even the environment. In all too many cases, however, socially responsible actions by corporations have occurred only under duress. These pressures have come from workers (unions) for better working conditions (including safety), health insurance, and higher wages. The various levels of government, but especially at the federal level, have had to apply a good

PANEL 11–1

"IN THE NAME OF PROFIT"

Source: Robert L. Heilbroner, "Controlling the Corporation," *In The Name of Profit,* Robert L. Heilbroner, *et al.* (eds.), (New York: Doubleday and Company, Inc., 1972), pp. 224–225.

Robert Heilbroner, an economist, has cited several illustrations of the deliberate decisions by corporations to sell products known to have detrimental side effects. Libby, McNeil & Libby, a major foodpacker

". . . found itself hampered by the imposition of a ban on cyclamates issued by the Food and Drug Administration in 1969. Over the next sixteen months, Libby sold some 300,000 cases of cyclamate-sweetened fruit to customers in West Germany, Spain and elsewhere. 'Fortunately,' the *Wall Street Journal* [February 11, 1971] quotes James Nadler, Libby's vice-president for international business, 'the older civilizations of the world are more deliberate about judging momentary fads that are popular in the U.S. from time to time.' The momentary fad to which he was referring was the upshot of nineteen years of increasingly alarming laboratory findings concerning the effects of cyclamates on chick embryos—effects that produce grotesque malformations similar to those induced by thalidomide. . . . Not that Libby is the only adherent to this principle. The *Journal* article goes on to report that Parke, Davis & Co. sells its Chloromycetin to foreign nations without some of the warnings concerning dangerous side effects it is forced to display here, and with a much wider range of recommended applications than it is allowed to mention here. The same double standard is true for Merck & Co's antihumantic drug Indocin, sold abroad under much less cautious description than at home."

deal of force to get corporations to integrate, to provide safe working conditions for employees, to provide safe products that fulfill
their advertising claims, to inform clients of the actual interest
rates, and to curb pollution. These efforts have been effective at a
minimum level for the most part. They have not met with as much
success as one would hope for, because Congress has rarely put
effective constraints on business.

It could be argued, on the other hand, that the profit motive that
drives corporations has indirectly accomplished a tremendous
amount of good for the society. Expansive organizations with high
rates of production have removed a very large portion of American
society from the compulsion and pressures of physical want.[17]
Although poverty remains a reality for millions of Americans, the
vast bulk of the population have relatively good jobs, leisure time,
and money for some luxuries. The money spent on leisure is one
indicator of affluence. Americans spent $58 billion in 1971 (an
average of $276 per capita) on leisure time pursuits, and the pros-
pect is for the amount to be $88 billion by 1976.[18]

The Unequal Distribution of Wealth

In theory, societies may range from a totally unequal distribution of
wealth (income and property) to total equality. The former is
present in a number of societies, but the latter, while a goal for
some, has never been fully attained. Since the American economy is
a mixture of capitalism and socialism, it is somewhere in between
the two extremes of inequality and equality. There are Americans
who live in wretched poverty without adequate food, clothing,
shelter, and medical attention (see Chapter 5). At the same time
there are Americans who are super rich. *Fortune* magazine, for
example, has estimated that 153 individuals in 1968 had fortunes in
excess of $50 million.[19] In between these extremes are the bulk of
Americans who are relatively affluent. In 1968, for example, 56
percent of all families had incomes of between $6,000 and
$14,999.[20] Consequently, while it is recognized that poverty exists
(10.3 percent of families had incomes of less than $3,000 in 1968),
it is commonly assumed that Americans are relatively affluent.
Moreover, most Americans believe that the wealth is gradually
being distributed more equitably. This, however, is a myth.

The facts are these: wealth is distributed unequally in the United
States and the gap between rich and poor is increasing. Table 11–2
provides the distribution of wealth among consumer units (families
of two or more persons and independent individuals).

According to these data, one-fourth of all American consumer units had wealth of less than $1,000 (wealth is defined as home and business assets, including the values of automobiles owned). This category, although almost 15 million units, had less than 1 percent of the total wealth. At the other end of the scale, however, slightly more than 2 percent of the units had wealth in excess of $100,000 (43 percent of all the wealth). These data clearly show the huge gap in wealth. The same conclusion is reached if we examine the statistics on income.

> The poorest fifth of the U.S. population receives only 4 per cent of the nation's annual income, and the next poorest fifth, only 11 per cent, while the richest fifth gets about 45 per cent, and the 5 per cent at the top, over 20 per cent.[21]

Not only is the distribution of wealth and income unequal in the United States, but it continues to worsen. A study prepared by two economists for the Joint Economic Committee of Congress noted the following about the unequal distribution of income in American society:

> In 1947 the average income of the richest 20 percent of all families was $10,565 higher than that of the poorest 20 percent of all

TABLE 11–2. Distribution of Wealth: December 31, 1962

Wealth	Consumer Units (millions)	Percentage Distribution Consumer Units	Wealth
Totals	57.9	100%	100%
Negative	1.0	2	*
Zero	4.7	8	*
$1 to 999	9.0	16	*
$1,000 to 4,999	10.8	19	2
$5,000 to 9,999	9.1	16	5
$10,000 to 24,999	13.3	23	18
$25,000 to 49,999	6.2	11	18
$50,000 to 99,999	2.5	4	14
$100,000 to 199,999	0.7	1	8
$200,000 to 499,999	0.5	1	13
$500,000 and over	0.2	*	22

* Less than ½ of 1 percent.
Source: Herman P. Miller, *Rich Man, Poor Man* (New York: Thomas Y. Crowell Company, 1971), p. 157.

families; in 1969 it was $19,071 higher (in 1969 dollars). The real gap between the poorest and richest 5 percent of all families rose from $17,057 to $27,605 (in 1969 dollars) . . .[22]

The differences in incomes between minority groups and the majority are particularly interesting because they highlight the seeming paradox of the minorities increasing at a faster rate than the majority while the gap continues to widen. From 1947 to 1969, average white family incomes grew from $5,194 to $9,794, while the incomes of the average black family rose from $2,660 to $6,191. Thus, while white incomes about doubled, black incomes almost trebled; the absolute difference, however, between black and white family incomes rose from $2,534 to $3,603.[23]

The discrepancy between males and females also follows the majority-minority distribution pattern. One difference is apparent, however. Whereas blacks and others have been gaining on the majority in percentage of income, women have not. In 1939 full-time female workers earned 58 percent of what males did. By 1969 the percentage had increased only one percent to 59. The real income gap between fully-employed males and females, therefore has increased from $1,570 (in 1969 dollars) in 1934 to $3,526 in 1969.[24]

A fundamental problem for the President and the Congress of the United States is the decision as to the degree of equality or inequality that is desirable in the American economy. The government can make the distribution of wealth more equitable in two ways: (a) taxing the more well to do, and (b) giving these monies to the poor through specially designed programs. A favorite device is the progressive income tax whereby the higher the income, the higher the tax rate. The inheritance tax is another useful technique that could, if total, eliminate inherited wealth. A third type of tax that aids in redistributing the wealth is the property tax, a device where property is taxed according to its value.

Using these tax monies, the government can institute programs designed to provide a more equitable distribution of income. The government could, for example, insure a minimum income through a negative income tax. Such a program would, in 1971, have cost $25 billion to provide a minimum of $3,600 income for a family of four and $71 billion if the minimum were to be a $5,500 income.*

Another possibility would be for the government to subsidize

---

* While these estimates are enormous, even the larger one is much less than the U.S. spends on defense, and much of it could be attained through tax reform.[25]

depressed industries such as coal mining or farming. Another governmental tactic would be to create public service jobs, similar to the WPA program instituted by President Roosevelt during the Depression years of the 1930's. That program not only provided millions of jobs to the needy, it ". . . constructed nearly 600 airports, built or rebuilt 110,000 public buildings, half a million miles of roads and city streets and more than 100,000 bridges."[26] Although costly, this program had the dual effects of redistributing income in a more equitable way and, through its accomplishments, provided services for the entire society.

But while the government could do these things, it has not, for the most part. Either by action or inaction, it has tended to be indulgent of the corporations and punitive to individuals, especially the poor and the wage earner. Panel 11–2 provides some interesting but depressing insights into how the government allows the common person to be abused by the corporations.

1. *Taxation and inequality.* Taxes are designed both to raise money and to have effects upon the distribution of wealth. To accomplish the latter they can be designed to increase inequality by taking a larger proportion of a poor person's income than a rich person's. This type of tax (called "regressive") is based on a more or less fixed amount of tax for all persons, regardless of income levels, which means, in effect, that the poor pay a larger percentage of their incomes. Social security taxes and sales taxes are two examples of regressive taxes. The latter is especially important because more than one-half of all state revenues come from this regressive source.

Progressive taxes, on the other hand, take a larger proportion of a rich person's income than a poor person's. In theory, progressive taxes should result in a leveling of economic differences. The federal income tax rates, for example, range from 20 percent to 70 percent (the wealthier paying the larger percentage). In practice, however, loopholes in the tax structure allow the wealthy to avoid paying high taxes. These loopholes occur because not all income is treated alike. Income from municipal bonds is totally exempt from taxes. Fifty percent of capital gains income goes untaxed (if the property is held over six months). Twenty percent of income received from oil also is not affected by taxes. These tax privileges benefit only the well-to-do. As Senator George McGovern has put it,

> Two taxpayers with the same annual income pay quite different taxes. A factory worker or a schoolteacher whose taxes are withheld from his wages cannot take advantage of loopholes. He may

369

expect to pay almost $1,000 in taxes on earnings of $10,000. A wealthy person who receives $10,000 income from state and local bonds will pay no federal taxes at all. Clearly this system is unfair.

And these inequities are not theoretical. On the basis of 1969 tax returns, the last year for which figures are available, some 21,317 people earning more than $20,000 paid no federal taxes whatso-

PANEL 11–2

"INSTITUTIONAL ABUSES OF UNCHECKED CORPORATE POWER"

Source: Ralph Nader, "A Citizen's Guide to the American Economy," *The New York Review of Books* 17 (September 2, 1971), pp. 14–18.

Ralph Nader, the consumer's advocate and leader of the consumerism movement, has devoted his life to stopping corporate and governmental abuses of the common citizen. The following are some of the major categories in which such abuses cause the consumer's dollars to be wasted and his taxes misused, as perceived by Ralph Nader:

1. *The involuntary sub-economy.* This refers to the billions that consumers would save if corporations would observe elementary standards of honesty, safety, and utility in production and sales. The consumers' cars have defects that are costly for them to repair. Deceptive advertising and promotion cost consumers because many products do not aid in losing weight, curing dandruff, or whatever the claim. All advertising costs, moreover, are passed on to consumers, for which they receive nothing of additional value.

2. *The transfer sub-economy.* This involves the high cost of changing goods from raw materials to finished products in the hands of consumers. This involves transportation, processing, and merchandising. At each level costs are entailed, taxes imposed, and profits made. The system is not efficient, and the costs are all transferred to the consumer.

3. *The controlled market sub-economy.* This refers to the thousands of arrangements that make it possible for corporations to avoid competition, thereby artificially keeping prices high.

> The Federal Trade Commission has estimated that if highly concentrated industries were broken up by the anti-trust laws into more competitive companies so that the four largest firms in any industry would not control more than 40 percent of that industry's sales, prices would fall *by 25 percent or more.* This estimate applies to such major industries as autos, steel, copper, aluminum, containers, chemicals, detergents, canned soups, cereals. (p. 15)

4. *The corporate socialism sub-economy.* This refers to the many special privileges granted by the government to corporations. These include the many tax loopholes that have been mentioned as well as the gross underpayment of property taxes. In Gary, Indiana, where the big company is U.S. Steel:

ever. That includes fifty-six people with incomes in a single year of $1 million or more.[27]

Such inequities exist because of the provisions in the tax law that permit the wealthy to exempt some types of income, but also such

Between 1961 and 1971 its property assessment only rose from $107 million to $117 million, although during that period the company installed $1.2 billion worth of capital improvements. U.S. Steel refuses to allow the city authorities to examine its books and it refuses to apply for building permits as required by city law, because this would reveal the size of its taxable investment.

U.S. Steel is able to get away with all this because it exerts raw corporate power in a company town. It is not in any way unusual. Timber companies in Maine, mine owners in Appalachia, paper mills and chemical plants in cities and towns that depend on them for employment—all flagrantly evade the constitutional provisions in their states for equal treatment under property taxes. (p. 16)

Governments also pay direct subsidies to business. Government subsidies to agriculture are well known. They also go to other businesses in the form of business promotion, research, and special equipment needed by government contractors. It is interesting to note, furthermore, that when a company bids to get a government contract (and many are not put out for competitive bids), when it gets the contract and then finds that it made a mistake in the costs, the government often bails the company out (Lockheed received $2 billion for a cost overrun on the C5A).

5. *The compulsory consumption sub-economy.* Nader refers in this case to the compulsory consumption of environmental pollution and compulsory exposure to occupation health and safety hazards. These cost in damages to health, cleaning costs, and in damage to property, resources, and agricultural crops. The costs to the unborn and to the environment of the future are incalculable.

Apologists for the present corporate system will argue that the subeconomies I have described so generally here are justified because they support industries, create jobs, generate income. But it should be clear that their operations and the kinds of needs they satisfy are, to a great extent, neither desirable nor socially responsible; in many cases they are not legal. . . . For most of this century there has been declared a national consensus in favor of competition, as well as numerous laws designed to encourage it, but both have been for the most part betrayed. When they have not, the benefits for the citizens have been dramatic. Indeed each of the subeconomies I have described subverts values that are deeply rooted in American life. (p. 18)

371

schemes as deferred compensation (the postponement of part of one's income until after retirement) and stock options (allowing part of salary to be taxed at capital gains rate since it is in the form of stock rather than a wage). As Gabriel Kolko has stated,

> The fantastic complexity of the tax law has not succeeded in dimming the sheer genius of tax lawyers, who have aided the economic elite to circumscribe, in a perfectly legal manner, many of the more onerous tax provisions. Their ultimate success, however, can be attributed neither to their ingenuity nor to the intricacy of the tax law; it results from the failure of political administrations over the past decades to enact tax legislation that seriously challenges the economic power of the wealthy. . . . The complexity of the effect of taxation should not be allowed to obscure the basic trends—the growing tax burden on the low- and middle-income classes, and the huge disparity between theoretical and actual tax rates for the wealthy. The conclusion is inescapable: Taxation has not mitigated the fundamentally unequal distribution of income. If anything it has perpetuated inequality by heavily taxing the low- and middle-income groups—those least able to bear its burden.[28]

The tax structure in the United States, we must conclude, is regressive. Joseph Pechman, an expert on such matters, has found that the *heaviest* taxed income group are persons with annual incomes of less than $2,000. These persons pay out 44 percent of their income in federal, state and local taxes, while those persons with incomes in excess of $15,000 pay out only a total of 38 percent of their income in taxes.[29]

2. *Government subsidies and inequality.* The tax loopholes just considered are in fact a form of subsidy—gifts to the wealthy, since the money not required is of course not given to the government but kept for private (or corporate) use. Some have called these subsidies "tax expenditures," because instead of becoming revenue, they are money lost. In 1968, for example, some of these tax expenditures amounted to:

$5.2 billion "spent" on deductions for mortgage interest and property taxes allowed persons who own homes.

$9.7 billion "spent" on investment tax credits, accelerated depreciation on buildings, the dividend exclusion, personal income tax, and other tax dodges.

$19.5 billion "spent" through deductions for medical expenses and for contributions to charities.[30]

These tax devices, although their advocates claim that they advance socially desirable objectives (e.g., home ownership, giving to charities, providing capital investment for business expansion), are subsidies to the middle and upper socioeconomic groups. If we add to this list the subsidies to the airlines (building of facilities), agriculture (tax credits, payment for not growing crops), the churches and other charitable organizations (their property is not taxed as we noted in Chapter 7), corporations through special tax credits and government contracts (e.g., defense), we must conclude that the beneficiaries are the well-to-do. As Leonard Ross has said,

> Federal transportation subsidies overwhelmingly aid the automobile, not the subway; farm programs sustain the squire, not the serf; urban renewal calms the middle classes, and dispossesses the poor. In general, government enterprise has proven little more effective than taxation in rearranging the American distribution of income.[31]

Perhaps the best example of a misdirected government subsidy designed to promote equality of opportunity is the California system of public higher education. Here the tuition costs, at least partly defrayed by the state, are intended to help everyone but in effect are subsidizing the well-to-do, as shown in Panel 11–3.

The conclusion to this section is obvious—there is a wide gap between rich and poor, with the wealthy being twice blessed (having disproportionate wealth to begin with, *and* special advantages to retain and pyramid it further). But what of the future? Will the gap continue to widen? Table 11–4 presents one forecast. (See page 376.)

The predictions in Table 11–4, if they are accurate, suggest that half of the population in 1985 will be at a level only the top three percent enjoyed in 1947 or the top 15 percent in 1970. Although Americans will enjoy greater affluence, three percent will earn below $5,000 annually while 15 percent will earn in excess of $25,000, a gap of at least $20,000. While the median income almost doubles in these 17 years, inequality remains. This is predicated on the assumption that governmental policies will remain the same during these intervening years. Will they?

The Future

The American economy has gradually shifted from laissez-faire capitalism (i.e., virtually unregulated) to a peculiar mixture of capitalism and socialism. The future economy, barring nuclear holocaust, can return to less governmental intervention, remain more or less the same, or move further in the direction of socialism.

Two important factors mitigate against increased socialism. First is the tremendous influence of the corporate rich in the public sector (as noted in Chapter 4). Second is the tendency for many Americans and especially persons in policy making positions to accept the present economic system as proper. The existence of the poor, in this view, is an aberration and the fault of individuals. Goodman has characterized the tendency to think in these terms as follows:

PANEL 11–3

"FREE PUBLIC HIGHER EDUCATION IN CALIFORNIA"

Source: W. Lee Hansen and Burton A. Weisbrod, "The Distribution of Costs and Direct Benefits of Public Higher Education: The Case of California," *The Journal of Human Resources* 4 (Spring, 1969), pp. 176–191.

The state of California subsidizes public higher education by providing tuition free schools. The irony of this apparent socialism is that the poor pay for the benefit of the more well-to-do.

California has three classes of schools—the junior colleges where all applicants (usually high school graduates) are welcome, the state colleges where the standards for admission are higher, and the universities where only about 15 percent of high school graduates meet the stiff entrance requirements. Education is also the most expensive at the university level, since these schools have the most prestigious faculties and the best research facilities. The other schools are less expensive in order.

The attendance at these types of schools is primarily based on socioeconomic status (because of the factors noted so frequently in Chapter 10). Consequently the children of the poor are least likely to complete high school. If successful in high school, they will probably not attend college, or if they do it will usually be at the junior college level. Finally, if they attend college, they are the least likely to receive a degree. The result, then, is a highly unequal distribution in the amounts of public subsidies received. In 1964, 41 percent received nothing, 44 percent received from $1 to $1,999 and 15 percent from $2,000 to over $6,500 in higher education subsidies. Table 11–3 summarizes the findings of Hansen and Weisbrod.

These data show clearly that those California families without children or with children not enrolled in schools of higher education pay their taxes but received no subsidy, while those families with children in higher education received subsidies *in excess* of the money they spent on taxes.

The economic system is right—something must be wrong with the people who don't fit it. Change the people who don't fit, cure *them* of *their* diseases . . . and the system will operate effectively.[32]

As long as this rationale of "blaming the victim" exists, fundamental changes will not occur. Despite the formidable opposition of the corporate rich and the "victim blamers," three current trends suggest that increased socialism might prevail. First there is an ever-

TABLE 11–3.   Who pays for and who benefits in the system of higher education in California, 1964

	Families without children in California colleges	Families with children in:		
		Jr. colleges	College	Univer- sities
1. Average family income of children in	$7,900	$8,800	$10,000	$12,000
2. Average annual state subsidy per student	$ 0	$ 720	$ 1,400	$ 1,700
3. Average state and local amount of taxes paid	$ 650	$ 680	$ 770	$ 910
4. Net gain (or loss) (Line 2 minus Line 3)	−$ 650	+$ 40	+$ 630	+$ 790

Source: Adapted from the Hansen and Weisbrod article, Table 10, p. 190.

Hansen and Weisbrod concluded their study by stating:

The general nature of the redistributive effects of the current method of financing public higher education in California is clear. Some low-income persons have benefited handsomely from the availability of publicly-subsidized higher education. But on the whole, the effect of these subsidies is to promote greater rather than less inequality among people of various social and economic backgrounds, by making available substantial subsidies that lower income families are either not eligible for or cannot make use of because of other conditions and constraints associated with their income position. . . . it is clear that whatever the degree to which our current higher education programs are rooted in the search for equality of opportunity, the results still leave much to be desired (p. 191).

increasing discontent among the majority of the people—not just students but intellectuals, blue-collar workers, farmers, small businessmen, and others. This is evidenced by the taxpayer's revolt, the consumerism movement, the ecology movement, and the appeal of populist political candidates. In each instance, the government and the huge corporations are the targets. There is a contempt for corporations without a social conscience—those who pollute the air and rivers, those who use misleading advertising. Taxes are always a provocative issue, and when the common wage earner learns he is paying the freight for the more well-to-do, he may vote for persons with viable tax reform proposals.*

A second trend is that a Republican President in 1971, whose political party stands for capitalism, instituted a ceiling on wages. This sets the stage for continued efforts along these lines to curb inflation. Organized labor opposed this practice, but will doubtless agree if prices and profits are also controlled, the logical next step. These socialistic measures (the essence of a planned economy) will probably occur in a Democratic administration if a ceiling is continued on wages.

TABLE 11–4.   Comparing Actual 1968 and Predicted 1985 Family and Individual Income in the United States

Percent	Families		Families and Individuals	
	1968	1985	1968	1985
Under $3,000	10%	4%	19%	9%
$3,000 to 4,999	12	6	14	8
$5,000 to 9,999	38	18	34	19
$10,000 to 14,999	25	23	21	21
$15,000 to 24,000	12	33	10	29
$25,000 and over	3	16	2	15
Mean Income	$9,600	$16,100	$8,500	$14,900
Median Income	$8,600	$14,700	$7,400	$13,500

Source: Adapted from Herman P. Miller, Rich Man, Poor Man (New York: Thomas Y. Crowell Company, 1971), p. 241.

* The two best tax reforms in this author's opinion are: (1) to rely exclusively on a progressive income tax (state and federal levels) with all sources of income treated alike; and (2) a 100 percent inheritance tax when the legacy is above a certain figure—e.g., $50,000. This would make the system much more equitable, with achieved status overriding ascribed status.

The third trend involves the general feeling by many Americans that national priorities need to be reordered. Presently military defense gets top billing, but the war in Southeast Asia has caused many to question this. Seymour Melman, director of the Center for Manpower Studies at George Washington University and an expert on defense spending, has said before a House of Representatives Committee that 64 percent of the 1972 tax dollar goes for the military budget and other war costs, past and present. In his judgment the 1972 defense budget of $79.2 billion can be cut by over $50 billion and not hurt security.[33] Such a difference could go a long way in solving social problems. Clearly many people feel the defense budget (and other governmental budgets) is full of fat that provides benefits to the corporate rich but not the common man.

These three trends will serve to pressure the government and the corporations to be more socially responsible. They will necessitate central planning, strong regulation to control business, and the enactment of laws that are fair to all segments of the society.

SUGGESTED FURTHER READING

Galbraith, John Kenneth, *The New Industrial State* (New York: Signet Books, 1967). An analysis of the shifting character of the American economy and the consequences that follow.

Heilbroner, Robert L., *et al.*, editors, *In the Name of Profit: Profiles in Corporate Irresponsibility* (New York: Doubleday and Company, 1972). This reader describes how the desire for profit sometimes leads to shameful decisions.

Hoch, Paul, *Rip Off the Big Game: The Exploitation of Sports by the Power Elite* (Garden City, New York: Doubleday Anchor Books, 1972). A Marxian interpretation of sport in American society that has implications for other institutional areas.

Lundberg, Ferdinand, *The Rich and the Super-Rich,* (New York: Bantam Books, 1968). This book makes a strong case for the extraordinary power of the wealthy in American society.

Nader, Ralph, and Mark J. Green, editors, *Corporate Power in America* (New York: Grossman Publishers, 1973). Several leading economists, political scientists, and lawyers present the arguments for restraining corporate power.

Newfield, Jack, and Jeff Greenfield, *A Populist Manifesto: The Making of a New Majority* (New York: Warner Paperbacks, 1972). Part II of this book deals with the negative consequences of having economic power highly concentrated. A number of specific proposals are presented to break up this concentration.

Stern, Philip M., *The Rape of the Taxpayer* (New York: Random House, 1973). This book indicts the taxation system because the middle and lower classes pay a disproportionate amount while the very rich pay comparatively little.

U.S. Government, *A Look at Business in 1990* (Washington, D.C.: U.S. Government Printing Office, 1972). A number of experts from business, labor, academia, and government deal with the challenge to business in a rapidly changing world.

NOTES AND REFERENCES

1. Karl Marx and Friedrich Engels, *The German Ideology* (New York: International Publishers, 1947); Karl Marx and Friedrich Engels, *The Communist Manifesto* (New York: International Publishers, 1930); and Karl Marx, *Capital: A Critique of Political Economy*, Volume I (New York: International Publishers, 1967).

2. Harold Wilensky, "The Early Impact of Industrialization on Society," in William A. Faunce (ed.), *Readings in Industrial Sociology* (New York: Appleton, 1967), pp. 78–79.

3. Emile Durkheim, *The Division of Labor in Society*, trans, George Simpson (Glencoe, Illinois: Free Press, 1947).

4. This section is dependent in part on the insights of Kenneth M. Dolbeare and Patricia Dolbeare, *American Ideologies: The Competing Political Beliefs of the 1970's* (Chicago: Markham Publishing Company, 1971), pp. 22–49.

5. Herbert J. Gans, "The New Egalitarianism," *Saturday Review* (May 6, 1972), pp. 43–46; and Max Ways, "Equality: A Steep and Endless Stair," *Fortune* 85 (March, 1972), pp. 79–81; 128–130.

6. John Kenneth Galbraith, *The New Industrial State* (New York: Signet Books, 1967), p. 14.

7. Daniel Bell and Irving Kristol (eds.), *Capitalism Today* (New York: Basic Books, Inc., 1970), p. viii.

8. Robin Williams, *American Society*, third edition (New York: Alfred A. Knopf, 1970), pp. 188–191.

9. Gans, "The New Egalitarianism," p. 43.

10. *Forbes* 109 (May 15, 1972), p. 142.

11. *U.S. News and World Report* 71 (December 20, 1971), pp. 29–30.

12. Raymond W. Mack, *Transforming America* (New York: Random House, 1967), pp. 86–87.

13. United States Bureau of the Census, *Statistical Abstract of the United States: 1970*, Table 684, p. 456.

14. C. H. Anderson, *Toward A New Sociology: A Critical View* (Homewood, Illinois: The Dorsey Press, 1971), pp. 187–188.

15. Gans, "The New Egalitarianism," p. 43.

16. John Kenneth Galbraith, *The New Industrial State* (New York: Signet Books, 1967), p. 79.

17. Galbraith, *The New Industrial State*, p. 16–17.

18. From a study conducted by the Midwest Research Institute, quoted in *Kansas City Star* (May 7, 1972), p. 5D.

19. Arthur M. Louis, "America's Centimillionaires," *Fortune* 77 (May, 1968), pp. 152–157. The number in this category is doubtless understated because some forms of wealth defy detection.

20. Census *Statistical Abstract: 1970*, p. 322.

21. Gans, "The New Egalitarianism," p. 43.

22. Lester C. Thurow and Robert E. B. Lucas, "The American Distribution of Income: A Structural Problem," (Washington, D.C.: U.S. Government Printing Office, March 17, 1972), p. 7.

23. Thurow and Lucas, "The American Distribution of Income," pp. 9–10.

24. Thurow and Lucas, "The American Distribution of Income," p. 11.

25. Leonard Ross, "The Myth that Things are Getting Better," *The New York Review of Books* 17 (August 17, 1971), p. 8.

26. *Newsweek* (May 8, 1972), p. 99.

27. George McGovern, "On Taxing and Redistributing Income," *The New York Review of Books* 8 (May 4, 1972), p. 7. For additional evidence of this see also: Ferdinand Lundberg, *The Rich and the Super-Rich* (New York: Bantam Books, 1968), pp. 388–464.

28. Gabriel Kolko, *Wealth and Power in America: An Analysis of Social Class and Income Distribution* (New York: Praeger Publishers, 1962), pp. 44–45.

29. Joseph A. Pechman, "The Rich, the Poor, and the Taxes they Pay," *The Public Interest* 17 (Fall, 1969), p. 43. See also Benjamin Okner, "Middle-Class Tax Reform?" *Trans-action* 8 (March–April, 1971), pp. 59–63.

30. Henry Aaron, "Tax Exemptions—the Artful Dodge," *Trans-action* 6 (March, 1969), pp. 4–6.

31. Ross, "The Myth that Things are Getting Better," p. 8.

32. Robert Goodman, *After the Planners* (New York: Simon and Schuster, 1971), p. 31. Goodman's book makes a strong plea for the opposing view that the structure is at fault, not the individuals who fail to fit the structure.

33. Quoted in the *Kansas City Star* (March 19, 1972).

CHAPTER 12

The American Polity

The polity is the societal institution especially concerned with maintaining order. The goal is societal order, but the key to that order is the legitimacy and effectiveness of the state in accomplishing it. Legitimacy is accomplished by achieving a consensus over the rules and social structures governing the society. This means maintaining the belief among the populace that the existing rules and structures are the most appropriate ones for the society and the ones most likely to be effective in accomplishing the basic functions of the polity. There is, for example, an underlying consensus among Americans that democracy is desirable and valid. Although election campaigns are often waged with considerable fury and fervor, when the returns are in, the people and the candidates accede to the results. Losing candidates and parties recognize the legitimacy of the process and do not use extra-legal means—e.g., forming guerilla groups that harass the government by blowing up bridges and kidnapping officials. Legitimacy is a most important variable because it means obedience to the powerful who are perceived as having the right to make such demands.

William Goode, a sociologist, has said that, "All social order and obedience to authority rests basically on legitimacy, on people's belief that the system is fundamentally decent, fair, honorable, and protective to its members."[1] The United States, however, is currently confronted with an authority crisis. Occasionally Americans find out that their leaders have lied to them, which of course leads to the destruction of credence, faith, and legitimacy. The actions of the police and other authorities, when guilty of taking bribes or police brutality, also shake the foundations of legitimacy. That an authority crisis is imminent is evidenced by the flaunting of some Supreme Court decisions (e.g., school desegregation, unconstitutionality of prayer in the public schools) and the violence that sometimes erupts when the President announces a controversial decision.

This chapter will focus on three topics: (a) the functions of the polity, (b) the distribution of political participation in American society, and (c) the political ideologies that prevail among various segments of the populace. We will omit the important consideration of the actual distribution of power, because that was the thrust of Chapter 4. Unlike the other institutional chapters, this one will not describe in detail how the political system works (e.g., federal system, checks and balances, rule of law) since American students have been exposed to these facts in elementary and secondary schools.[2]

THE FUNCTIONS OF THE POLITY

The polity must accomplish at least four things if the society is to be maintained. First, it must provide for a relatively stable distribution of power. Power is never equally distributed in a society. Some persons and some roles will have more authority (legitimate power) than others. Thus, the polity legitimates the unequal structure of power, thereby contributing to the maintenance and the predictability of the system.

A second function of the polity is to provide mechanisms for the orderly changing of the system. The polity must, under penalty of anarchy if it fails, provide for the orderly transfer of power. With regard to this function, there is presently a crisis of legitimacy regarding America's political mechanisms. Not only have they been unable to keep up with the accelerated pace of change, but they tend to be intransigent about change. Political parties,* the electoral

* An exception was the restructuring of the Democratic Party in 1972. Remarkable reforms were instituted following the 1968 convention debacle that allowed for minority group representation in relationship to their approximate proportion in society:

	1968	1972
percentage of women	13.0	39.7
percentage of blacks	5.5	15.2
percentage under 30	4.0	21.0

The result was the diminution in the power of the "old guard" party leaders (union leaders, governors, mayors, state committeemen).

college system, and the seniority system in Congress are but a few examples of over-aged and entrenched political mechanisms that defy change. There appears to be a kind of law of inertia operating (the tendency of matter to remain in a fixed condition—either at rest or in motion—without change), and the resulting conditions have caused many persons in American society to question the legitimacy of the system. We will return to this important topic later in this chapter.

PANEL 12–1

"POLITICAL SURVEILLANCE IN THE UNITED STATES"

Source: Frank Donner, "The Theory and Practice of American Political Intelligence," *The New York Review of Books* 16 (April 22, 1971), pp. 27–39.

The government in its desire to maintain law and order has tended to equate dissent with subversion, thereby denying that the demand for social change is based on real social, economic, or political conditions. College dissenters, black liberation groups, union organizers, and other "agitators" have consequently become the targets of political surveillance. Donner has listed the most important federal agencies engaged in intelligence activities:

—the FBI, with an estimated 2,000 agents in the field, together with a huge staff operating a dossier bank of 25 million "personalities,"
—the CIA,
—the Internal Revenue Service (for several weeks in 1970 its agents requested access to the circulation records of public libraries in a number of cities in order to learn the names of borrowers of books on explosives and other "militant and subversive" subjects, a practice which it defended as "just a continual building of information"),
—the Intelligence Division of the Post Office,
—the Secret Service (where names of 50,000 "persons of interest" are on file),
—the Customs Bureau of the Treasury Department,
—the Civil Service Commission (15 million names of "subversive activity" suspects),
—the Immigration and Naturalization Service,
—the Navy, Air Force, Coast Guard,
—the Passport Division of the State Department,
—the Department of Justice Community Relations Service, which feeds information into its computerized Inter-Divisional Intelligence and Information Unit,

A third necessary function of the polity is providing for the welfare of the citizens. This includes protection against outside interference, both militarily and economically. The polity also has the task of trying to promote prosperity, as well as protection from the wide swings of economic cycles, and even protection from floods, famine, and other disasters.

The polity, most important of all, has the function of maintaining order within the society. This includes the resolution of conflict

—civil rights and poverty projects sponsored by the Department of Health, Education and Welfare and the Office of Economic Opportunity. The Executive Department agencies cooperate with and are supplemented by the Congressional anti-subversive committees (pp. 27–28).

Political surveillance occurs at the local level also. The changing role of the police in carrying out surveillance was described a few years ago by Inspector Harry Fox of the Philadelphia Police. In his Senate testimony, he said:

"Police have now become watchdogs and observers of vocal, subversive and revolutionary minded people. This function has been institutionalized in Philadelphia in a civil-disobedience unit composed of selected and highly trained plainclothesmen. They cover all meetings, rallies, lectures, marches, sit-ins, laydowns, fasts, vigils, or any other type of demonstration that has ominous overtones. . . . These officers know by sight the hard core men and women who lead and inspire demonstrations. They know their associates, family ties, techniques, and affiliations with organizations leaning toward Communism both on and off the Attorney General's list. They see them day in and day out recruiting, planning, carrying signs, and verbally assaulting the principles of democracy. Yes, the police role has become one of . . . surveillance, taking photographs, identifying participants, and making records of the events. On this basis, local police are able to piece together this jigsaw puzzle and see the widespread activity of the hard core demonstrators and instigators" (p. 30).

As Donner points out, "The FBI plays a central role in coordinating the intelligence system; it exchanges information with other agencies, performs investigative work for intelligence groups with limited jurisdiction, and trains intelligence agents for service in other agencies. Its intelligence techniques and political standards serve as a model for local operations. It compiles albums of photographs and files of activists which are transmitted to agencies throughout the United States" (pp. 29–30).

between various factions (e.g., racial conflict, management-union conflict), the control of persons who deviate from societal norms, and the regulation of abuses by individuals and corporations.

Social control is inherent in any institution. Education, religion, the family, and the economy each require individuals to behave in certain ways and refrain from others. The polity has this social control function as a primary responsibility. The mechanisms for achieving conformity (the goal of social control) are varied. They can occur subtly in the socialization process, so that persons feel guilty or proud, depending upon their actions. They can occur in the form of rewards to reinforce certain behaviors (medals, prizes, honors, prestige). Most common, however, are the negative sanctions that are enforced by the agents of the government. Punishments such as fines, imprisonment, loss of citizenship, deportation, and death are used to enforce conformity. Fear of punishment is often cited as a powerful deterrent against deviant behavior. The government can raise or lower these fear levels by a number of acts. Surveillance (see Panel 12–1), Congressional anti-subversive probes (e.g., the famous or infamous hearings by Senator Joseph Mc-Carthy in the 1950's), passage of laws requiring loyalty oaths, security clearances, and police harassment are techniques for such a purpose.

While recognizing the necessity of law and law enforcement, we should be aware of two fundamental problems associated with the governmental sanctions on private citizens. The first can be stated in the form of a question—Who monitors the monitors? There are always the possibilities that some of the agents of social control are corrupt (accepting graft) while others may abuse their authority (e.g., police brutality, arbitrary justice).

The second and related problem is the danger of equating dissent with lawlessness and treason. Persons, groups, and political parties in power, even in a democracy, tend to want to remain in power. They tend to equate their own goals with that of the society. When faced with a threat, they tend to become extremely aggressive, and will act without hesitation to undermine democratic rights. All efforts that challenge the appropriateness of the government's policies are interpreted as giving aid and comfort to its enemies. Serious criticism is thus defined as treachery.* This desire to keep the status quo results in two governmental activities to enhance stability—propaganda and repression of dissent. In the first in-

---

* These insights come from a penetrating examination by Robert Michels of the tendency for democratic organizations to become oligarchic—"the iron law of oligarchy."[3]

stance, the government spends millions of dollars presenting its version of history and politics to Americans. One example of this, as noted in Chapter 4, is that the Pentagon spends millions of dollars on public relations and maintains hundreds of lobbyists to deal with Congress.[4] Free films and speakers are supplied by the Defense Department to schools and various organizations. Another example is the President's use of free television in prime time to win public opinion to his view.

The repression of dissent is especially offensive because it is unAmerican. The Bill of Rights protects citizens if they wish to dissent. As the esteemed historian Henry Steele Commager has stated,

> Corruption of language is often a first sign of a deeper malaise of mind and spirit, and it is ominous that invasions of liberty are carried on, today, in the name of constitutionalism, and the impairment of due process, in the name of Law and Order. Here it takes the form of a challenge to the great principle of the superiority of the civil to the military authority. Here it is the intimidation of the press and television by threats both subtle and blatant, there of resort to the odious doctrine of "intent" to punish anti-war demonstrators. Here it is the use of the dangerous weapon of censorship, overt and covert, to silence troublesome criticism, there the abuse of power of punishment by contempt of court. The thrust is everywhere the same, and so too the animus behind it: to equate dissent with lawlessness and nonconformity with treason. The purpose of those who are prepared to sweep aside our ancient guarantees of freedom is to blot out those great problems that glare upon us from every horizon, and pretend that if we refuse to acknowledge them, they will somehow go away. It is to argue that discontent is not an honest expression of genuine grievances but of willfulness, or perversity, or perhaps of the crime of being young, and that if it can only be stifled, we can restore harmony to our distracted society.[5]

POLITICAL PARTICIPATION IN AMERICAN SOCIETY

Of interest in a democracy are questions such as—who votes and how do different categories of voters vote? A basic assumption of sociologists intrigued with voting behavior is, in the words of Lewis Coser, that:

> Political views are not arrived at through dispassionate study or in isolation—they are products of the associations men form with one another. . . .

> . . . [E]ven though certain attitudes and values may be partly formed in the early stages of life, they continue to be molded, and remolded, in later years. The variety of groups with which a man affiliates in his later life, his occupational associates, his religious or class loyalties, his ethnic affiliation, all these, and not only his specifically political associations, in some measure determine his political orientations.[6]

Thus, a number of variables are assumed to be important in individual decisions (to vote or not vote, to work actively for the election or defeat of a particular candidate, to vote a strict party line or mixed). The list Coser has provided is not exhaustive. Age, sex, region, size of community, political events, also affect political decision making at the individual level.

In sociology the unit of analysis is not the individual but a collectivity. This approach is not concerned with explaining individual voting decisions, but rather accounting for the differences in rates, if consistent, between different social groups (organizations) or social categories (i.e., persons with similar social characteristics). So, comparisons are made among social classes, occupational categories, regions, and communities. These comparisons result in group rates which do not allow us to predict the behavior of any one individual from the group—only probability statements (e.g., the greater the number of organizational memberships, the greater the likelihood of one's participation in an election).

Sociologists have one other interest in political behavior—the collective behavior aspects. Those include public opinion, the effects of manipulation of the masses through propaganda and techniques of crowd manipulation, and social contagion such as the "bandwagon effect." Sociologists interested in these phenomena focus on shifting attitudes, shifting allegiances, the coalescing of public opinion in the light of important events that occur within or outside the society. Events such as an assassination attempt, a decision to intensify or decrease the war, or an increase in protests tend to activate particular categories of persons. Additionally, the way a particular candidate or issue fires the imagination of a portion of the electorate is also of interest.

The empirical research on the effects of social variables on political behavior are consistent (we will note some of these findings shortly). The people are, for the most part, predictable. Their social "locations" (age, sex, race, social class) have influenced their interpretation of events, issues, and candidates in a particular direction for a long enough period that they have developed partisan attachments (political party identification and/or adherence to a particular set of political beliefs). The stability of party identification is seen in Table 12–1.

These data from Table 12–1 were taken from national samples in the fall prior to each of four presidential elections. Although the first two surveys preceded the election of a Republican President and the last two preceded a Democrat's election, the percentages are remarkably stable.

At least two exceptions temper the assertion that political behavior is stable. First, there is the obvious fact that some persons do change their opinions. Shifts in loyalties or beliefs may occur because of persons who have changed their economic situation or have moved to a different locality. Changes may also have occurred for idiosyncratic reasons or because of the intrusion of particular events, issues, and candidates.

In the 1972 election, for example, political behavior was unstable because of the way in which the two candidates were perceived. Party identification made little difference, as evidenced by the unprecedented level of ticket-splitting in that election. While President Nixon was winning in a landslide (61 percent), his party had a net loss of two senators. In several states he won over two thirds of the votes, but the Democrats elected a Governor or a Senator by an equally wide margin. Even in the home state of the Democratic candidate, South Dakota, President Nixon won, but the usually Republican state elected a Democratic Governor and Senator. Analysts of that election are in basic agreement that the presidential

TABLE 12–1.   The Distribution of Party Identification in the United States

Party Identification	1952	1956	1960	1964
Strong Democrat	22%	21%	21%	24%
Weak Democrat	25	23	25	22
Independent Democrat	10	7	8	7
Independent	5	9	8	10
Independent Republican	7	8	7	5
Weak Republican	14	14	13	17
Strong Republican	13	19	14	11
Apolitical (do not know)	4	3	4	4

Source: Adapted from Philip E. Converse, "The Concept of a Normal Vote," Elections and the Political Order, Angus Campbell, Philip E. Converse, Warren E. Miller, and Donald E. Stokes (New York: John Wiley and Sons, Inc., 1966), p. 13.

387

candidates made the difference, not party labels. McGovern was believed to be too radical, too permissive, too naive, and too vacillating, while Nixon was viewed typically as stable, decisive, and politically astute.

The second imponderable are those persons who are faced with "cross-pressures." This refers to the situation when the motives affecting a political decision are incompatible.[7] These cross-pressures may be attitudinal or affiliational. An example of an attitudinal cross-pressure is when the potential voter agrees with one party or candidate on foreign policy but prefers the other on domestic policy. If his race benefits from the policies of one party but his occupation is favorably affected by the policies of the other, he is faced with affiliative cross-pressures. The possibilities for affiliative cross-pressures are numerous between the differing views and/or interests between one's family members, friends, job associates, church members, or clients.

The effects of cross-pressures are well documented. Persons faced with these conflicting political pressures tend to split their ticket, make up their minds late in the campaign, and quite often do not vote at all. Although persons faced with cross-pressures are somewhat unpredictable in their political behavior, other categories of persons are not. In the remainder of this section we will examine the voting patterns of several important social categories—social class, age, and race-ethnicity.

Social Class and Political Behavior

William Erbe found some 18 studies which showed that socioeconomic status affects an individual's propensity to participate in political activities.

> Whether the specific measure used is income, education, occupation, home ownership, rent, race, some status hierarchy of religious affiliation, or some combination of any or all of these indices into a measure of "social class," the results are most uniform: the higher the social status, the more likely to register, to vote, to be interested in politics, to discuss politics, to belong to politically relevant organizations, and to attempt to influence the political views of others.[8]

Table 12–2 provides one example of this generalization. It is an analysis of the relationship between structural variables and political involvement in a sample of adults in four Wisconsin cities (N = 1,635). The dependent variable (political involvement) consists of the degree of interest in political activities, amount of information, attendance at meetings, and if one voted or not in the local election. To be considered high in political involvement, one had to be in the upper half of at least three of these four areas. Only 28 percent of the sample met these criteria.

Several important and related implications are found in the data in Table 12–2. Local elections are notorious for their low turnouts. This means that few of the poor vote, while a much higher proportion of the better-off vote—the result of which is *de facto* community leadership for the well-to-do. This does not bode well for the poor, because well-off and secure persons view the problems of the community and the solutions to these problems very differently. One source of the political apathy of the less well-to-do is that they see no reason for voting. Most communities do not have proportional representation or even district representation. The poor, therefore, almost never have a candidate who will speak for them.

Blue-Collar Politics

In 1968, ten million Americans (13.5 percent of the voting electorate) voted for George Wallace. In 1972, the day after he was shot by a would-be assassin, Wallace won over 50 percent of the Democratic primary vote in Michigan and in Maryland. His strength,

TABLE 12–2.   Local Political Involvement and Social Status

Status Variable	*Percent high in local political involvement.*		
	Eleven or less years	High school graduate	Some college or more
Education:	13%	23%	43%
	Manual	Nonmanual	
Occupation:	16%	37%	
	Less than $6,000	$6,000 or more	
Income:	16%	32%	

Source: Adapted from Robert R. Alford and Harry M. Scoble, "Sources of Local Political Involvement," *American Political Science Review* 62 (December, 1968), p. 1195.

although primarily southern, has grown in the North. Lipset and Raab report some data that hint at his appeal in the North in Table 12–3.

These data in Table 12–3 suggest that Wallace's greatest support came from blue-collar workers, with no more than a high school education, making between $3,000 and $10,000. These findings are supported by Pettigrew and his associates, who studied Gary, Indiana, and Cleveland. They found in Gary, for example, that men with annual family incomes between $7,900 and $10,000 were six times more likely to prefer Wallace than those families under $5,000. "Wallaceites combine low educational attainment and modest occupational statuses with relatively high incomes."[9]

But why does a candidate like George Wallace appeal to relatively well-off blue-collar workers? For one thing, Wallace addressed himself to the "common man." His speeches typically pictured the common man as a victim—a victim of the federal bureaucrats, intellectuals, mass media, student demonstrators, and the welfare chiselers. Wallace's appeal was simple—"us common folks against them" (see Panel 12–2). Some clues as to why this appeal worked is found in the survey conducted by *Newsweek* of what they called the "white majority"—whites with annual incomes between $5,000 and $15,000.[10] They found this category, which represents 61 per-

TABLE 12–3.   1968 Presidential Voting in the Non-South

Status Variable	Percentage Voted for Wallace	Seriously Considered Wallace	Total % for Wallace
Occupation			
Non-manual	5%	5%	10%
Manual	9	13	22
Education			
Grade School or less	7	10	17
High School or less	7	9	17
Some College	5	4	9
Income			
Less than $3,000	5	5	11
$3,000–$6,999	10	9	19
$7,000–$9,999	6	11	17
$10,000–$14,999	6	8	14
$15,000 plus	3	7	10

Source: Adapted from Seymour Martin Lipset and Earl Raab, "The Wallace Whitelash," *Trans-action* 7 (December, 1969), p. 28.

cent of Americans, as very bitter and resentful for the following reasons:

1. This category feels that they pay the bulk of the taxes, since the rich have the loopholes and the poor do not pay.
2. Since they tend to be on fixed incomes, they are the hardest hit by inflation.
3. Many are home owners and have had to sacrifice a good deal for this privilege. They fear that blacks moving in their neighborhoods will lower the value of their homes. Persons in this income bracket live in neighborhoods that are the most susceptible to black inroads, since the homes are in a modest price range.
4. They feel that the government's priorities are all wrong when they spend for war, space, foreign aid, and welfare.
5. They fear change. The cherished virtues are being attacked— the work ethic, patriotism, premarital chastity, gratitude to parents for their sacrifices, traditional religion.
6. They feel that the persons in power cannot or will not cope with the crises facing America—urban crisis, international monetary crisis, crisis in international relations, inflation, unemployment, lawlessness.
7. There is a feeling of powerlessness among these persons. Somehow powerful others make the decisions that determine the course of events.
8. This group is insecure financially because of the fear of layoffs, strikes, plant relocations, and automation.

In sum, this category, although quite heterogeneous, is united by its discontent. They are increasingly seeing themselves as an oppressed majority. That is why many of them favor the populist rhetoric of George Wallace.* The desire of many of these persons is to restore *order*. They want to bring back the time-honored values of love of country, hard work, sexual morality, traditional religion;

---

* While blue-collar workers tended to favor the populist ideology and policies of George Wallace, they did not find the populist rhetoric of George McGovern appealing. When Wallace was sidelined from the 1972 campaign, his supporters went en masse to President Nixon, the candidate most likely to favor the wealthy. The reason goes beyond populism to fear and racism. McGovern represented change in defense policies, in domestic priorities, and in the distribution of wealth. While such policies should have encouraged blue-collar workers, it brought ridicule instead. Most important were the changes McGovern advocated in the area of race relations. Busing to promote integrated schools, racial quotas in jobs, and increased welfare were perceived as reforms that would help blacks at the expense of white blue-collar workers. The irony of this is that the very persons who would have benefitted from McGovern's plans to redistribute the wealth and to make government more responsive to the needs of the common man chose rather the candidate of the status quo. Apparently economic grievances about the system were outweighed by fears about McGovern's remedies for those grievances.

they want to halt crime; they want to stop the revolutionaries (black militants, student protestors, demonstrating clerics); they want to prosecute criminals, anarchists, and communists. In other words, they wish to stop the erosion of law and order.

Many of the persons experiencing these fears and concerns seek a candidate outside the mainstream who will bring about meaningful change. George Wallace is perceived as that candidate. There are two additional reasons for his appeal among the blue-collar category. First, there is evidence that they believe the condition of the average man is getting worse, not better. Pettigrew and his associates found that 42 percent of the Wallace supporters agreed there is slippage in their condition, while only 33 percent of the Nixon backers and 25 percent of the Humphrey backers did so. This is why they fear change, why they wish to restore order.*

---

* This phenomenon is called "relative deprivation." It is the psychological mechanism that explains why status inconsistency (low education, moderate occupation, and relative high income) predisposes persons to the radical right.[11]

PANEL 12–2

"THE APPEAL OF GEORGE WALLACE"

Source: News release from the Wallace Campaign Headquarters, Montgomery, Alabama, 1972.

The following are a series of quotes from George Wallace during his campaign for the Democratic Party nomination for President in 1972. These quotes are representative of the grievances that Wallace and his constituency were registering with the establishment. Busing, welfare, foreign aid, and the decline of familiar American values and morality were his targets, and the "average man in America" was the source of his political clout.

"The Democratic Party leaders in Washington have paid attention to the intellectual snobs and catered to the exotic for too long. They have forgotten the working American who pays his taxes and holds this country together. They only remember him on tax paying day."

"The working man is tired of seeing his tax dollars wasted away on foreign aid projects thousands of miles away in countries that aid our enemies and attack us in the United Nations. He is tired of paying twice his share of the tax burden while the super-rich with their multi-billion and multi-million dollar foundations remain sheltered almost free from taxation."

"The average man is tired of watching his country relegated to a second-rate military power while he knows that the only way to insure

Another possible explanation for the attractiveness of candidates like George Wallace for blue-collar workers is the phenomenon of "working-class authoritarianism." There is a good deal of evidence that blue-collar workers are especially intolerant.[12] Of all occupation categories, they tend to be most opposed to civil liberties (i.e., the freedoms expressed in the Bill of Rights), less tolerant of deviant behavior, and most likely to place persons and ideas into either one category or another (i.e., no gray area or indecision).

Three reasons for the working class having these tendencies are posited by researchers in this area. In the first place, they lack economic security; therefore change is especially distasteful. Second, they are less likely to participate in formal organizations and less likely to be interested in elections and to vote. Each of these characteristics is related to attitudes toward democracy. Third, blue-collar workers are the most likely of any occupational category to be unsatisfied with their jobs and therefore alienated (see Table 12–4).

Table 12–4 shows a wide variance between professional and working-class occupations in job satisfaction. Within the latter

a lasting and meaningful peace is to be so strong militarily that our enemies will only want to talk."

"He also realizes the economy can best be stimulated through a reduction in taxes, which will result in increased buying power for the average man, thereby creating a demand for more consumer goods. This will create more jobs, reduce unemployment, and stimulate the economy of our country without runaway inflation."

"The average working man is tired of his children being trifled with by social schemers who write guidelines while sitting a thousand miles away. He wants quality education for all without discrimination, but he wants an immediate halt to this senseless forced busing of public school children."

"The average man is sick and tired of seeing his hard-earned tax dollars go to pay those who refuse to work. I have always been for helping the handicapped, the maimed, the sick, the elderly and those in need, but if we continue to pay those able bodied who refuse to work, it is going to break us as a nation and destroy our moral fiber."

"We should use the money we are giving away and pouring down rat holes overseas to solve the problems in our cities—use it for rapid transit, for increased social security benefits to our senior citizens, and to solve pollution and environmental problems."

"The people can do anything because the politicians will listen to the people. The national politicians have their eyes and ears turned to the people now, and they will hear clearly when the people send them a message by electing George Wallace."

category especially, assembly-line work appears to be very distasteful. The worker in that capacity has little room for advancement, he is easily replaced, and he has little control over the pace of work. Lipsitz found when comparing assembly-line workers with two other blue-collar jobs—repair and skilled maintenance workers—that the former were the least sympathetic and tolerant of the three groups. They more strongly blame the poor for being in poverty, they approved the dropping of atomic bombs on Japan, they recommended a policy of toughness toward Russia, and they were more likely to favor capital punishment.

> These findings are worth noting largely because they tend to confirm previous conclusions about authoritarianism and social class. Within this group of workers, punitive attitudes are associated with work frustration and lack of control over work life. These facts point to the possible significance of everyday frustrations in conditioning attitudes toward out-groups.[13]

While candidates with the programs and ideology of a Wallace find most of their support among blue-collar workers, this category is strongly identified with the Democratic Party. In the past, unions have delivered the vast majority of their vote for Democratic candidates, who in turn worked for legislation and policies that benefitted organized labor. In 1968, for example, Richard Nixon, the Republican candidate for President, received but 33 percent of the blue-collar vote. The 1972 election, however, found Nixon getting 50 percent of the votes from this category. The AFL-CIO went on

TABLE 12–4.   Proportion in Various Occupations Who Would Choose Same Kind of Work if Beginning Career Again

Professional Occupation	%	Working-Class Occupation	%
Mathematicians	91	Skilled printers	52
Physicists	89	Paper workers	52
Biologists	89	Skilled automobile workers	41
Chemists	86	Skilled Steelworkers	41
Lawyers	83	Textile workers	31
Journalists	82	Unskilled steelworkers	21
		Unskilled automobile workers	16

Source: Robert Blauner, "Work Satisfaction and Industrial Trends in Modern Society," Labor and Trade Unionism, Walter Galenson and S. M. Lipset (eds.), (New York: John Wiley & Sons, 1960), p. 343.

record as not favoring either presidential candidate, while a number of their affiliates and the powerful Teamsters Union actually supported President Nixon. This switch occurred for a variety of reasons: (1) McGovern had alienated many Union officials; (2) the working class were especially suspicious of the counterculture issues that McGovern more or less espoused (amnesty, abortion, marijuana); and (3) the working class feared social changes that would aid blacks. Out of this mixture, President Nixon emerged as the champion of the status quo, as the advocate of a strong defense and peace with honor, and the leader who favored the time-honored values of the work ethic, law and order, morality, and patriotism.

Nixon's inroads into the blue-collar vote most probably do not signal a trend away from the Democratic Party, but rather a reaction against a candidate whom they feared. The defection of this many blue-collar workers to a Republican president suggests that in the near future the Democratic Party must appeal to "middle Americans" if they desire victory.

Youth and Politics

In 1970, the 26th Amendment to the Constitution was ratified, lowering the voting age to 18. This meant that in 1972, approximately 25 million persons were newly eligible to cast a vote (this includes persons from 18 to 24). If any group ever held the swing vote in an election, it was that group in 1972 (since they comprised about 20 percent of the electorate). Moreover, youth had the chance to have a special impact in local elections, particularly in college communities. At first glance, this group would appear to lean toward the Democratic Party and candidates that espouse liberal causes. This impression arises from the publicity that college students command. Fully two-thirds of the 25 million persons eligible to vote for the first time, however, were not in school. These persons would tend to be more traditional in political outlooks. But youth itself is an interesting variable in political behavior. Empirical research has shown that youth has certain political propensities. First, there is a probability that the youngest voters will be more liberal than those senior to them. Table 12–5 presents data from two Gallup polls (samples of about 1,600 cases in each) taken just prior to the presidential election in 1964 that illustrate this point.

In each of the cases presented in Table 12–5, the data show the younger citizens to be the more liberal. These data, coupled with the influx of 25 million possible new young voters in 1972 appeared to bode well for the Democratic Party. There is contrary evidence, however, which demonstrates that youth tend to take extreme political positions of the left *and* the right. Analysis of the 1968 election reveals that those young people (under 30) who were interested in politics were more likely than the older voters to reject the political mainstream. For example, Lipset and Raab reported the findings of Gallup and Harris polls conducted in October, 1968, which revealed that 25 percent of persons 21 to 29 in age were for George Wallace, while only 20 percent of persons in older categories favored that political conservative.[14] *Fortune* magazine conducted a poll of persons aged 18 to 24 also in October of 1968 and found that education was a most significant variable affecting the appeal of George Wallace among young people. Whereas 25 percent of those not in college were found to favor Wallace, only 7 percent of college students preferred that candidate.[15] Students, moreover, were found to be likely to lean toward the opposite end of the political spectrum from Wallace—radical left politics. But while the most visible students are radicals of the left, it should be remembered that the state of campus opinion cannot be inferred from observing demonstrations. Even during the heyday of campus revolt (1965 to

TABLE 12–5.   Age and Political Attitudes

Political Attitude	21–29	Age 30–49	50+
Ideology			
Very liberal	47%	44%	42%
Moderately liberal	22	23	19
Middle of the road	23	20	21
Moderately conservative	5	7	9
Very conservative	3	6	9
Government Power			
Too much power	19	26	29
About right	40	37	34
Should use more	36	31	28
Party Identification			
Republican	19	20	31
Democratic	47	52	48
Independent	31	25	19

Source: Adapted from Lloyd A. Free and Haley Cantril, *The Political Beliefs of Americans: A Study of Public Opinion* (New York: Simon and Schuster, 1968), pp. 216, 218, and 233.

1970), only about 10 to 15 percent of the students were "activists."[16] Thus we may conclude that while young persons are more extreme in their political wishes than their elders (to the left if college-educated and to the right if not), the overwhelming majority of young persons, whether blue-collar workers or college students, fit in the political mainstream. These persons accept the system and seek only to find their place in it. But this greater tendency for youth to take more extreme political positions than their elders should not be taken lightly, since they have such great potential to affect the outcome of elections. Lipset has an excellent statement of the possible reasons why youth are so inclined to zeal rather than to caution.

> The propensity of youth to zealously pursue an ideal can be seen as a direct outgrowth of the socialization process. Societies teach youth to adhere to the basic values of the social system in absolute terms. This emphasis on absolute values, on idealism, has understandable consequences for the beliefs of youth.
> The real world, of course, necessarily deviates considerably from the ideal, and part of the process of maturing is to learn to function in a world of conflicting values, roles, interests, and demands. Compromises which are dictated by contradictory pressures and are justified in the eyes of many adults are viewed by idealistic youth as violations of basic morality. Young people tend to be committed to ideals rather than institutions. Hence events which point up the gap between ideals and reality often stimulate them to action, though cynicism and withdrawal occur as well if they see no appropriate way to act.[17]

While youth often choose commitment, some, as Lipset noted in the above quote, are apathetic when it comes to politics. Research has shown that young persons are the least likely (tied with the elderly) age category to vote.

> During the 1960s, for example, only about half of those who were between twenty-one and twenty-four and qualified to vote cast ballots in Presidential elections. The turnout was around 66 percent for those twenty-five to thirty-four years old, but even that is still below the 75 percent participation by people thirty-five to sixty-five years old, and only equals the turnout of those over sixty-five.[18]

But is the new generation of youth different from their predecessors? Panel 12–3 makes the case that the new generation may help usher in "the new politics."

The youth vote in the 1972 election did not have the impact

nationally that had been anticipated. McGovern won but 52 percent of their votes. Several factors probably accounted for McGovern not sweeping two-thirds of the youth vote as had once been predicted. First, many potential voters were apathetic because the nation was so overwhelmingly pro-Nixon (or anti-McGovern). Second, among many liberal college youth, McGovern lost popularity because he backed away from his original views on marijuana, abortion, and $1,000 for every citizen. Moreover, he proved to be like other poli-

PANEL 12–3

"THE NEW GENERATION OF VOTERS"

Source: Frederick G. Dutton, *Changing Sources of Power: American Politics in the 1970s* (New York: McGraw-Hill Book Company, 1971), especially Chapter 3, "The Politics of the New Generation." Dutton was a senior advisor to George McGovern in his 1972 Presidential campaign.

In 1964 over 10.5 million persons became eligible to vote for the first time. In 1968 this number jumped to about 12 million. The number in 1972, however, was in excess of 25 million, thus giving youth the possibility of having a tremendous impact on the direction of politics in American society. But are these young persons different from the youth of earlier times? Dutton has cited a number of ways in which this new generation is considerably different from their predecessors and therefore will be at the forefront of a shift toward "the new politics." Moreover, he has argued that because they are different, they will not ease up as they grow older. In Dutton's view, this new generation is different for the following reasons:

1. These persons knew the Depression only as an episode in history textbooks. They grew up, rather, in a prolonged period of affluence. One consequence of this is that this generation is significantly less concerned with economic matters and more enthused with social problems than earlier generations.
2. This generation is the first baby crop to be nurtured by television. Television gave these persons heavy doses of violence, fantasy, and vicarious participation in instant history (including the civil rights struggle and the war in Indo-China).
3. This generation is more educated in length of schooling and degree of acceleration and enrichment than any previous group. In 1950 only 20 percent of high school graduates attended college, while in the 1970s, well over half will at least spend some time in college. One consequence of this is that the more educated the individual, the more likely to be informed and active in politics as well as to favor civil rights, civil liberties, and social welfare.

ticians in making supplicating visits to Mayor Daley, Lyndon Johnson, and Wall Street. Third, young people in 1972 made their political choices much like older voters, being affected by similar events and propaganda in similar ways. The centrist position of President Nixon was obviously appealing to many young people and most of their elders.

But what is the fate of the "new politics?" Did it die with McGovern's electoral burial? Clearly, Americans in 1972 were not

4. This generation is the first to participate solely in an unpopular war. The older generation may not have cared for the American involvement in Indo-China either, but they could recall the popular causes of World War II and the Korean War. As a result of this difference, the new generation is much more likely to question governmental policies and not to take their patriotism as seriously as their elders.
5. These persons were the first to grow up entirely within the setting of the nuclear age.
6. These persons have experienced change at a much more rapid and accelerated pace than their elders.

These fundamental differences in the generations lead Dutton to predict that the "new politics" will prevail. Some of the shifts that will likely occur are, to quote Dutton:

—While the prevailing personal goal of Americans in recent decades has been *security*, the objective may gradually shift not back to the older cry for *opportunity* but to *fulfillment*.

—While there have been pretensions recently of striving for the Great Society and a law-and-order society, the growing want among young people is simply a *humane society*.

—While there has long been a preoccupation with *national* purpose, the rising concern is again with *individual* purpose. And not even *purpose* so much as *being*.

—While most practical attention has long been on *special-interest politics*, the scope must be expanded not just in rhetoric but in substance to include the elusive and difficult *politics of values*. And while the primary emphasis of politics and government has long been on *programs and laws*, the balance is unmistakably shifting toward a concern with *process, variety, and spontaneity*.

—While the public frame of reference has long been *city, state, and nation*, the loyalty evoking increasing response is *mankind*.

—While the public pace which has long been extolled is *gradual progress*, there will be increasing insistence on *now* (pp. 55–56).

ready for change. The youth were, but only by a narrow margin. If this generation truly is significantly different, as Dutton suggested in Panel 12–3, then they will presumably remain different as they grow older. Moreover, each new election will bring additional millions into the electorate with an outlook which may favor a more humane and democratic society and the reforms necessary to achieve those goals. The "old politics" of clichés, smoke-filled rooms, and power by the special interests will die very hard. The result will doubtless be some form of synthesis forged out of the reaction of powerful individuals and groups to the thrusts of the idealistic young, the demands for equality by minority groups, and the Wallace movement offensive.

Race and Ethnicity

Americans have typically believed in the "melting pot hypothesis," that is, Americans of all origins are becoming more alike through the process of assimilation. If anything, however, race and ethnicity have increased in salience to members and non-members alike in recent years.[19] Most of the thrust of the black power movement, for example, was to instill pride in being black and in having a unique heritage. So, too, with the American Indians, Chicanos, Jews, Italians, Poles, the Irish, and others.

Although there are important differences between these groups, several generalizations can be made about the role of ethnic groups in the American political system. First, as a category, ethnic (used broadly to include race as well) minorities are less likely to be interested enough to vote in elections than members of the majority. This is partly a social class phenomenon, since ethnics are found disproportionately in the lower socioeconomic strata. It is also the result of discrimination. Many feel their input will not make a difference in changing an unjust system.

A second generalization is that ethnics have overwhelmingly identified with the Democratic Party. This party is believed to be the one most partial to the interests of the "common man" through its support of unions and social security.

Although the above has been true, ethnicity itself may often transcend political party affiliation (see Panel 12–4). Black Democrats will likely cross over to vote for a black Republican over a white Democrat. For this reason, political parties, especially in urban places, carefully provide a slate of candidates with the right balance of ethnic representation.

Just as ethnics tend to vote for persons of the same social identity, they vote against persons because they are from either the majority group (WASP) or from some competitive ethnic group. Conversely, ethnicity is also a salient variable for persons who are WASPS, but most often negatively. Antipathy for blacks, Jews, Poles, or whatever, is, unfortunately, the reason for voting for many.

Finally, ethnic groups are an important source for changing the system. Because they are often victims of discriminatory institutions, ethnic groups tend to produce radical leadership. Leaders like Cesar Chavez or Martin Luther King, Jr., can move their people to act in concert, thereby creating power where there was none. Sometimes through violence, sometimes through moral persuasion, leaders of deprived ethnic groups have forced the system to change (albeit grudgingly).

POLITICAL IDEOLOGIES

At the end of the 1950's, sociologist Daniel Bell proclaimed the death of ideology:

> For the radical intellectual who had articulated the revolutionary impulses of the past century and a half, all this has meant an end to chiliastic hopes, to millenarianism, to apocalyptic thinking—and to ideology. For ideology, which once was a road to action, has come to be a dead end.[20]

Obviously Bell did not foresee the ideological decade of the 1960's. The civil rights movement, the black power movement, the student protest movement, and the counterattacks by the protectors of the status quo were in sharp contrast to the apathy that characterized the 1950's. At the risk of being wrong, as Daniel Bell was for predicting from the recent past, this book's author believes that we will continue to live in an age of competing ideologies. The increasingly swift tempo of change that characterizes society is going to increase the probability of diversity—diversity in life style and beliefs. The chance for increased polarization in the near future appears relatively strong.[21]

This section on ideology is an appropriate ending to the chapter on politics and to a book on American society for several reasons. First, political ideologies (i.e., distinctive belief systems) have an impact on the institutions of the society (the degree of structure in the polity, assumptions about the economy, tolerance for deviance, and the "necessity" of inequality). Second, they are the source for action (and inaction). They drive people to strive for certain things and to defend against the encroachment of others. As such, they are perhaps the most important source of social change. Third, ideology is not only a prime mover, but it serves as a "perceptual screen." Persons, groups, and political parties perceive events, persons, and issues in ways shaped by their ideology. Moreover, these perceptions, as they are shaped by certain assumptions about the nature of man, suggest the source of blame for social problems and hence the way they should be solved. Fourth, the degree to which people hold any political ideology affects the way they perceive the structure. If they are students of society (whether professional sociologists or amateurs), their political ideology affects research (not in objectiv-

PANEL 12–4

"THE PERSISTENCE OF ETHNIC VOTING"

Source: Robert Lorinkas, Brett Hawkins, and Stephen Edwards, "The Persistence of Ethnic Voting in Rural and Urban Areas," Social Science Quarterly 49 (March, 1969), pp. 891–899.

In an effort to test the salience of ethnicity in voting patterns, the researchers asked Polish respondents in Chicago and in a rural area in southern Illinois to fill out a ballot that included, among other things, a list of fictitious candidates for a fictitious office. The Chicago sample was asked to list their preference between Stanley J. Lipinski and Michael E. Harper for "Sanitary Canal District Committeeman." The rural sample was asked to choose between these same "candidates" except the office was "Southern Illinois University Board of Trustees." One-third of the ballots labelled Lipinski a Democrat, one-third a Republican, and one-third had no party labels. Candidate Harper was always listed as a member of the opposite party except on the ballots where no labels were provided.

The use of fictitious candidates is a useful technique, since the respondents cannot be influenced by the candidate's personality, office prestige, or short-term election issues. This allows the researcher to control for the variables that are essential to the research—candidate ethnicity and political party.

The findings for the Lipinski-Harper "election" are in Table 12–6.

ity, hopefully, but in problem selection and interpretation). At any rate, people should recognize the impact of their own ideas on what they perceive "out there in the real world."

A final reason for ending this book with a section on political ideology is that the distribution of power, the role of the economy, and the belief about inequality are all integral parts of a political ideology—and these have been special foci of this book.

The remainder of this section will be devoted to the political ideologies that are most prominent in contemporary American society. By necessity we will have to paint each of these with broad brush strokes, acknowledging that not all adherents to a particular ideological label would agree totally. We will examine five ideologies, starting with the dominant one, "capitalism-liberalism." Two reform ideologies, "reform liberalism" and "conservatism" will be compared to the mainstream ideology. Finally, we will examine revolutionary ideologies from the political left ("The New Left") and the right ("The Radical Right").

TABLE 12–6. The Effects of Ethnicity and Party Labels in a Fictitious Election

Percent Voting for Lipinski as:

Type of Ethnic	Democrat	Republican	No Label
Urban Ethnics			87.2%
Voting Democratic	61.7%	23.5%	
Voting Republican	38.3	76.5	
Rural Ethnics			65.5
Voting Democratic	65.5	56.3	
Voting Republican	34.5	43.7	

There are two important findings from these data. First, in the absence of party labels, ethnic voting increases. Second, urban ethnics find ethnicity to be more salient than do rural ethnics. The rural ethnics, although somewhat partial to Polish candidates, are much more affected by political party affiliation. There is one important consideration that may account for this difference. Urban ethnics are much more in competition with other ethnic groups. They also have formed their own communities with ethnic churches, radio programs, veterans' organizations, and newspapers—all of which contribute to the reinforcement of ethnic awareness and the saliency of "us versus them."

The Orthodox Ideology—Capitalism-Liberalism

This is the ideology held by the majority of Americans, including Republicans and Democrats alike. It has dominated the political process in the United States throughout the twentieth century.

This ideology accepts the status quo. The class structure, the economic system, the political system are judged to be proper, since they have combined to create an affluent society characterized by freedom, individualism, civil liberties, due process of law, and democracy. It is believed, therefore, that social change is acceptable only by working through the existing societal institutions. Change occurs most frequently through compromise and bargaining between competing legitimate interest groups. Law and order (stability within the system) are of utmost importance.

The economic system, although mixed, is primarily capitalist. Great affluence has been accomplished ("the greatest good for the greatest number") by individuals seeking their own ends with a minimum of governmental influence. The government's main activities are to provide a good climate for business by protecting American interests at home and abroad.

Reform Ideology I: Conservatism

Although there are several strands of conservatism, there is agreement on several key points. First, there is a tremendous respect for the past; next, a belief in the Constitution, the Bible, and other sources that provide *the* set of principles by which man should be guided. These are eternal truths by which current policies and programs are measured (and found to lack a perfect fit). Among these principles are the importance of private property, freedom, and respect for authority. These principles lead its adherents to strongly favor laissez-faire capitalism, to accept social inequality as the fruits of competition and hard work, and to rigidly oppose socialism and communism.

This ideology is for the most part reform-oriented (we will examine the revolutionary segment later). Although it grudgingly accepts some use of the government for social purposes, it is reformist because it seeks to shift the government to programs and policies consonant with conservative ideology.

Reform Ideology II: Reform Liberalism

This ideology, which could also be called "democratic socialism," is impatient with the status quo, with compromise, and with society's inability to cope adequately with social problems. This impatience has not led to the advocacy of overthrowing the system; hence it is categorized as an ideology of reforming, not transforming, the established order.

This ideology emphasizes equality. There is less stress on self-interest and more on group goals. For this ideology, unlike the conservative one, human rights supersede property rights.

A second tenet of this ideology is the acute concern for the social problems of poverty, racism, pollution, and war, along with the conviction that established procedures cannot or will not solve these problems. Hence, there is a willingness to attempt new governmental programs for social improvement, and most importantly, for the reduction of inequality.

Revolutionary Ideology I: The Radical Right

Since the early 1950's there has been a resurgence of extremist conservative groups. Organizations such as the John Birch Society, the Christian Crusade, the Christian Nationalist Crusade, the Minutemen, the National States' Rights Party, and the American Nazi Party have emerged, each with a fanatic following of varying size and importance.[22] Although these organizations differ somewhat in beliefs, we can summarize a number of views they have in common. First, they reject the present political system. They reject the government's use of compromise; they reject the government's playing into the hands of the Communists; they question the integrity and patriotism of those who lead the government (and other institutions such as the churches, and the schools). Furthermore, they reject those governmental programs designed to solve social problems. They warn that the moral fiber of the United States is breaking down (as evidenced by the permissive climate where anything goes). For each of these groups there is a specific enemy or enemies. Generally their enemies are the Communists, the plutocrats, the intellectuals, the corrupt government, foreigners, Jews, blacks, and Catholics. Whoever the enemy, the collapse of the country is believed to be imminent. This collapse was blueprinted by Lenin and is about to be precipitated by a vast network of Commu-

PANEL 12–5

"THE VALUES OF THE NEW LEFT"

Source: "The Port Huron Statement," *How Democratic Is America?* Robert A. Goldwin (ed.), (Chicago: Rand McNally & Company, 1971), pp. 5–8.

The following is a selection from "The Port Huron Statement," the first official statement of the Students for a Democratic Society (SDS) at their convention in Port Huron, Michigan, June 11–15, 1962. The SDS has since splintered, with some persons advocating violence as the means to achieve the goals, while others advocated peaceful means. This statement, growing out of a first draft by Tom Hayden, is an excellent declaration of the New Left ideology.

"We regard *men* as infinitely precious and possessed of unfulfilled capacities for reason, freedom, and love. In affirming these principles we are aware of countering perhaps the dominant conceptions of man in the twentieth century; that he is a thing to be manipulated, and that he is inherently incapable of directing his own affairs. We oppose the depersonalization that reduces human beings to the status of things— if anything, the brutalities of the twentieth century teach that means and ends are intimately related, that vague appeals to 'posterity' cannot justify the mutilations of the present. We oppose, too, the doctrine of human incompetence because it rests essentially on the modern fact that men have been 'competently' manipulated into incompetence— we see little reason why men cannot meet with increasing skill the complexities and responsibilities of their situation, if society is organized not for minority, but for majority, participation in decision-making.

Men have unrealized potential for self-cultivation, self-direction, self-understanding, and creativity. It is this potential that we regard as crucial and to which we appeal, not to the human potentiality for violence, unreason, and submission to authority. The goal of man and society should be human independence: a concern not with the image of popularity but with finding a meaning in life that is personally authentic; a quality of mind not compulsively driven by a sense of powerlessness, nor one which unthinkingly adopts status values, nor one which represses all threats to its habit, but one which has full, spontaneous access to present and past experiences; one which easily unites the fragmented parts of personal history; one which openly faces problems which are troubling and unresolved; one with an intuitive awareness of possibilities, an active sense of curiosity, an ability and willingness to learn.

This kind of independence does not mean egotistic individualism— the object is not to have one's way so much as it is to have a way that is one's own. Nor do we deify man—we merely have faith in his potential.

Human relationships should involve fraternity and honesty. Human interdependence is contemporary fact; human brotherhood must be willed, however, as a condition of future survival and as the most appropriate form of social relations. Personal links between man and man are needed, especially to go beyond the partial and fragmentary bonds of function that bind men only as worker to worker, employer to employee, teacher to student, American to Russian.

Loneliness, estrangement, isolation describe the vast distance between man and man today. These dominant tendencies cannot be overcome by better personnel management, nor by improved gadgets, but only when a love of man overcomes the idolatrous worship of things by man. As the individualism we affirm is not egoism, the selflessness we affirm is not self-elimination. On the contrary, we believe in generosity of a kind that imprints one's unique individual qualities in the relation to other men, and to all human activity. Further, to dislike isolation is not to favor the abolition of privacy; the latter differs from isolation in that it occurs or is abolished according to individual will.

We would replace power rooted in possession, privilege, or circumstance by power and uniqueness rooted in love, reflectiveness, reason, and creativity. As a *social system* we seek the establishment of a democracy of individual participation, governed by two central aims; that the individual share in those social decisions determining the quality and direction of his life; that society be organized to encourage independence in men and provide the media for their common participation.

In a participatory democracy, the political life would be based in several root principles:

that decision-making of basic social consequence be carried on by public groupings;

that politics be seen positively, as the art of collectively creating an acceptable pattern of social relations;

that politics has the function of bringing people out of isolation and into community, thus being a necessary, though not sufficient, means of finding meaning in personal life;

that the political order should serve to clarify problems in a way instrumental to their solution; it should provide outlets for the expression of personal grievance and aspiration; opposing views should be organized so as to illuminate choices and facilitate the attainment of goals; channels should be commonly available to relate men to knowledge and to power so that private problems—from bad recreation facilities to personal alienation—are formulated as general issues.

The economic sphere would have as its basis the principles:

that work should involve incentives worthier than money or survival. It should be educative, not stultifying; creative, not mechanical; self-directed, not manipulated, encouraging independence, a respect for others a sense of dignity and a willingness to accept social responsibility, since it is this experience that has crucial influence on habits, perceptions, and individual ethics; (continued)

nist subversives or dupes of the Communists. Finally, the radical conservatives oppose a number of things on the basis of their being unpatriotic, Communist-inspired, immoral, socialistic, and in danger of bringing the downfall of the Republic. A partial list of these would include: collective bargaining, the union shop, civil liberties, social security, integration, the Supreme Court, the State Department, the Central Intelligence Agency, federal aid to education, the graduated income tax, the city-manager form of government, the National Council of Churches, fluoridation of water, urban renewal, the Revised Standard Version of the Bible, the Federal Reserve System, the United Nations, the Tennessee Valley Authority, foreign aid, and sex education in the schools.[23]

Revolutionary Ideology II: The New Left

As with the Radical Right, the New Left is not a monolithic movement. As a political ideology it consists of many diverse strands. But there are some distinctive features. Unlike reform liberals who accept the system, the New Left adherents locate the source of problems (racism, poverty, materialism) in the structure and in societal institutions. Hence, there must be a restructuring of the

PANEL 12–5 *Continued*

that the economic experience is so personally decisive that the individual must share in its full determination;

that the economy itself is of such social importance that its major resources and means of production should be open to democratic participation and subject to democratic social regulation.

Like the political and economic ones, major social institutions—cultural, educational, rehabilitative, and others—should be generally organized with the well-being and dignity of man as the essential measure of success.

In social change or interchange, we find violence to be abhorrent because it requires generally the transformation of the target, be it a human being or a community of people, into a depersonalized object of hate. It is imperative that the means of violence be abolished and the institutions—local, national, international—that encourage nonviolence as a condition of conflict be developed.

These are our central values, in skeletal form. It remains vital to understand their denial or attainment in the context of the modern world."

system itself. The system is dehumanizing (rigid hierarchies, bureaucratic unresponsiveness, property rights taking precedence over human rights) and therefore alienating to its members. The concentration of wealth is deplored. Large corporations (often monopolies) dominate the economy, thereby preventing competition. The profit motive supersedes humanitarian concerns at all levels (governmental, business, and personal). The wealthy, moreover, have strong linkages with the government. The result is that the "haves" dominate the less well-to-do.

The goal of the New Left is to restructure society so that persons are free to pursue their desires. This newly created society will be organized on the basis of cooperation and brotherhood—not competition and struggle. This would necessitate the return of the institutions of society to the control of the people (participatory democracy). Not just the polity but the economy, family, education, and religion also require restructuring to meet the criteria of participatory democracy (see Panel 12–5).

All the ideologies from mainstream to revolutionary address themselves to the proper relationship between the economy and government, the source of current social problems, the desirability of social inequality, the nature of man, and the nature of social relationships. The consistent (or not so consistent) ideas that individuals have on these questions provides the rationale for political acts. Political ideology, therefore, supplies the fuel for either maintaining the politico-economic system or changing it. The future of American society as either a mass society or a free one rests squarely in the struggle among these (or perhaps other) political ideologies.

SUMMARY FOR PART III

The study of a society's institutions provides a description of the way a people have organized over a long period of time to cope with the perennial problems of societal maintenance. We have tried to show not only how American institutions provide for social integration, but how they are also the sources of social problems and conflict. In this regard, institutions illustrate the duality of social life. They provide the stability that man and society demand. Because of this, however, they are slow to change and even resistant to change.

Part II of this book focused on inequality in American society. Institutions are part of this mix. Institutions have power—the power to keep the status quo where certain categories of persons benefit while others are disadvantaged. Institutions are not viewed by most persons as the source of social problems, however, because Americans are socialized to believe that individuals are to blame for their misfortune. But beginning in the 1960's, blacks, welfare mothers, students, and others began to focus on societal institutions as the primary source of social problems. The result is a small but ever-widening body of dissatisfied persons who challenge the existing social arrangements. The importance of this shift cannot be overlooked because American institutions are in crisis. They increasingly cannot cope with social problems because of the rapidity of social change. More and more persons are promoting and living alternatives to the existing institutional expectations. What happens to these persons and the institutional alternatives they propose will be a vital clue as to whether American society will become a free or a mass society.

SUGGESTED FURTHER READING

Benello, C. George, and Dimitrios Roussopoulos, editors, *The Case for Participatory Democracy: Some Prospects for a Radical Society* (New York: Viking Press, 1971). A reader that presents alternatives to current political institutions.

Burkhart, James A., and Frank J. Kendrick, editors, *The New Politics: Mood or Movement?* (Englewood Cliffs, New Jersey: Prentice-Hall, 1971). An excellent collection of articles that provide insight to a number of important political problems of contemporary American society.

Dolbeare, Kenneth M., and Patricia Dolbeare, *American Ideologies: The Competing Political Beliefs of the 1970's* (Chicago: Markham Publishing Company, 1971). This book provides a concise treatment of seven political ideologies.

Lipset, Seymour Martin, and Earl Raab, *The Politics of Unreason: Right-wing Extremism in America, 1790–1970* (New York: Harper and Row, 1970). A comprehensive analysis of the political "right" in American history. Of special interest are the chapters on McCarthyism, the John Birch Society and George Wallace.

Litt, Edgar, *Ethnic Politics in America* (Glenview, Illinois: Scott, Foresman and Company, 1970). This book traces the political influence of race, nationality, and religion in American society.

NOTES AND REFERENCES

1. William J. Goode, "We Can Expect More Atticas," *New York Times* (September 20, 1971).

2. For a refresher course of the political process in American society see Robin Williams, *American Society*, Third Edition (New York: Alfred A. Knopf, 1970), pp. 242–262.

3. Robert Michels, *Political Parties* (Glencoe: The Free Press, 1949). This book was first published in Germany in 1911.

4. J. William Fulbright, *The Pentagon Propaganda Machine* (New York: Vintage Books, 1971).

5. Henry Steele Commager, "Is Freedom Dying in America?" *Look* 34 (July 14, 1970), p. 18.

6. Lewis A. Coser, "Introduction," *Political Sociology: Selected Essays*, Lewis A. Coser (ed.), (New York: Harper Torchbooks, 1967), p. 4.

7. See especially the first study that empirically verified the consequences of this phenomenon, Paul F. Lazarsfeld, Bernard Berelson, and Hazel Gaudet, *The People's Choice: How the Voter Makes up His Mind in a Presidential Campaign* (New York: Columbia University Press, 1944).

8. William Erbe, "Social Involvement and Political Activity: A Replication and Elaboration," *American Sociological Review* 29 (April, 1964), p. 198.

9. Thomas F. Pettigrew, Robert T. Riley, and Reeve D. Vanneman, "George Wallace's Constituents," *Psychology Today* 5 (February, 1972), p. 92. This is precisely the finding of my study of Lawrence, Kansas, D. Stanley Eitzen, "Status Inconsistency and Wallace Supporters in a Midwestern City," *Social Forces* 48 (June, 1970), pp. 493–498.

10. "The Troubled American," *Newsweek* (October 6, 1969), pp. 29–73.

11. Thomas F. Pettigrew, Robert T. Riley, and Reeve D. Vanneman, "George Wallace's Constituents," *Psychology Today* 5 (February,

1972), p. 49. Also see D. Stanley Eitzen, "Status Inconsistency and Wallace Supporters in a Midwestern City," *Social Forces* 48 (June, 1970), pp. 493–498.

12.   For a review of the studies see Seymour Martin Lipset, *Political Man: The Social Bases of Politics* (Garden City, New York: Doubleday and Co., Inc., 1960), pp. 87–126.

13.   Lewis Lipsitz, "Work Life and Political Attitudes: A Study of Manual Workers," *The White Majority*, Louise Kapp Howe (ed.), (New York: Vintage Books, 1970), p. 159.

14.   Seymour Martin Lipset and Earl Raab, *The Politics of Unreason: Right-Wing Extremism in America, 1790–1970* (New York: Harper and Row, Publishers, 1970), p. 367.

15.   "What They Believe," *Fortune* 79 (January, 1969), p. 70.

16.   Seymour Martin Lipset, "Youth and Politics," *Contemporary Social Problems*, Third Edition, Robert K. Merton and Robert Nisbet (eds.), (New York: Harcourt Brace Jovanovich, Inc., 1971), p. 771.

17.   Lipset, "Youth and Politics," pp. 744–745.

18.   Frederick G. Dutton, *Changing Sources of Power: American Politics in the 1970s* (New York: McGraw-Hill Book Company, 1971), p. 19.

19.   Edgar Litt, *Ethnic Politics in America* (Glenview, Illinois: Scott, Foresman and Company, 1970); Michael Parentic, "Ethnic Politics and the Persistence of Ethnic Identification," *American Political Science Review* 61 (September, 1967), pp. 717–726.

20.   Daniel Bell, *The End of Ideology: On the Exhaustion of Political Ideas in the Fifties*, Revised Edition (New York: The Free Press, 1962), p. 393.

21.   A good portion of this section is dependent upon the discussion of political ideologies in Kenneth M. Dolbeare and Patricia Dolbeare, *American Ideologies: The Competing Political Beliefs of the 1970s*, (Chicago: Markham Publishing Company, 1971).

22.   One source lists some 1,150 conservative, anti-communist American organizations (of course, not all would be classified as radical). Laird Wilcox, *Guide to the American Right* (Kansas City, Missouri: U.S. Directory Service, 1970).

23.   J. Allen Broyles, *The John Birch Society: Anatomy of a Protest* (Boston: Beacon Press, 1966); Benjamin R. Epstein and Arnold Forster, *The Radical Right: Report on the John Birch Society and Its Allies* (New York: Vintage Books, 1967); Daniel Bell (ed.), *The Radical Right* (Garden City, New York: Doubleday and Company, Inc., 1964); Donald Janson and Bernard Eisman, *The Far Right* (New York: McGraw-Hill Book Company, 1963); Mike Newberry, *The Yahoos* (New York: Marzani and Munsell, 1964); Robert A. Rosenstone, *Protest from the Right* (Beverly Hills, California: The Glencoe Press, 1968); Seymour Martin Lipset and Earl Raab, *The Politics of Unreason: Right-Wing Extremism in America, 1790–1970* (New York: Harper and Row, Publishers, 1970).

Epilogue

Any analyst of American society has the option of emphasizing either the social system as a smoothly functioning unit or the disunity and lack of harmony within it. American society for the most part does work rather smoothly. If we examine the whole of history, we must conclude that the system is improved in many respects. But this society has severe problems—the persistence of poverty, racial discrimination, injustice, violence, and the intransigence of the institutions to change, to name but a few. We must recognize that American society has many paradoxical dichotomies—unity and disunity, affluence and poverty, freedom and oppression, stability and change.

The topics selected for this book, the order in which they were presented, and the emphases have tended to focus on the problems, faults, and weaknesses of American society. This strategy was employed because they are often minimized in other books, but more important, because the society needs reform. Since institutions are man-made, they can be changed by men. As long as there are problems we cannot be content with the status quo. A full understanding of the complex nature of society must, however, precede the implementation of social change. That has been one goal of this book.

The primary purpose of any sociology book is to make the reader more perceptive and more analytical regarding social life. It is the author's hope that readers have gained new perspectives and new insights about our society from the reading and thinking required for analyzing American society. Hopefully, readers will build upon this knowledge in a life-long quest to understand better this complex system called American society and to work for its improvement.

APPENDIX

1970 Census

Sources: Pages 416–419: Bureau of the Census, *General Population Characteristics: United States Summary,* (Washington, D.C.: U.S. Department of Commerce, 1972), p. I-258, I–259, I-261, I-262. Pages 420–425: Bureau of the Census, *Number of Inhabitants: United States Summary* (Washington, D.C.: U.S. Department of Commerce, 1971), Figures 14, 15, 21, 22, 24, 31, 38. Pages 426–432: Bureau of the Census, *General Social and Economic Characteristics: United States Summary,* (Washington, D.C.: U.S. Department of Commerce, 1972), Figures 46–57, 66, 74, 75, 77, 78.

Population by Race and Residence

NUMBER IN MILLIONS

 WHITE NEGRO OTHER RACES

UNITED STATES

177.7   22.6   2.9

Total

Percent Change, 1960 to 1970

WHITE ▮ 11.9%
NEGRO ▮ 19.7%

URBAN and RURAL RESIDENCE

URBAN   128.8   18.4 2.2

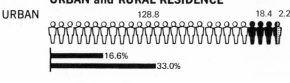

▮ 16.6%
▮ 33.0%

RURAL   49.0   4.2 0.7

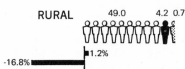

▮ 1.2%
-16.8% ▮

METROPOLITAN and NONMETROPOLITAN RESIDENCE
(SMSA's=Standard Metropolitan Statistical Areas)

INSIDE SMSA's total   120.6   16.8 2.1

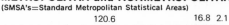

Inside Central Cities   49.4   13.1 1.2

Outside Central Cities   71.1   3.6 0.8

OUTSIDE SMSA's total   57.2   5.8 0.8

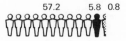

416

Population by Age: 1970 and 1960

NUMBER IN MILLIONS

1970	1960	YEARS
7.6	5.6	75+
5.4	4.7	70–74
7.0	6.3	65–69
8.6	7.1	60–64
10.0	8.4	55–59
11.1	9.6	50–54
12.1	10.9	45–49
12.0	11.6	40–44
11.1	12.5	35–39
11.4	11.9	30–34
13.5	10.9	25–29
16.4	10.8	20–24
19.1	13.2	15–19
20.8	16.8	10–14
20.0	18.7	5–9
17.2	20.3	0–4

PERCENT CHANGE, 1960 to 1970

EACH ● = 5%

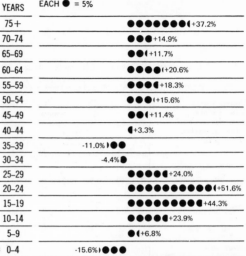

YEARS	PERCENT CHANGE
75+	+37.2%
70–74	+14.9%
65–69	+11.7%
60–64	+20.6%
55–59	+18.3%
50–54	+15.6%
45–49	+11.4%
40–44	+3.3%
35–39	-11.0%
30–34	-4.4%
25–29	+24.0%
20–24	+51.6%
15–19	+44.3%
10–14	+23.9%
5–9	+6.8%
0–4	-15.6%

Sex Ratio: 1900 to 1970

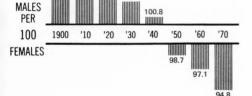

MALES
PER
100
FEMALES

1900	'10	'20	'30	'40	'50	'60	'70
104.6	106.2	104.1	102.6	100.8	98.7	97.1	94.8

Marital Status by Sex: 1970

≡ MALE

■ FEMALE

14 YEARS AND OLDER

SINGLE

MALE 28.6%

FEMALE 22.4%

MARRIED

MALE 65.8%

FEMALE 61.3%

WIDOWED and DIVORCED

MALE 5.7%

FEMALE 16.3%

417

Table 47. Summary of General Characteristics: 1970

[For minimum base for derived figures (percent, median, etc.) and meaning of symbols, see text]

United States Size of Place Metropolitan and Nonmetropolitan Residence	Population										Households			Population in group quarters	
	All persons							Persons 14 years and over — Percent married		Persons 18 years and over — Percent male					
	Number	Percent change 1960-70	Percent Negro and other races	Percent under 18 years	Percent 18 to 64 years	Percent 65 years and over	Fertility ratio[1]	Male	Female		Number	Percent change 1960-70	Persons per household	Number	Percent of total
SIZE OF PLACE															
Total	203 211 926	13.3	12.5	34.3	55.9	9.9	352	65.8	61.3	47.5	63 449 747	19.7	3.11	5 812 013	2.9
Urban	149 324 930	19.9	13.8	33.3	56.9	9.8	341	65.0	59.5	46.9	47 562 681	25.0	3.04	4 715 341	3.2
Urbanized areas	118 446 566	24.6	14.8	33.5	57.2	9.4	339	65.1	59.5	46.8	37 814 089	28.6	3.05	3 067 985	2.6
Central cities	63 921 684	11.7	22.5	31.8	57.5	10.7	336	62.5	56.1	46.2	21 410 602	17.3	2.90	1 881 073	2.9
Urban fringe	54 524 882	44.0	5.7	35.4	56.7	7.8	342	68.3	63.8	47.7	16 403 487	50.7	3.25	1 186 912	2.2
Other urban	30 878 364	5.0	9.9	32.9	55.7	11.4	348	64.6	59.3	47.1	9 748 592	9.2	3.00	1 647 356	5.3
Places of 10,000 or more	16 618 596	2.8	10.7	32.3	57.0	10.8	336	63.0	58.1	47.4	5 221 333	6.9	2.98	1 054 224	6.3
Places of 2,500 to 10,000	14 259 768	7.6	9.0	33.6	54.2	12.2	363	66.5	60.6	46.9	4 527 259	11.9	3.02	593 132	4.2
Rural	53 886 996	-0.3	9.1	36.8	53.1	10.1	387	67.7	66.7	49.2	15 887 066	8.0	3.32	1 096 672	2.0
Places of 1,000 to 2,500	6 656 007	2.5	7.8	33.9	52.6	13.6	376	68.5	62.0	46.7	2 162 478	7.4	3.01	152 512	2.3
Other rural	47 230 989	-0.7	9.3	37.2	53.2	9.6	388	67.6	67.5	49.6	13 724 588	8.1	3.37	944 160	2.0
METROPOLITAN AND NONMETROPOLITAN RESIDENCE															
Total	203 211 926	(NA)	12.5	34.3	55.9	9.9	352	65.8	61.3	47.5	63 449 747	(NA)	3.11	5 812 013	2.9
Metropolitan	139 418 811	(NA)	13.5	34.0	56.7	9.2	345	65.5	60.5	47.2	43 862 993	(NA)	3.09	3 727 720	2.7
Urban	123 007 271	(NA)	14.5	33.5	57.1	9.4	340	65.1	59.6	46.9	39 196 005	(NA)	3.05	3 333 862	2.7
Central cities	63 796 943	(NA)	22.5	31.8	57.5	10.7	336	62.5	56.1	46.1	21 382 260	(NA)	2.90	1 867 870	2.9
Other urban	59 210 328	(NA)	5.9	35.4	56.7	8.0	345	67.9	63.7	47.8	17 813 745	(NA)	3.24	1 465 992	2.5
Rural	16 411 540	(NA)	5.9	37.9	54.1	8.0	379	68.4	67.9	49.5	4 666 988	(NA)	3.43	393 858	2.4
Nonmetropolitan	63 793 115	(NA)	10.4	34.8	53.9	11.3	370	66.3	63.0	48.1	19 586 754	(NA)	3.15	2 084 293	3.3
Urban	26 317 659	(NA)	10.2	32.6	55.7	11.7	344	64.6	58.8	46.9	8 366 676	(NA)	2.98	1 381 479	5.2
Rural	37 475 456	(NA)	10.5	36.4	52.6	11.0	390	67.4	66.2	49.1	11 220 078	(NA)	3.28	702 814	1.9

[1]Children under 5 years per 1,000 women 15 to 49 years.

Table 48. **Race by Sex: 1900 to 1970**

[For years prior to 1960, small segments of several racial groups were not identified separately in the tabulations for Alaska and Hawaii. These persons are included in the residual class, "All other." For minimum base for derived figures (percent, median, etc.) and meaning of symbols, see text]

United States Size of Place, 1970 Metropolitan and Nonmetropolitan Residence, 1970			Negro and other races								Percent distribution				
					Other races								Negro and other races		
	Total	White	Total	Negro	Total	Indian	Japanese	Chinese	Filipino	All other	Total	White	Total	Negro	Other
SIZE OF PLACE															
Total															
1970	203 211 926	177 748 975	25 462 951	22 580 289	2 882 662	792 730	591 290	435 062	343 060	720 520	100.0	87.5	12.5	11.1	1.4
Urban	149 324 930	128 773 240	20 551 690	18 367 318	2 184 372	355 738	523 651	418 779	292 712	593 492	100.0	86.2	13.8	12.3	1.5
Urbanized areas	118 446 566	100 951 502	17 495 064	15 692 685	1 802 379	241 699	445 578	387 312	250 455	477 335	100.0	85.2	14.8	13.2	1.5
Central cities	63 921 684	49 546 571	14 375 113	13 144 798	1 230 315	158 115	283 847	295 170	165 248	327 935	100.0	77.5	22.5	20.6	1.9
Urban fringe	54 524 882	51 404 931	3 119 951	2 547 887	572 064	83 584	161 731	92 142	85 207	149 400	100.0	94.3	5.7	4.7	1.0
Other urban	30 878 364	27 821 738	3 056 626	2 674 633	381 993	114 039	78 073	31 467	42 257	116 157	100.0	90.1	9.9	8.7	1.2
Places of 10,000 or more	16 618 596	14 838 518	1 780 078	1 567 639	212 439	55 600	49 101	22 258	21 278	64 202	100.0	89.3	10.7	9.4	1.3
Places of 2,500 to 10,000	14 259 768	12 983 220	1 276 548	1 106 994	169 554	58 439	28 972	9 209	20 979	51 955	100.0	91.0	9.0	7.8	1.2
Rural	53 886 996	48 975 735	4 911 261	4 212 971	698 290	436 992	67 639	16 283	50 348	127 028	100.0	90.9	9.1	7.8	1.3
Places of 1,000 to 2,500	6 656 007	6 139 580	516 427	420 240	96 187	39 577	15 409	2 692	14 712	23 797	100.0	92.2	7.8	6.3	1.4
Other rural	47 230 989	42 836 155	4 394 834	3 792 731	602 103	397 415	52 230	13 591	35 636	103 231	100.0	90.7	9.3	8.0	1.3
1960	179 323 175	158 831 732	20 491 443	18 871 831	1 619 612	523 591	464 332	237 292	176 310	218 087	100.0	88.6	11.4	10.5	0.9
1950	151 325 798	135 149 629	16 176 169	15 044 937	1 131 232	357 499	326 379	150 005	122 707	174 642	100.0	89.3	10.7	9.9	0.7
1940[1]	132 165 129	118 357 831	13 807 298	12 865 914	941 384	345 252	285 115	106 334	98 535	106 148	100.0	89.6	10.4	9.7	0.7
1930[1]	123 202 660	110 395 753	12 806 907	11 891 842	915 065	343 352	278 743	102 159	108 260	82 551	100.0	89.6	10.4	9.7	0.7
1920[1]	106 021 568	94 903 540	11 118 028	10 463 607	654 421	244 437	220 596	85 202	26 634	77 552	100.0	89.5	10.5	9.9	0.6
1910[1]	92 228 531	81 812 405	10 416 126	9 828 667	587 459	276 927	152 745	94 414	2 767	60 606	100.0	88.7	11.3	10.7	0.6
1900	76 212 168	66 868 508	9 343 660	8 834 395	509 265	237 196	85 716	118 746	[3]	67 607	100.0	87.7	12.3	11.6	0.7
Male															
1970	98 912 192	86 720 987	12 191 205	10 748 316	1 442 889	388 691	271 300	228 565	189 498	364 835	100.0	87.7	12.3	10.9	1.5
Urban	71 958 564	62 210 243	9 748 321	8 657 231	1 091 090	171 941	240 185	220 078	158 511	300 375	100.0	86.5	13.5	12.0	1.5
Urbanized areas	57 035 148	48 751 475	8 283 673	7 384 180	899 493	116 276	205 395	203 007	134 731	240 084	100.0	85.5	14.5	12.9	1.6
Central cities	30 409 942	23 642 104	6 767 838	6 151 899	615 939	75 157	132 490	155 515	88 328	164 449	100.0	77.7	22.3	20.2	2.0
Urban fringe	26 625 206	25 109 371	1 515 835	1 232 281	283 554	41 119	72 905	47 492	46 403	75 635	100.0	94.3	5.7	4.6	1.1
Other urban	14 923 416	13 458 768	1 464 648	1 273 051	191 597	55 665	34 790	17 071	23 780	60 291	100.0	90.2	9.8	8.5	1.3
Places of 10,000 or more	8 051 809	7 196 050	855 759	748 323	107 436	27 432	22 178	12 180	12 028	33 618	100.0	89.4	10.6	9.3	1.3
Places of 2,500 to 10,000	6 871 607	6 262 718	608 889	524 728	84 161	28 233	12 612	4 891	11 752	26 673	100.0	91.1	8.9	7.6	1.2
Rural	26 953 628	24 510 744	2 442 884	2 091 085	351 799	216 750	31 115	8 487	30 987	64 460	100.0	90.9	9.1	7.8	1.3
Places of 1,000 to 2,500	3 201 271	2 954 445	246 826	198 947	47 879	19 083	7 212	1 354	8 466	11 764	100.0	92.3	7.7	6.2	1.5
Other rural	23 752 357	21 556 299	2 196 058	1 892 138	303 920	197 667	23 903	7 133	22 521	52 696	100.0	90.8	9.2	8.0	1.3
1960	88 331 494	78 367 149	9 964 345	9 113 408	850 937	263 369	224 828	135 549	112 286	114 905	100.0	88.7	11.3	10.3	1.0
1950	75 186 606	67 254 991	7 931 615	7 300 755	630 860	186 062	169 899	94 052	89 658	91 189	100.0	89.5	10.5	9.7	0.8
1940[1]	66 349 730	59 538 616	6 811 114	6 269 262	541 852	177 215	154 967	73 561	80 835	55 274	100.0	89.7	10.3	9.4	0.8
1930[1]	62 395 484	55 991 138	6 404 346	5 856 053	548 293	175 938	156 986	76 388	94 834	44 147	100.0	89.7	10.3	9.4	0.9
1920[1]	54 086 116	48 481 746	5 604 370	5 209 717	394 653	125 068	135 616	70 141	22 083	41 745	100.0	89.6	10.4	9.6	0.7
1910[1]	47 501 233	42 233 361	5 267 872	4 886 439	381 433	140 818	118 741	85 210	2 502	34 162	100.0	88.9	11.1	10.3	0.8
1900	38 968 689	34 245 559	4 723 130	4 386 856	336 274	119 484	71 116	110 750	[3]	34 924	100.0	87.9	12.1	11.3	0.9
Female															
1970	104 299 734	91 027 988	13 271 746	11 831 973	1 439 773	404 039	319 990	206 497	153 562	355 685	100.0	87.3	12.7	11.3	1.4
Urban	77 366 366	66 562 997	10 803 369	9 710 087	1 093 282	183 797	283 466	198 701	134 201	293 117	100.0	86.0	14.0	12.6	1.4
Urbanized areas	61 411 418	52 200 027	9 211 391	8 308 505	902 886	125 423	240 183	184 305	115 724	237 251	100.0	85.0	15.0	13.5	1.5
Central cities	33 511 742	25 904 467	7 607 275	6 992 899	614 376	82 958	151 357	139 655	76 920	163 486	100.0	77.3	22.7	20.9	1.8
Urban fringe	27 899 676	26 295 560	1 604 116	1 315 606	288 510	42 465	88 826	44 650	38 804	73 765	100.0	94.3	5.7	4.7	1.0
Other urban	15 954 948	14 362 970	1 591 978	1 401 582	190 396	58 374	43 283	14 396	18 477	55 866	100.0	90.0	10.0	8.8	1.2
Places of 10,000 or more	8 566 787	7 642 468	924 319	819 316	105 003	28 168	26 923	10 078	9 250	30 584	100.0	89.2	10.8	9.6	1.2
Places of 2,500 to 10,000	7 388 161	6 720 502	667 659	582 266	85 393	30 206	16 360	4 318	9 227	25 282	100.0	91.0	9.0	7.9	1.2
Rural	26 933 368	24 464 991	2 468 377	2 121 886	346 491	220 242	36 524	7 796	19 361	62 568	100.0	90.8	9.2	7.9	1.3
Places of 1,000 to 2,500	3 454 736	3 185 135	269 601	221 293	48 308	20 494	8 197	1 338	6 246	12 033	100.0	92.2	7.8	6.4	1.4
Other rural	23 478 632	21 279 856	2 198 776	1 900 593	298 183	199 748	28 327	6 458	13 115	50 535	100.0	90.6	9.4	8.1	1.3
1960	90 991 681	80 464 583	10 527 098	9 758 423	768 675	260 222	239 504	101 743	64 024	103 182	100.0	88.4	11.6	10.7	0.8
1950	76 139 192	67 894 638	8 244 554	7 744 182	500 372	171 437	156 480	55 953	33 049	83 453	100.0	89.2	10.8	10.2	0.7
1940[1]	65 815 399	58 819 215	6 996 184	6 596 652	399 532	168 037	130 148	32 773	17 700	50 874	100.0	89.4	10.6	10.0	0.6
1930[1]	60 807 176	54 404 615	6 402 561	6 035 789	366 772	167 414	121 757	25 771	13 426	38 404	100.0	89.5	10.5	9.9	0.6
1920[1]	51 935 452	46 421 794	5 513 658	5 253 890	259 768	119 369	84 980	15 061	4 551	35 807	100.0	89.4	10.6	10.1	0.5
1910[1]	44 727 298	39 579 044	5 148 254	4 942 228	206 026	136 109	34 004	9 204	265	26 444	100.0	88.5	11.5	11.0	0.5
1900	37 243 479	32 622 949	4 620 530	4 447 539	172 991	117 712	14 600	7 996	[3]	32 683	100.0	87.6	12.4	11.9	0.5
METROPOLITAN AND NONMETROPOLITAN RESIDENCE															
Total															
1970	**203 211 926**	**177 748 975**	**25 462 951**	**22 580 289**	**2 882 662**	**792 730**	**591 290**	**435 062**	**343 060**	**720 520**	**100.0**	**87.5**	**12.5**	**11.1**	**1.4**
Metropolitan	139 418 811	120 578 729	18 840 082	16 770 610	2 069 472	307 867	505 522	405 546	289 781	560 756	100.0	86.5	13.5	12.0	1.5
Urban	123 007 271	105 137 365	17 869 906	15 940 477	1 929 429	256 473	479 801	397 391	271 858	523 906	100.0	85.5	14.5	13.0	1.6
Central cities	63 796 943	49 430 443	14 366 500	13 140 331	1 226 169	157 897	282 507	294 843	164 156	326 766	100.0	77.5	22.5	20.6	1.9
Other urban	59 210 328	55 706 922	3 503 406	2 800 146	703 260	98 576	197 294	102 548	107 702	197 140	100.0	94.1	5.9	4.7	1.2
Rural	16 411 540	15 441 364	970 176	830 133	140 043	51 394	25 721	8 155	17 923	36 850	100.0	94.1	5.9	5.1	0.9
Nonmetropolitan	63 793 115	57 170 246	6 622 869	5 809 679	813 190	484 863	85 768	29 516	53 279	159 764	100.0	89.6	10.4	9.1	1.3
Urban	26 317 659	23 635 875	2 681 784	2 426 841	254 943	99 265	43 850	21 388	20 854	69 586	100.0	89.8	10.2	9.2	1.0
Rural	37 475 456	33 534 371	3 941 085	3 382 838	558 247	385 598	41 918	8 128	32 425	90 178	100.0	89.5	10.5	9.0	1.5
Male															
1970	**98 912 192**	**86 720 987**	**12 191 205**	**10 748 316**	**1 442 889**	**388 691**	**271 300**	**228 565**	**189 498**	**364 835**	**100.0**	**87.7**	**12.3**	**10.9**	**1.5**
Metropolitan	67 545 062	58 575 636	8 969 426	7 933 326	1 036 100	150 037	232 585	212 482	158 189	282 807	100.0	86.7	13.3	11.7	1.5
Urban	59 293 875	50 820 467	8 473 408	7 509 494	963 914	124 000	220 848	208 249	146 905	263 912	100.0	85.7	14.3	12.7	1.6
Central cities	30 343 327	23 580 350	6 762 977	6 149 156	613 821	75 020	131 920	155 310	87 829	163 742	100.0	77.7	22.3	20.3	2.0
Other urban	28 950 548	27 240 117	1 710 431	1 360 338	350 093	48 980	88 928	52 939	59 076	100 170	100.0	94.1	5.9	4.7	1.2
Rural	8 251 187	7 755 169	496 018	423 832	72 186	26 037	11 737	4 233	11 284	18 895	100.0	94.0	6.0	5.1	0.9
Nonmetropolitan	31 367 130	28 145 351	3 221 779	2 814 990	406 789	238 654	38 715	16 083	31 309	82 028	100.0	89.7	10.3	9.0	1.3
Urban	12 664 689	11 389 776	1 274 913	1 147 737	127 176	47 941	19 337	11 829	11 606	36 463	100.0	89.9	10.1	9.1	1.0
Rural	18 702 441	16 755 575	1 946 866	1 667 253	279 613	190 713	19 378	4 254	19 703	45 565	100.0	89.6	10.4	8.9	1.5
Female															
1970	**104 299 734**	**91 027 988**	**13 271 746**	**11 831 973**	**1 439 773**	**404 039**	**319 990**	**206 497**	**153 562**	**355 685**	**100.0**	**87.3**	**12.7**	**11.3**	**1.4**
Metropolitan	71 873 749	62 003 093	9 870 656	8 837 284	1 033 372	157 830	272 937	193 064	131 592	277 949	100.0	86.3	13.7	12.3	1.4
Urban	63 713 396	54 316 898	9 396 498	8 430 983	965 515	132 473	258 953	189 142	124 953	259 994	100.0	85.3	14.7	13.2	1.5
Central cities	33 453 616	25 850 093	7 603 523	6 991 175	612 348	82 877	150 587	139 533	76 327	163 024	100.0	77.3	22.7	20.9	1.8
Other urban	30 259 780	28 466 805	1 792 975	1 439 808	353 167	49 596	108 366	49 609	48 626	96 970	100.0	94.1	5.9	4.8	1.2
Rural	8 160 353	7 686 195	474 158	406 301	67 857	25 357	13 984	3 922	6 639	17 955	100.0	94.2	5.8	5.0	0.8
Nonmetropolitan	32 425 985	29 024 895	3 401 090	2 994 689	406 401	246 209	47 053	13 433	21 970	77 736	100.0	89.5	10.5	9.2	1.3
Urban	13 652 970	12 246 099	1 406 871	1 279 104	127 767	51 324	24 513	9 559	9 248	33 123	100.0	89.7	10.3	9.4	0.9
Rural	18 773 015	16 778 796	1 994 219	1 715 585	278 634	194 885	22 540	3 874	12 722	44 613	100.0	89.4	10.6	9.1	1.5

[1]Data for 1910 through 1940 include the small number of residents in certain outlying areas of sovereignty or jurisdiction. [2]Partially estimated. [3]Included with "All other."

POPULATION OF THE UNITED STATES: 1790-1970

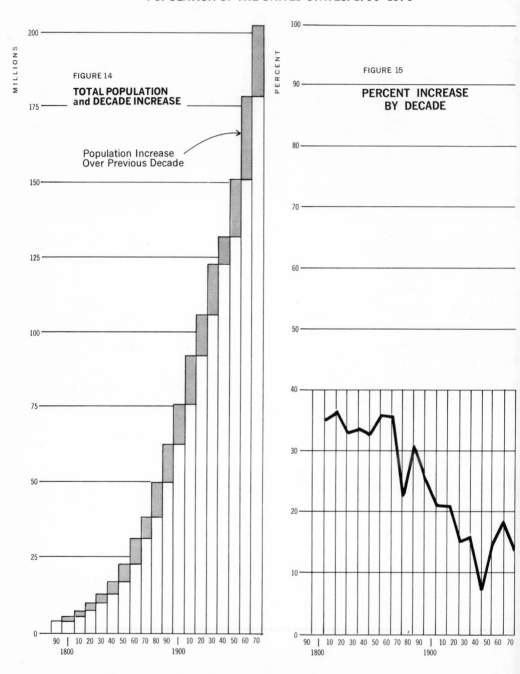

MILLIONS

FIGURE 14

**TOTAL POPULATION
and DECADE INCREASE**

Population Increase
Over Previous Decade

PERCENT

FIGURE 15

**PERCENT INCREASE
BY DECADE**

FIGURE 21 **STATES RANKED BY TOTAL POPULATION: 1970**

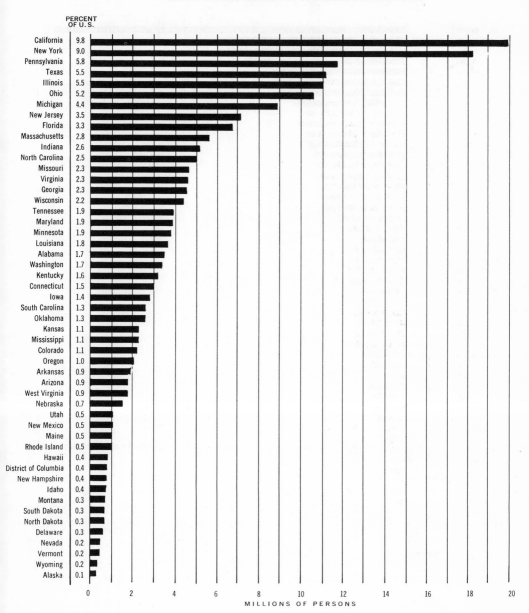

	PERCENT OF U.S.
California	9.8
New York	9.0
Pennsylvania	5.8
Texas	5.5
Illinois	5.5
Ohio	5.2
Michigan	4.4
New Jersey	3.5
Florida	3.3
Massachusetts	2.8
Indiana	2.6
North Carolina	2.5
Missouri	2.3
Virginia	2.3
Georgia	2.3
Wisconsin	2.2
Tennessee	1.9
Maryland	1.9
Minnesota	1.9
Louisiana	1.8
Alabama	1.7
Washington	1.7
Kentucky	1.6
Connecticut	1.5
Iowa	1.4
South Carolina	1.3
Oklahoma	1.3
Kansas	1.1
Mississippi	1.1
Colorado	1.1
Oregon	1.0
Arkansas	0.9
Arizona	0.9
West Virginia	0.9
Nebraska	0.7
Utah	0.5
New Mexico	0.5
Maine	0.5
Rhode Island	0.5
Hawaii	0.4
District of Columbia	0.4
New Hampshire	0.4
Idaho	0.4
Montana	0.3
South Dakota	0.3
North Dakota	0.3
Delaware	0.3
Nevada	0.2
Vermont	0.2
Wyoming	0.2
Alaska	0.1

MILLIONS OF PERSONS

0   2   4   6   8   10   12   14   16   18   20

421

FIGURE 23   **STATES RANKED BY PERCENT OF POPULATION CHANGE: 1960-1970**

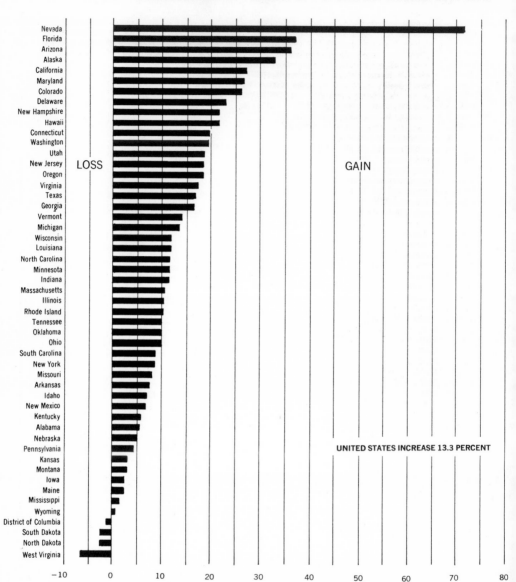

LOSS   GAIN

UNITED STATES INCREASE 13.3 PERCENT

PERCENT POPULATION CHANGE

FIGURE 24 **STATES RANKED BY POPULATION DENSITY: 1970**

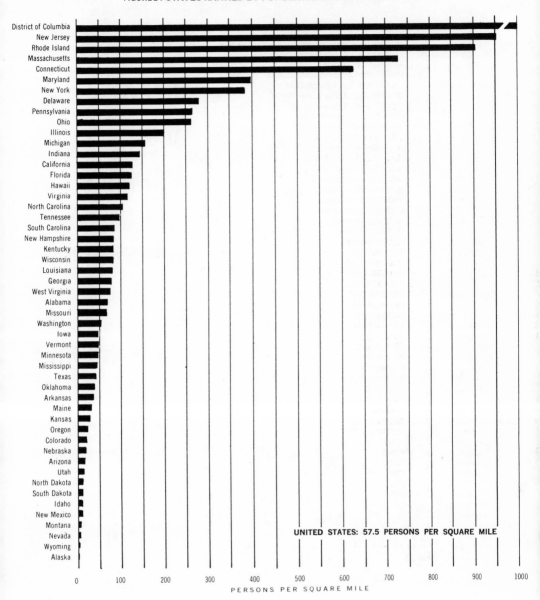

FIGURE 31 **POPULATION BY SIZE OF PLACE: 1970**

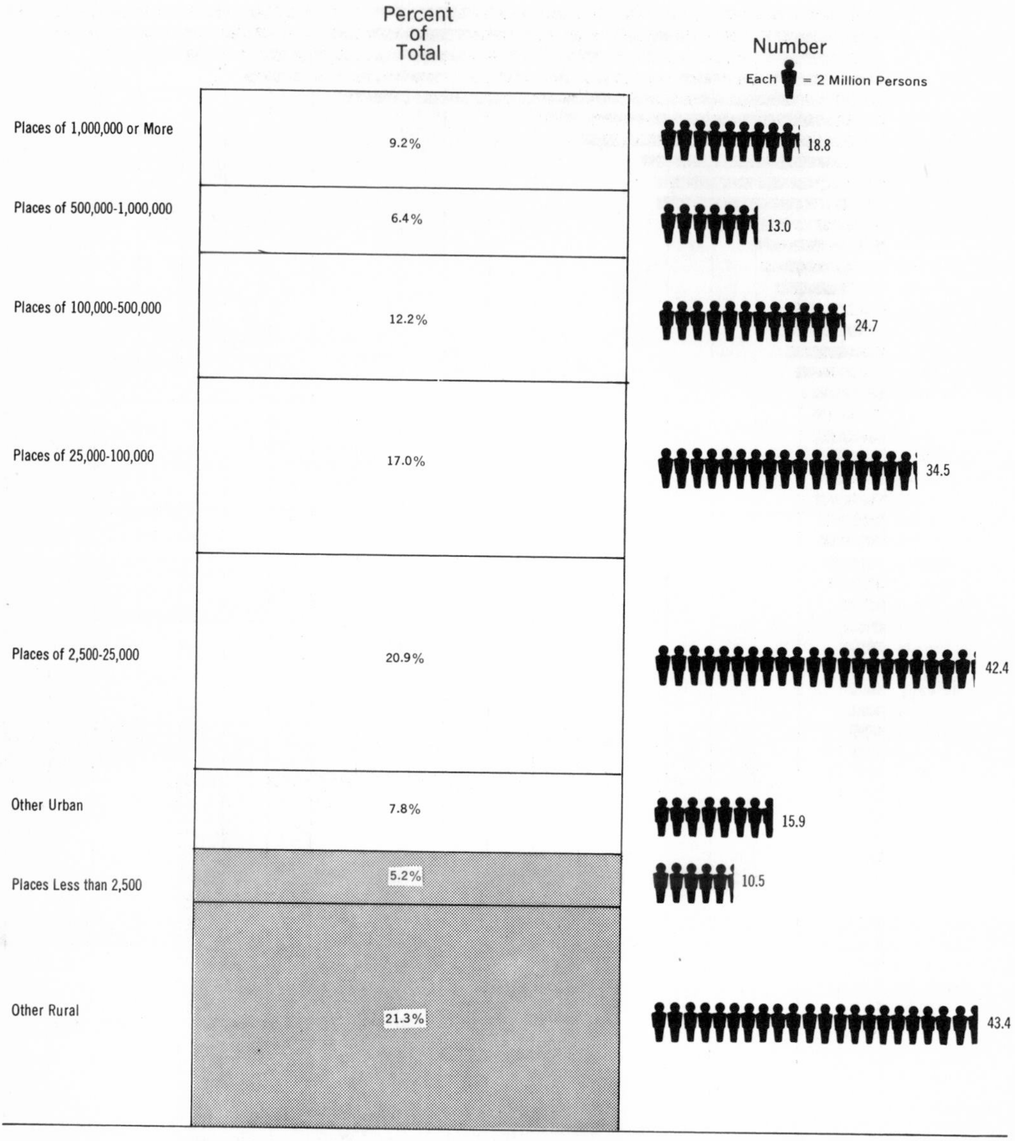

FIGURE 38

POPULATION INSIDE and OUTSIDE SMSA'S: 1970 and 1960

Number in thousands

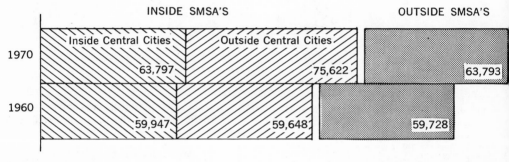

Percent

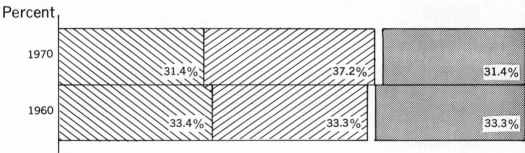

FIGURE 46

PERSONS OF SPANISH ORIGIN: 1970

- ☐ Under 50,000
- ▨ 50,000–99,999
- ▧ 100,000–249,999
- ▩ 250,000–499,999
- ▦ 500,000 or More

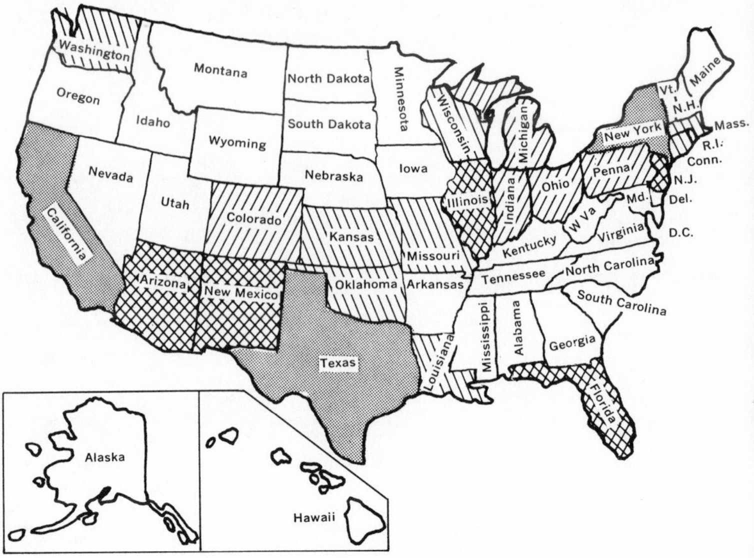

FIGURE 47 NATIVE POPULATION BORN IN STATE OTHER THAN STATE OF RESIDENCE: 1900–1970

EACH SYMBOL=2 PERCENT

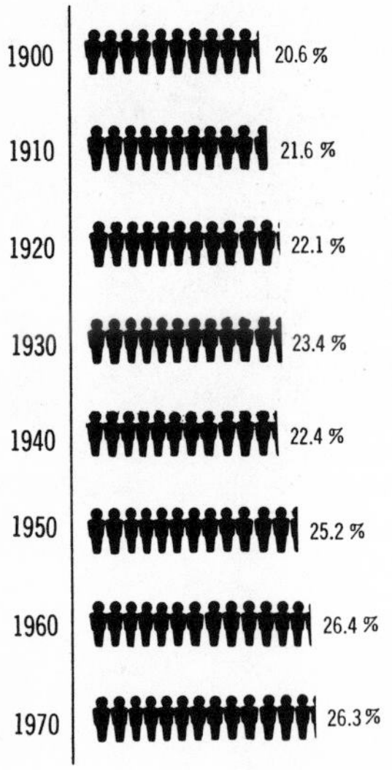

Year		Percent
1900	👥👥👥👥👥👥👥👥👥👥	20.6 %
1910	👥👥👥👥👥👥👥👥👥👥	21.6 %
1920	👥👥👥👥👥👥👥👥👥👥	22.1 %
1930	👥👥👥👥👥👥👥👥👥👥	23.4 %
1940	👥👥👥👥👥👥👥👥👥👥	22.4 %
1950	👥👥👥👥👥👥👥👥👥👥	25.2 %
1960	👥👥👥👥👥👥👥👥👥👥	26.4 %
1970	👥👥👥👥👥👥👥👥👥👥	26.3 %

FIGURE 48 RESIDENCE IN 1965 FOR PERSONS 5 YEARS OLD AND OVER, Urban and Rural: 1970

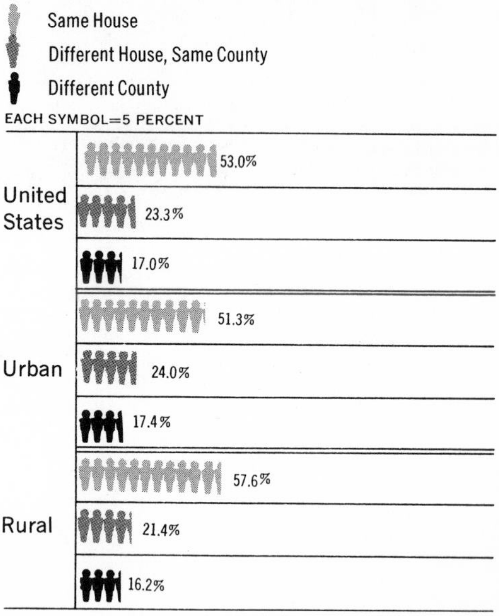

- Same House
- Different House, Same County
- Different County

EACH SYMBOL=5 PERCENT

		Percent
United States	Same House	53.0%
	Different House, Same County	23.3%
	Different County	17.0%
Urban	Same House	51.3%
	Different House, Same County	24.0%
	Different County	17.4%
Rural	Same House	57.6%
	Different House, Same County	21.4%
	Different County	16.2%

FIGURE 49 RESIDENCE IN 1965 FOR PERSONS 5 YEARS OLD AND OVER
By Race and Spanish Heritage: 1970

PERCENT DISTRIBUTION

Legend:
- ☐ Same House
- ▦ Different House, Same County
- ▨ Different County
- ⧄ Abroad or Moved, Residence Not Reported

	Same House	Different House, Same County	Different County	Abroad or Moved, Residence Not Reported
United States	53.0%	23.3%	17.0%	6.7%
White	53.3%	22.5%	18.0%	6.2%
Negro	51.4%	29.8%	9.5%	9.3%
Spanish Heritage	42.5%	30.4%	14.7%	12.4%

FIGURE 50 MOVERS, 1965–1970, By States: 1970

Legend:
- ▦ 55.0% and Over
- ▨ 50.0%–54.9%
- ⧄ 45.0%–49.9%
- ☐ Under 45.0%

Movers are persons who were not living in the same house in the United States in 1970 as in 1965

UNITED STATES AVERAGE=47.0%

Washington 55.0%
Oregon 55.3%
Idaho 51.3%
Montana 49.6%
North Dakota 43.6%
Minnesota 43.2%
Maine 41.7%
Vt. 40.4%
N.H. 45.1%
Nevada 63.8%
Wyoming 51.8%
South Dakota 42.9%
Wisconsin 42.2%
Michigan 44.7%
New York 40.9%
Mass. 45.0%
R.I. 42.6%
Conn. 42.5%
California 56.5%
Utah 46.1%
Colorado 57.1%
Nebraska 46.1%
Iowa 42.9%
Illinois 46.2%
Indiana 45.2%
Ohio 36.3%
Pennsylvania 39.6%
N.J. 42.4%
Del. 46.0%
Md. 48.5%
D.C. 52.7%
Arizona 58.7%
New Mexico 50.3%
Kansas 48.9%
Missouri 47.9%
Kentucky 46.4%
W.Va. 39.6%
Virginia 49.7%
North Carolina 46.2%
Oklahoma 52.3%
Arkansas 49.4%
Tennessee 47.4%
South Carolina 45.3%
Texas 52.5%
Louisiana 44.2%
Miss. 44.6%
Alabama 45.5%
Georgia 51.4%
Florida 55.9%

Alaska 73.1%
Hawaii 54.1%

NUMBER OF CHILDREN EVER BORN PER 1,000 WOMEN 15-44 YEARS OLD

FIGURE 51 **By Age: 1940–1970**

FIGURE 52 **By Age and Race: 1970**

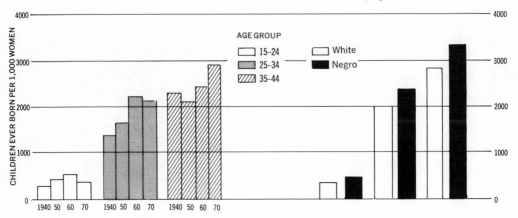

AGE GROUP
- 15–24
- 25–34
- 35–44

White
Negro

FIGURE 53 **FERTILITY RATIO: 1890–1970**

FIGURE 54 **POPULATION REPLACEMENT INDEX: 1970**
See text for definition of replacement index

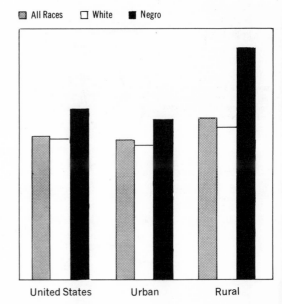

All Races   White   Negro

United States   Urban   Rural

FIGURE 55 **PERCENT ENROLLED IN SCHOOL**
By Age: 1910–1970

5 and 6 Years Old

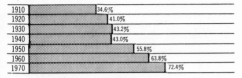

1910	34.6%
1920	41.0%
1930	43.2%
1940	43.0%
1950	55.8%
1960	63.8%
1970	72.4%

7 to 13 Years Old

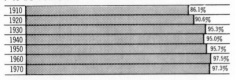

1910	86.1%
1920	90.6%
1930	95.3%
1940	95.0%
1950	95.7%
1960	97.5%
1970	97.3%

14 and 15 Years Old

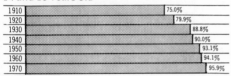

1910	75.0%
1920	79.9%
1930	88.8%
1940	90.0%
1950	93.1%
1960	94.1%
1970	95.9%

16 and 17 Years Old

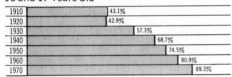

1910	43.1%
1920	42.9%
1930	57.3%
1940	68.7%
1950	74.5%
1960	80.9%
1970	89.3%

18 and 19 Years Old

1910	18.7%
1920	17.8%
1930	25.4%
1940	28.9%
1950	32.3%
1960	42.1%
1970	56.6%

20 to 24 Years Old

1910	NA
1920	NA
1930	7.4%
1940	6.6%
1950	12.9%
1960	14.6%
1970	21.3%

FIGURE 56 **MEDIAN YEARS OF SCHOOL COMPLETED,**
By Regions and Divisions: 1970

Persons 25 Years Old and Over   YEARS

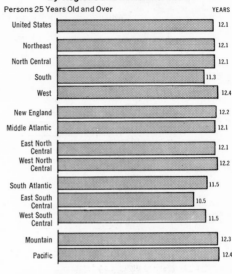

United States	12.1
Northeast	12.1
North Central	12.1
South	11.3
West	12.4
New England	12.2
Middle Atlantic	12.1
East North Central	12.1
West North Central	12.2
South Atlantic	11.5
East South Central	10.5
West South Central	11.5
Mountain	12.3
Pacific	12.4

FIGURE 57 **MEDIAN YEARS OF SCHOOL COMPLETED**
By Race: 1940–1970

Persons 25 Years Old and Over

TOTAL

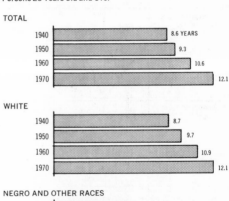

1940	8.6 YEARS
1950	9.3
1960	10.6
1970	12.1

WHITE

1940	8.7
1950	9.7
1960	10.9
1970	12.1

NEGRO AND OTHER RACES

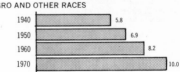

1940	5.8
1950	6.9
1960	8.2
1970	10.0

FIGURE 66 MAJOR OCCUPATION OF EMPLOYED PERSONS By Race and Sex: 1970 and 1960

WHITE ☐   NEGRO AND OTHER RACES ■

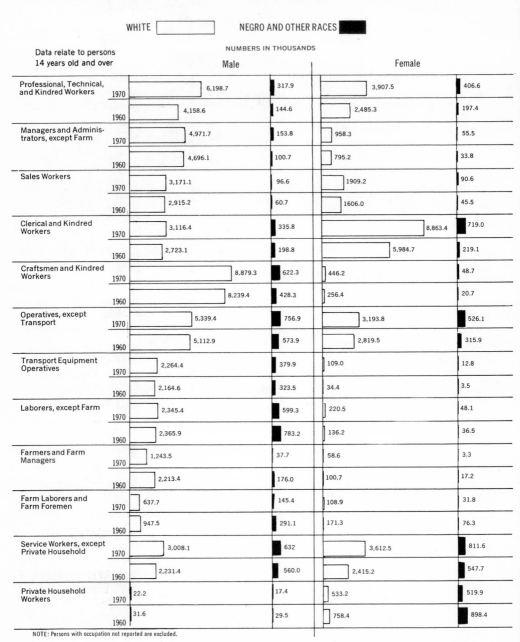

Data relate to persons 14 years old and over

NUMBERS IN THOUSANDS

		Male		Female	
		WHITE	NEGRO AND OTHER	WHITE	NEGRO AND OTHER
Professional, Technical, and Kindred Workers	1970	6,198.7	317.9	3,907.5	406.6
	1960	4,158.6	144.6	2,485.3	197.4
Managers and Administrators, except Farm	1970	4,971.7	153.8	958.3	55.5
	1960	4,696.1	100.7	795.2	33.8
Sales Workers	1970	3,171.1	96.6	1909.2	90.6
	1960	2,915.2	60.7	1606.0	45.5
Clerical and Kindred Workers	1970	3,116.4	335.8	8,863.4	719.0
	1960	2,723.1	198.8	5,984.7	219.1
Craftsmen and Kindred Workers	1970	8,879.3	622.3	446.2	48.7
	1960	8,239.4	428.3	256.4	20.7
Operatives, except Transport	1970	5,339.4	756.9	3,193.8	526.1
	1960	5,112.9	573.9	2,819.5	315.9
Transport Equipment Operatives	1970	2,264.4	379.9	109.0	12.8
	1960	2,164.6	323.5	34.4	3.5
Laborers, except Farm	1970	2,345.4	599.3	220.5	48.1
	1960	2,365.9	783.2	136.2	36.5
Farmers and Farm Managers	1970	1,243.5	37.7	58.6	3.3
	1960	2,213.4	176.0	100.7	17.2
Farm Laborers and Farm Foremen	1970	637.7	145.4	108.9	31.8
	1960	947.5	291.1	171.3	76.3
Service Workers, except Private Household	1970	3,008.1	632	3,612.5	811.6
	1960	2,231.4	560.0	2,415.2	547.7
Private Household Workers	1970	22.2	17.4	533.2	519.9
	1960	31.6	29.5	758.4	898.4

NOTE: Persons with occupation not reported are excluded.

430

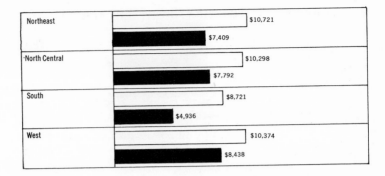

FIGURE 74
**MEDIAN INCOME IN 1969
OF FAMILIES
By Race Of Head, By Regions**

☐ White

■ Negro and Other Races

Northeast	White	$10,721
	Negro and Other Races	$7,409
North Central	White	$10,298
	Negro and Other Races	$7,792
South	White	$8,721
	Negro and Other Races	$4,936
West	White	$10,374
	Negro and Other Races	$8,438

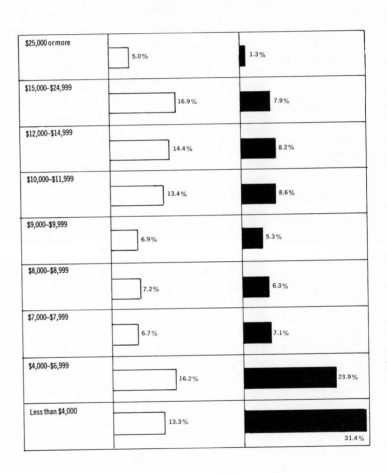

FIGURE 75
**INCOME IN 1969
OF FAMILIES
By Race of Head**

☐ White

■ Negro and Other Races

	White	Negro and Other Races
$25,000 or more	5.0%	1.3%
$15,000–$24,999	16.9%	7.9%
$12,000–$14,999	14.4%	8.2%
$10,000–$11,999	13.4%	8.6%
$9,000–$9,999	6.9%	5.3%
$8,000–$8,999	7.2%	6.3%
$7,000–$7,999	6.7%	7.1%
$4,000–$6,999	16.2%	23.9%
Less than $4,000	13.3%	31.4%

FIGURE 77 **PERCENT OF PERSONS BELOW POVERTY LEVEL IN 1969**

PERCENT OF SPECIFIED GROUP

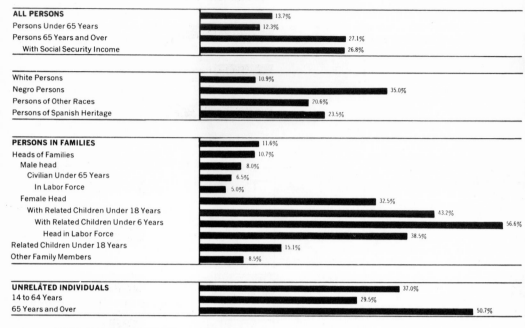

Group	Percent
ALL PERSONS	13.7%
Persons Under 65 Years	12.3%
Persons 65 Years and Over	27.1%
With Social Security Income	26.8%
White Persons	10.9%
Negro Persons	35.0%
Persons of Other Races	20.6%
Persons of Spanish Heritage	23.5%
PERSONS IN FAMILIES	11.6%
Heads of Families	10.7%
Male head	8.0%
Civilian Under 65 Years	6.5%
In Labor Force	5.0%
Female Head	32.5%
With Related Children Under 18 Years	43.2%
With Related Children Under 6 Years	56.6%
Head in Labor Force	38.5%
Related Children Under 18 Years	15.1%
Other Family Members	8.5%
UNRELATED INDIVIDUALS	37.0%
14 to 64 Years	29.5%
65 Years and Over	50.7%

FIGURE 78 **RATIO OF INCOME IN 1969 TO POVERTY LEVEL**

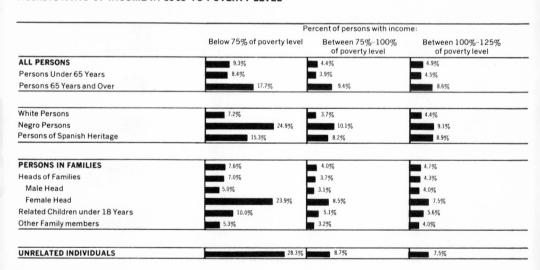

	Percent of persons with income:		
	Below 75% of poverty level	Between 75%–100% of poverty level	Between 100%–125% of poverty level
ALL PERSONS	9.3%	4.4%	4.9%
Persons Under 65 Years	8.4%	3.9%	4.5%
Persons 65 Years and Over	17.7%	9.4%	8.6%
White Persons	7.2%	3.7%	4.4%
Negro Persons	24.9%	10.1%	9.1%
Persons of Spanish Heritage	15.3%	8.2%	8.9%
PERSONS IN FAMILIES	7.6%	4.0%	4.7%
Heads of Families	7.0%	3.7%	4.3%
Male Head	5.0%	3.1%	4.0%
Female Head	23.9%	8.5%	7.5%
Related Children under 18 Years	10.0%	5.1%	5.6%
Other Family members	5.3%	3.2%	4.0%
UNRELATED INDIVIDUALS	28.3%	8.7%	7.5%

Index

Proper names of persons in this index are limited to social researchers, to whose work the text devotes substantial quotation and/or conceptual discussion. For extensive references to individuals and their research, see the chapter-end reference sections.

434